ALSO BY GERALD LINDERMAN

Mirror of War

Embattled Courage

THE FREE PRESS

New York London Toronto Sydney Singapore

THE
WORLD
WITHIN WAR

America's Combat

Experience in World War II

GERALD F. LINDERMAN

For Katherine Ehle
1903–1994

THE FREE PRESS
A Division of Simon & Schuster Inc.
1230 Avenue of the Americas
New York, NY 10020

THE FREE PRESS and colophon are trademarks
of Simon & Schuster Inc.

Designed by Carla Bolte

Manufactured in the United States of America

10 9 8 7 6 5 4 3 2 1

Library of Congress Cataloging-in-Publication Data

Linderman, Gerald F.
    The world within war : American soldiers' experience of combat in
World War II / Gerald F. Linderman.
        p.   cm.
    Includes bibliographical references and index.
    ISBN 0-684-82797-2
    1. United States.   Army—History—World War, 1939–1945.
    2. Soldiers—United States—History—20th century.   3. World War,
1939–1945—Campaigns.   I. Title.
    D769.2.L56   1997
    940.54'1273—dc21   97-36361
                                                    CIP

CONTENTS

ACKNOWLEDGMENTS

I began work on this book while a visitor at Fort Leavenworth's U.S. Army Command and General Staff College, in an atmosphere that, to my benefit, combined comradely feeling with open, vigorous debate and criticism. Binford Peay III, Richard Swain, and Bob Berlin, hosts cordial and unvaryingly considerate, made me welcome and often acted in support of my efforts. Sam Lewis and Tom Huber opened to me German and Japanese perspectives on World War II. Discussions with Roger Spiller were most rewarding; he also made available to me a number of his excellent working papers on World War II topics. The visits of Peter Maslowski and Edward Drea seemed always to advance the organization of my thoughts.

No persons were more helpful in the book's subsequent stages than Robert Wiebe and Tom Collier. The astuteness of the former's ideas was equalled only by the generosity with which he shared them. The latter was unstinting in placing at my disposal his encyclopedic knowledge of World War II; when I needed help, he offered it.

At many junctures, colleagues and friends provided particular assistance or support of less tangible but no less important qualities: Mary and Rick Bendix; Grant Burns; Bob Domine; Kate and Michael Gass; Yvonne Gillies; Lou Guenin; Roger Hackett; Charles Heftman; Rachel and David Hsiung; Matt Klimow; Beth Kodner; Keith Lee; Carolyn McCormick; Joe Mendes; James Morgan; Beth O'Brien; Bradford Perkins; Evan Rosen; Tom Shaw; Janice Shimmel; Jim Tobin; Theresa Wirtz; Jean Wyman; Sue and Bruce Zellers.

Staff members at four libraries greatly eased extended research: at the

CGSC Library, Fort Leavenworth, Pat Wells; at the University of Michigan's Graduate Library, Joanne Spaide; at Michigan's School of Business Administration Library, Thirza Cady; and at the U.S. Army Military History Institute (with its uniquely valuable Veterans Survey Project), Richard Sommers.

The weekly meetings of the Department of History's War Studies Group pointed me to new sources of information, spurred the refinement of my ideas, and guarded me against writer isolation. I am grateful to its members—and especially to Jonathan Marwil, for his special aid, astute advice and regular reminders of analytical excellence.

My editor, Bruce Nichols, buoyed me with his early enthusiasm and, by the firmness of his own ideas, challenged me to think carefully of the form that the book should assume. Carol de Onís responded to numerous queries with patience, good will, and high helpfulness.

Jeanette Diuble was extraordinarily proficient in her preparation of the manuscript; her sallies and laughter joined those of Janet Fisk, Connie Hamlin and Lorna Altstetter, also of the Department of History, in repeatedly bolstering my morale.

My daughters, Karen and Kathy, took an interest in the project and voiced occasional concern for their father's equipoise. Perhaps they need not have worried, for Barbara Linderman continued to bring to our life a grace and a spirit that immunized me against most of war's incursions.

INTRODUCTION

Combat soldiers—Army infantrymen and Marine riflemen—fought as the vanguard of the military power with which the United States stood against the Third Reich and the Empire of Japan in World War II. It was they who grappled with the forces of the enemy, staking their bodies in tasks for which large war machines did not suffice, in order to expel the Germans and Japanese from conquered territories and force them back on their homelands.

For so indispensable a role in the American accomplishment, their numbers were small. From a population of 132 million, the military drew into service 16.3 million persons; fewer than 1 million, probably no more than 800,000, took any part in extended combat. In numerous theaters, fighting men comprised 10 percent, or less, of the full military complement. Infantrymen, constituting 14 percent of American troops overseas, suffered 70 percent of the casualties.

This study is an attempt to see World War II through the eyes of those American combat soldiers. It suggests how combat registered in their minds and memories; how so profound an experience impressed itself on their relationships with their enemies, their comrades, their commanders, and even their families; and how battle exacted its costs of them.

Regrettably, limitations on and within sources of information do not make for easy identification of their experience. Military regulations prohibited the keeping of diaries. Letters from soldiers to their families were multitudinous, but their writers ordinarily chose reassurance over realism. Besides, cultural constraints, notably the American veneration of individualism and self-sufficiency, made it difficult for soldiers to own to their loneliness and

1

vulnerability. Reliance on soldier memoirs, even those few published during or shortly after the war, posed problems of selective memory, for often the repression of painful remembrance began with the first respite following episodes recognizable as central to the combat experience.

This exploration relies on the interplay between letters and recollections published by approximately 500 combat soldiers, some few of the few. I began research with a vivid interest in the conditions of combat, a disposition to heed with full care and concern all that soldiers were able to impart, and a conviction that the application of E. M. Forster's maxim "Only connect" would reveal a clear, representative, and virtually full portrait of the combat experience. I was mistaken in what I thought that I would find.

It is often said that combat remains beyond the grasp of those not a part of it, but so it is too for many who did engage in battle. So relentless were the poundings of combat that World War II soldiers, however remarkable their efforts to adapt, seldom achieved more than fragmentary accommodations and thus became vulnerable to deep disorientation. Those trying to describe their own experience, even those for whom memory may not have been a conclusive problem, collided with another obstacle to articulation. In the confusion and distress generated by battle, they tried to speak from depths dark and complicated. Their language strained to express the inexpressible; their generalizations failed to span their numerous voids. Historians struggle to reckon with those blanks—and then again with the accessible fragments: the narrative form confines them to presenting separately and sequentially much that they know occurred simultaneously in combat. For soldiers, observers, and analysts, much that happened remains distressingly elusive.

And warfare continues to guard many of its secrets. Why, in war after war, do soldiers first approaching battle remain convinced that the loss of their own lives is an impossibility? Why do so many soldiers, having discovered the realities of warfare, still persevere in battle? Why, of those whose experience of training and battle appears virtually identical, do some but not others succumb to neuropsychiatric collapse? Or, following the war, suffer post-traumatic stress disorder? As soldiers approaching France's Mediterranean shoreline in landing craft waited for the Germans' guns to open on them, infantryman Audie Murphy contemplated the "little men, myself included, who are pitted against a riddle that is as vast and indifferent as the blue sky above us."

In the pages that follow I do not hesitate to draw conclusions supported by a coalescence of soldier testimony, but such judgments are offered in the spirit of those always aware that they continue to circle a mystery.

1 BATTLE
Expectation, Encounter, Reaction

One expects to find in war a killing power. What American soldiers in World War II failed to foresee was that battle also possessed a power to impose thorough and dramatic change on those whom it did not kill. To continue in combat exposed the body and the mind to the hammerings of a behemoth; its blows seemed to pound away individual variation, to compel submission, and to portend a collective, ever-pliant combat personality.

In the event, even amid coerced change, American soldiers demonstrated an adaptability that, weighed against the force bearing hard on them, was often astonishing. They reacted in a medley of ways; sometimes they invested in logic, sometimes in magic, often in both. Even when those longest in combat felt that they were losing all efficacy, they continued to make choices.

The passages below try to describe the collision of American soldiers with the forces of the battlefield and to trace the repercussions of the combat experience, particularly in infantrymen's feelings of abandonment and expendability. The chapter that follows explores how soldiers attempted to withstand battle, and measures the outcome of their efforts.

In light of the American public's initial view of the war as a distasteful necessity, soldiers anticipated combat with what today seems an unlikely receptivity. Following basic training, they believed themselves ready for battle, were impatient to engage the enemy, minimized their adversaries' capacities to oppose them, and seldom worried about the results either for themselves or for their country. An exuberant aggressiveness infused their words and actions.

Most felt a powerful impulse to close on the enemy without delay. Private Mario Sabatelli spoke for those Marine Raiders with whom he moved toward the invasion of Tulagi: "We wanted to get our hands on Japs." A seaman whose combat station was a machine-gun mount on a light cruiser declared en route to Guadalcanal that "I came out here to see action and I hope this is the biggest battle of all time. . . . I . . . don't care how many Japs I run into." Army private Morton Eustis worried that there would not be combat enough to satisfy him: "I'm so scared Germany may sue for peace before we have a chance to take a crack at her. . . ." Such sentiments drew their keenness from dissatisfaction with the pre-combat present, from soldiers' confidence that they would realize the gratifications of combat and from the conviction that battle, entered upon as quickly and as unrestrainedly as possible, represented the fastest "road back to America."[1]

Impatience to fight trailed closely the conviction of many that their training ensured success in battle. Said Sabatelli on the eve of Tulagi: "We felt good. . . . I felt cool and confident. My feeling was that it was going to be tough, but after the training we'd had I felt this was my business and I was ready for it." When the troops with whom Ernie Pyle was traveling—as a correspondent for the Scripps-Howard newspaper chain—landed on Sicily and encountered no enemy resistance, there was disappointment, for they thought themselves "trained to such a point that instead of being pleased with no opposition they were thoroughly annoyed."[2]

Others, whatever they considered their training's effectiveness, simply could no longer tolerate its irksomeness. Eustis wrote from England in April 1944: "I don't credit the Army with being sufficiently far-sighted to make their training so boring that men are really anxious to go into combat just to get away from it, but that is actually what happens." And the simple termination of training did not suffice; the interval between training and battle—mere waiting, in the men's view—was worse, one of the war's most unendurable stages. Eustis spoke to this point, too: "I don't believe there's a man in our company who wouldn't rather be under enemy fire than in garrison over here [in England]. And I know that they're itching to get going and get this over with, rather than to sit around for months and even years."[3]

To those who thought themselves ready to fight, activity designated to fill the interim was intolerable make-work. When a Marine private refused orders to continue laboring in the hold of a ship anchored off Guadalcanal, the captain to whom his dereliction was reported was curious. "You volunteered, you know. You didn't have to come out here. Why did you enlist?" "To fight, Sir. . . . I've been working all the way across [the Pacific], swabbing decks, cleaning heads. I've spent twelve hours down there in the hold today, while some of them goldbricks that ain't done a tap got to go ashore with the first detail. I've done more than my share and I ain't taking any more pushing around." He had come to the southwest Pacific "to get me some Japs—not work as a stevedore." Others like him looked forward to battle as relief from camp or shipboard life, as action that would deliver them from insufferable inaction.[4]

Some found ways other than insubordination to quell their impatience. Basic training taught no lesson more convincingly than "Don't volunteer!" and James Johns "knew better" than to do so, but when Admiral William Halsey himself asked for fifty men to offer to service Marine aircraft in the eye of combat on Guadalcanal, he stepped forward. Geddes Mumford, a messenger at battalion headquarters, hastened his way into the fight. "[E]very time he was given a message to deliver, he wandered off with his rifle to hunt for Germans or to attach himself to a rifle company in the lines."[5]

Those compelled to wait envied those who were about to see or had already seen battle. Eustis, eager for combat but counting days in a North African replacement depot, was jealous of two tent-mates—"the lucky devils"—who were sent to the front. A Marine private, a replacement on Guadalcanal, complained that "Other guys . . . have [already] had personal, hand-to-hand fights with the Japs, but not me. Somehow, I don't get those breaks." In a Honolulu bar, James Jones, while a soldier training in Hawaii, met crewmen of the carrier *Yorktown,* which had just fought in the Battle of the Coral Sea and was doomed soon to go down at Midway. All three sailors were "curiously sun-blackened and with deep hollow eyes" and "drunk as hoot owls" at nine o'clock in the morning. At his first glance, Jones realized that they were "different from me." He stayed with them for hours, listening to their battle stories. They "had already passed on into a realm I had never seen." Jones, an enlistee in the peacetime Regular Army, was not as impatient as most to enter battle's domain, but as for those fighting sailors, "The whole encounter had been immensely romantic for me" and "More than anything in the world I wanted to be like them."[6]

Such comments reflected minds unintimidated by the prowess of the enemy or the prospect of death. To very few did their opponents appear formidable; indeed, Americans approached their enemies with a nonchalance edging on disdain. So little concerned with the opposition's lethal power was

Joseph Miller, an engineer officer in North Africa, that he found the opening round of German machine-gun and artillery fire "just sort of exciting" and carried on with his sergeant "a race" to determine who would become the first wounded and thus "get the first Purple Heart." Morton Eustis deemed the Italians worth hardly a thought. It was "humiliating" that Italian soldiers—"if you can dignify them by the name"—cried "like sniveling babies" and were so eager to surrender. As for the Germans, Eustis hoped that he and his friends "can each knock out at least a hundred Jerries apiece . . . just as a starter." He would dedicate the first German cut down to his mother and the second to his brother. "If I don't kill at least ten personally, I shall be most unhappy!"[7]

In the Pacific, Army sergeant Myles Standish Babcock, embarking for Guadalcanal, said much the same about his enemy. "Intensely desirous of going into combat . . . I'd like to kill ten Japs, then become a casualty of sufficient importance to justify convalescence in New Zealand or even the United States of America!" Aboard another vessel bound for Guadalcanal, U.S. correspondent Richard Tregaskis listened as Marines loaded cartridges into machine-gun belts. "One of them kept time with the clink of the belter. 'One, two, three, another Jap for me,' he said. Others tried other ideas. . . . Another boy said, 'Honorable bullet take honorable Jap honorable death. So solly.' 'I've got a Jap's name written on each bullet. There's three generals among 'em.' 'Which one's for Tojo?'. . . 'Oh, Hell, the first one's got his name on it.'"[8]

Partner to this insouciance sometimes bordering on frivolousness was sterner stuff—a hard, comprehensive, but very abstract vindictiveness. When family members wrote to Eustis of their misgivings about the American bombing of German towns, he disparaged all qualms. "God knows, I don't advocate the wholesale slaughter of enemy civilians in cold blood, though, in the case of Germany, some of that medicine won't do them any harm. But if civilians must be killed to attain your objective, why then there's nothing to do but kill them. . . . I think the Germans . . . should suffer. . . . The simple solution of the problem—complete extermination of the German people—is, I realize, a consummation that can never be realized, however devoutly [I wish it]." It is difficult to measure the depth of conviction to which such disdain and vengefulness reached, but those soldiers who offered dire prescriptions seldom expected them to receive serious consideration, nor was any ordinarily given. Much of what soldiers said was intended to bolster the exuberance of their war talk.[9]

Equally emboldening was the soldier's conviction that he need not worry much about his own death in battle. Psychiatrist Jules Masserman has identified faith in personal survival as one of the master beliefs undergirding the individual's psychic defense against war's destructiveness, and there is persuasive evidence of World War II recruits' certainty of their invulnerability. "You hear of casualties, see casualties, and read of casualties," explained a member of an Army ordnance unit in North Africa, "but you believe it will never happen to you." In a letter written on the eve of the invasion of Iwo Jima, Marine private James Bruce assured his wife that "[N]othing could make [him] really, fundamentally believe that a bullet or chunk of bomb or shell might suddenly rip the life out of [him]." Roger Hilsman remembered how his group of twelve, aboard a ship sailing for Bombay and destined for grim service with Merrill's Marauders in Burma, hooted at a suggestion that any one of them could be wounded in the approaching fighting. All comprehended intellectually that woundings and dyings constituted war, but those not yet under fire proceeded as if each had been granted some fundamental exemption.[10]

Soldiers who survived first combat realized how profound had been their conviction of imperishability. Just ashore on Guadalcanal, Marine Grady Gallant deliberated on what would happen if Japanese aircraft attacking American ships in the roadstead shifted targets. "What horror it would be . . . if they [were to] strafe our beachhead and bomb it. . . . The men and supplies were still confined to a rather small area. . . . Bombs and machine guns could kill most of us, or wound us, and there would be no help for us against a thing we could not fight, or stop, or avenge. This possibility froze my blood." As Marine Eugene Sledge realized, "The fact that our lives might end violently or that we might be crippled while we were still boys didn't seem to register."[11]

With many so resistant to any thought of personal jeopardy, the few in whom disquietude appeared early were ordinarily able to draw reassurance from within (". . . if I die . . . [But] that is stupid thinking, a part of myself told the other part, you are not going to die. That is the way to look at it, the only way") or from friends ("You know somebody's going to get it, but not [us].")[12]

Widespread enthusiasm for closing and grappling with the enemy and obliviousness to one's own mortality did not relieve soldiers of all anxiety. One immediately pressing concern was peculiar: Convinced that he would not die in battle, the soldier still worried that those important to him could. "The other fellow will get it, not me." But what if the other fellow were a comrade? Even this was a source of only minor alarm. Bonds among those approaching battle were weaker than they would become as a result of battle.

The emphasis remained on death passing by the self rather than striking others close by, and the soldier's anticipation of the destruction of friends served principally to reassert the certainty of his own survival. As Marine private Allen Matthews put it, "Of course we knew that fatalities might and probably would occur, but in our mind's eye we saw ourselves grieving over the loss of friends and we never could picture our friends grieving over us." One story, as popular as it was apocryphal, illustrated how the soldier accommodated the certainty that he would survive with the certainty that war killed soldiers. Prior to an assault, a battalion commander "stood in front of his men . . . and painted a picture of impending doom. 'By tomorrow morning . . . every man here, except one, will be dead.' The remark bit deeply into every man present, and each glanced at his comrades with undisguised compassion. 'Gee,' each man thought to himself, 'those poor fellows.'"[13]

A more pressing concern of the soldier was his own performance in battle. Morton Eustis, just assigned to an armored division, included in a letter home an apprehension that many felt. He was worried "not whether I'm killed, wounded or taken prisoner . . . but how well I acquit myself when I come up against the real thing." The conception of combat as a test of the individual had lost most of its specificity and some of its gravity since Theodore Roosevelt and his Rough Riders had demonstrated its centrality to the combat of the Spanish-American War, but an aura of its influence remained and some of its precepts continued to circulate: that combat was the ultimate test of the soldier's courage and manhood; that it tried the soul but would purify successful participants; that it confirmed character by strengthening the strong and by diminishing further the already weak. Such beliefs no longer received serious attention at home. No one had challenged departing soldiers to "Be brave!" as had family and friends at the outset of the Civil War. The test had largely lost its social dimension. Still, it remained a source of private, painful curiosity within many soldiers. "We had questions about ourselves that could be answered only in combat," said platoon leader Harold Leinbaugh, a lieutenant in Company K, 333d Infantry Regiment, 84th Division. When, in another unit, the captain announced that "Tomorrow night we attack the Siegfried Line!" platoon leader Howard Randall welcomed the news: an assault would end the uncertainty and enable the men to answer the question, "How would we stand up under really rugged action?"[14]

Randall's alacrity, like the anticipation of so many American soldiers entering battle, hinged on a critical assumption—that the consequences of combat would be determined by the effectiveness of the soldier's own reasoning and of his consequent responses. This conviction incorporated another

of the beliefs Jules Masserman held fundamental to the functioning soldier—that there was a connection between his actions and what happened to
him—but moved beyond it to assert the soldier's ability to control his own
fate. Writing from an infantry training camp, Geddes Mumford told his parents that "[W]orrying about my getting killed . . . is foolish. I have no intention of doing anything but returning. Most men get killed in battle because
they forget to take cover or make some such tactical mistake. I'll make no
mistake like that." Such certainty, circulating widely in the view that soldiers
were rarely hit if they did not lose their heads, propelled Mumford's efforts
to attach himself to a rifle company whenever opportunity offered and ultimately to transfer from clerk-messenger to combat scout.[15]

Like Mumford, a soldier in Fort Benning's officer training program revealed the unexplored and unchallenged major premise, the assumption of
individual control. Officer Candidate Bodine knew who would dominate his
encounter with the enemy. "It keeps coming back just when I'm falling off to
sleep . . . how it'll be to draw a bead on a living man and take his life away. I
really can't wait to get over." He would act rather than be acted upon. He
would place others in his sights, not find himself in others' sights. "If I just
act in the right ways, from the right values," American soldiers reasoned, "all
will be well." "It's good to have courage," thought poet and airman John
Ciardi; "nothing happens to the brave."[16]

Soldiers also anticipated that the war they would control would be the war
that they desired, one of personalized, individualized combat. They spoke as if
battles would be decided by hand-to-hand fighting; their talk was of immediate, close-quarters applications of physicality. "I just know I want to get in
there and kill some Japs." "[My] last hope before going to sleep was that our
boys might have left a few Japs for me." A Marine aboard a troop transport
bound for Guadalcanal found intolerable the laborious instruction in sector
maps and unit roles: "I just want to kill a Jap, that's all." When, on Guadalcanal, a Japanese soldier ran toward the beach in flight from American tanks
moving through a palm grove, Marines began firing at him. The colonel, concerned that American bullets might strike the tanks, shouted an order to cease
fire, but the Marines continued to shoot. "As usual, each Marine was eager to
kill *his* Jap." Even those pledges to kill ten Japs or one hundred Jerries retained
that personal quality, as if those foes were to be dispatched serially. It seemed as
if each American soldier, so intent on accomplishing one or another individualized battle goal, were going into combat alone.[17]

The mode of combat that best fit soldiers' expectations was the bayonet
fight. No phase of basic training had left a more powerful impression than

bayonet instruction. Military leaders who ordered it bore no illusion that the bayonet retained importance in a war dominated by artillery and aircraft, tanks and machine guns; but however anachronistic, its use, they thought, implanted that fierce martial spirit they wished to fix in the men. Few trainees had not been awed. Nothing seemed closer to real battle than charging, shouting—as instructed—"Kill! Kill! Kill!" and lunging at straw-sack enemies with bayoneted rifle extended. Hired to write the script for a film about GIs and touring military installations to gather "enough facts, honest-to-God true facts, to make a soldier picture which soldiers would sit through . . . without once laughing in derision," the young Arthur Miller visited an infantry replacement center and there joined trainees in crawling through an infiltration course and launching a climactic bayonet charge. "[E]verybody crouches in the trench with the bayonets set, and [the lieutenant] yells let's go! and you crunch your shoes into the dirt and clamber over the top and run faster than you ever ran before until you hit into the straw-filled potato bags set up on frames and zam, that blade goes in deep, and you're through." But Miller was surprised at his own reaction. "Funny, you felt like giving it another jab. . . . It felt good when the blade went in. It felt very good."[18]

"We always saw ourselves," Marine Grady Gallant said later, "charging through enemy . . . set up just like the bayonet course."[19]

Dedication to the bayonet remained strong as troops moved toward combat. International News Service correspondent Richard Tregaskis, sailing for Guadalcanal, reported that "all over the ship" sharpening bayonets "seemed to be a universal pastime." On Tulagi, a Marine Raider approaching his first battle "saw red when he thought of [the Japanese]. He'd take a bayonet and dance around the place, sticking it into the air and saying, 'I'm going to rip them and stick them like this!' You knew he wasn't kidding." For many, the bayonet was the weapon of a truly devoted bellicosity.[20]

For its distinctive impress the bayonet owed much to several values embedded in the culture of 1940s America. Bayonet combat was highly personal, "the most intimate fighting in the war," as army correspondent Ralph Ingersoll observed. It also promised to be a highly individualistic instrument, for it postulated one-against-one conflict replicating the pattern in which most soldiers had fought the opponents of their youth. And bayonet duels, placing decisive premium on the personal skills of the combatants, promised not only drama but fairness. Said Ingersoll, "If ever there might be a perfect balance between offense and defense, you would expect to find it in this most primitive conflict." Primitive, yes, though in soldiers' thought more elemental than savage, more quintessential than uncivilized. Indeed, it was so

connected in American minds with man-to-man struggle that it opened to
soldiers achievements that the culture considered among its most meritori-
ous. Bayonet clashes, requiring the direct application of personal virtues and
energies, all seemingly offered in dedication to country, embodied the highest individual heroism.[21]

Peculiarly, in the end a wartime situation far removed from the bayonet
charge surpassed it in demonstrating the values which Americans brought to
battle. Indeed, for reasons that will become clear, it is necessary to leave land
warfare and go to another medium to find episodes in which Americans actually realized the values they pursued in the war. An instance of aerial combat described by Robert Scott in his 1943 bestseller, *God Is My Co-Pilot,*
attained the acme of that personalized warfare desired by so many. A solitary
Japanese Zero strafed the airfield at Hengyang, China, and was challenged
by a P-40 piloted by Tex Hill.

> As the two fighters drew together in this breathtaking, head-on attack, I saw
> their tracers meeting and for a second I didn't know whether the ships ran to-
> gether or both exploded in the air. As the smoke thinned I saw the P-40 flash on
> through and out into the clear, but the Jap crashed and burned on the field. . . .
> Hill and the Jap had shot it out nose to nose, and once again I thought of the
> days of Western gunplay. We landed and waited for Tex to come over. As we
> stood around the burning enemy ship, I saw Hill striding across the field from
> his fighter. Hanging low on his right leg was his army forty-five [pistol]. . . .
> Tex's blond hair was blowing in the wind, his eyes were looking with venomous
> hate at the Jap, his jaw was set. I had opened my mouth to congratulate him, for
> he had shot down two enemy ships that day, when . . . Tex strode over close to
> the fire and looked at the mutilated Jap where he had been thrown from the
> cockpit. Then, without a change of expression, he kicked the largest piece of
> Jap—the head and one shoulder—into the fire. I heard his slow drawl: 'All
> right, mister—if that's the way you want to fight it's all right with me.' Tex
> calmly left the group and walked back to his ship and into the alert shed for his
> cup of tea. None of us said anything.

If American fighting men had been able to create episodes embodying
their expectations of combat and the bearing to which they aspired, here was
the kind of encounter they would have designed.[22]

World War II, like wars before and after it, confounded the expectations of
those who entered upon its battles. Few other human activities are as certain

as combat to alter substantially those who participate, and American soldiers who survived more than a brief span of the fighting found themselves propelled through changes overthrowing, one after another, propositions that they had regarded as both fundamental and assured.

The organizing proposition that soldiers brought with them to battle and that at times survived at least some combat could be understood as "War is neither killing nor dying." Marine private Russell Davis approached his first battle, the amphibious attack on Peleliu, he later realized, with no serious thought of either one, as if no lives were ending on the island.[23]

The early experience of battle, however, compelled soldiers to jettison their maiden proposition, first by replacing "War is neither killing nor dying" with "War is killing." While the sense of one's own invulnerability remained intact, the killing of others seemed suddenly to render one's own survival less automatic. Grady Gallant on Guadalcanal struggled to adjust. "The thought of dying had not occurred to [the Marines]. They had not been taught to die. They had been taught to kill. Dying had not occurred to them. They did not look upon war as dying. War was killing. Seeking out the enemy and killing. . . . There was no plan to die." His worried, repetitive, dogmatic phrases were those of soldiers to whom battle sights had just brought the powerful insistence that all men were mortal. Even the most confident had to begin to wonder about their own fates. Earlier certainties had to be compromised. There was no more hooting at the idea of being wounded. Now the soldier let himself think of being shot at, though not yet of being shot at and hit. And, once exposed to battle, many soldiers sought and offered reassurances where none had been necessary before. William Owens, who was in the Pacific theater, remembered a conversation in December 1944. Although "Rarely among soldiers I knew was there talk of death, of 'getting it,'" just prior to the American return to the Philippines, one of his friends proposed that "The way for me to go in is to know I am not going to get it. The Japs ain't got a bullet with my name on it." "Hell, yes," agreed another. "You've got to go in knowing you'll come out alive. You know somebody's going to get it, but not you. You don't, you might as well stand up and let 'em shoot you down."[24]

When an American regimental commander in Italy noticed one of his young soldiers "shaking with nerves," he walked to him, placed a hand on his shoulder, and said, "Don't worry, son. Tell yourself that it won't happen to you. It is always the other fellow, you know." As soldiers began to repeat to themselves and to their comrades, "Remember, it never happens to you," a seemingly perfect assurance dwindled to incantation.[25]

With certitude disappearing, soldiers admitted and gave name to the first imponderable: They conceded a role to luck. Such terms as "odds" and "chances" and "fortune" and "Lady Luck" became the currency of their conversations. Infantryman Grady Arrington tried to cheer a fellow private who was becoming fatalistic: "Stacker, I've been with this outfit since basic training [and] have not even been scratched yet. Your chances are as good as everyone's."[26]

The third stage—"War is killing—and dying"—was the most painful to enter upon, for it insisted on the actual overthrow of that world of pre-battle assumptions. It necessitated especially the abandonment of invulnerability. "It can't happen to me" became perforce "It *can* happen to me." And it required emotional acceptance of what were to distant civilians mere truisms: that those on the other side killed too and that those whom they killed were dead. It was a mark of the intensity of resistance to the obvious that soldiers frequently testified to their surprise that someone actually desired to cause their deaths. Paratrooper Robert Houston, en route to Normandy, watched antiaircraft fire climb toward his C-47 and was surprised that "anybody actually hated us enough to want to kill us." Such was disbelief in the enemy's lethal intent that soldiers often thought that the Germans, or the Japanese, "cannot realize what they are doing to us."[27]

Grady Gallant, that Marine who on Guadalcanal was shaken by the realization that Japanese aircraft bombing American ships might at any moment turn on him ("What horror it would be . . ."), there grasped that he had previously had no understanding of death on any personal level. Yes, it had possessed a certain theoretical possibility, but it had remained remote. "My own death had never been considered by me. But now, that very real possibility flooded my mind with crystal clarity. . . . It came to me that a Japanese would no more hesitate to kill me than I would hesitate to slay him. He *would*. I could expect no mercy. There would be no negotiation. It would either be I would kill him, or he would kill me. . . . [One] of us would kill the other. . . . Death might come to me, personally."[28]

Edwin Hoyt caught the sense of surprise among American soldiers landing in Morocco against stiff Vichy French resistance in November 1942: ". . . and then for the first time in their lives they came under artillery attack. Real guns were firing at them, and trying to kill them!" Acceptance of that reality, thought Hoyt, was the first step in becoming a combat soldier.[29]

Soldiers struggled with their new vulnerability and often tried to confine it. Some envisioned that they could be wounded but refused to contemplate their own deaths. Some considered the loss of an arm or leg, but drew a line against the possibility of a head wound causing brain damage. Some granted that they might be killed but placed the event in a future that would never arrive; it would happen later, always later.[30]

Such resistance was sometimes overturned, as in Gallant's experience, by an event so dramatic that it toppled pre-combat assumptions, sometimes by "minor" incidents that any veteran would recognize as unexceptional but that could carry for initiates a traumatic power compelling them to confront the unreality of their presuppositions. For Marine Russell Davis, it was the wounded's cry of distress, so urgent with need: "Corpsman!" It reverberated in him as "the worst Greek chorus of the war," whose memory continued to frighten him years later. For others, it was the sort of convulsion experienced when a British officer in North Africa, caught in a shelling and clutching the earth at the bottom of an excavation, looked up and saw a small blade of grass gently moving in the breeze. "I watched it, fascinated!—'You're too small to be hit!' At that moment there was a thud and glow as a white-hot piece of shrapnel plunked into the wall of the trench and glared at me. I looked up. The grass was gone. Oh God!"[31]

One pattern of experience provoking rapid reconsideration was that of the non-infantry specialist, trained in the delivery of his own species of destructive power, suddenly finding himself subjected to that very power—the artilleryman shelled, the fighter pilot strafed, the bomber pilot bombed.

For ground soldiers, a common series of experiences of mounting impact—seeing for the first time enemy dead, American dead, the body of a person the soldier knew, the body of a comrade—often, in any one of its steps, forced reappraisal. It came to artilleryman Frank Mercurio with the sight of a German soldier dying on an Italian beach.

> I looked down at my feet and there lay a long stretched body clad in a green uniform; his face was white and sulky, with streaks of red blood dripping over his face and blond hair, a wounded German! The beach was crowded with maddened foot soldiers running to their advanced positions [but] I couldn't see or hear anything [but] the groans of this twisted and mangled body. His arms stretched upward, and a leg folded back under his body. I was stunned, frozen; I couldn't move; I realized that this could happen to me. My mind started to go round and round like a whirlpool of shooting stars; I realized that I too could be a victim of death. . . . Fear grew more intense now, for now I saw things about death I had only imagined.

While at first some viewed enemy dead with satisfaction—"They aren't going to kill anybody anymore"—or with indifference—"The dead . . .

looked . . . like bad stage props . . ."—many lost their composure. A Marine platoon leader, Paul Moore, Jr., newly arrived on Guadalcanal, "heard a couple of shots . . . and as we walked along the path . . . I saw this dead Japanese soldier. It was the first dead soldier that I had ever seen. That was a pretty traumatic experience. He looked to be about fifteen years old, like a nice little kid, and to see him dead there was pretty bad." But soon the first sight of a dead American intensified his distress. "I saw . . . a body in Marine Corps combat dress lying on a stretcher, and I thought he was wounded, but then I saw a fly crawling across his ear. The ear didn't move. The head didn't move. So I knew he was dead. . . . [T]hat was the first time I saw dead Marines [and it was] even more traumatic than seeing dead Japanese."[32]

Moving ashore at Oran, Lieutenant John Downing of the 1st Division's 18th Infantry "came upon a dead American soldier. he was lying on his back, a hole through his head, with hands raised toward his head. There was an expression of tension engraved on the dirty face. A staff sergeant. A dead dogface. [Downing] thought he was going to be sick. So the maneuvers were over. This was war. There would be no recall bugles in the evening. It was going to go on for a long time, and the only way out was to be carried out on a stretcher, or to lie in a ditch like this sergeant."[33]

Even more certain to jolt the soldier was the death of a comrade. Nothing brought home more rapidly the finality of death—"For the first time I truly understood that the dead . . . were dead"—and that dying could not be depended upon to overtake only other people.[34]

The artillery barrage, particularly, shook the body, the spirit—and the mind's assumptions. Ernie Pyle described an Anzio shelling: "There was debris flying back and forth all over the room. One gigantic explosion came after another. The concussion was terrific. It was like a great blast of air in which my body felt as light and as helpless as a leaf tossed in a whirlwind." Combat engineer Henry Giles also testified to the overpowering effect of the cannonade. During a bombardment by German 88s, one shell "got louder and louder until it was right on top of us and a thousand boxcars with locomotives attached couldn't have been noisier. . . . Then we heard a thud and I came as close to dying from fear as I ever will. . . ." Wounds inflicted in such barrages or elsewhere often came to constitute the decisive event. U.S. correspondent Keith Wheeler described the moment he was hit: "A violence nothing had ever taught me to believe possible smashed against the right side of my face." And when a mortar fragment tore into cartoonist Bill Mauldin's foot, he too was shocked: "It can't happen to you. But . . . suddenly the war became very real to me."[35]

While a few soldiers could continue to slough off for a time injuries witnessed and even suffered, most completed quickly the transition to the realities of combat. Battle bore little relationship to civilian life and its presumptions. What the soldier first saw in battle, William Shirer noted, made little sense to him because "It did not fit into anything." Or, as paratroop commander Laurence Critchell put it, "Combat is foreign to all other experience; nothing in ordinary life reminds one of it." But once pushed to the other side, they began transforming themselves—swiftly. An English captain judged that in most cases he witnessed nothing beyond the first exposure to battle was required: the "baptism of fire" was sufficient to instill the "undefinable something" that differentiated the veteran from the newcomer, "almost as though a knowledge of war were some secret rite." American participants agreed that the transition was a rapid one. After a single night on Tulagi, Raider Sabatelli noticed that "All the boys seemed a little quieter, even a little older. You knew right there what war was like." Initiated into battle in Germany's Huertgen Forest, Lieutenant Paul Boesch said to himself, "So this is combat. I've had only one day of it. How does a man stand it, day in and day out?" One of James Jones's soldiers in the Pacific, conscious of the fear and helplessness that had arrived with a mortar sliver in the hand, decided that no one required more than two days of combat.[36]

Marine pilot Samuel Hynes summarized how change swept over so many fighting men. "The reality of death comes to you in stages. First it is an idea—all men are mortal, as in the syllogism. Then it is something that happens to strangers, then to persons you know, but somewhere else, and at last it enters your presence, and you see death. . . ."[37]

Whatever their variety and tempo, the events that confronted these men with death's reality also brought home to them another harsh truth: their loss of control over events. Battle introduced them to the immensity of the force that would be brought against them, infused them with feelings of diminution and even helplessness, and ultimately denied them their sense of order and purposiveness.

Efforts to describe the force to which the battlefield subjected soldiers pushed them to the limits of their imaginations. The might of the artillery barrage was a special challenge. "To me," wrote Marine Eugene Sledge, "artillery was an invention of hell. The onrushing whistle and scream of the big steel package of destruction was the pinnacle of violent fury and the embodiment of pent-up evil. It was the essence of violence and of man's inhumanity to man." "It was," proposed Private Lester Atwell, "as if an enraged giant were hurling with all his force an entire string of trains, screaming locomotive and all." Infantryman Walter Bernstein thought that "something about heavy artillery . . . is inhuman and terribly frightening. . . . It is like the finger of God."[38]

Now, soldiers knew they were facing forces beyond their control. "When I heard the whistle of an approaching [shell]," Sledge reported, "every muscle in my body contracted. I braced myself in a puny effort to keep from being swept away. I felt utterly helpless." "We were reduced to the size of ants," Atwell submitted. "I felt cowardly and small," said Bernstein; "I felt like a fly about to be swatted."[39]

Often GIs caught in shellings could no longer command their muscles and were wracked sometimes by spasms, sometimes by paralysis. Geddes Mumford told his father that he had watched "men cry like babies after they have been under [artillery fire] too long. I've seen men almost unable to walk just from nervous exhaustion." But the physical toll was frequently less menacing than the prospect of psychological disintegration. Eugene Sledge feared that "if I ever lost control of myself under shell fire my mind would be shattered. I hated shells as much for their damage to the mind as to the body." Others were visited by what Sledge dreaded. Ernie Pyle reported that in the wake of prolonged artillery barrages, he saw "many pitiful cases of 'anxiety neurosis.'" Nightmares of being shelled were numbered among the battle dreams that most haunted those in Army hospitals. "It's the whine and crunch of shells and [their mutilation of the] bodies of your buddies," Mumford knew, that ". . . tears a man to pieces."[40]

Bombing attacks, too, brought sensations of overwhelming force and threats of demoralization and even nervous collapse, but the sense of powerlessness was not often as profound as in the artillery barrage. Doubtless the aerial assault was painful. As a British lieutenant reported from the North African desert: "It is demoralizing for an infantryman to be attacked by something he can see . . . but which is too fast or too high to form a target." A Marine captain in the Pacific wished that he could relieve the strain of Japanese air attacks by firing his pistol or even by throwing rocks at his tormentors. Still, the soldier could see aircraft; strafing runs sometimes brought them within range of the infantry's machine guns; and even rifle fire might on rare occasions bring down a plane.[41]

The artillery barrage seemed far more malign. No weapon, no missile, no human agent was visible to its targets, and thus there could be none of the psychological relief to be derived from infantry retaliation. Correspondent-photographer Margaret Bourke-White had survived bombing attacks on Barcelona, Chunking, and London and "had not minded [it] too much," but she found cannonades different. "Shelling was like a dentist with a drill. And with me, those shells had found the nerve"—largely because she felt so helpless. "In many forms of anger you can do something about it, and that is your salvation. . . . But with shelling, you simply can't do anything. . . . You are pinned to your ditch . . . like a fox in a trap. You are at the will of the enemy."[42]

Soldiers at first responded with small gestures of defiance. "Occasionally, as an act of bravado and to signal an insult to their enemies, a GI would clamber out of his foxhole as shells burst nearby. 'Here we were, pinned down by shellfire and you see some guy going out in the middle of a field to take a crap. It broke the tension and brought a laugh to most everyone.'" Others found some alleviation in simply shouting out their fury. But gestures were seldom repeated—they cost lives—and on whom was the soldier's anger to be trained? Enemy artillerymen miles away? It expended precious energy simply to shape protest in the imagination, and no result would diminish the shelling's impact or lift for more than a moment the shelled soldier's sense of impotence. As Captain Laurence Critchell discovered, the infantryman "must listen in silence, generally without moving, while the heavy shells explode with a shattering thunder . . . all-encompassing in [their] violence. . . . With each roar the earth shakes. . . . What is worse, each explosion is anticipated by a high, thin and unearthly shriek—unearthly because it comes from something moving faster than instinct comprehends. . . . [T]here is nothing a man can do to help himself."[43]

Almost as debilitating was the American soldier's experience with German mines. Preconceptions of combat came close to assuming that if the soldier could see no enemies, they could not injure him; but mines, like long-range artillery, demonstrated that his destruction did not require the enemy's presence. "They were planted a few inches below the soil," explained platoon leader George Wilson, "and covered by leaves or natural growth that left no sign. Not a bit of ground was safe. They went off if you stepped on them with as little as five pounds of pressure, or if you moved their invisibly thin trip wire. The only defense was not to move at all. A mine usually blew off one leg up to the knee and shattered the other, which looked like it had been blasted by a shotgun at close range. If a man was not killed instantly, he needed immediate attention due to shock and loss of blood."[44]

Mines were more trying than bullets. "The German machine guns and rifles were different," decided infantry officer William Dreux; "at least I thought I could cope with them and I had a chance. Behind each such weapon was an enemy and I might get him before he could get me." It was the antipersonnel mine that he "dreaded most." And in some ways mines were worse than shells. That "high, thin unearthly shriek" that agitated Critchell had at least warned him that a shell was on its way. As the war moved forward, the Germans developed mines whose only metal was in the detonator and then glass and plastic mines that were undetectable by early-war metal detectors, so often the first and only sign of their presence was the explosion that killed or maimed. The psychological impact on those who could do no more than "Be careful!" in searching for (often non-existent) tell-tale signs was enormous. Sometimes even to escape produced severe demoralization. One can only try to imagine what a group of 84th Division infantrymen felt when they realized that they had just walked across a field sown with German stake mines, but though some of them had actually stumbled against canisters, they had been spared even a single explosion because American artillery shells had miraculously cut every one of the tripwires.[45]

Lieutenant George Wilson summarized a characteristic American reaction to mines: "It was there in that green forest [overlooking the Siegfried Line near Miescheid] that we ran into the most frightening weapon of the war, the one that made us almost sick with fear: *antipersonnel mines.* By now I had gone through aerial bombing, artillery and mortar shelling, open combat, direct rifle and machine-gun firing, night patrolling, and ambush. Against all of this we had some kind of chance; against mines we had none. They were viciously, deadly, inhuman. They churned our guts. . . . Soon each of the line companies had lost men to mines, and the rest of us were afraid to walk anywhere."[46]

In the eleven months between the Normandy invasion and the German capitulation, save for several brief periods of rapid breakout advances, American soldiers in lead units were seldom able to evade the lethal circles of German mines.

The average combat soldier thus lost his sense of invulnerability—and discovered how accessible he was to death. He lost too his sense of control over battle—and discovered his helplessness in the face of shellings and minefields. And these revelations abraded other, related propositions that soldiers had confidently brought with them into combat.

One of the first to disappear was the determination to close with the enemy. Encountering in battle more exhaustion than vitalization, more physical discomfort than excitement, more confusion than clarity, more fear than gratification, soldiers who failed to find what they had expected realized that they had not been trained for what they did find. Some began to think of battle as an experience so extraordinary that it allowed of no preparation, but most were angry, muddled, and defeated. The "ruling passion" of Canadian soldier Farley Mowat—his intense desire for combat—"collapsed like a pricked balloon." "What [am] I doing here?" infantry private Lester Atwell asked himself. "Panic came over me and for a wild moment I thought of marching into the new Company Commander's tent and saying, 'Look. There's been some big mistake. I'm here, but I haven't had the same training as the others and I have no idea what to do in combat. What do you intend to do about it?'"[47]

A frequent early reaction, drawing on that new, frightening sense of personal jeopardy, was to dismiss bravery and to summon what a British tank officer, Robert Crisp, called "judicious discrimination"—shorn of euphemism, the resolve to be ever careful, ever cautious. Dashing to close with the enemy now seemed the way to certain death.[48]

Occasionally, a soldier was so imbued with martial spirit and so fortunate in his first experience of combat that he was able to defer reconsideration or even to reaffirm pre-combat propositions. Morton Eustis, one of those soldiers so eager to get into action, found a job—in an armored division's reconnaissance battalion—that enabled him to do so. His first combat, in Sicily, was largely reassuring: "I got through the campaign without a scratch, save for those on my hands from crawling through bushes, scouting. . . . I enjoyed the campaign immensely. It's a fascinating game, particularly when you're the first element out front. And the fact that the stakes are high makes it all the more engrossing." He flirted briefly with fatalism ("If you're going to be hit, you're going to be hit and there's not much you can do about it"), but he was able to confine his fear ("You really haven't time to think about being scared for the most part"), and by the date his division was sent to England to prepare for the campaign in Western Europe, his assumptions seemed once more as they had been prior to battle. He was impatient for "more action."[49]

In France, Eustis was at first exhilarated by his rides in tanks and by the accompanying sensation "that nothing can stop you." He soon decided, however, that "This campaign is a good deal nearer the real thing than Sicily was," a conclusion swiftly underscored by two telling experiences. After "many, many close shaves" ("At times you get a little bit fed up with being under fire, usually when you are just sitting under artillery fire and can't fire back"), he ran "smack into the enemy lines" and survived only because the Germans were too startled to fire. Shortly thereafter he escaped an enemy ambush. ("For a few moments I thought we'd never get out.") His thought turned decisively.

> I shouldn't mind . . . if the whole [war] wound up before many more weeks are passed, as your luck can hold out just so long in this type of game, and sooner

or later someone's aim is going to be good, especially when you are sitting out most of the time in the point vehicle.

Three days later, riding exposed in the turret of a lead reconnaissance tank, he was killed instantly by a German *Panzerfaust.*[50]

Most soldiers, however, moved much faster and, when reconsidering their pre-combat convictions, seldom returned to them. With studied non-chalance, Geddes Mumford told his parents, "Your dear little boy has finally seen the more gruesome side of this man's war. I celebrated my [nineteenth] birthday by coming as close to getting killed as I ever want to. I felt the machine gun bullets passing my shoulder. Two of my buddies were hit by the same burst. It's a great life if you like excitement." Some repudiated explicitly their earlier expectations. Captain George Hunt declared that although those in his Marine unit "might have been stirred once by a parade, a cheering crowd and a brass band, they knew now that fighting was a dirty business in which the glamour that might have existed once in [their] imagination was lost." Once he had been in battle on Guadalcanal, rifleman John George reported derisively, the memory of his impatience to enter the fighting "provided me with numerous laughs, especially on many occasions when I was able to think back on it from a hot spot in the middle of a raging fire fight."[51]

Sadly, more authentic perceptions of combat could neither comfort the soldier nor mitigate the problem confronting him. The loss of desire to close with the adversary in no way altered the reality that, from summer 1942 to the end of the war, forcing battle on the enemy was the primary mission of the American military forces. Engagement, no longer the soldier's desire, remained his job—through one captured town after another; through one island invasion to the next; through countless enemy dead replaceable in ways that seemed always to present him with a solid front of opposition.[52]

Another casualty of battlefield experience was the soldier's fascination with personalized combat. Weapons technology dictated that soldiers would not often see the enemy; combatants were able to destroy their opponents without bringing them within sight. That the range and lethality of their weapons separated antagonists and eliminated mass movements surprised many soldiers. Atwell was stunned: "This wasn't anything as I had imagined actual combat, this lonely little string of men. When I thought of it at all, I saw a battlefield and rows of men advancing shoulder to shoulder, cannons firing, the first ranks being mowed down. I realized I had been thinking of [Civil War soldiers in] scenes from *The Birth of a Nation*." No less taken aback was correspondent Eric Sevareid. "Never were there masses of men in olive drab locked in photogenic combat with masses of men in field gray."

What one observed, in apparently unrelated patches, [were] small, loose bodies of men moving down narrow defiles or over steep inclines, going methodically from position to position between long halts, and the only continuous factor was the roaring and crackling of the big guns. One felt baffled at first by the unreality of it all. Unseen groups of men were fighting other men that they rarely saw. They located the enemy by the abstractions of mathematics, an imagined science; they reported the enemy through radio waves that no man could visualize; and they destroyed him most frequently with projectiles no eye could follow. When the target became quiet, that particular fight would be over and they moved ahead to something else. . . . It was a slow, spasmodic movement from one patch of silence to another.

Battle was becoming, as Lee Kennett has observed, an environment in which no enemy and few friends were discernible.[53]

Soldiers found perturbing the invisibility of the enemy. A Canadian was both wistful—"If I could only see [the Germans], as in battles long ago, at close range, before engaging them"—and aggrieved—"The warring sides are getting farther and farther apart and [thus] war is getting more and more meaningless for field-warriors. . . . It is already a very impersonal thing." Groused Audie Murphy, an infantryman whose actions won him a record twenty-eight decorations, "Maybe my notions about war were all cockeyed. How do you pit skill against skill if you cannot even see the enemy?" Ralph Ingersoll, climbing a Tunisian hill to his first battle, registered in his mind "the sounds of the firing and that feeling of excitement and wanting to get quickly to where I could see what was happening." But the reality was eerie: "The scene in the valley looked even more peaceful than the scene on the hilltop." Though around him German rifle bullets zinged off rocks and automatic weapons barked, "I couldn't see any enemy at all."[54]

Near the German town of Kogenbroich, someone in Lieutenant Harold Leinbaugh's company shot a German trying to move from a log dugout to a concrete pillbox. Private Joe Namey was "pretty sure" that Paul Coste had killed the enemy soldier. But if so, Coste remained unwitting: "I finally got to fire my [Browning Automatic Rifle], but I never had a target. I laid down fire when someone told me to, but I literally never aimed at anyone." Later, enemy fire pinned down another member of the company, Mel Cline. "This German machine gunner was directly to our front. . . . We could see [him] come up from his hole, fire, and duck down again. I adjusted my sights, got the range, and squeezed off several clips before I finally hit his gun and put him out of action. When we reached his hole, I found [that] the bullet had glanced off his machine gun and mangled his arm." "That was," Cline later recalled, "the only time in combat that I fired aimed shots like we did on the range in training."[55]

In the Pacific, even more than in the European theater, the low visibility of the enemy became what Tregaskis called "a perfectly normal condition." The density of the foliage, the rarity of prisoner-taking, and the Japanese resort to underground fortifications kept sightings uncommon. Eugene Sledge described the Marines' struggle to seize Hill 140 on the island of Peleliu: "If we moved past a certain point, the Japanese opened up suddenly with rifle, machine gun, mortar, and artillery fire. It was like a sudden storm breaking. More often than not we had to pull back, and not a man in the company had seen a live enemy anywhere."[56]

These dramatic alterations in the men's conceptions of war, and their new, intense desire to remain outside the sweep of the enemy's weapons, precluded any renewal of interest in the bayonet charge as the acme of the combat experience. During the Battle of the Bulge, the German American paratrooper Kurt Gabel was astonished to hear the command, "Fix bayonets!"

> I felt the shock of it jerk my body. Surely this was some kind of psychological game they played in Company F! Fix bayonets? That's World War I stuff. Bayonets were for opening C-ration cans. Sometimes you threw them at trees while imitating Errol Flynn or John Wayne, and of course in basic training you had to pretend how fierce you were as you thrust them into sandbag dummies. But here? I searched for the lieutenant, expecting to see a big grin on his face as he enjoyed this stupid joke.

When Lieutenant George Wilson's regimental commander wished to learn the type and strength of an opposing unit near Saint-Lô in Normandy, he ordered Wilson to organize a combat patrol whose mission was "to engage the Germans in a fight—using trench knives, bayonets, and grenades. We were to inflict as much damage as possible, then quickly take a prisoner and get out." Wilson was appalled. Was the colonel aware "that it would be difficult to find more than two bayonets in the whole company and very few more trench knives"? Angrily, the colonel demanded explanations, insisted on inspections by company commanders, and ordered that the mission proceed. The "asinine patrol" came to nothing. Wilson had been aware from the outset that "hand-to-hand combat was about the last thing [the men] wanted to do."[57]

John Toole of the 3d Infantry Division later remembered that "Small arms fire . . . terrified me. It meant that the Germans were firing directly at me or my buddies and that they would soon close in for hand-to-hand combat. [Here he paused to reconsider.] Actually, we practically never engaged in hand-to-hand combat.* . . . The automatic and semi-automatic weapons eliminated the bayonet as it was used in World War I."[58]

Vernon McHugh, an NCO in General Patton's Third Army, remembered that his company commander had urged the riflemen to throw away their bayonets—on grounds that if a soldier were close enough to stick an enemy, he was close enough to shoot him. McHugh could have told the homefolks that while bayonet duels remained one of the most prominent features of World War II films, they had largely disappeared from World War II combat.[59]

Ironically, in light of higher officers' insistence that combat soldiers hold fast to the bayonet, the semiofficial American handbook on *How the Jap Army Fights,* published early in the war, found incomprehensible the place accorded it in the Imperial Japanese Army as the "most essential weapon" carried by the Japanese soldier.[60]

Even the prominence of the Cause suffered in battle. Consideration of principles and larger aims diminished drastically as soldiers realized that they had no bearing on battle. Convinced that they made war in a good cause, GIs did not miss that the Germans and the Japanese often fought very well in behalf of what Americans were certain was a bad cause. It was not surprising that amid this deflation a few soldiers found grounds to repudiate their commitment to the Cause. Artilleryman Frank Mercurio, caught on that invasion beach and reasoning with a mind going "round and round like a whirlpool of shooting stars," realized that if he were killed, he would be unable to benefit from the precepts for which he was risking his life. "So why fight for them, if I can't live to go home and enjoy them? I didn't want any part of it." Overwhelming numbers of soldiers, however, remained convinced of a cause that to them possessed rock-solid justification. No less persuasive, it simply became, in both European and Pacific combat, extraneous to absorbing daily pursuits and consequently virtually disappeared from their thoughts.[61]

Another canon—the assumption of American material superiority—also suffered, though here the issue was factualness rather than pertinence. Seldom were there grounds to question the quality of resources made available to the U.S. Navy—beyond the flawed torpedoes that did constitute a se-

---

*Toole made an exception for the close fighting on the densely packed Anzio beachhead.

rious problem in the war's early stages. American aircraft yielded some elements of superiority to the Japanese Zero, but only at the outset, and to the German ME-262 jet aircraft, but only in the last days of the war; otherwise, American planes, in their quality and especially in their numbers, dominated those of their opponents.

American sailors and airmen, then, lacked cause to complain about the weapons given them to fight the war. Combat soldiers, however, had grounds for grievance. American technological accomplishment was weakest where it affected them most. True, their semi-automatic M-1 rifle was a better basic weapon than the landser's bolt-action Mauser; the military historian Russell Weigley had described the M-1 as the best standard shoulder arm of the war. German machine guns and antitank missiles, however, were conspicuously superior to their American counterparts, and Weigley, for one, maintains that the Wehrmacht squad consequently possessed a firepower greater than that of the U.S. Army squad. Of those forces working in support of the infantry the Americans possessed more artillery, but the German 88 was, by common consent, the most effective artillery piece of the war. Tanks posed a special problem. In 1944, Nazi production chief Albert Speer boasted that "one Tiger II [tank] has . . . the same effect as 25 to 30 Shermans." Americans disputed the numbers—an American tank commander told combat engineer Henry Giles that "it took four of our Shermans to equal one of their Panthers and about eight to equal one of their Tigers"— but combat soldiers conceded, often with bitterness, the fundamental truth beneath Speer's claim: German tank supremacy.[62]

Field surgeon Brendan Phibbs watched as an American tank caught a Panther in its sights and fired three 76-mm rounds that struck the enemy vehicle "swiftly and accurately, right on the front slope-plate"—and bounced away. As a tanker screamed over the radio net, "Ping-Pong balls! Goddamn fucking Ping-Pong balls!" a shell from the Panther traversed the length of the American tank, destroying it and at least one of its crew. Phibbs, who learned to approach burned American tanks from upwind because of the odor of charred flesh, could hardly restrain his anger.

Even German prisoners of war sympathized with the victims of so unmistakable a technological disparity.

> Ronsons, you know. Ronsons, yes, like for a cigarette. Our [German] gunners see your tanks coming . . . and they say to each other, "Here comes another Ronson." Why do the Americans do this for us? Bang! and it burns like twenty haystacks. All the people [inside], my God.
>
> Those funny tanks with the little guns, and so high and straight we can see

them from a long way in our gunsights. Those square sides, and thin, the armor. We know if we hit one it goes up.

Why does the country of Detroit send their men out to die in these things?[63]

Fortunately for the Allies, the Wehrmacht lacked the numbers of tanks that might have proven decisive, and the superiority of German manufacture was in the end overcome by the plenitude of Shermans and, more decisively, of artillery support.

Still, American soldiers in Europe were often confronted, as GIs and Marines in the Pacific almost never were, with recurring instances of a local enemy weapons superiority. Coupled with soldiers' diminishing sense of control within their own sphere, the consequences were disheartening. Infantry medic Frank Irgang contemplated the SS troops blocking his unit's advance: "Yes, we were well fed and equipped, but they had a match for everything we had, and it usually went one better." Giles decided that "One thing you have to give the Krauts. Some of their equipment is damned good and a lot of it beats the hell out of ours." His conclusion was bleak: "If they hadn't been fighting for five years before we got here and hadn't had a two-front war on their hands at that, we'd have had a hell of a time licking them. They've been hard enough, the way it is."[64]

Failing to find in combat much that they had expected, finding much that they had not expected, and quickly losing the exuberant, confident aggressiveness with which most had approached battle, soldiers began manifesting the strain of their lives in combat. The most visible sign was physical aging.

Young soldiers had looked forward to war altering them physically and emotionally. En route to maturation, no station would be more significant, and battle would be the decisive rite of passage, entered upon as a boy, releasing one as a man. It seemed reasonable, too, that physical exertion, exposure to the elements, and irregular sleep would exact some physical costs. But the reality revealed a process moving much faster and further than soldiers had foreseen, and they struggled in their description of the results. One of them spoke of taking on "the look and movements of middle age." Some agreed that they were losing youthfulness but thought the result an indeterminate ageless appearance. Others simply concluded that they were growing old too soon. But all would have identified with George Hunt's observation of his Marine comrades: "Every face seemed older than it should have been, more hard-bitten."[65]

Equally confusing was the rapidity of the metamorphosis. Grady Arrington thought that a friend had "aged immeasurably" in his first three hours of combat. A cook in Harold Leinbaugh's company noticed that soldiers re-turning for hot food after their first battle "hardly looked like the same men." A sailor described those who debarked for, and later re-embarked from, Pacific island battles: "Going, they are young and in the best of health. Returning, they are old and beaten shells that once were men." Replace-ments gingerly surveyed old-timers and wondered, "Are we going to look like that?" Veterans saw that question in the glances of new men; with cer-tain knowledge—"Their youth will decay; they'll become tired and aged"—but with a certain pity for an innocence they knew would be lost, they seldom tendered the answer: "Yes, very soon."[66]

Grady Arrington barely recognized a college companion who had re-cently seen combat; but by his friend's reaction when he hailed him, Arring-ton realized that he would have to introduce himself: his friend had entirely failed to recognize him.[67]

The availability of mirrors in airbase barracks and the opportunity—in-deed, requirement—for daily grooming often brought home battle-aging to airmen faster than to ground troops. Bomber pilot Bert Stiles said of himself and of those air-crews around him at a base in England that in the mirror they were all "like old men."[68]

Volubility disappeared as rapidly as youthfulness. Based on his observa-tions of Americans at Normandy, Richard Tobin, correspondent for the *New York Herald Tribune,* concluded that Londoners would no longer find famil-iar those Yanks so recently in their midst. In fact, Tobin himself "scarcely rec-ognized the G.I. whom I had met in such loquacious quantities aboard my troop transport. . . ." "The first thing that has happened to him is that he has stopped talking." He "did not often look up or say anything at all. . . ." In the wake of its first experience of battle in Luxembourg—of 180 men, 16 had been killed and 30 wounded—Howard Randall's Company K became "a solemn and greatly changed group of men." Gone were their earlier horse-play and loud talk. And seldom did soldiers, even with the lifting of somber post-battle moods, recover their talkativeness.[69]

The experience of the 16th Infantry Regiment made plain that such changes were neither superficial nor transient. Brought to England to pre-pare for the Normandy invasion, its men were ordered, for purposes of secu-rity, to conceal their participation in combat in North Africa and Sicily and their affiliation with the 1st Division; so, "Unit patches were ripped off uni-forms, combat decorations and theater ribbons were forbidden, and the big red '1' on their helmets was painted over with brown paint. They were to [tell others] that they had [just] come fresh from the United States." The men of the 16th complied. (Obedience was never more onerous than when earlier arrivals, who though without battle experience considered themselves "old hands," shouted at the columns of the 16th, "Hey, what took you guys so long in getting over here?" and "Waiting for the war to end [so you can] cash in on the glory?" and "Were you afraid to leave your mommas?" and "Careful now, girls, don't stub your toes.") But not even stiff will and model discipline could carry the ruse. The 16th Regiment had lost its ebullience to battle. There was no bonhomie, no persiflage, no boasting of what the men would do in combat. And civilians, grasping the similarity between the 16th and young English veterans of their acquaintance, knew immediately that these were Americans who had been in battle. They were "too quiet."[70]

Those who had seen combat talked to new arrivals in their own ranks diffidently and differently. Many campaigners clung to silence on the grounds that replacements would "find out soon enough for themselves." Many replacements resented the veterans' reserve and, no less, some of what *was* said. In the light of subsequent experience, it sometimes seemed that the old-timers had given them false information. From North Africa Morton Eustis wrote home that "Everyone here who has been [at the front] says that you're scared absolutely sick the first time that you're dive-bombed or shelled, but that gradually you get accustomed to it, particularly as you realize how rarely you get hit, especially if you don't lose your head." No veteran believed in the diminution of fear or the ability of rationality to fend off casualties, but false assurances were not always offered from cruelty or trickery, except when beginners were intolerably brash. Often the governing intent, behind the gruffness, was sympathetic consideration. Why alarm them? Learning for themselves would be hard enough. True, replacements justifiably curious and genuinely concerned to learn of battle did, in their ardor, still send out signals that they knew it all. And in response, many veterans— in pained combinations irritated, offended, sympathetic, and despairing of their ability to communicate to others the realities of battle—were most likely to shelter beneath a laconic "Just wait and see."[71]

Reticence, in fact, rose to a level meriting at least semi-official attention. Colonel Samuel Lyman Marshall, a journalist and military commentator who at war's end became the Army's chief historian of European theater operations, complained that while German and Japanese soldiers talked to one another in battle, thereby joining force and multiplying strength, American soldiers remained silent, threatening small units with a loss of control due to the failure of "close-up communications." He blamed "a definite blind spot in our training"—the inability to impart awareness that it was "when you talk to others and they join with you that your action becomes important." The United States, he lamented, had committed to battle against the Axis "about the mutest [army] we ever sent to war." True, at or near the front it was not a talking, shouting, or singing army, but no one had ever testified to the reluctance of American soldiers, prior to combat, to express themselves in mess hall, on bayonet range, or in any other military or social setting. Their reserve was another acquisition of combat.[72]

The loss of volubility was a further component of the soldier's sinking sense of control and thus of a heightening awareness of his own fragility. An acute manifestation appeared among a group of 9th Infantry Division riflemen during furious fighting in the Huertgen Forest. Convinced that death was imminent, they debated whether it would remain at bay long enough for them to finish smoking the carton of cigarettes they carried with them. Or a pack? Or the single cigarette just lighted? Confidence in survival had given way to deep pessimism, and it was here that soldiers seeking ways to contend with the change yielded the ruling role in their calculations to luck. Wrote Morton Eustis to his mother: "It's luck, pure and simple, this game. There's no other way you can look at it." Only chance could explain life-and-death episodes in which no soldier's action, wise or stupid, could account for the outcome—and battle abounded in such occurrences.[73]

As the vehicle carrying Franklyn Johnson, a member of an anti-tank unit, drove through a dirty Tunisian creek, he glanced behind just as the water cleared to reveal, midway between the tire tracks, a German teller mine. Ten minutes later, farther along the road, another truck struck an identical mine, killing two Americans. In Luxembourg, platoon leader Howard Randall realized that he had inadvertently pulled the trip wire of a German booby trap—"I tried to think of a prayer—[and] couldn't"—but with a sudden drop in temperature, a small bead of ice had so formed that it kept the firing device, a cotter pin, slightly spread. There was no explosion. Why did an enemy shell snuff out the lives of one group of Americans and another, landing in the midst of a similar group, fail to detonate? Why, at that moment, was a particular soldier in the second group rather than the first? "You were where you were and the men who were being killed were where they were," one of writer Harry Brown's soldiers tried, and failed, to explain. Private Lester Atwell pondered artillery deaths on his second day of fighting: "Some men had been killed [by German 88-mm shells] because they were in foxholes; some because they were not. Still others had been hit by our own artillery falling short of its mark." "It seemed dehumanized to me, a matter of purest chance." Battle drew almost all American soldiers into agreement with James Jones's observation that "We pretty much lived by superstition. We had to. When all of knowledge and of . . . experience had been utilized, the outcome of . . . a defense or an attack depended largely on luck."[74]

The first adjustment to luck's new prominence, a reorientation from "I'm in control and won't get hit because I won't make a mistake" to "I may not be in control, but I still won't get hit because I'm a lucky bastard," was no less painful than the surrender of any other cherished certainty and, moreover, had to be accomplished rapidly. In combat's early stages, soldiers remained unwilling to grant luck unfettered play in their lives—no one, after all, believed that all luck was good luck—so they resorted to the notion of odds, used both as a hedge and as a charm against any unfavorable turn of luck. And while still new to battle, they tended to very optimistic estimates of the odds. Wrote Eustis: "[W]e knew . . . that your chances of getting hit, even under direct machine gun fire, were slight." "It's always a help to be under fire and to realize how great the odds are against being hit." As casualties mounted, however, calculations became less confident. American combat doctor Klaus Huebner counted the replacements who arrived to replenish his battalion: "Approximately two hundred and fifty new faces appear. I now realize that we have already lost and replaced one half of the battalion since starting our push up the Italian peninsula [forty-nine days ago]. Thus far, my chances of [remaining] alive have been about fifty-fifty." Soon combat lieutenants were computing the life spans of platoon leaders following arrival in their theater of operations. (In Western Europe, the average was thirty days.) The soldier's god, professed James Jones, was "a Great Roulette Wheel."[75]

Next came a fear that the odds protecting one were daily growing less favorable and that one's own luck was running out. It was one thing to say of unit members just killed, "Well, luck can last only so long"; it was quite another for the soldier to stand and face a new conviction that *his own* luck was being expended. Sometimes triggered by the death of a soldier who was a favorite in the company or whose friends thought him indestructible ("Until today, I thought maybe there was a chance of getting through alive. But when Horse-Face got it, I gave up"), the moment of confrontation could be shattering. Eugene Sledge, approaching Kunishi Ridge on southern Okinawa, "plodded along through the darkness, my heart pounding, my throat dry and almost too tight to swallow[;] near-panic seized me. Having made it that far in the war, I *knew* my luck would run out. I began to sweat and pray. . . . I wanted to turn and run away." No one caught this critical juncture

more perceptively than Robert Crisp, the British tank officer who fought in
the North African desert campaign:

> I had had half a dozen tanks knocked out under me, I had seen tanks alongside
> me turned into incandescent tombs for the men trapped inside them, I had
> been sprayed with lead particles and God knows how many times I had escaped
> death by the smallest fraction of deviation in some gunner's aim; I had passed
> more or less unscathed through air filled with the flying steel of shell explosions
> and the indiscriminate hail of machine-gun fire. I tried to console myself by
> thinking that each battle presented exactly the same chances of individual sur-
> vival or obliteration. But I felt my chances were running out; that I had used
> them all up. . . . [Our] next objective was the rear of the enemy position at
> Gazala, and I had a frightening certainty that I was going to be particularly in-
> volved in a way that would not affect anybody else. I had been afraid often
> enough before, but it had always been tempered by the conviction that, what-
> ever happened to anybody else, disaster could not come to me. "It could not
> happen to me." It was, in fact, the basis of most of my actions. Now, in a mo-
> ment of realisation that made me very afraid, I knew I had lost my immunity.[76]

Ironically, as the soldier came to feel his complete loss of control and
thus his complete vulnerability, success—i.e., staying alive—veered to reinforce pessimism rather than confidence in survival. Another British officer,
after suffering in fighting within Germany "several more narrow shaves," remembered that six months earlier he had found close-by shell explosions
"slightly exhilarating, just as when one has ridden in a number of steeple-
chases without a mishap, it does one's nerve good to have a harmless fall."
No longer. "[Now] I have seen too much. . . ." Last autumn dodging mortar
shells had seemed an amusement. No longer. "But [now] it wasn't fun at all."
Each escape from death seemed less assured, more miraculous, and thus increasingly unlikely to repeat itself, so he and his men were going into battle
"knowing perfectly well that [we] are dicing against the mathematical odds.
. . . For an officer to go into a dozen actions without being killed or badly
wounded is like a coin coming down heads six times running. He knows that
his luck cannot possibly last. . . ."[77]

It was here roughly, as soldiers were compelled to concede the loss of all
protection, that their thought, increasingly fatalistic, narrowed down to two
final formulations: the conviction that "War is dying," and an almost full acceptance of "It is going to happen to me."

Infantrymen felt more acutely than others in the war zone this new and
unconquerable conviction of their own expendability, for time in battle also

brought convincing evidence that they stood almost alone, that the supporting arms could not be relied upon, and that many on their own side were willing to see them killed.

Infantrymen found out that tanks were a motley benefit, even when working in direct support of foot soldiers. Soldiers could not live with them or without them, decided Frank Irgang and his comrades. Tanks' firepower was of course welcome and their battering power could sometimes demolish enemy-held buildings or hedgerows, but they regularly attracted enemy artillery fire. In Italy, a soldier of the 10th Mountain Division, John Bassett, expressed a common infantry reaction: "Halfway up the hill the line stopped and we stooped down beside a protective . . . hedge. There were tanks going by . . . and then they stopped. Those bastards, I muttered. They'll draw more artillery fire on us." In France, Vernon McHugh decided that despite their "wonderful support," he "wanted no part of tanks. They are moving foxholes easy for the Jerries to spot."[78]

Foot soldiers in Europe were well aware that the American tank was inferior to the German and was especially vulnerable to its 88. "[In] a tank-against-tank battle we were decidedly mercenary and bet on the Jerries, unless our tanks outnumbered them something fierce. A Tiger could sit all day just like a chunk of solid steel, soaking up the punishment, and then blast off one 88 and put 'paid' to the pestering Sherman. . . ." But because tankers still seemed so much better protected than they, infantry often derided the cautiousness of the armor. Even worse was what appeared the behemoths' lumbering obliviousness. Just as SS troops in the French village of Saint-Benôit began to wave white flags at dug-in GIs, two Shermans "clanked into the field . . . took no time to ask questions [and] opened up on the village with their .50-caliber turret guns and their 75-millimeter cannon. White flags and Germans [seeking new cover] disappeared in a cloud of dust." Often tanks supposed to shield infantry required shielding *by* the infantry. "'Tank-chasing' [use of foot men to protect tanks]," reported a Marine on Okinawa, "became one of the most dreaded chores of the riflemen."[79]

Infantrymen frequently protested that the tankmen deserted them and, specifically, that they were too quick to withdraw when they drew enemy fire. A Bill Mauldin cartoon pictured a tanker popping genially from his hatch to tell five nearby GIs crouching in their holes, "We'll go away an' stop botherin' you boys now. Jerry's got our range." Infantry also grumbled that the tankers' insistence on nightly behind-the-lines "maintenance" of their machines owed less to mechanical necessity than to the desire for sound sleep. Accordingly, ground soldiers sometimes resorted to manipulation to overcome what they deemed tanker timidity. As part of an effort to persuade armor to move up, Don Lavender of the 9th Infantry Division understated to the tankers the size of the German tanks opposing them.[80]

In truth, however, at its heart the infantryman's estrangement drew less on complaints of inadequate support—by any comparative measure American infantry-armor cooperation was very good—and more on the grievance caught by Mauldin: Foot soldiers stayed in battle, tankers departed. Lavender told his story with deep-seated resignation: "We had moved only a few hundred yards when a German anti-tank gun fired on our tanks[,] which were moving abreast of us on the road below. . . . We continued on without our tanks." The infantry's presence was required always; that of the tankers seemed sporadic and always conditional. Medic William Tsuchida told of a fight near the Saar Basin against German pillboxes, "a mess of concrete and steel":

> . . . [Our] demolition squad crawled up with TNT on their backs and blew the door in. And the infantry guys took a beating while they did it. Even the tanks had pulled back after their firing point-blank at the pillboxes had failed. But this one company of guys with just rifles had to stick it out. You figure it out. We can't.[81]

The artillery's support of the infantry was massive, constant, and critical. No factor was more important to success in Europe than the infantry's ability to call down artillery fire to break up German attacks or to cripple German resistance to its own assaults. Foot soldiers generally recognized the relationship, comprehended its importance, and were grateful. Often they expressed, at least to one another, their relief that the artillery had been able to extricate them from a trap or reduce the danger to one of their withdrawals by interposing between them and oncoming enemy an impenetrable barrier of destructive power.[82]

Still, aggravation, crystallizing around certain kinds of episodes, persisted. Batteries arrived in the midst of infantry, set up, shelled the enemy, and quickly withdrew—leaving the foot soldiers to absorb the counterbattery fire. (When each morning in Belgium a British twenty-five-pounder rushed up, fired ten rounds, and scurried away, an infantryman-mechanic one day removed its mobile unit's rotor arm, thereby forcing the artillerymen to sample the ripostes of the German 88s to which they daily exposed the ground soldiers. The infantry "weren't troubled again.") Then, too, American artillerymen committed errors, in calculation or communication, that inflicted casualties on American infantry. Such lapses triggered outrage: *"Our own artillery* is coming in *on us!*" Particularly infuriating were instances when, during full-scale bombardments, single pieces were improperly ranged and the short-shelling that was wounding and killing GIs was not stopped because, amid so many cannon, the offender could not be located nor the whole barrage halted.[83]

Finally, there were matériel shortages that infantrymen, understandably but unjustifiably, blamed on artillerymen. Russell Weigley has described the situation: "Various basic calibers of artillery ammunition were in scarce supply in northwest Europe from soon after D-Day and virtually throughout the rest of the war. American corps and division commanders repeatedly requested allocations of artillery ammunition for bombardments to precede attacks and could not get what they wanted." This problem filtered to foxholes in stories of artillerymen who, having fired a few rounds at advancing enemy and just found the range, then told the infantry: "Sorry, we have used up our quota for today."[84]

Still, as with armor, it was less what the artillery did or failed to do and more the other arm's relationship to the fighting that agitated infantrymen. The foot soldier, conceded a rifleman who fought on Guadalcanal, "[envied] the Artilleryman, a thousand yards to his rear, [with all] the additional safety and comforts back there." Such envy frequently quickened into anger—and sometimes into disdain. Combat medic Keith Winston told those at home that while battle losses in the 3d Division had turned over front-line soldiers five to seven times, an attached artillery unit had suffered "only one casualty in ten months of combat—and this from their own ack-ack. This is not hearsay, this is fact—from the [artillery] boys themselves. They're also called combat boys and get the same battle star credit for combat as the doughboy who sleeps in a wet foxhole risking his life every second." In the Pacific theater, William Manchester was persuaded, there was "a certain fairness—if anything in battle can be fair—in one rifleman fighting another. Each [has] a chance. . . . But there [is] something grotesque and outrageous about a man safely behind fortifications, miles away, pulling a lanyard and killing other men who cannot see him, let alone reach him." But infantrymen did not truly wish that the artillery receive less recognition or suffer higher casualties or kill the enemy in some more equitable fashion; they were simply deploring once again what they were believed was the war's maldistribution of sacrifice, with their own lives the forfeit.[85]

Contact with the Air Force was more complex than with armor or artillery, and far less frequent. In general, air actions were beyond the front-line soldier's range of vision—and when they were close enough to see, they were close enough to do him injury. Again, another arm's mistakes claimed their victims largely among foot soldiers. From the Philippines: "Not long after moving inland we set up . . . in a small Lingayen town. We were sleeping peacefully when we heard sirens, a roar, and machine guns. One of our planes got mixed up in the moonlight and buzzed up and down the highway tearing up a convoy of our trucks . . . [with] tragic consequences. . . . A few days later we watched as Mustangs dive-bombed a village tucked into a copse of trees. . . . Unknown to the careless pilots, our own soldiers had moved into the village and were being killed and wounded by the attack." From Germany: "Then suddenly something went wrong. We heard a fast rate of fire from multiple guns. . . . We looked up and there was one of our own planes diving with his guns blazing, . . . strafing our area. . . . The pilot [then] came in from east to west and dropped one bomb[,] . . . zoomed around . . . [and dropped] a second bomb."[86]

Such episodes generated infantry fury—and violent fluctuations of attitude. Lieutenant Paul Boesch and his comrades near Brest

> watched in awe . . . as [our P-39s and P-47s] delivered huge demolition bombs, smaller fragmentation bombs, machine-gun fire, and Napalm bombs which exploded in a great, spectacular gush of flaming oil. The planes zoomed low over our heads as they streaked for Jerry's lines to support our attacking units, and we were loud in our praise of the airmen we had so often vilified during training because we thought they had an easy life. Taking back most of the mean things we had said about them we were ready to admit they were our allies. We were even ready to admit out loud that they were soldiers, which was quite a concession for infantrymen.

But then—

> Just as we were shouting the airmen's praises without restriction, a pair of Thunderbolts roared out of the sky. To our horror we could see their bombs release and come screaming straight at us. . . . [They] landed about a hundred yards away with terrific blasts. I had no sooner scrambled shakily to my feet and checked my platoon . . . when the P-47s returned to strafe. . . . The planes zipped past, spitting blatant messages of death. . . . We stood up, brushed off and hardly had time to cuss before two others roared out of the sky on a bombing run. Again we hugged the earth . . .

Those fellow soldiers of the air instantaneously became "those crazy bastards [who] are after us." "God bless our Air Corps, but . . ." "We'll kill the dumb bastards if they do it again." A soldier in the 104th Division chidingly called several Air Force officers members of the "Ninth Luftwaffe." They had killed more Americans than Germans, he claimed, and thus ought to be awarded Iron Crosses.[87]

Tragic incidents provided occasion for infantry to recapitulate the whole slate of their grievances against airmen, for they were convinced that they sacrificed far more and were remunerated far less than pilots and their crews. Airmen, after all, returned "home" after every mission, while, in infantryman Orval Faubus's testy words, "for the front-line soldier there is no surcease from danger and hardship." At airbases, growled rifleman John George, "men are usually sure of a cot to sleep on and warm food to eat." In early 1944, Ernie Pyle visited an Air Force facility in Italy.

> Now our airmen have wood stoves in their rooms, they sleep in sleeping bags on folding cots, they have shelves to put their things on, they have electric light, they eat at tables, sitting on stools, and have an Italian boy to clear the dishes away. They have an Italian barber, and their clothes are clean and pressed. They have a small recreation room with soldier-drawn murals on the walls. They can go to a nearby town of an evening and see American movies, in theaters taken over by the Army. They can have dates with nurses. They can play cards. They can read by good light in a warm room.

Pyle considered pilots "as a class . . . the gayest people in the Army. When they came back from a mission they were usually full of high spirits. And when they sat around together . . . nine-tenths of their conversation was exuberant and full of howling jokes. There was no grimness in their conduct to match that of the infantrymen in the line."[88]

One day a Marine fighter pilot over Rabaul, the Japanese base on New Britain, cast himself as an action hero and was immediately joined on the squadron's communications net by others no less familiar with comic books and radio serials. "I'm the Green Hornet! Bzzzzzzz! Bzzzzzzz! Watch me sting this Jap." . . . "Here comes Jack Armstrong, the A-a-a-all American Boy! Rat-a-taaaaaat! Rat-a-taaaaaat!" "Which way'd they go, Sheriff? Thataway, pardner. Yippeeeeeee! The Lone Ranger rides again!" . . . "Dick Tracy's the name. Flat-top . . . you're a goner—Rat-a-a-taat! Rat-a-taaaaaaaaa!" It was the sort of fun that infantrymen thought the daily fare of American fighter pilots. Ernie Pyle's cautionary note—"Don't get the wrong impression. Their life is not luxurious. At home we wouldn't consider it adequate. It has the security of walls and doors, but it's a dog's life at that"—must have had line soldiers wondering, if that was a dog's life, what lower-order existence was theirs in the Liri Valley? Anger was inevitable. Combat soldiers who stared at aircraft passing overhead and were convinced that their pilots would, in an hour's time, be showered, shaved, shining in clean clothes, and hailing a taxi to Cairo, Rome, or London, called flyers the "Brylcreem Boys."[89]

To the infantryman, ground warfare was impossibly chaotic, while the airman's life appeared neatly ordered and almost completely governable during as well as between combat missions. From the ground, bomber formations looked faultlessly patterned, so precise and tidy, and the movements of fighter aircraft carried equal appeal for the opposite reason: their great swoops, tight turns, and steep dives seemed to trace with drama the pilot's ability—and freedom—to act exactly as he willed.

Airmen, ground soldiers were certain, received for their less strenuous war lives far more than their share of pay, promotions, and citations. Infantry lieutenant George Wilson of the Army's 4th Division respected the Air Force's "awesomely effective job," but he never ceased to resent airmen's comfortable lives and "extra pay." A colonel in the 35th Division protested flyers' "double pay for flying, while the Infantry, with the hardest lot of all, gets nothing extra no matter what they do." Air Force promotions, by infantry standards, came early and often. A Mauldin cartoon depicted a neatly dressed, curly-haired, adolescent Air Force colonel moving excitedly to embrace a scruffy infantry private whom he greeted as "Uncle Willie!" Another pictured a crewman explaining to Willie and Joe, loaded up and ready to emplane, that "Ya might hafta catch a boat. One of them kids ya chased off th' field wuz the pilot." Asked by a replacement why aircraft had not destroyed a German roadblock holding back the infantry's advance, a sergeant in Audie Murphy's platoon adopted the tone common to ground soldiers. "Are you kidding? The air force is taking the day off to run off a new batch of medals. Bunch of flyers knocked out a Jerry latrine day before yesterday and go gliding home through the wild blue yonder to get their medals. And what do you know? There wasn't a medal left. Plumb broke the spirit of them flyers. No, we can't depend on the air corps."[90]

There was reality beneath the infantrymen's complaints of inequitable treatment, although some of the disparities reflected Army remissness rather than Air Force advantage. Promotions and thus pay were more generous in the air arm, and the gap in supplemental compensation remained unclosed even after Congress authorized combat pay for ground soldiers. Recognition, too, came easier to airmen; a study of awards for performance in the European theater in spring 1945 revealed that airmen received fourteen times as many medals as combat troops.[91]

Yet some of the better treatment of airmen was carefully considered. The Air Corps monitored far better than the ground forces the physical condition and psychological equipoise of its personnel. Flight surgeons watched for symptoms of psychoneurosis, made prompt diagnoses, and ordinarily introduced timely therapy. That institutional concern was rooted in the Air Force's desire to guard against explosions of aberrant behavior with far greater potential for damage, jeopardizing highly trained crews and costly machinery, than were those of unhinged infantrymen; the result was a program, far more diligent than the Army's, to identify and pull from combat those close to collapse. Sometimes rests sufficed to restore injured psyches. Sometimes transfers to other kinds of aircraft or to other theaters or to instructor positions brought relief. (Rare was the infantryman, infirm or fit, who was thought to have gained from combat any knowledge sufficiently important to be imparted to others.) Finally, the sting of every disparity was intensified by the American public's idolization of pilots as leather-jacketed, bescarfed, brave, rollicking hero-adventurers.[92]

Still, though there were grounds for some of the infantry's complaints, others rested on profound misconceptions. Foot soldiers understood airmen's lives less accurately than flyers comprehended the experience of ground combat. Although there existed an Air Corps–infantry exchange program in which, as infantryman James Fry described it, "some of our officers visited Air organizations in the rear, and Air Force officers visited the front . . . an excellent plan to improve understanding and cooperation," it included no enlisted men and drew far more air than infantry participants.[93]

Even aviators whose comprehension relied on views from thousands of feet up thought that they saw enough to prefer their war—and to sympathize with those below. Bert Stiles glanced from the cockpit of his B-17 on D-Day and felt a powerful compassion for "those poor bastards down on the beach." "[M]ost of the time you don't live with death in a [Flying Fortress] the way they must in a ditch." Flyers appreciated, too, the comfort they returned to each day. Slumped in his chair contemplating a just-completed mission in support of ground forces imperiled by the Germans' Ardennes offensive of Christmas 1944, a pilot suddenly spoke out: "I was just thinking. All of us guys flying planes are such lucky pricks. We go through hell but then we come back to a bed and a hot meal and a good night's sleep. But those poor goddam bastards in the fucking infantry . . ." Ten thousand miles away, air gunner John Ciardi's ruminations were similar: "It's the boys in the foxholes that are sweating out this war. I'm part of the exclusive Saipan Hunt Club— hunting parties twice weekly (weather and mechanics permitting)."[94]

Most of this fellow feeling was lost on infantrymen who, seeing airmen only from afar, regularly exaggerated the contrasts between ground war and air war and underestimated the latter's costs. Seldom were they aware of the price paid by those aviators who alone carried the war to the enemy in Western Europe between mid-August 1942 and early June 1944. "Our own war . . . the exclusive war," Stiles called it. Air crews, explained B-17 pilot Philip Ardery, "felt that they had borne the whole war [there] for a long time, and they longed for assistance on the ground to speed things up." This was more than a matter of misery seeking company; bombing raids, unbearably costly during the summer and fall of 1943, brought air crews to near desperation. The Germans were able to destroy 30.5 percent of the 177 B-24s sent to bomb Ploesti; 19.1 percent of the bombers that attacked Regensburg-Schweinfurt; 26.2 percent of those returning to Schweinfurt. At the same time, James Doolittle, commander of the Eighth Air Force, became convinced that it was "wasteful . . . to send crews home just when they had become full-fledged professionals, combat-hardened," and he consequently increased the number of missions requisite for relief from twenty-five to thirty to thirty-five. (It was later extended to fifty.) Doolittle conceded that the changes were "highly unpopular at first," but he claimed that "the air crews came to agree as our loss rate steadily decreased and the chances of survival correspondingly increased." Yet, little improvement appeared before the early summer of 1944 and Doolittle's measures at first simply heightened the airmen's despair.[95]

B-24 pilot John Vietor estimated that in 1943 and early 1944, "it was seldom that more than ten percent of the squadrons flying from England would complete the twenty-five missions necessary for the Lucky Bastard Ribbon (Distinguished Flying Cross) and return to the States." In April 1944, the Army Air Corps' commanding officer, Henry "Hap" Arnold, warned the Joint Chiefs that "the massive likelihood of death was beginning to affect his crews—the loss rate was currently 85% of the total force over a tour of twenty-five sorties." The historian Michael Sherry calculated that, overall, only 27 percent of air crews were able to complete twenty-five raids over Germany. Ultimately, 52,000 of America's 290,000 battle deaths were those of air personnel, and the loss rate of bomber crews reached a level exceeded only by the infantry.[96]

Pilots were seldom told theater statistics, but they counted losses within their own units and were desolated. William Cubbins' B-24 squadron arrived in Italy during the spring of 1944. "Within less than four months, [it] had lost over 100 percent of [its] normal complement of aircraft and crews. . . . The original . . . crews had dwindled to a few. None had completed the required fifty missions, and air crew prospects for survival were grim." "Mathematically," Philip Ardery decided, "no one had a chance of getting through a tour." John Muirhead, whose war would end when his B-17 was shot down and he was made a prisoner of war, alternated between slight hope and no hope. "Nine missions was maturity; up to fifteen or more was to be regarded with awe; beyond that was magic, luck to be touched, to be near and favored beyond anything else." "Completing fifty missions was too implausible to even consider." "Our lives were defined by a line from the present to a violent moment that must come for each of us." Worrying before every mission whether he would return, Ardery wondered each morning whether he should open early the Christmas presents that had arrived from home.[97]

The actual air losses were of course concealed on grounds of military security and morale, so infantrymen retained a sense of the disparity of their own sacrifice. To them, it continued to appear as if all those in the Air Corps could "look forward to a trip home. All they have to do is complete so many missions. [But] what do we have to look forward to?" Ernie Pyle spent most of his time with the Air Force in the company of fighter pilots and chose not to go along on long-distance bombing runs; continuing to write from the infantry perspective, he persisted in his sanguine views of life in the air arm. Air personnel came to the war zone, fought with a zest and ease denied ground soldiers, stayed a relatively short time, and, with inappreciable exceptions, survived to be transferred beyond harm. "It would be unusual for a combat airman to be overseas more than a year, at the present rate." He cited the Air Corps "system of relieving pilots after a certain number of missions," as if that were simply a matter of course. He visited a squadron of tactical fighter-bombers and weighed its odds. Fifty pilots had entered combat six months earlier; twelve had become casualties, thirty-five had returned home, and the last three were about to follow. His mistaken conclusion: "[A] a new pilot . . . has about a seventy-five percent chance of coming through safely. . . ." And even those few who died maintained an advantage over dog soldiers: "A man approached death rather decently in the Air Forces," as someone who, well-fed and clean-shaven, "was at the front only a few hours a day . . . came back to something approximating a home . . . and still had some acquaintance with orderly life," not someone like the ground soldier, who "had to become half beast [to try] to survive."[98]

The view from the ground was misleading. True, the time over the target was brief, but it was terrifying. "We were under [antiaircraft] fire for twelve minutes," recalled B-24 gunner James McMahon. "It is the most terrible experience you can have. It is just like going 'over the top' into an artillery barrage. I saw two [other American aircraft] blow up this day, and one go down by fighters." B-17 pilot John Bennett likened a bomber over a German city to a person burdened by two heavy cans of gasoline trying to run rapidly through a dark alley while thugs aimed firecrackers at the open containers. Sometimes the flak bursts were so dense that a pilot "had the feeling he could step out and walk on them," and the rare ground soldier who became their target was as likely to be terrified as an Air Force officer caught in a mortar barrage. One English ground-signals lieutenant, Anthony Cotterell, profoundly regretted that he had agreed to go along on a night RAF raid against Frankfurt; he found it "maddening . . . that [amidst the flak] the pilot didn't seem to make any effort to go any faster or dodge about. We just mooned drearily forward."[99]

Like most ground soldiers, Cotterell supposed that flyers were always able to exercise more control over their fates than could infantrymen, but bomber crews singled out feelings of helplessness as among the most frequent and daunting of their reactions. While gunners worked frenziedly to ward off enemy fighters, pilots had to hold their planes rigidly in formation, mooning drearily forward and praying that paths of aircraft and shells or bullets would not intersect. "It makes a guy so damned mad," McMahon protested, "and you can't do anything about it." Bennett too deplored that "the bomber pilot can't fight back, but must sit there and take it." Moreover, however short the time over target, the missions themselves were often protracted; the average round trip from the Marianas to Japan consumed fourteen hours, from English bases to Germany eight hours. Mechanical failure was common. Would a malfunction send the ship hurtling to earth or sea? Would the damage inflicted by flak or fighter prove fatal during the long return? Pilots could only fly on. And even when one's own craft seemed to be operating adequately, "you feel so . . . helpless when the others get in trouble. . . . I could spare any of them one engine and five hundred gallons of gas if I could just get it to them. It makes you feel so damn helpless."[100]

The pilots' sense of their own powerlessness, real despite the immense destructive power their bombers released upon the earth, was the root of at least one of the disconnections between bomber and fighter pilots, all of which remained beyond the ken of the infantry. As John Bennett told it, the bomber pilot's incapacity to return blows explained "why there is such a difference between the bomber and fighter boys. The men in this latter group can match their skill against the enemy. [The fighter pilot] carries a club of his own with which to fight back. I do not find the light-hearted devil-may-care spirit on the bomber station. . . . Our men go about their grim business with sober determination." "We are all afraid. . . ." Infantry, then, did not understand that bomber pilots might envy fighter pilots as ground soldiers envied all flyers. Muirhead was one of the wistful: "P-38s slid over the formation, drifting toward the southeast. Every time I saw them, I felt the same yearning to be as free as they were, to move as they did in soft, curling patterns above the bombers, or to roll away in a flash of motion as though abandoned to some impulse of delight. The sky was more a playground for them than a battlefield. . . . I knew they fell and died as we did, but theirs must have been a brighter heaven." Nor could ground troops appreciate that such pilots sometimes fought against that cavalier imagery. When a B-17 group commander in Europe, leafing through an American magazine, came upon an advertisement whose banner asked: "Who's afraid of the new Focke-Wulf?"* he clipped it, signed his name, and posted it. After all of his pilots, in avowal of their own fear, had added their signatures, he mailed the page to the advertiser.[101]

Beginning in spring 1944, the fundamental situation confronting American bombers over Germany changed rapidly. The arrival of the 108-gallon drop-tank extended decisively the range of the P-51 Mustang and for the first time permitted bomber missions round-trip fighter protection. This development, conjoining with the Germans' failure to replace experienced pilots who had died and the enemy's dearth of aviation fuel, so sapped the Luftwaffe's power that bomber losses in daylight raids fell from 20-25 percent to 6 percent. Still, veteran pilots who had begun their bomber tours with little fighter protection were unable to shake off their consciousness of acute peril. When Stiles' crew completed the required number of missions, "They all seemed to be in a quiet daze. . . . [They] wouldn't believe it for hours, maybe days."[102]

Nor was there much lightening of the burden borne by B-29 crews in the Pacific. John Ciardi, evincing no less helplessness than crewmen in Europe, spoke of the new dangers to which the shift early in 1945 to incendiary bombs had exposed him: "The new policy is to go in lower and lower. The object—as it should be—is to wipe out targets. But the terrific underlining of our complete expendability . . . doesn't help much. . . . I'm frankly afraid of these lowered-altitude runs. And I'm frankly afraid that Wing's refusal to

---

*A German high-altitude interceptor

tell us how many missions we're to fly means that we're here to be used up. . . . I do my job and keep cool. But this waiting to be expended does me down." "We are motes in a current. . . . And we wait with dread fringing all our consciousness." "We were [over Japan] to destroy . . . factories and Japanese factories had a price tag attached. We were the price and neither longing nor the will to live mattered in the final balance."[103]

Even at a distance, a few combat soldiers of unusual perceptiveness were able to grasp some of these strains in airmen's lives. Henry Giles, learning that the man who had married his fiancée's daughter was about to become a bomber pilot, thought carefully about life in the air:

> . . . brother, I don't envy him. It takes guts to sit up there and ride through that flak and I'm damned sure I don't have that kind. I've watched them plow through when it was as thick as a carpet under them and you couldn't see how any of them could make it. And some didn't. I've never watched one of our planes fall that it didn't make me sick at my stomach. The worst is when they spin down in flames. Somebody is being fried to a crackling and he hasn't got a chance. I don't begrudge a single one of those boys his easy life between missions, for when they fly it's rough.

Lieutenant Paul Boesch was another ground soldier whom events propelled to contemplate the indecency of the airmen's deaths rather than the decency of their living conditions. With his unit committed to the siege of Brest, he and his men watched as American squadrons bombed the German defenses.

> One day we had two separate attacks by . . . B-17s. My boys were so elated . . . that they got out of their foxholes and cheered lustily as the bombs fell in clusters toward the German positions. The cheers suddenly caught in our throats however as we saw one of the planes swerve into another. . . . Both . . . ships seemed to fall apart in the air, and pieces hurried earthward as harbingers of the remains. It seemed to take forever for the main body of the planes to crash to earth, and yet not a parachute appeared. [Untutored] as we were in the problems of the men in the sky, it seemed that some of the crews should have been able to escape, and we prayed to the last for the billowing silk that would indicate they had succeeded. The tragedy made us feel closer to the men of the Air Corps and impressed on us that we had no monopoly on death.[104]

But an understanding of airmen's lives—that there was a frightfulness in trying to withstand flak and in contending with death by fire; that access to civilian amenities could touch off longing and almost as much pain as pleasure; that there were in airmen's lives battle aging, sleeplessness, and combat nerves mirroring their own desperation—seldom entered the consciousness of ground soldiers. They could see only dimly the realities of the lives of bomber crews, and they continued to covet what they believed to be the relative ease of the air war. James Fry described with assurance the views of his fellow infantrymen:

> We were envious of airmen. Although we appreciated the courage it took to face enemy anti-aircraft fire, the average infantry combat soldier would have gladly exchanged places with the men [of] the Air Force. Each aviator's brief bombing mission, if successful, ended up with the crew far in [the] rear of the battle lines. There the dangers of the day could be followed by a congenial drink under conditions that would permit one to forget the whole grim affair[,] to relax mind and muscle.

Fry went on, as would many infantrymen, to contrast the civilized smoothness of air effort with the onerousness of infantry life: foot soldiers seldom received hot food or fresh clothing; they slept on the ground; they were never spared awareness "of the imminence of enemy action and violent death." For them, "there would be no chance to relax, no opportunity to forget what had taken place." So once again, continuities in the two experiences of warmaking went unrecognized, and obvious contrasts worked to raise an envy and resentment intensifying the infantry soldier's sense of isolation from the other branches of the American military.[105]

The final stamp on the infantry's conviction that it had been set apart was its estrangement from the high command of its own army.

Some disaffection was inevitable, for there were in all armies opposed perspectives, purposes, and powers in top and bottom ranks. Whereas those with combat experience were moving to define "victory" in terms of personal survival, for their commanders it continued to mean the pursuit of military success, battle and campaign triumphs that envisioned and accepted the destruction of certain numbers of platoons. But a high command victory was no victory to the GI whose death it encompassed, and surviving soldiers found increasingly remote and irrelevant prior assurances that battlefield victories promised the earliest possible return home. Their focus narrowed drastically to whatever they deemed would sustain continued existence; and to that, larger military success and failure were almost equally subordinate. Margaret Bourke-White became unhappy with those many infantrymen who failed to develop "a vision of their contribution to the basic scheme of battle," but here she ignored that in the distillation of their concerns to survival they had excluded interest in the cause, in developments in other theaters, and ultimately in combat beyond their own purview. Such tensions found lodgement in every army.[106]

There was, however, in the U.S. Army's policy governing relief from battle a problem of greater magnitude, one that created a divide greater than in the militaries of other nations. At the outset, the government's Victory Program had foreseen an army of 215 divisions; but with the nation's focus first on the war of industrial production, there materialized only eighty-nine—a total, as it proved, dangerously close to the minimum number necessary to win the war. With so slender a margin, the high command thought there was no option but to commit its divisions to combat indefinitely and to maintain their strength through a system of individual replacements. But casualties in Europe exceeded estimates, and not even continual service in the line could hold off a crisis in the late summer of 1944: the shortage of combat riflemen became acute. Indeed, S. L. A. Marshall claimed, extravagantly, that on August 6 "the entire reinforcement pool for infantry forces in Europe— . . . infantrymen ashore in France and ready to go into battle—consisted of one lone rifleman." Only the very rapid conversion of manpower from antiaircraft units, from Army and Air Force support units, and from ASTP* units of young soldiers enrolled in American universities—all of them trained or being trained for duties elsewhere—bridged the gap, often with tragic results for many so ill-grounded in infantry tactics.[107]

Almost all other armies established systems of rotating units out of the line. Even the Wehrmacht, with enemy armies pressing on the homeland from east and west, managed practically to the war's end to withdraw combat formations for days and weeks of refitting and relaxation or at least respite. An English officer in North Africa made clear what departure from the line, with its opportunity to clean and rest oneself, meant to his tankers: "The psychological magic of it moved us right out of the desert and its battles into some oasis of the mind in which just being able to wash and change our underclothes produced as complete a metamorphosis as being suddenly transposed to a breakfast in bed in a luxury hotel. . . ." GIs gained only brief pauses when their regiment was that one of the division's three held in reserve near but not on the line, and hard-used divisions were sometimes, but infrequently, shifted to quiet sectors. In November 1944, the U.S. Army established a program of recuperation leave in the United States but its numer-

---

*Army Specialized Training Program

ical limit—5,500 men a month—opened it to no more than one man in each company and assured that it would be greeted with derisive calculations of the eight, nine, or ten years that would be required to provide everyone in the unit a furlough at home.[108]

In the early stages of the war many infantrymen were able to accept such high command reasoning as that which Brigadier General Theodore Roosevelt, Jr., set out for his wife in a letter from North Africa in March 1943: "In this war no units in the line get relief. We just go on and on. I believe that the very fierceness of this fighting means that later resistance will be softened." Many ground soldiers, however, soon decided that they could not take the long view, that the "later" of diminished enemy opposition would arrive too late to help them evade death; and they were in any case appalled to realize that high command policy offered them no alternative less painful and costly than a serious wound or a nervous collapse. Said one infantry scout who fought in Sicily: "Men in our division gave up all hope of being relieved. They thought the Army intended to keep them in action until everybody was killed[,] that [the Army] would simply replace casualties. . . . All the men have hope of getting back, but most of the hope is that you'll get hit someplace that won't kill you. That's all they talk about." And even that hope soon evaporated: "You give up. You feel that you'll never get back anyway. You just try to postpone it as long as possible." Bitterness prevailed. "They stick us here," cried Irgang's friend Brinker, "and here we stay until we are either burned out or shot to hell." "It is a world no civilian can ever know," Orval Faubus wrote home. "Civilians can hide from the storm and wait and pray for its passing. We must go into the hell and finish the job. With sickened souls, despairing hearts and hate in our minds we must stick it out to our finish (in one way or another) or the war's finish. There must be a hell hereafter for men who willfully make such hells here for us."[109]

During the campaign to wrest the Huertgen Forest from the Germans, company commander Paul Boesch was ordered to assault the town of Huertgen. He protested: extended combat had reduced the unit to less than one-quarter strength and those who had survived were exhausted. Battalion reiterated its order but did send reinforcements, two squads of engineers armed with flamethrowers. Boesch quickly organized an attack, but when one of the engineers fired his weapon prematurely and alerted the enemy, overpowering German machine-gun fire wounded two Americans and left Boesch no option but to withdraw the men to their foxholes.

That night the engineers' section leader approached Boesch. "Lieutenant, isn't it time for us to go back? My men are getting cold in these holes." Boesch did not hesitate: "My men have been cold in the same kind of holes for about two weeks now, Sergeant. I expect to use you and your men later tonight[;] you'd better stand by." The sergeant retired—but was soon back. "Lieutenant, I'd like to take my men now and return to the company area." Boesch, irritated, replied that the assault was imminent, that the engineers were to have an important role, that they could not be spared. "Well, gee whiz, Lieutenant, they didn't tell me we were going on no suicide mission." Boesch bristled: "What the hell do you think about the rest of us? Don't you think we get a little sick of suicide missions too?" "But Lieutenant," came the sergeant's reply, "you all are *infantry.*"

> I sighed out loud. My God, we were infantry. That apparently meant [that] we were a race apart. Maybe we weren't supposed to feel, to hurt, to shiver, to be frightened, to react like other human beings. They were engineers, supply clerks, quartermasters, signalmen, ordnance repairmen—they were above this kind of miserable thing. But as for us, we were infantry.
>
> I started to tell the man to get back to his hole, that I wanted to hear no more from him, that he and his men had better be ready when I gave the word to move forward. Then I changed my mind. These men had tasted too much warm food and slept in too many dry spots to be of any real use to us. To hell with them.
>
> "You're goddamned right we're infantry," I said. "As for you, you take your men and your fancy equipment and get the hell back to the rear where you belong. We want no part of whiners. We'll get along without you. Don't you worry about that."[110]

The soldier's exuberant, impatient aggressiveness of those days before battle; the certainty that he would control all that befell him; the ability to dismiss any possibility of his own death—combat toppled them all. He could then trace in his own worn face and increasingly anxious thought the advance of a new and fearsome vulnerability. He looked to the other arms for help, but their seeming inability to improve the odds confronting him further devitalized him—by pressing on him first a sense of the infantry's isolation and then of its expendability.

2 BATTLE
Coping with Combat

In contending with their initial experience of battle, soldiers grasped for ways to fortify themselves against its concussions. They devised, or gravitated to, a diversity of methods for coping: acquiring a specialized battle knowledge; ascertaining and applying the lessons of the battlefield; fostering combat intuition; soliciting intercession; numbing-coarsening; and finally, harboring in fatalism.

One palliative, however, they had brought with them from civilian life—the concept of the job. It gave comprehensible shape to their reactions to combat and, beyond battle, to the whole of their military experience; indeed, it occupied a central position in their consciousness and, by serving so many functions, acted as the prism through which they tried to view the war. For many combat soldiers, "the job" defined war aims; sustained the vital link between themselves and those at home; regulated their relationship with the rear echelon; provided a rationale for their participation in the fighting; established a framework for their actions in battle; and assuaged some of the guilt their actions engendered.

The notion of the job served initially to translate the nation's aims and purposes in World War II to the most personal level of meaning, and here the immediate historical background was crucial. For a decade, the actuality or menace of joblessness had oppressed uncountable individuals; at the depth of the depression one of every four Americans lost employment. That blithe little song sung by the Dwarfs in the 1937 Walt Disney film *Snow White and the Seven Dwarfs*—"Hi-ho, Hi-ho, It's off to work we go"—must have carried for millions the very different sounds of a supplicatory chant. Even when the economy began its decisive upward turn in 1939, unemployment's grip, loosening very grudgingly, ensured that young men would relate military service to the search for a job. Henry Giles enlisted "in the old army back in 1939. . . . [The] depression hadn't ended down our way [Kentucky] and I was sick . . . of scrabbling and [of] the shame of the commodity [relief] lines and [of] no jobs but the WPA. You couldn't find a day's work in a month of Sundays." His first vision of the Army was that of a job. "Nobody knows what the army meant to me—security and pride and something fine and good. . . . [For] the first time in my life I was *somebody*." Ensign Robert Edson Lee had not traveled during the 1930s—his Iowa family had no money—but Navy service opened to him opportunities to tour the length of the East Coast. Stationed at the South Boston Navy Yard and watching each day a careworn woman who worked nearby in a "nauseous-smelling fish factory," he pondered the likelihood that she would never travel—and then suddenly realized "that Iowa had been *my* fish factory and that I had been rescued by the war."[1]

So contemplating the future, young Americans brought with them into the service the values they attached to work. "I had a strong view," Philip Ardery declared, "of the rightness of things like work and saving money." The indispensability of a job and the military's ability to provide one produced a disposition favorable to soldiering, or at least a forceful tendency to acquiesce in military service. The recruits' conviction that every adult male should have a job and perform it satisfactorily provided a less exalted but still practicable substitute for that concept of duty so much more powerful in other armies. Granted that the utter subordination that the military tried to impose on the individual came as a nasty shock, the fact that the job had required, in working-class positions, obeying orders, and, in the majority of middle-class posts, no less than "taking direction," inclined recruits to acquiesce in the enforcement of military discipline.[2]

When the Japanese attack on Pearl Harbor provoked in almost all Americans the conviction that action was essential, "The nation has a job to do" became a reasonable, acceptable, and ultimately satisfying way to think and talk about the vast and complex effort ahead. "More motivating [than patriotism]," Lee reported, "was the sense of a certain work that had to be done; we knew no more why it had to be done than . . . why we had been born, but there was a feeling of: Get the job done and then we can get on to something else; and so we labored and won the war." In similar vein, Air Force general James Doolittle explained his success in the 1942 B-25 raid on Tokyo that brought him fame: "If you are put in a position where you have a responsible thing to do, you don't do that for God and country—you do that because it's your job." And at home, if families asked of a husband, father, or son, "Why does he have to go?" an admissible, though not always easily embraceable, answer came back: "He's a man, and he has a job to do." Even women frightened for the lives of men they loved found some reassurance in the familiarity of the job: "Just do your job and come home to me."[3]

Conceptions of the job proved equally useful further afield. As they had eased civilian acceptance of military service, so did they allow servicemen to invoke civilian employment, and by pairing it with their new military jobs maintain a distinction important to them, that between themselves and military professionals. Lieutenant Robert Bass spoke of those around him in the 99th Infantry as "a bunch of soda jerks and grocery clerks. . . . [T]hat's what all these American soldiers are. They're not professional military men but just a bunch of guys over here doing a job, and a darn good one, and proving themselves much the superior soldier to the German, who has spent the better part of this life pursuing military training."[4]

Following the men's departure for war, the job continued to link war front and home front; mutual dedication to it would survive long after soldier and civilian experience of the war diverged dramatically. When the homefolk said, "Sure glad to see you again, Ben. We've been reading about you in the newspapers and magazines and been hearing you on the radio. We folks are sure proud of you, Ben," and Ben despaired of describing what had really happened to him in battle, he could still reach out to pluck the common chord: "I just did my job." From bottom to top, from Ben to Doolittle's "I was just doing my job," it was everywhere the same. In August 1943 Johnny Stradling, an Army draftee from Arizona, wrote to his family words of such generic quality that his letter might have been any one of a hundred thousand:

> It was really swell to be home for a week and to be able to see all of you again. It was refreshing and inspiring and it makes it real easy to go back to work again and to look forward to the time when our job is done and we can come back for good. Until the job's done, tho', we'll all have to take it, and like it, and just do our best to finish it up . . . so we can come back home just like we left it.[5]

Admittedly, conceptualizing a titanic, intensely violent global struggle as a job was prosaic. As one of Army sergeant Harry Marsden's friends observed at the time of Pearl Harbor, "It's different from the last war. No rah rah stuff.

Just a tough job to do." That unimaginative, mundane approach to the war caught the attention of foreign observers—and drew a rebuke from the French pilot-writer-philosopher Antoine de Saint-Exupéry. Distressed by Americans' formulation of the war as a "thankless, necessary job" conveying no "poetry, color, love" or "sense of spiritual meaning," he was critical of much that he saw about him in the United States, particularly its degraded "conveyor-belt activity."[6]

Saint-Exupéry was right to believe that Americans thought the job an uninspiring one. A Marine, Sergeant Francis Cockrel, wrote from the Pacific: "I had wondered what it would be like on the front. . . . It's like work. It *is* work. . . . [The] whole is no more or less than dangerous drudgery—mean, exhausting work. . . ." Infantryman Orval Faubus wrote from Europe: "I think all soldiers look upon the war as a desperately dirty and dangerous job which we have to finish. . . ." And Saint-Exupéry was right to invoke an assembly-line imagery. One could hear in the words of GIs echoes of the industrial process; each Pacific atoll seized, every European city captured or province occupied was an additional piece fitted to the final product, victory. But Saint-Exupéry missed that these were the grounds on which Americans felt most fully at home. Fighting the war as a process of industrial production *was* gratifying to Americans because it seemed to restore work of which the depression had deprived them. They appeared to say that this, this war of production at home and the fighting of it abroad as an integral job activity, was like that which they had once done, done well, and were anxious to resume. True, they saw in it little poetry, color, or love, but once seized of its importance, they were often buoyantly and determinedly impatient to be at it. As Faubus said, "[T]he sooner we get started the sooner we will see the war's end."[7]

In war zones, the notion of the job worked to stabilize relationships between fighting formations and support units. Sometimes, to be sure, it was used to rebuke rear-echelon types insufficiently respectful of the distinction between themselves and the risk takers. When an Air Force captain whose tour had passed in debriefing pilots realized embarrassedly that he was about to return home with no idea what it was like to fly a bombing run, he asked John Muirhead (abruptly and intrusively, Muirhead decided), "What's it like?" Muirhead replied sharply: "I'm employed to fly a bomber from here to there. I drop some bombs there, and then I come back here—if I'm lucky. That's my job. . . ." But ordinarily support personnel were able to use respect for the job to bolster their self-worth; it was their vehicle for soliciting greater recognition of their contributions to the war effort.[8]

In 1944, Captain Earl Nelson wrote an editorial, "Heroes Don't Win Wars," for the Seventh Air Force's weekly magazine. "Why don't [the press and radio] talk about the guy who is just a soldier? Why doesn't anybody ever mention the poor bastard who got dragged into the Army, got stuck out here [in the Pacific in] one of these God-forsaken holes, and is doing nothing but his job?"—a truck driver named Chuck, for example. Nelson went on to claim for the support services equivalence with the combat arms—and more. What aircraft mechanics did was just as important as what pilots and gunners did. Indeed, "The guys whose jobs have become so regulated and monotonous . . . are the real heroes of this war. . . ." Drivers, supply clerks, cooks, mechanics, all were winning the war simply by doing their jobs. Few rear-echelon personnel actually pressed for parity—they knew what combat exacted of front-line soldiers and were not avid to join them—but all those in the support forces drew purpose and status from the concept of the job. Fighting GIs had somehow received their jobs, they reasoned, and we received ours. Combat troops were doing their jobs, and we, no less, were doing ours.[9]

Combat soldiers in their turn resorted to the job to explain battle not only to their families but to themselves. The job, rather than the killing of human beings and the destruction of buildings and bunkers, provided the framework within which they contemplated their actions. What were you thinking and feeling in battle? "Trying to do our job," replied Staff sergeant Dewey Hill, an Army replacement in the Pacific. "Not thinking much[,] only how to stay in one piece and get [the] job done." How did you react to your baptism of fire? "Fear," answered PFC Robert Neimeyer of the 10th Mountain Division. "[I just thought] do your job—get it over with." Drawing on his experience as a forward artillery observer in Europe, Bradford Perkins reported that "The great majority [of those at the front], though acting with such prudence and caution as they could, simply did their jobs, even when it was dangerous."[10]

Indeed, when the situation was most perilous, the job to be done became, to those whose thought it focused, highly preservative. George Lucht, an enlisted man in Harold Leinbaugh's company, seeking "to make combat more manageable," concentrated on his assignment "like football back in college. Like playing weak-side halfback on defense—I did my job and didn't worry about anyone else. It was zone coverage, and I covered my zone." One of those in the invasion force approaching Peleliu would not look at the shore: "Buck had no curiosity that was not necessary for his job." Soldiers and Marines, the high command understood, would not be overwhelmed even by operations of mammoth scale when they were broken down into hundreds and thousands of small-unit jobs. Conversely, to be a fighting man with no clear sense of job invited demoralization. The Anglo-Australian Alan Moorehead knew what it was for prospective participants to contemplate the Normandy invasion before they learned how they were to fit within the grand design:

> Just waiting, waiting until your number turned up. . . . What you had to do, your job, your place in the machine, was everything [but you] were given no idea of your place in the plan. . . . You were driven back into yourself to the point where you lacked even a normal companionship with the others, who after all were in exactly the same situation. It was not fear that oppressed you, but loneliness. A sense of implacable helplessness. You were without identity, a number projected in unrelated space among a million other numbers.

To be told the plan and one's job within it, he went on, was to welcome a "wave of relief."[11]

Front-line enlisted men were at a disadvantage relative to their superiors. Privates had roles *vis-à-vis* others but no specific actions to perform until NCOs or officers issued orders. It thus seemed to John Hogan of the Army's 9th Amphibian Force in the Pacific that "if you haven't got stripes, you aren't doing anything. . . . Every day I see the problem mounting and more and more maladjustment building up." Marine Russell Davis eyed his squad's radioman: "He had a job, something to do with his mind and hands, and I envied him." Up the ranks, experienced company officers were grateful for their substantial, detailed job prescriptions; engrossed in performing up to standard, they were better able to push away doubt, worry, and fear. Cyril Joly used his "whole-minded concentration on duties [that were] close to becoming second nature" to smother a premonition of his own death in battle; he and his fellow British officers appreciated that they could turn to their duties "with a single-mindedness which was an effective blanket to our other thoughts and desires." When soldiers felt themselves under professional obligation to view dangerous battle situations as problems they had to solve, they had little time to consult their terror or deterioration. In a period of static warfare, Paul Boesch realized that even his officer tasks were insufficient to occupy him "outside my hole," and that he was manifesting the timidity and acute apprehensiveness of "a serious foxhole complex." "That same day I discovered an antidote"—volunteering for the duties of a rifle-company commander. "Taking charge of a patrol to search a wooded area on our flank, I found that the greatest cure for concern over my own safety was to have something to do."[12]

To no group was the concept of the job more indispensable than to combat medics. They faced directly the disasters that befell individuals in battle; to place the job between themselves and the suffering and destruction to which they were recurrently exposed became a requisite of their survival. Medic Klaus Huebner concentrated on the task of bandaging. "One chap has a shrapnel wound that destroys the sinus beneath his right cheek, and half of his eye is hanging loose. This is a tough case to bandage in a hurry. Another chap has his lower jaw missing, and you can see his entire bloody gullet and vocal cords; he has no chin to hold a bandage." Also required was that the caregiver sustain a focus intense enough to confine his reactions to the job. When shivering American tankers and artillery observers built a fire to warm themselves and a German gun crew dropped a shell in the center of the flames, the results came before surgeon Brendan Phibbs:

> One trained oneself to think with a cold, steely, ferocious concentration on each specific motion; one chanted to oneself: " There is nothing in this aid station except this one [bleeding artery], and all I've got to do in the whole world for the rest of my life is to clamp it," and every skill one had focused on sponging the blood and torn tissue, finding the ripped end of the artery and sealing it with as much care as if one had all day in the finest operating room in the United States. This kind of savage exclusion of the terror and pain around us meant speed, and our speed meant men's lives.[13]

As "savage exclusion" served the survival of the wounded, so did it shield the stability of their doctors—by fostering undifferentiated, almost rote job responses. To reach American wounded, Huebner had to enter fields he knew the Germans had mined. "After several missions and for some peculiar reason, I suddenly become completely indifferent to either life or death. Survival now is only a lucky break. [But] the wounded must be treated, shelling is very heavy, and cover is simply not available. Automatically and without realizing it, I must have done things that later were called heroic." (He was awarded the Bronze Star.) It was also essential that jobs be compartmentalized to limit the responsibility of medical personnel and to curtail their susceptibility to sympathy. "[Once] I have seen a casualty with a serious wound, I will never see *it* again," Huebner knew; "I do not have . . . opportunities for follow-up [once casualties are evacuated to the rear]." Assured that he would not again encounter soldiers he had tended, he no longer needed to think of them.[14]

Finally, the job provided a way of easing the guilt that might otherwise have distressed combat soldiers. Boesch collided with a German in the Huertgen Forest. "Just as I emerged from the house, one of the Jerries stopped, turned, and raised his machine pistol to fire. . . . I instinctively opened fire with my carbine. . . . The German fired, but his burst of bullets flew past me. . . . Loud screams told me my own shots had found a mark." The German, shot in the chest, "moaned pitifully" and "obviously had not long to live. . . . Looking at him and knowing that it was I who had done this thing to him, I realized I should have felt some kind of compassion, yet I had none. Here . . . is the first man I can truly say without doubt that I killed. . . . Yet I could stand there and watch him die and feel absolutely no qualms of any kind. . . . It was as if I were a carpenter and had driven home a nail which secured one beam to another, the job I was assigned to do."[15]

The soldier's ability to establish connections between the job and the battlefield reduced military operations to comprehensible scale; brought a modicum of order to the otherwise overwhelming confusions of combat; and buttressed psychological equilibrium by delimiting horror and guilt. Brought from home, but rich in reassuring metaphorical possibilities for the battlefield, the concept of the job worked with other ways of coping acquired in combat to blunt some of combat's exactions.

Battle's surprises—so numerous, so intimidating—immediately alerted soldiers to the gap between what they knew and what they needed to know. Harold Leinbaugh's introduction to battle fixed in him so profound a disgust for the inadequacies of basic training that he refused to concede it *any* value. "You know nothing," he warned, "when you enter combat." On the battlefield soldiers had to seek out new ways to preserve themselves, and nothing seemed to promise a greater increase in the margin of survival than a rapid mastery of the specialized knowledge of combat.[16]

Battle sounds—"mean, nasty, personal," Paul Boesch called them—constituted an unmistakable first lesson. Soldiers had to lift each one from battle's background noise, identify it, and fix it in mind. "One of the protections an infantryman needs," Boesch explained, ". . . is an ability to distinguish the various sounds of battle and recognize those that mean danger to him. . . . Uncertainty means delay, and sometimes the difference of a split second is all that separates life from death."[17]

Shell sounds carried the highest priority. Learning to identify outgoing artillery fire spared the soldier unnecessary alarm and expenditure of the energy to throw himself to earth. Recognizing incoming shells, and differentiating their sounds, established imminent danger. In North African combat, infantryman George Abend "learned to distinguish shells by the different sounds of their flight and explosion." To judge the peril in which Japanese shellings placed him, Marine Grady Gallant cultivated a sophisticated discrimination between air and impact sounds. Flight: "If the shell is low and about to hit the earth, it has a tearing sound; if it is higher, but will strike soon, it has a rushing, ghostly cry; if it is absolutely safe, very high and very fast, it leaves behind it a *whish-whish-whishing* sound." Explosion: "If the shell strikes very, very close, it combines the tearing sound with a metallic scream followed instantly by brittle cracking noises ended by a deafening explosion . . . sounds . . . in rapid sequence, blended into each other." And to outgoing-incoming and flight-explosion variations, soldiers added a third set: the cannon's-mouth noise of the propellant charge ("a deafening roar as if the sky were falling") versus that of the shellburst ("a sharp ripping crack, not so loud but much more menacing").[18]

No one compiled a catalogue. Metaphorical imaginations varied, and one man's "rushing, ghostly cry" was another's "fierce, trailing bark of a giant hound," but most combatants did develop associations that allowed them to gauge the danger of a shell and to reach agreement with their immediate comrades. "When they whistle they're not on you. What you got to watch for is when they hiss soft. . . . Like that one. See?" Experience also taught the limits of this schooling in sound—discovering, for example, that German 88 projectiles did not announce their approach. During a barrage in Normandy, paratrooper Ross Carter "first calculated that a direct-firing 88 shell traveled about three hundred yards ahead of its sound. A man had no time to duck before it arrived." In Normandy, too, a British combat veteran used a destroyed 88 fieldpiece to instruct his companions: "That's the deadliest bastard that's come out of this war so far! You can hear all the rest coming, but that sod's too quick. The shell explodes, you hear it coming, and only then do you hear the report as it's fired. Keep away from tanks [with 88s] if those bastards are about!"[19]

Other battlefield noises were hardly less significant than shell sounds. Was that explosion a grenade? A rocket? A mortar round ("[an] awful . . . thump which vibrated not just your eardrums, but your entrails")? Was that a light machine gun—a Bren, a BAR, or a German MG 34—or a heavy Vickers, Browning, or MG 42? Such sounds supplied witting infantry with more than that critical index of immediate danger ("when the rifle bullets were zipping they were on your flank, and when . . . cracking, they were overhead"). They also told the soldier how battle beyond sight was unfolding. Writer-correspondent John Hersey learned on Guadalcanal the *tatatatat* signature of the American machine gun and the *bubububub* of the Japanese; as he and a group of Marines listened to duelling exchanges of fire, they were able to identify the last burst as Japanese and thus knew what that "one of our guns was knocked out." ("It was awful.") In the end, the lesson perhaps most salutary to the tyro terrified by battlefield din was that such sounds, however unnerving, were not all lethal.[20]

The soldier's nose could teach him almost as much as his ears. Learning to detect the presence of the dead was simple; soldiers could not escape, in William Dreux's version of a common description, that "peculiar half-sweet odor which is like no other." But other smells were useful in distinguishing among the lifeless. Sergeant William Ogden of the 29th Division was confident that "If there was a dead man on the other side of the hedgerow, you could always tell by the smell whether he was German or American." An English officer agreed: "I became aware . . . that German troops *en masse* carried a peculiar odor, different from that of British or American troops. . . . [Troops] of every nation have a national aroma peculiar to themselves. Even the trenches occupied by one nation smell odd to the troops of another. . . ." Though there was no consensus on the source of divergence—differences in diets, shaving soaps, decomposing uniform materials, cigars, and cigarettes were all put forward—soldiers agreed that odor was a source of vital information. Some maintained that the typical German smell, "pungent" and "oily," helped GIs actually locate the enemy—on night patrols, for example. In the Pacific, the matter was less clear; the terrain itself, especially rain forests, emitted so many unfamiliar aromas. But Marine Al Schmid, for one, believed that he had isolated the odor of the Japanese ("part of it came from a powder they put in dishes and burned beside their beds"). That "Jap stink" disgusted him: "Those rotten buggers, I couldn't stand . . . to sleep in a place that smells like this!"[21]

Another crucial class of information was that which soldiers drew from the lessons of their early combat. "Each day," Frank Irgang observed, combat soldiers "learned a bit more," most indelibly from the fates of those around them. The easiest acquisitions came from evidence that a precept with which their instructors in basic training had pummeled them occasionally possessed a validity after all. No one had forgotten "Don't bunch up!" but soldiers seeking security in the combat zone and thinking to find it in proximity to others often ignored the injunction. So it was likely that Staff Sergeant George McLemore and his men of the 3d Armored Division, crowded together in a sunken Norman road, paid no more than passing attention when Captain James Nixon, on his way to a command conference in a small outbuilding nearby, glowered at them and growled, "Don't bunch up there. One shell will get you all." But when, moments later, a single German shell struck the shed squarely, destroying Nixon, killing or wounding all but one of the divisional task force leaders, and abruptly vaulting Sergeant McLemore to company commander, "Don't bunch up!" required, for those crouching close by, no further iteration.[22]

From casualties, soldiers also derived new precepts. Irgang and his friends found fascinating a replacement dedicated to living by the book. He took every precaution to maintain fitness; each day he stimulated his scalp, brushed his teeth, massaged his gums, changed his socks. "'No, sir,' the replacement said to Irgang; 'No trench mouth or trench feet for me. I've read too much about it to be dumb enough to let it get a start on me.'" But the next morning he took a bullet through the forehead. "Yes, he had read all about trench mouth and trench feet," Irgang reflected, "but somewhere along the way he had forgotten to read about raising his head above the level of the earth when the enemy was in view. No, I had never read it either, nor had anyone told me. I merely lived long enough to learn through experience and observation. Baker was not given that chance." During an American assault on a town in Luxembourg not far from the Siegfried Line, a fragment of a German artillery shell struck Howard Randall's best friend. Medical aid was prompt but was thwarted by spillage from the man's rent stomach, fatally contaminating the wound. "If he had not eaten before the attack, he might have been saved"—a caution Randall took to himself.[23]

Casualties also provided an education in the enemy's battle tricks. Irgang recalled that "Ordinarily, at night, when we saw the tracer bullets of a machine gun arching up overhead, we would feel free to maneuver about beneath them. [Then,] however, the enemy . . . synchronized [with the first] another machine gun . . . that fired without tracers. It raked a path just above the ground, thus getting the unsuspecting soldiers who were in its way."[24]

Finally, casualties instructed combat participants in gauging the severity of wounds. No one, of course, learned more rapidly than the medics. By mid-1944, surgeon Klaus Huebner was ready with his own guide to treatment: "Direct hits with 20-mm shells are no problem because the victim is dead. Most men felled with penetrating head wounds from machine-gun bullets are also dead [or soon will be]. Shrapnel from 88s and 'Nebelwerfers' [rockets] is disabling, but many victims will survive if their wounds are in the extremities." Soldiers were just as concerned as doctors not to expend energy or even attention on those whose condition was hopeless. Lieutenant John Downing of the 1st Division knew what he needed to know of the stricken soldier before him: "[The infantryman] was alive, but his face already had that greenish tinge which . . . said the poor guy wasn't going to make it."[25]

Battlefield experience that on occasion revitalized training precepts sometimes also broadened their usefulness. Paratrooper Kurt Gabel was able to apply "Don't bunch up!" to another problem, that of combat troops not commonly told where they were going but anxious to gauge the dangerousness of their new locale. He had noticed that if drivers of trucks delivering the infantry kept their motors running, slammed tailgates as the last GI jumped out, and sped away even before the foot soldiers had formed up, the location was unsafe. And by the end of a ride into Luxembourg following the Battle of the Bulge, he had developed an additional index: If, after dismounting, infantrymen were permitted to sit down without being ordered to spread out, "things could not be as bad as the rapidly disappearing convoy would have [had] us think." Similarly, battle endorsed training's emphasis on seeking shelter by burrowing into the earth ("Nobody has to be told to dig any more!"), but experience also taught the soldier *how* to dig his role—in such shapes that a shell landing nearby would not blow out his eardrums.[26]

Battlefield wisdom, however, continued to overthrow more training precepts than it confirmed. Instruction had ordained an intense, unwavering resort to firepower whenever the enemy might be within range, and as a result Americans at first "fired everything . . . at anything that moved." Officers of regimental level and above remained committed to this "relentless process" of destruction, but there soon emerged what battalion commander Charles Cawthon called "an unwritten soldiers' maxim": "If you shoot at the enemy, he is likely to shoot back." So what training had espoused unconditionally—the use of weaponry all-out—became highly relative, subject to "a fine calculation of the odds." Soldiers weighed their resources against what they knew of the immediate opposition's, and, unless directly ordered to do so, hesitated to risk that their M-1 fire would provoke German machine gunners or that their 37-mm shells would draw the attention of a Tiger tank's 88.[27]

Lessons ranged from the As of surviving battle to the Zs of bringing to a foxhole existence some slightly enhanced measure of comfort. Did the soldier know that it was possible to fire *through* trees to destroy enemies sheltering behind them? That on patrol he could stop a sneeze by pressing a finger against his upper lip or suppress a cough by pushing against his Adam's apple? That the original bazooka, while ineffective as the tank-stopper it was designed to be, again became a valuable weapon in street fighting, especially against snipers firing from dormer windows? That the red circle on the package of Lucky Strike cigarettes was exactly the color and size to fit behind the lens of the GI flashlight and thus to produce the perfectly dimmed light? That toothpowder could serve to scour his rifle barrel—and to substitute for baking powder when he made pancakes? That howitzer recoil oil was a satisfactory substitute for shortening in the preparation of french fries? That the standard cellophane gas cape should not be thrown away when he pitched out his gas mask but used to wrap his bedroll? That in welcoming his first shower in two months, he was also washing away the layer of grime and body grease that, however unaesthetic, protected him against the European cold?[28]

In the end, however, it was not the feebleness of organized field instruction or even the encyclopedic nature of that which was there to be learned that contributed most to the demoralization of the American soldier; it was the chill recognition that most of those who died had committed no error, that no superior knowledge would have saved them.

Soldiers who learned enough and lived long enough developed intuitive reactions to the dangers with which combat accosted them. "Any man who has been through numerous battles," observed U.S. correspondent Jack Belden of his own experience, "has a kind of instinct that enables him to sense a dangerous situation. . . ." Antiaircraft gunner George Abend claimed that he and his comrades learned "by instinct to trace . . . [the] course [of German shells] in the air and figure where they would fall. Our muscles developed a new reflex that thrust us forward on our faces. . . ." James Jones, describing the young Marine whose face was frozen in the "Two-Thousand-Yard Stare" symptomatic of acute neuropsychiatric distress (he "has had all, and more than, he can take"), was certain that if shots were fired nearby or "a mortar round came shu-shu-ing in," the immobile Marine would move "quick as a cat" to seek cover. "His trained instincts are by now something he can depend on. . . ."[29]

Fifty years ago, the word "instinct" conveyed a more direct connection with the world of nature than it retains today. A 1947 dictionary defined it as "a natural impulse or innate propensity that incites animals (including man) to the actions essential to existence, preservation and development; animal intuition." Soldiers welcomed reactions that they felt drew them toward identity with nature. Marine Raider Anthony Coulis was impressed that he and all four of his tentmates snapped awake, dressed, and hurried to the shelter before anyone sounded a warning of Japanese air raids about to break over Guadalcanal; it was, he said, "nature's warning of danger." Grady Gallant discovered, also on Guadalcanal, that Marines could "sleep through bombardments, air raids, small-arms fire—anything," no matter how clangorous, until the violence came close enough to threaten the sleepers' safety. That was part of "an adjustment of Nature"; the Marines had fitted themselves "into Nature's pulsating movement of life. . . . We were absorbed by our environment and the dangers we found in it."[30]

But combat soldiers were discomfited by any implication that their association with nature linked them with animals. However welcome the nonrational reactions they came to believe their lives depended on, any imputation of their own animalization deeply troubled them. In this perspective, the development of instinct subordinated rational thought, a hallmark of their individuality; it deprived them of one more element of control and it threatened to reduce them to a level beneath that of human beings. They feared that they would become what continuous confrontation with death had made of Erich Maria Remarque's World War I protagonist, Paul Bäumer, who grieved that war had "transformed us into unthinking animals in order to give us the weapon of instinct."[31]

Still, the immediate value of intuitive-instinctive reaction was beyond question. Surviving combat soldiers developed what John Muirhead called "a sensitivity learned from peril." Reactions to danger came faster and faster until they seemed automatic. Naval lieutenant John Walsh described the process as one in which "Your mind and body react mechanically, performing their duties from trained habit as swiftly and efficiently as when you're more conscious of your acts." So, in assaults, the infantryman might always be looking, without consciousness of his constant calculation, for the next hole into which he could throw himself, and would, if suddenly brought under shellfire, find himself in it before he became aware that his mind had registered danger.[32]

American soldiers often described such movement as "reflex action," thus raising once more the prospect that the unwilled impulse was displacing thought in the governance of their reactions. No one claimed immunity from reflexive motions; all knew that eyes blinked in defense against threatening gestures, and that bullets hissing by drove the body to dodges patently futile. "I recall," wrote Orval Faubus, ". . . how each man would duck quickly when a bullet would whiz close . . . I ducked . . . as a bullet zipped into the road beside me. . . ." He was troubled: "But the ducking was not of one's own volition. It was an involuntary reaction [to] the angry whine of the close flying lead." It was this loss of control at which Bill Mauldin took aim in his cartoon depicting several dogface soldiers who have thrown themselves flat in mud and water. Joe, the sole soldier still sitting upright, has been fiddling with his jacket and has just said blithely to Willie, prone and tensed for the impact of a shell, "Ever notice th' funny sound these zippers make, Willie?"[33]

Intuition also operated to alert soldiers to the presence of the enemy. In Italy, Jack Belden felt himself "gripped by that indefinable sense of danger, which he called a sort of smelling of the enemy, as it were." (He was right; as he attempted to withdraw by climbing a wall, a German bullet "hammered" into his leg.) Marine company commander George Hunt explained that "When all your senses are alert you can feel [danger's] approach. On patrol through jungle trails where you are liable to meet Japs head-on, where they wait in ambush, where they bivouac, you can feel when they are near. A sharp, prickling sensation runs up your back; you slow down your patrol and approach with infinite caution and silence." On Peleliu, one of his men, coming on two friends resting in a quiet area and sitting down to talk with them, suddenly prickled with that "premonitive feeling." Quietly scouting the pillbox against which the Marines were sitting, he used his Thompson submachine gun to kill the Japanese inside, five of them, whom he had detected. To combat pilot John Muirhead, the sky "became, in time, as familiar as any habitat of sea or land." Such intimacy abetted "a primitive awareness that often transcended his perceptions," and aided him to anticipate peril. On the return from a raid against Piombino, in Italy, he "felt it." Although the roads below were empty and the landscape devoid of signs of military activity, "I knew it. There was something ahead of us, some threatening presence." Muirhead broke radio silence—"Group Leader, I smell flak" and the colonel—"Yes, I smell it too"—ordered a turn that moved beyond danger all aircraft save the B-17 on Muirhead's left wing; ground fire sent it down in flames.[34]

So, in spite of their misgivings, American soldiers came to rely on intuitive signals and responses. Grady Gallant described how Marines on Guadalcanal "became conditioned" to the sounds of Japanese artillery shells. "The proper reactions to them became reflex movements done without thinking."

> I was standing near a truck one day . . . when a Marine unloading the vehicle reached into the truck bed and took hold of a wooden box and pulled it toward the tailgate. . . . On the bottom, it had a bent nail [that] pressed hard against the steel [truck bed] and [emitted] a metallic scream. At this sound not one man remained standing. Everyone hit the deck, even the Marine pulling the box. . . . It had sounded like a close hit by an artillery shell. . . . We hit the deck, fast and hard.

Gone was Mauldin's sense of the ridiculous. "When we realized what had happened, we felt somewhat foolish," Gallant conceded, "but not the least bit sorry we had done it. . . . Our reflex to that sound had not allowed us to think." But Gallant was accepting of that condition, even grateful, because

"There usually wasn't time to think." "Total intuitiveness," counseled Harold Leinbaugh; "you need it to survive."[35]

Few narratives fail to include the successes of those who came to submit to such advice. Marine radioman Henry LaCoy "frequently felt a warning from nowhere to move. He always obeyed that feeling. In one instance he was sitting behind a rock on [Peleliu] and suddenly felt this urge. No sooner had he jumped to another spot when a bullet snapped into the rock exactly where his back had been resting." George Hunt was "in a hole among the rocks, and for no reason at all other than a quick hunch I moved thirty yards away to another [hole]. Immediately a mortar shell burst about five feet from where I had left. The shrapnel flew alarmingly near . . . my near position but did not touch me." In French hedgerow country, George Wilson "was lying . . . beside one of our tanks. . . . I suddenly got the urge to move—and did crawl ahead some ten feet closer to the hedge. There was no purpose in this move, just a compulsion. The next moment, a machine gun cut up the very ground I had just left."[36]

Soldiers received only one intuitive warning with greater solicitude than those signals that enemy were nearby or that the soldier stood in imminent danger—the premonition that the soldier himself was about to die. Again, the narrative literature is replete with classic confirmations. On the eve of the 1st Division's North African landing in the face of Vichy French resistance, one of Corporal John Moglia's friends, Smitty, spoke to him in private. "I just wanted to say goodbye, John." "What do you mean, goodbye? [It's] going to be a long war." "Not for me. Tomorrow I die." Ten minutes later another comrade, Bill, shook Moglia's hand: "The last time, buddy. Tomorrow I will have had it." And within the hour a third friend, Mike, said that he too was destined to die. The next day, Smitty, Bill, and Mike were all killed in action. An "exceptionally close friend" told George Hunt that he was certain he would die in the Marines' landing on New Britain. "It was not long after the first shots had been fired," Hunt reported, "that I saw him carried out on a stretcher with the telltale pallor on his face."[37]

Still, soldiers were seldom able to reduce combat tension by entrusting themselves to their intuitive awareness; they continued to question its reliability. On the level of rapid, reflexive battlefield reactions to escape shell bursts, it was welcome; but few could extend full confidence to advance warnings of danger or of imminent death. Soldiers were aware of, but rarely recorded, those many occasions when they had felt the "sharp, prickling sensation" up the spine, had sensed the enemy close by—and had been wrong. Posterity received no reports from those who divined danger, moved quickly, and, once in their new spots, were immediately shot dead. Some with pre-monitions of rapidly closing death did die, but how many times was the foreboding cited by his friends only the dead soldier's last of several identical warnings? Prior to the Okinawa invasion, Ernie Pyle met on Guam his fel-low correspondent Robert Sherwood, there as "a sort of unofficial reporter for President Roosevelt." Pyle, who knew personally and communicated di-rectly with the president, spoke with high emotion: "Tell him I love him." Sherwood promised to do so and spoke warmly of seeing Pyle again soon. The correspondent shook his head: "I am not coming back from this one." Sherwood laughed: "You said that about Sicily, Normandy, and every other operation—and you are still alive." "I always believed it when I said it," Pyle replied, "and I believe it now, and sometime I have got to be right." This time, he was, but such portents likely confounded a fundamental pessimism with intuitive acuity.[38]

Another problem lay in the possibility that some soldiers worked to ful-fill their own presentiments of destruction. Hunt recalled that on New Britain one of his sergeants, who had received a powerful premonition of his death in battle, proceeded to take "incredible chances, as though to say, 'Come on, let's get it over with.'" And consider too those soldiers who, with identical forewarnings, survived unscathed. They seldom spoke or wrote about their misperceptions, but a few offered glimpses of the problem. An-thony Casamento, a Marine corporal with little bent for introspection, was left more bemused than chastened:

> The more we kept going forward [over and beyond Guadalcanal's Tenaru River], the more . . . the snipers were coming out to meet us. Somehow, just after we cross . . . the bridge, something comes into my mind. It's the funniest feeling. My time's up, I think. Right now, today. . . . I had that hunch. You know how it is when you get something like that. It's whacky, but you can't help believing it. I try to shake it away [as] we keep going forward.

Soon the Marines ran against the Japanese main line of resistance.

> It was awful. . . . Boy, the Japs gave it to us! They weren't fooling. They got every one of my fourteen men, killed or wounded them—everyone except me! How do you figure that out?[39]

The soldier's belief that he had gained access to intuitive awareness and reactions drawing on translogical forces helped him to cope with battlefield stress, but there remained vexing questions of intuition's independence of reasoning, its uncontrollable elements, and its reliability.

As combat soldiers lost confidence that they could control their lives in war, conceded the likelihood that they would suffer injury, and began to fear that harm could not long be kept at bay, they increasingly entreated supernatural forces to intercede in their behalf.

Most soldiers invoked God's protection. Asked what helped them "when the going was rough," American combat troops both in Europe and in the Pacific cited prayer more than any other source of support, beyond ideology, group solidarity, and hatred of the enemy. Eighty-three percent of line infantrymen in four divisions fighting in Italy professed that prayer "helped a lot." In the early stages of combat, soldiers seem to have offered up simple supplications that God would safeguard their welfare ("I just asked the old man above to lead the way and take care of me"), but when they became uncertain of survival, prayer grew both more fervent and more complex: soldiers proposed the terms of bargains that they hoped God would accept. In firefights they whispered, "God, if I ever get out of this, I promise that I will"—go to church as soon as I get home and thank you on bended knee, or begin to live a truly moral life, or become a minister, or behave as a dutiful son, faithful husband, or proper parent. And as they became more and more pessimistic, they pared back what they asked of God, as if to enhance their chances that the essential, continuing life, would be granted. Will you, please, God, spare this soldier for another day? Will you help ensure that injury, when it comes, will be only as severe as an arm or leg wound?[40]

Soldiers believed that the supportive actions of those at home reinforced their prayers. On Peleliu, George Hunt suddenly snapped awake to see a tree beginning to topple upon him, but after a terrifying moment of paralysis he was able to roll away just as the trunk crashed to the spot on which he had been lying. "Someone must be doing a lot of prayin' for you, Skipper," offered a fellow Marine, and Hunt replied, "Yes . . . there's several prayin' for me [and] I'm beginning to think it must do some good." Many soldiers looked to their home churches to mediate the conditions of their bargains with God. Morton Eustis, always appreciative of his mother's prayers, sent her money to be given, via the church, to St. Anthony, one of the patron saints of travelers. Later, when the wish that propelled that offering (unspecified in his letters but surely turning on his safety) was realized, he gratefully sent an additional $50. Soon, another request prompted the dispatch of $100, with the promise of a like sum if that desire were also granted. Other soldiers asked that their names be included in hometown church prayer services.[41]

Chaplains sometimes found what they knew of the men's negotiations with the Deity offensive to their own convictions. Too many fighting men were turning to God only because they wished to be delivered from fear for their lives, decided Arthur Glasser, an evangelical Protestant serving with Marines in the Pacific. He saw the devil's work in those who, to his disappointment and anger, held to the Christian message as "just something to give courage to . . . men who are afraid to die." But such flurries were fruitless, and soldiers continued to find in their highly personalized religious faiths an important source of support, especially at moments of acute battle stress. "I sure prayed when I was in a tight spot. . . . When I was hit in the leg I asked [God] above to heal [it]. We had prayers sometimes before going into action. It helps a lot" . . . "I used to pray a lot. You just automatically pray to yourself when you're going [into combat] and when you're in. . . . You know the saying that there are no atheists in a foxhole." In a 1945 survey, 79 percent of men with time in combat believed that their military experience had increased their faith in God.[42]

Soldiers who petitioned God did not hesitate simultaneously to solicit luck, although their differing conception of faith and fortune necessitated contrasting approaches. Combatants thought of God as a positive, male force whose protection might save them if they appealed for it and were found worthy of it; they considered luck a potentially malevolent female force that, if not propitiated, would turn on them. So it was necessary to find ways to appease, in John Muirhead's acrid words, "that insolent, wayward bitch, luck, who ruled our lives with her gambols and all the bloody things that amused her." Luck

> moved from plane to plane, and those she chose not to destroy, she visited in her way, leaving vile reminders of her malice. Sometimes she would barely touch you, which was her way of saying she would be back; sometimes she played games smashing things around you: pipe, cable, instrument panels, turrets, and a Thermos of tomato juice splattered around the flight deck like a joke for blood. She tore a gunner's parachute harness away from his body, and scratched his belly with her nails. Oh, she was quite a girl!

In their attempts to placate her, the men found it unnecessary to distinguish between rites spiritual and secular.

> We did everything we could to please her: we showed her trinkets, crucifixes, St. Christopher medals, the foot of a rabbit, vials of holy water, small pieces of paper with prayers written on them, lucky coins, sacred photographs in gold lockets, a pair of loaded dice, a pressed flower from a girl, a picture of a child in an embossed leather case, and many other beloved charms.[43]

That closing word, with its intimations of magic, often embarrassed those who were nonetheless intent on calling forth any powers it might possess. After the war, Marine pilot Gregory "Pappy" Boyington spoke defensively of a small medallion he continued to wear around his neck. "Unlike so many flyers I know, even those in my own outfit, I have not always worn a good-luck charm. Today, as we know, a good many so-called charms are on the bottom of the [Pacific]. So I do not consider this medallion . . . as such. At least not in the ordinary sense, for it represents to me something even bigger than that. . . ." With his plane shot down and his raft bobbing in turbulent waters, Boyington had found in a pocket a prayer card sent to him by a nun.

> [Why] now on the raft I had it in my hand, water-soaked though it was, I never will know. Yet, for some peculiar reason, I now looked at it more closely than I had before. It was a picture of a lady with a baby in her arms, and there was a boat on a stormy sea. On the back . . . I could make out the blurred lettering of a lengthy prayer. I read it over time after time, while drifting . . . probably . . . forty or fifty times, and it seemed to give me a great deal of company, and I was sickly unhappy when later the Japanese, after taking me, also took the card. . . .

At the end of the war the nun sent him the medallion in lieu of the lost card, and Boyington, whose meditations on the card had brought him to a first awareness of "a Higher Power," overrode his sheepishness about amulets and vowed that he would never part with the medallion.[44]

Combat correspondent Keith Wheeler devised his own magic formula, writing on the eve of each invasion of a Pacific atoll a "last" letter that served, he thought, as "a form of insurance." With those letters he would propitiate fate, though he confessed that composing them was "like repeating the litany of a conjuring trick, having no faith in it, but afraid to neglect it."[45]

Since at stake here were exemptions from the luck that soldiers assumed would eventually turn against them, what were required were not pledges to lead better lives but minor, though very regular, obeisances. Luck, said Muirhead, had to be "constantly adored." Many thought that simply obtaining and holding fast to a talisman would protect them. PFC Alphie Gregoire of a mortar company fighting its way into Germany told a friend that "If my lucky rabbit's foot doesn't fail me for a while longer, I'll make it to the Rhine"—and then he reached into his shirt pocket to be certain his amulet was in its place. Marine platoon sergeant Johnalson "Big" Wright remained calm as Japanese aircraft rained down bombs on the Wake Island garrison. When explosions converged on his antiaircraft gun emplacement, he ordered his men to the bomb shelter while he remained in the gun pit. Concussions jolted him, but he was unhurt. "Hey, Godwin!" he yelled to a sergeant in the shelter during each raid; "Don't you worry, Godwin! I'm squeezing my lucky dollar for you!"

> Then the Japs were gone, and Big Wright stood up, dusting off the sand. He put his dollar back in his pocket. The men came crawling out of the shelter and somebody said the lucky dollar had worked again. "It always works," Wright said. . . . Men could argue endlessly whether there could be such a thing as a good-luck charm, a magic talisman. Most of them said it was a lot of bunk, but when the bombers came, even the scoffers felt easier being near Big Wright as he squatted in the . . . pit and squeezed his lucky dollar. . . . [He said] he didn't need a bombproof as long as he had his dollar [and] there was one argument nobody could answer—they were still alive and how could anybody prove it wasn't the dollar that did it?

PFC Bernard Dodge was so impressed that he acquired a lucky coin of his own, a fifty-cent piece, and in subsequent raids he crouched in another pit, squeezing it.[46]

Combatants conjured an amazing variety of magical formulas. A B-29 crew in the Pacific became convinced that if all eleven wore the same sort of cap at the start of every bombing mission, "we'll be all right." Major Robinson occasionally forgot his, but each time the enlisted men sent someone to retrieve it prior to takeoff. Pilot Beirne Lay, Jr., just before every departure, patted the blanket at the foot of his bed—"for good luck." Other rituals included leaving beds unmade, making dates for the next night, going out clean-shaven—all on the assumption by crews that making clear to Fortune that they expected nothing out of the ordinary would thereby ward off the extraordinary. Those "last" letters of Keith Wheeler took the opposite tack: they granted the worst. "If, openly and by the written word, you acknowledge the fact of death, then death, being elusive, may deny you." One of Russell Davis's Marine comrades was of similar mind: Luck was so perverse that it would forgo striking down the soldier expecting, and prepared, to die. "[Buck] thought that if he talked about the worst it wouldn't happen."[47]

Many soldiers bargained with luck as they had with God; they invented capricious, idiosyncratic "tests" for themselves, on the understanding that if they passed, luck would agree to hold good for them. "For some strange reason," remembered a member of Leinbaugh's company, Fred Olson, "I had persuaded myself that if I could live through my nineteenth birthday, I could make it all the rest of the way through the war; that somehow everything was going to be all right."

In *The Thin Red Line,* James Jones explored other types of tests:

Something had happened to [Bell] with the wounding of Peale. Perhaps it was the sheer accident of it. There was no earthly reason why that bullet should have struck Peale and not someone else. But . . . when he saw that little hole in Peale's leg with its trickle of blood running down the white thigh, the actuality of his own death, perhaps sometimes soon, perhaps not, had become a reality to Bell. It terrified him. Bell understood the superstitious talisman he had made of never having anything to do with any other woman after being called up; he would not even have conversations with them for fear of feeling some desire. Now he added to that first superstition a second which was that if he and Marty both remained true to each other, he could make it back with his genitals intact.[48]

Other prohibitions acquired broader appeal and emerged as taboos. Marines in the Pacific, because they associated the stretcher with injury and death, agreed that no fit person should bed down on one. From his friend Giddons, George Hunt received a well-hedged offer. "Would you like a stretcher to sleep on, that is if you're not superstitious? I know a man who fell asleep on a stretcher and died on it without ever waking up." Here one Haggerty intervened: "I wouldn't sleep on a stretcher if I was paid to, unless it's by necessity [i.e., if wounded]." Hunt, however, decided to "take a chance on it." That night the falling tree barely missed him. In the morning, Giddons eagerly returned to the subject: "Do you think you'll ever sleep on a stretcher again?" "No," replied Hunt, "I guess I won't, unless I absolutely have to." "I hate to say I told you so," Haggerty summed up, "but those things are strictly taboo"—and more strictly so after Giddons and Haggerty circulated Hunt's story.[49]

Finally, soldiers alive, unwounded, and anxious to ward off that adverse turn of luck they feared was approaching sought ways to reinforce the relatively advantageous status quo. Observers have described GIs as the war's most avid souvenir seekers. So much fascinated them; so little answered any of their practical needs; so much was rapidly discarded. Numerous apparently purposeless repetitions suggested a psychological quest; souvenirs—like the dates airmen arranged for those evenings following their return from bombing raids—seemed to promise a future. Luck would not turn against a soldier so assured that he was stocking postwar artifacts.

Combat soldiers often tried to forestall luck's perfidy by sheltering within the orbits of those whose chances of survival they thought better than their own. Ed Stewart, a squad leader in Leinbaugh's company, felt a magnetism drawing him to Mario Lage, a fighter who "always kept his cool" in battle. Soon the connection became so compelling to Stewart that Lage unknowingly became his mystic protector. "I still remember thinking, 'If Lage is all right, you're all right. Don't worry.'"50

In the end, none of these efforts succeeded in providing the assurance that soldiers sought. Particular devices often failed spectacularly. When Japanese dive bombers again attacked Wake Island, Big Wright kept his gun crew at work until the last moment, then ordered them to the shelter, squatted in the pit, and shouted to Godwin his ritual message. This time, however, bombs exploded on the battery's position, sending up clouds of sand and smoke, and when the men called out to Big Wright, there was no answer; he was dead. He had neither lost nor forgotten his lucky dollar. There it was "still tightly clutched in his hand." After Wright's burial, Bernard Dodge "walked down to the lagoon alone. He stood there a moment turning his lucky fifty-cent piece between his fingers. Then he flung it as far out into the lagoon as he could and walked back to the guns." Human talismans proffered no better protection. When Lage was promoted to lieutenant, Stewart, assuming that Lage's guardianship had been extended to all within his new command, was upset by the death of a company soldier. Suddenly, he could no longer be certain that Lage would survive the war and that "If Mario makes it, I'll make it." Now it was the converse that overwhelmed him. "My God, what happens if [Lage] is killed?" "If Mario doesn't come through, I won't either."51

The insurmountable problem was the soldier's inability to find ways to defend himself against what was, by any human standard, the utter capriciousness of war's life-and-death decisions. A Messerschmitt's cannon shell struck the ball turret of John Muirhead's B-17. Its path took it between the legs of the gunner, who was saved from bleeding or freezing to death by the exertions of the waist gunner and radioman. On landing, Muirhead pummeled his crew chief with indignant, unanswerable questions. "Why wasn't he killed? Look at the goddamn thing! Just look at it! Look at the size of that hole, right by the gun handles! Christ!" Just then another aircraft landed, and its crew, who had not notified the base of any casualties aboard, began removing a body. "It's the bombardier, Sully," someone told Muirhead. "We don't know what happened. He's dead. There's not a mark on him. No wounds—nothin' but he's dead." The men finally discovered just under the hairline a one-and-a-half-inch "thin red crescent" where the tiniest fragment of a shell had entered Sullivan's head. The copilot was incredulous: "A little piece like that—Christ!"52

One man on whom war's destructiveness had descended spectacularly and who was, by ordinary indices, doomed had survived; a second man who appeared to have escaped the violence and whom others were certain had survived had died slightingly. Muirhead was furious: "I felt overwhelmed, like a man trapped in a circumstance from which there was no escape, where every way was blocked except the only hopeless way before him." John Muirhead thus reached the point at which many combat soldiers had arrived before him: "Nothing gave me peace; nothing gave me any understanding."[53]

Combat pared away the emotional sensitivity of the soldier. Robert Jay Lifton's study of Japanese survivors of atomic bomb explosions revealed that, caught up in a devastating event, they underwent an emotional desensitization that very quickly brought them to the sole state in which they could continue to function, one of unfeeling, virtually mechanical response. Soldiers on the battlefield were caught up in a similar process, albeit with notable distinctions. Infantrymen who remained unhit suffered not a single, catastrophic onslaught but a series of lesser shocks. Because their reactions to the initial concussions of combat left them anguished, weakened, and vulnerable, and because they foresaw additional shocks no less painful, they—unlike later Hiroshima and Nagasaki survivors—began working to advance their own desensitization. Margaret Bourke-White, noticing in Italy the insentience of American infantrymen, construed it as a sign of low morale and even of inattentiveness to the work at hand; they had contracted, she feared, a "fatal numbness." But she misunderstood. The soldier's willingness to league himself with the dulling process, though costly, was not destructive behavior; its role was defensive and preservative.[54]

Numbing appeared at first an automatic process, one that acted upon all soldiers reacting to the shocks of battle. John Steinbeck believed it to be largely physiological. In combat, he wrote in one of his dispatches from Italy,

> The ductless glands pour their fluids into the system to make it able to stand up to the great demand on it. Fear and ferocity are products of the same fluid. Fatigue toxins poison the system. Hunger followed by wolfed food distorts the metabolic pattern already distorted by the adrenalin and fatigue. The body and the mind so disturbed are really ill and fevered. . . . Under extended bombardment or bombing the nerve ends are literally beaten. The ear drums are tortured by blast and the eyes ache from the constant hammering. . . . At first your ears hurt, but then they become dull and all your other senses become dull, too. . . . In the dullness all kinds of emphases change. . . . The whole world becomes unreal. . . . [Later] you try to remember what it was like, and you can't quite

manage it. . . . A woman is said to feel the same way when she tries to remember what childbirth was like. . . . The system provides the shield and then removes the memory, so that a woman can have another child and a man can go into combat again.

Artilleryman Ben Waldron agreed that numbing arrived independently of the soldier's will, but he thought it fundamentally psychological rather than physiological. Made a prisoner of the Japanese on Corregidor, he subsequently became convinced that he and his mistreated comrades had passed the point "where, even though we saw all of these sights, our minds would block out the horror of what we saw. It seemed as though we were numb and were walking in some sort of trance. I guess the human mind has the ability to turn itself off when it confronts something too horrible to comprehend."[55]

Soon, however, soldiers decided that they could, and would, push forward their own numbing. Intense feeling—sympathy, hurt, fear—in their first reactions had left them weakened and exposed. They sensed too that an unconfined imagination could be dangerous. Airman John Ciardi narrowed rigorously his thought of dead friends: "It hurts when the smiling boys go down. . . . [But] you can't sympathize, by definition, until you feel a thing yourself. . . . The trouble with wakening the imagination is that it makes you afraid in advance." En route to their jump into Normandy, paratrooper Ross Carter and his companions "sat quietly and smoked cigarettes, trying as best we could to confine our reflections and mental images within the vacuum of nothingness. . . . Imagination given free play could ruin a man under such tensions; therefore I kept tight rein on mine."[56]

Some fighting men viewed the problem as one of regulating the emotions, of reducing the emotional pulse beat and then monitoring its maintenance at a low level. Writer Masayo Umezawa Duus detected the emotional flatness of Japanese American soldiers fighting through the forests of the Vosges: "There was no joy or sadness or hatred or even despair in their eyes. They seemed hollow and dried out." A lieutenant in Jones's *The Thin Red Line* asks an infantry NCO, "Didn't you feel *any*thing [when your men got hit]?" Culn shoots back: "[The] Service nor nobody pays me any extra 'Feeling Pay' for feeling. Like they pay flyers "Flight Pay' for flyin. So I figure I ain't required to feel. I figure I won't feel any more than's just absolutely necessary." Other soldiers actually contemplated the elimination of feeling and strove for a state of emotionlessness, Carter's "vacuum of nothingness" rendered permanent. Combat artist Tom Lea reported that on Peleliu, "I was without emotion of any kind. I saw everything around me in sharp focus, yet it no longer crashed into my consciousness. My mind blanked itself for my body's sake."[57]

In their efforts to numb themselves, soldiers found a powerful ally in exhaustion. After her escape from Bataan to Corregidor, evacuation to Australia by plane, and return to the United States by boat, Army nurse Juanita Redmond welcomed the rapid resumption of strenuous hospital duty: "When I have work to do, I can get too tired to lie awake remembering the soldiers, the doctors and nurses and corpsmen who are my friends and who are [now] prisoners of the Japanese." But the infantryman's depletion was of another order, a steady-state, seemingly endless, bone-deep weariness, and it was this kind of exhaustion that Guy Sajer, an Alsatian fighting in the Wehrmacht, invoked in describing an episode on the Eastern Front. A Russian plane, struck by German fire, fell from the sky but in crashing smashed into a convoy of Wehrmact vehicles and crushed a truckful of wounded landsers. "No one [elsewhere in the column] cried out: in fact, almost no one looked. We simply picked up our burdens and went on. We were all too exhausted to react, and almost nothing stirred our emotions."[58]

Soldiers still sentient tried in several ways to deaden themselves. The first attempt was ordinarily the effort to refuse horrific scenes entry into the consciousness. "I won't think about this." British lance corporal Peter Huntley, a stretcher bearer, took part in the 53d Welsh Division's campaign in the Reichswald Forest, near the Dutch border, carrying wounded from front to treatment center, again and again returning for more. "You just couldn't let yourself think about it. You couldn't dwell on the fact that you were carrying a man whose legs had just been blown off or who had some really devastating wounds from shrapnel." Learning "to amputate [the pain] at the root," James Jones called this tack—but few soldiers were able to master it. When Audie Murphy's friend Elleridge, the platoon intellectual, pondered a grisly battlefield incident and worried aloud that ". . . maybe I caught too much before I could get the guards up," Audie Murphy replied resignedly, "Who didn't?"[59]

Soldiers unable to bar the mind's door could still try to efface dire developments by denying their reality. "This can't be real" laid out the course that Anton Myrer explored in his book *The Big War*. The battle deaths of three friends haunted Marine Alan Newcombe with horrifying images—"Klumanski rolling in anguish, rolling and writhing, Diebenkorn crying in thick, fuzzy moans, the cratered horror of Hansen's head—a sickening montage of smashed bones and spilled viscera and steel baited with blued guts, screams and blood-red frothing rage and clammy fear." Sinking, Newcombe sought to catch himself: "What *stupidity!* It could not be: he would not let it, that was all. None of it existed, all were the passes of subjective imagination . . . idiocy and lies, all of it, lies and idiocy . . . and there was no need to accept any of it, [it] needed only to be willed out of existence, *willed away.*" George Hunt of the 1st Marine Division also sought to dissolve unendurable battle scenes. "My thoughts wandered to the dead men lying on the slope of the Point. So many lives had been snuffed out so quickly that it seemed impossible and incredible. Once again I thought of a fantastic dream with no logic, only a pattern of grotesque, lugubrious shapes and a background of tuneless music and uncontrolled rhythms."[60]

Ultimately, whatever the efficacy of such efforts to displace intolerable images into a world of illusion, there always remained some thoughts soldiers felt they simply had to learn to banish without hesitation. Henry Giles was in the Liège replacement center—far, he thought, from the war's destructiveness—when one of the Germans' new buzz bombs landed nearby, killing passing Belgian civilians, including a little girl. "Well," he ordered himself, "some things you just have to put out of your mind." "Just forget it" was an everyday, front-line exhortation. A German shell landed twenty yards from Audie Murphy, who remained burrowed in. His friend Thompson, however, peered above ground—and saw an American soldier blown into two pieces, the upper part of his body still clutching a rifle. Thompson's face went "white with horror." "I saw it happen." "Saw what happen?" "He was lying there flat." "Forget it. Come on." "He was just lying there flat." "Come on." "I can't." "Goddammit, you've got to. You can't stay here." "Who was it?" "Fellow named Ward. Come on." "He was just lying there." "I know, I know. Let's move now. We've got to get some cover." "Is he dead?" "Half of his body is missing. Can't you see?" "I don't want to look. I got a headache. I got a bad headache." Here, as Thompson's teeth began to chatter and his lips to twitch, his friend slapped him. "Now come on. If we stay here, we'll both get hit." With Thompson calming, Audie Murphy pushed home his point: "You've got to learn to forget what you see."[61]

When soldiers tried and failed first to exclude and then to expel the unbearable, they often attempted next to build in the mind a distance between the self and the insupportable experience. Seeing oneself, for example, as a spectator rather than a participant could dispel some of the menace. "This isn't happening to me. I'm only watching."

Near Würm, heavy German fire forced an American infantry squad into a shallow ditch. "We tried to keep going," Harold Leinbaugh recalled, "but were pinned down with point-blank fire only thirty or forty feet away. The fire was constant, blasting our eardrums, spraying the lip of our hollow with sheets of mud. We couldn't get off more than one shot at a time. We were trapped; we couldn't move forward or backward. I figured that was the end. We'd had it. [But then] I was looking down from above and watching the episode unfold in slow motion. I remember feeling completely detached, but terribly sorry for the guys spread-eagled in that little muddy ditch." (Then American machine gunners arrived and opened fire, sending the Germans into flight.)[62]

Soldiers who could not prevent the entry of daunting facts, deny their reality, or dissociate themselves from them sometimes tried to engineer another escape: postponing consideration of them. "I won't think about this now."

As American infantryman John Bassett moved into battle in Italy, his contemplations threatened to demoralize him: "We thought the Krauts were evil; but we were evil too. I was prepared to kill a man . . . for a crime . . . he . . . may not have committed. Should it be right for me to kill a middle-aged Kraut who loved his family and believed in God, not in Hitler, but who was drafted by the Third Reich to serve his country? I could not stop to think it out. . . ."[63]

The combat soldier's final resort was to so concentrate on affable thought that it would bar or oust menacing thought. "I'll think about other things." In *A Walk in the Sun,* Harry Brown described the effort of soldiers in one platoon. "A man could exist on [those memories of life before the war had come along;] he could withdraw into them, he could construct them into an unpierceable shell. They were his defense against the violence of his world. Every man in the platoon had his own thoughts as he walked along, and they hovered unseen over the little group, an indefinable armor, a protection against fate, an indestructible essence."[64]

By working to numb himself, the soldier tried to diminish his sensitivity to what battle did to him, and what he did to others, but he soon discovered that numbing was but a phase of a larger process. It carried him first to a toughening and then to a coarsening of his tastes, manner, conduct, and sensibility.

He welcomed the results—initially—for he wished and worked to toughen himself, both as a way of rising to warfare's physical demands, and, once in battle, as another means of limiting his emotional vulnerability to the prospect of seeing, causing, and suffering death.

It was his introduction to battle near Saint-Lô that fixed in George Wilson, the 4th Division platoon commander, his determination to harden himself. He lost his first man when the soldier foolishly tried to duel a German half-track. "I felt sick." He soon shot his first German soldier; that shook him again. "I'm glad I didn't kill him." Then, as he and his men were resting against a hedgerow, they heard an American tank bearing down on them from the other side. Yells alerted the dozers, and all scrambled away—except for one sergeant: "he just sat in a daze as the tank plowed through [the hedgerow] and buried him alive. [We] dug him out at once, but it was too late." Pained and agitated, Wilson set out both to numb and to toughen himself:

> Thus my second man was gone—and he as needlessly as the first. I knew then I'd never survive if I let myself get tied in with every case. It was vital for me to build some sort of protective shield within myself and concentrate only on what had to be done in the present and how to do it. I forced myself to suppress all thoughts of prior losses and gruesome mental pictures of the tragedy of war.[65]

Wilson's resolve was astute: battle often made very dangerous temperate thoughts or gestures. "Tenderness must die," declared Marine Grady Gallant, or the horror would grow unendurable and "[we] would become mad." More was at stake than the soldier's psychological stability: his very survival. "The gentle die in battle," concluded one of writer John Horne Burns's soldiers. In the course of combat along the Siegfried Line, Wilson and his men watched as an American lieutenant stood in the open and urged a dozen Germans in facing positions to surrender. Continuing to hold forth in a loud voice, he began to walk toward the enemy line. GI spectators decided not to intervene. "Let the nut go on. It looks easier than fighting." The lieutenant maintained his march into the midst of the Germans—until one of them killed him. Sympathy became a sentimental, fatuous, deadly indulgence. When a fellow pilot charged him with "callous indifference to the losses in the squadron," John Muirhead tried to explain his want of pity: "[A]ll men in combat must come to [insensitivity]. To feel sorrow, to grieve for the dead, to weep in despair, was not what we were asked to do. To kill, to maim, to destroy, to die, these were our tasks, and we were to do them without too much fuss."[66]

Soldiers required toughening first to inure themselves to unaccustomed sights, as in Wilson's case, and then to enable them to take unaccustomed action. Almost all succeeded. Army machine gunner Frank Mathias reported that during the American return to the Philippines,

> [Japanese] bodies sprawled here and there along the road. We became used to seeing them. I sat alongside the road one day eating K-rations. Five or six

bloated bodies were in a ditch below me. I absent-mindedly watched bubbles of gas and liquid moving around under their tightly stretched skins as I munched my crackers. The June sunlight was bright and hot. They were in their world and I was in mine. I had to eat, didn't I?

Aboard the USS *Montpelier* on patrol in waters off Saipan, Seaman James Fahey confided to his war diary on July 13, 1944: "Today the water was full of dead Jap bodies, you could see them floating by, men, women, and children. . . . One Jap was floating face up and he had a goatee; an arm also floated by. I never saw anything like it for bodies floating around. The water is full of them; the fish will eat good." On July 16, 1944: "Mass was in the morning. . . . It was the first time I ever went to church services and saw dead bodies floating by. . . . The ships just run over them." In Italy's Po Valley, combat doctor Klaus Huebner came upon the aftermath of an American aerial assault—blasted enemy vehicles, charred horses, torn bodies. "Here's a picture to remember. It's that of a dead German. His grimaced face is bloated and his head lies in a pile of dust. His leg wound stinks and crawls with flies and maggots. What a degrading sight! [But] no one seems to give a damn. How calloused we have all become! Our men don't even give this guy a second look, but just walk over him."[67]

As the men added layers of callus, they were able to begin acting as they would not have done as civilians but in a way that now seemed unexceptional. They began to "requisition" supplies and equipment that they told one another had been withheld by self-serving rear-echelon personnel or stalled by needless bureaucratic niceties or monopolized by other units. The result, Ernie Pyle gently pointed out, was that "Our men have less regard for property than [they were] raised . . . to have. The stress of war puts old virtues in a changed light."[68]

Seeking souvenirs sounded prosaic, but the evolution of battlefield practice broke down numerous civilian restraints. On Peleliu, Eugene Sledge saw his first enemy dead, a Japanese medic and two foot soldiers. "I stared in horror, shocked at the [medic's] glistening viscera bespecked with fine coral dust. This can't have been a human being, I agonized. It looked more like the guts of the many rabbits or squirrels I had cleaned on hunting trips as a boy. I felt sick as I stared at the corpses." But then,

A sweating, dusty . . . veteran came up . . . slung his M-1 rifle over his shoulder and leaned over the bodies. . . . [He] deftly plucked a pair of hornrimmed glasses from the face of the corpsman. This was done as casually as a guest plucking an hors d'oeuvre from a tray at a cocktail party. "Sledgehammer," he said reproachfully, "don't stand there with your mouth open when there's all these good souvenirs laying around." . . . He then removed a Nambu pistol, slipped the belt off the corpse, and took the leather holster. He pulled off the steel helmet, reached inside, and took out a neatly folded Japanese flag covered with writing. The veteran . . . rolled the corpse over, and started pawing through the combat pack. The veteran's buddy came up and started stripping the other . . . corpses. His take was a flag and other items. . . . The first veteran said, "See you, Sledgehammer. Don't take any wooden nickels." He and his buddy moved on.

I hadn't budged an inch or said a word, just stood glued to the spot almost in a trance. . . . Would I become this casual and calloused about enemy dead? I wondered. Would the war dehumanize me so that I, too, could "field strip" enemy dead with such nonchalance? The time soon came when it didn't bother me a bit.[69]

Always present was the impulse to take the succeeding step. Staff Sergeant Myles Babcock began removing teeth from the skulls of Japanese corpses; he saved them as souvenirs.[70]

Where precisely lay the line separating necessary toughening and coarsening was difficult to determine, but soldiers whose insensibility *vis-à-vis* the enemy subsequently spilled over into their relationships with compatriots had clearly crossed it. At three o'clock one morning, American sailor James Johns returned to his camp on New Caledonia.

By this time we [had] been working without food or rest for over eighteen hours. I told Arkie that I was going to find us something to eat, and I headed for the cook's shack to beg some chow. The cooks were already up preparing the breakfast mess. I asked the first cook if we could make us a Spam sandwich. We must have looked pretty mean and hungry, because he shrugged his shoulders and said to go ahead. We had just finished gulping down the sandwich when I spied a cake that they must have just finished baking. I asked for a piece for me and Arkie, but the cook said "Hell no." I walked over and started cutting a piece and when I did, the cook picked up a butcher knife and told me to stop or he would stop me. It was at that moment that I realized that the war was already changing me. Without even thinking about it I unstrapped the holster of the .45 Colt I was carrying. I told the cook to suit himself. He backed away and Arkie and I ate our cake. It was the best food I had ever tasted.[71]

These expedients proved less protective than the men assumed, and desired, they would be. Neither numbing nor coarsening rooted itself so deeply that those who experienced it could expect to remain immune to deep feeling. In the end, infantrymen could not foresee or control all of battle's shocks; dread and repugnance constantly threatened to erupt and often did, sometimes without any actuating event. "[And] then as I shaved," British intelligence officer Jocelyn Pereira recalled, ". . . a nauseous wave of ideas about war went flooding through my mind and I was nearly sick." Guy Sajer and his German comrades thought that they had buried a series of battlefield images—surrendered Soviet soldiers whom they had killed; tanks driving over flesh; Hitler Youth caught under a Russian artillery barrage. "[But] we suddenly felt gripped by something horrible, which made our skins crawl and our hair stand on end." On the other hand, the wellspring of Charles ("Commando") Kelly's paroxysm was unmistakable.

> The next morning I went over to find out what had happened to the fellow in the other foxhole, and when I pulled him out half his body remained behind. I began to feel things churning inside of me—which was bad, because it's better if you can close your mind to emotion. Picking up a shovel and covering what was left of him in the hole, I got hot and cold flashes. When the hot ones hit me, I was full of red rage. The cold ones took the heart out of me and drained away my confidence. I managed to beat the disheartened feeling down, but some of the rage stayed in me.[72]

Kelly's spasm was no rarity. American soldiers were seldom able to close down their reactions to the sight, for example, of dead compatriots. Eugene Sledge "had heard and read that combat troops . . . became hardened . . . to . . . their own dead," but he "didn't find that to be the case at all. . . . Marine dead brought forth regret, never indifference." Many, it is true, insisted that they had become invulnerable. James Fry considered himself "numbed beyond being bothered by the sight of . . . dead comrades" and thus able to pass by their bodies as if they were bundles of rags. Marine George Hunt "had seen so many of my men killed or wounded that I was left benumbed. Seeing them fall right and left had become a regular part of a day's work." Paul Moore, Jr., claimed that his fellow Marines were "fairly impervious to the death of [their] colleagues—not that you don't regret it . . . but you don't burst into tears when you see this guy you've worked with for a few months lying there dead." Moore's first consideration? "So he's dead. I wonder who I'll get to replace him . . . in the line." But even those confident that they had steeled themselves remained susceptible to sudden flashes of tumultuous feeling.[73]

John Bassett was preparing for guard duty on the Italian front.

> It could have been a very pleasant two hour stretch. I was comfortable enough lying back in the shallow trench, and the day was warm and sunny. A cupful of

cereal and water and some candy-coated peanuts were by my side, waiting to be eaten. I was reading a week-old issue of *Stars and Stripes* and not worrying much because the Krauts seemed to have called it quits for a while. But there was something on my mind, and it bothered me. Just before I got into the trench, I had made an unpleasant discovery. Coming out here last night, I must have passed close to it. I was hard; I was tough now, but still a shiver went through me. It was only another GI corpse. But why—at this time—did I have to see it? Just when I was about to relax for two hours? I knew it was thawing in the warm sun [and] at night it would grow stiff again. I tried to concentrate on the paper, but my interest somehow was gone. The branches swaying gently in the breeze attracted my eye and when I thought of the cereal, I wasn't hungry at all.[74]

Also powerfully invasive were sights that caught some of the anomalies of the war: a block of houses that, amid a town's utter destruction, remained untouched; a farmer milking his cows at the center of a firefight; and so on. In France, American infantrymen came upon hundreds of horses caught by an artillery barrage. "They look at us with puzzled, unblaming eyes, whinnying softly as their torn flesh waits for life to drain from it. We are used to the sight of dead and wounded men, but these shuddering animals affect us strangely. Perhaps we have been in the field too long to remember that innocence is also caught in the carnage of war." A Texan, who shot the suffering animals that could not survive, was deeply disturbed: "I've known horses all my life and there's not one dirty, mean thing about them. They're too decent to blast each other's guts out like we are doing. Makes you ashamed to belong to the human race."[75]

Soldiers could not rely on achieving a state of permanent insentience. They could only continue cultivating a more and more comprehensive detachment, trying to make smaller and smaller any opening to the consciousness and perhaps ultimately to prevent any entry. "The inner self walling itself in," Theodor Plievier called this effort in his book *Stalingrad.* To some soldiers it yielded an order of indifference that those at home would not have believed possible. In the Bois de Fragette, the German American paratrooper Kurt Gabel, battered by battle, reported: "Without interest I waited for the Germans to storm over us and plunge a bayonet into me." At the end of the clash, he looked out over the survivors of the rifle platoons, wounded awaiting evacuation, snow-suited German prisoners, and described them as "white clumps of misery . . . next to dark lumps of misery, neither caring who won or lost."[76]

But no soldier's wall was without holes. In James Jones's portrayal of the problem, his Pacific theater soldiers too sought insensibility; Sergeant Welsh's "calculated hope and belief [was] that [numbness] might really become a permanent and mercifully blissful state. It was all he asked." In the segmented combat of island-hopping, numbness seemed to persist a little longer after each campaign—but never long enough. After six days out of the line, the men of the company, alarmed that their sensibility and thus their fears were reviving and that, with rest, they could no longer count on exhaustion's dulling power, began a desperate search for alcohol to reinforce the impenetrability they had failed to sustain after battle, for when numbness "went away [it left them] again a quivering mass of jelly."[77]

While the soldier's wall failed to keep out all that he was anxious to repel, it closed out much to which he wished to remain open. He could not insulate himself against battle shocks without affecting his relationships with those around him. To reduce one's accessibility to terror was to diminish one's ability to feel sympathy. Watching replacements moving into battle, Audie Murphy and his mates in the platoon scanned them "with casual interest. Pity is a luxury we cannot afford. We have survived our stretch at the front. Now it is up to them to save their [own] hides. . . ." George Hunt's indifference drew much closer. When the deaths of comrades were "as common as head colds," he said, "the wounded were simply ineffectives who must be replaced . . . at once." Soldiers of diminishing ability to offer sympathy received less sympathy. No one found a way to reduce sensitivity selectively.[78]

In other ways, too, the cost of numbing was high. Soldiers ordinarily described their numbed state in pejorative terms: as a trance; as a stupor (the ultimate expression of which was Tom Lea's painting of the Marine whose face was frozen in the Two-Thousand-Yard Stare); as a petrification of the self; as a drugged or anesthetized condition. "We just slogged along like zombies, walking through all the bodies." Many felt themselves reduced to automatons functioning, as counter-intelligence officer J. Glenn Gray described the state in his World War II study *The Warriors* (1959), "like cells in a military organism, doing what is expected of them because it has become automatic." "My own actions," George Hunt realized, "had become those of a machine, as though my muscles and mind had been trained and coordinated since my birth to perform mechanically the activities of fighting, at the mere fall of a switch." Common to soldiers' reactions was a distress that, anxious as they had been to feel less acutely the fates of friends and their own fears, numbing had cost them something of what made them human.[79]

When Russell Davis reached the top of that hill on Peleliu, his fingers were crushed and burned, but I felt no pain. I crawled and scrambled forward and lay still, without any feeling toward any human thing. In the next hole was [another Marine] rifleman. He peered at me through red and painful eyes. Then we both looked away. I didn't care about him. He didn't care about me. I thought he was a fool and he probably thought I was the same. We had both resigned from the human club. . . . We were no longer even human beings.[80]

Combat troops with the insight to grasp that they could not choose when to numb themselves might also soon realize that the sequence of changes that began with numbing did not halt with coarsening but proceeded to brutalization.

The boundary between coarsening and brutalization was not clear, but there was a rough confirmation of completed passage: the appearance in the soldier of a malice in no way essential to his survival.

Anthony Coulis and the Marines around him on Guadalcanal experienced an "extreme delight in firing [bursts] of machine-gun fire into already dead Japanese. . . . Their bodies sprawled, their lifeless eyes staring into nothingness, their sagging jaws open, gold teeth gleaming in the sun, their sardonic grinning mouths—these sights somehow impelled us to fire volley after volley. As the bodies jerked and quivered, we would laugh gleefully and hysterically. Only when the bullets tore open the corpses, emitting a stench that stung our nostrils and turned our stomachs, did we snap back. . . ."[81]

In the Philippines, a sailor who came upon a Japanese bomber that had crashed on the beach cut off the pilot's genitals and carried them off as a souvenir.[82]

Lieutenant Harold Bond, a replacement mortar platoon leader, described the aftermath of a battle near Cassino on the Italian front:

The Germans had been badly hurt, and one man in particular screamed and screamed. The shooting had stopped, and the whole battlefield around me was quiet except for this man's horrible screams. The enemy in their emplacements, the New Zealanders, the Americans, all surrounding this amphitheater, thousands of invisible eyes were all looking out on the scene, and ears taking in the awful sound. I was stunned.

[One of my sergeants, Jim] Haney grabbed the phone from my hand and gave orders to the [mortar] platoon down below to fire more rounds. "Don't . . ." I started to say, but before I could stop him he had given the command and the men busy at the guns had twelve more shells in the air, and then again twelve more. The shells landed furiously and filled the valley with violent sound. Then everything was quiet. The screaming of the wounded German had stopped, and there was only the black smoke from the shells drifting away. "Why did you do that?" . . . "I know, Lieutenant. I don't like it either." . . . "But he was hurt." . . . "If you don't kill them now you'll have to do it later."* . . . "But the attack was stopped." . . . "They'll kill you if you don't kill them. . . . I've been with this a long time, Lieutenant."

Bond, told in effect that Haney's way was the way things were done at the front, was "sickened by our shelling of those wounded, crying men." He "loathed what we had done." But he recorded no subsequent objection, and soon agreed that the sergeant was right.[83]

Correspondent Eric Sevareid saw throughout the length of the peninsula what he was convinced was a comprehensive brutalization:

> For weeks we would be halted before one of these old cities, and we would shell it without pause until it was rubble. Why? The shelling killed only a very few of the enemy, it wasted countless tons of supplies, and yet in almost every case it was only through the final attack by armor and infantry that the Germans were routed from the rubble, which proved better protection for them than the buildings and which merely impeded the movement of our own vehicles. Shelling upon specific objectives could not be avoided, but this wholesale devastation seemed wanton and senseless to me. Frequently one stood with an artilleryman and listened to remarks like this: "I'm getting tired of seeing that big white building there. Knock the goddamn thing down." He did not know, and would not have cared, whether it was an enemy headquarters, a family home, or a famous museum. It had become a kind of obsession to destroy, to fire for the sake of firing.[84]

The combat soldier worked to accelerate his numbing and toughening, and then acceded to the battlefield evolution toward coarsening and ultimately brutalization. The cost—described by James Jones as "the peculiar numbness of soul that combat caused in everybody"—was high. The returns were not.[85]

Combat soldiers sought a final refuge in fatalism. Ultimately, two metaphorical constructions dominated their thoughts about battlefield death. The first was the notion that bullets and shells carried on them the names of their victims. "If the bullet's got my name written on it, there's

---

*Germans seriously wounded were unlikely to escape, and both sides in the Italian campaign regularly took prisoners, incarcerating them for the duration rather than exchanging them.

nothing I can do" . . . "I'm going to die if a bullet has my name on it." The insistence that missiles were individually targeted did not reflect a belief that the war lay in the hands of a controlling power. No supernatural force etched names on casings. What happened happened. Chance also informed a second imagery, that of a lottery fixing soldiers' deaths as their numbers came up. "That was the raid that had my number" . . . "If your number's up, you'll get it one way or another." Minor variants appeared from time to time—e.g., each GI's appointed day to die—but framing all discussion was the conviction that projectiles hit individuals preordained to die, and that such lives ended on established schedules. Lester Atwell reached to the acme of this fatalism as he watched a wounded soldier be brought in on a stretcher and worked over feveredly by doctors, and then die. That life, Atwell declared, "had been aimed like a guided missile . . . through childhood and school days, through the first pair of roller skates, the first two-wheel bike, through Christmases at home, through high school and baseball and first dates, [at this moment] to meet death here, frightened and bewildered, among strangers in a dark barn, on New Year's Eve in Belgium."[86]

Fatalism was a necessity for those in battle. It provided the sole remaining basis on which the soldier could bring himself to act when the action required was one whose consequences he could not control, one he was offered no opportunity to refuse, one he wished fervently not to take. It was the final summons for a calm sufficient to overcome the fear that one was about to be maimed or killed.

Though vital to soldiers' continuing ability to function in battle, the watchwords they exchanged seemed no more than hoary truisms. During heavy fighting in Italy, John Bassett told himself, ". . . don't worry about it[,] boy. If it's going to get you it's going to get you no matter where you are." William Dreux fended off his fear of parachute jumps: "You adopted a fatalistic attitude—'What will be, will be.'" Morton Eustis too found comfort in the obvious. Battle, he decided, was not so frightening once he adopted "a philosophy that, if you're going to be hit, you're going to be hit." A march behind enemy lines to assault a German position on the only axis from which it was vulnerable terrified Ralph Ingersoll—until he assured himself that the operation "was just happening and it was happening the way it would happen and there was nothing I could do about it except tag along. We were all tagging along. . . ."[87]

Howard Randall received orders for a night patrol required to determine whether the Germans had mined a vital snow-covered road. He had "a hell of a lot of questions," but he knew that "it wouldn't do any good to ask them." In the end he could think of only one way to test the road. Ordering his men to shelter behind trees, he began walking its length. When no explosion hurled him into the air, he shouted for the others, and, although he feared a mutiny, they came and followed him, at one-hundred-yard intervals. When they reached the river and realized there were no mines, they joked and threw snowballs at one another. A soldier like Randall could act as he did because his conviction that he would die when he was meant to die and that, once it was scheduled, he could do nothing to avert his rendezvous with death seemed also to promise that he would die *only* when he was meant to, the thought holding his fear in rein. "Don't worry. . . . If it's going to get you it's going to get you no matter where you are" had as its reassuring converse: "Don't worry. If it's not going to get you, it's not going to get you no matter where you are." Yes, you died if your number was up, but if it were not, you would live no matter how perilous your immediate situation. In a curious way, fatalism thus offered even the soldier in utmost danger a back-door hope of survival.[88]

In the Normandy invasion, Joseph O'Connell of the 4th Infantry Division was the only member of his platoon to reach the shoreline alive. Terrified and desolately lonely, he longed for the shelter of the farmhouse ahead, but he hesitated to cross the intervening open space. "I lie in the grass pondering whether to take the chance. Yes-no-yes-no. My brain keeps whirling." Then he decided: "I must go on, for I'll be killed only when my time comes." (To his relief, he was able to run untouched through the danger zone and to find other Americans there in the house.) Infantryman Carl Damsky applied the same reasoning in a subsequent Allied advance. "I had always heard about booby traps, etc., but it is amazing how you disregard things like that when you get the feeling that nothing will happen to you unless your number is up, and if it is, you'll get it one way or another, so you might as well do what you please."[89]

The helplessness explicit in these formulas, though troubling to soldiers, was not without redemption. At Salerno, correspondent Jack Belden was wounded in the leg; medics placed him on a stretcher, bound his leg to it, and before moving on left him in a stone building to await an ambulance. As he lay there, the tide of battle reversed and columns of German tanks clattered down the road, passing just feet away. Belden found in his powerlessness a way to stave off panic. "I think if I had been in the same position but not wounded, I would have been more frightened than I was then. As it was, I couldn't influence matters. I had no will and no responsibility. Anything that happened was just up to fate." And as helplessness relieved Belden of accountability for what he might otherwise have done, it relieved soldiers of responsibility for contributing to or causing their own deaths. Paul Boesch recited a poem to his men as they sat in their foxholes:

> It does not matter when I go.
>   Nor how nor why.
> Each day a million roses blow,
>   A million die.
> For every bird that lives to sing,
>   A song is stilled.
> I go . . . a brief remembering . . .
>   My place is filled.
> I'll live and love and dine and drink
>   The while I may,
> And when my number's called, I think
>   I'll say "O.K."[90]

Following the New Britain campaign and just before the Peleliu landing, Robert Leckie and his Marine friends singled out in turn each of their number, circled the target, and, to the tune of "Funiculi, Funicula" with changes of name, repeatedly sang:

> Ya-mo, ya-mo, Playboy's gonna die
> Ya-mo, ya-mo, Playboy's gonna die
> He's gonna die, he's gonna die, he's gonna DIE
> So what the hell's the use.
> You're gonna die, you're gonna die.

"A ghoulish serenade," Leckie acknowledged—but a deliverance from all individual responsibility for one's death in battle.[91]

Fatalism similarly helped to lift from soldiers the burden of comrades' deaths. As one Canadian soldier, Donald Pearce, explained: "When a soldier is killed or wounded his buddies, shaking their heads, merely say, 'Poor old Joe. He got it. Just as he was going up that hill, he got it.' As if to imply that he was merely in the wrong place at the wrong time, and that life and death are only matters of luck and do not depend on the calculations of human beings at the other end of [a] gun." No one accused God of placing Joe at the fatal spot, and neither should anyone rebuke a soldier for failing to extricate a comrade *from* the fatal spot; the dead man was, after all, *meant* to be at that wrong place at that wrong time.[92]

Gunner John Ciardi watched others' planes explode in the air or plummet into the ocean, and he himself "did not expect to get off Saipan alive." But a personnel officer, requiring what he called a "grammarian," sifted through personnel files, discovered that Ciardi was a writer, happened on an issue of the *Atlantic Monthly* that carried several of Ciardi's poems, and reassigned him to headquarters to write award and decoration citations and letters of condolence. On their third mission following his transfer to desk duty, the remaining members of Ciardi's original crew were destroyed in a direct hit on their aircraft over Tokyo Bay. He "attributed his survival to simple good luck, the kind no one in his position had a right to expect . . . exactly [the] sort of randomness . . . of blind luck . . . that had contributed so largely to his fears in the first place."[93]

As often as soldiers turned to fatalism to contain fear, to ease their sense of liability for disasters occurring around them, and to prevent being overcome by the forlorn hope of protecting themselves against deaths of such variety, fatalism, like other ways of coping, proved inadequate to their needs.

Sometimes American soldiers seemed to invest themselves in a fatalism as profound as that of their Japanese and German counterparts. "Over in some dry grass by a tree," as Tom Lea recalled an arresting experience during the landing on Peleliu, "I stood a moment looking down at the face of a dead Marine. He seemed so quiet and empty and past all the small things a man could love or hate. I suddenly knew I no longer had to defend my beating heart against the stillness of death. There was no defense." James Jones carried further the accommodation with death. In describing what he called "the evolution of a soldier," Jones proposed as its last stage the GI's "final full acceptance of the fact that his name is already written down in the rolls of the already dead. Every combat soldier, if he follows far enough along the path that began with his induction, must . . . be led inexorably to that awareness. He must make a compact with himself or with Fate that he is lost. Only then can he function as he ought to function, under fire. He knows and accepts beforehand that he's dead, although he may still be walking around for a while."[94]

But combat soldiers rarely espoused for long either the Lea or Jones perspective. Rarely did they move to the point of accepting that there was "no defense" against death or that they themselves were "already dead." As formidable as were the forces pressing on them in battle, as dire as was the situation in particular units during particular periods, soldiers were loath to acknowledge that they had lost control, to admit the impossibility of initiative, or to accede to their destruction. Americans continued to struggle fiercely against death, even when there was little likelihood of living.

Eugene Sledge recognized in himself and the Marines around him on Peleliu the limits of their fatalism. "As [battle] dragged on and on and casualties mounted, a sense of despair pervaded us. It seemed that the only escape was to be killed or wounded. The will for self-preservation weakened. Many men I knew became intensely fatalistic. Somehow, though, one never could quite visualize his own death." Masayo Duus discerned the same boundary behind the words of GIs fighting in the European theater. "Some soldiers said with bravado, 'When I'm going to die, I'm going to die. If the bullet's got my name written on it, there's nothing I can do. No need to get upset about it.'" But Duus noticed that "when the going got rough they pulled their helmets down and hugged the ground. They dug their foxholes deep and did whatever else they could to protect themselves. All the soldiers . . . had but one thought. They did not want to die." And James Jones himself, after adding that the final evolution of the soldier required his acceptance not only of death but of anonymous death, admitted that "I don't think I ever learned this one of the last steps . . . and I think it was just there that my [evolution] stopped short of the full development." So was it with almost all American combat soldiers.[95]

At most, they were able to accept that they would suffer wounds in battle. Sledge could envision no fatal assault on his body, but he could imagine non-lethal injury: ". . . getting wounded did seem inevitable." Acceptance of the wound bespoke a disposition not thoroughly fatalistic, for Americans viewed such injury not as Japanese soldiers did, as a preliminary to death, but as a potential passport from combat, as the *saving* of one's life.[96]

It was easy for field officers to accept the fatalism of absolution for orders that killed rank-and-file, and soldiers for their unwillingness or inability to save their stricken fellows; but the fatalism of certain death was another matter. Rarely can one find in American narratives a fighting man who based practice on fatalistic precept. In reality, GIs drew from their circumscribed fatalism what relaxation of tension it offered and continued to contend with death far more determinedly than with the enemy. Cautiousness became the hallmark of veteran combat soldiers. They sought out every way of enhancing the odds of their survival. They evaded, and sometimes resisted, orders they deemed unreasonable. They followed reasonable orders—and moved not one iota beyond. "Just do whatever everybody else is doing." They learned how to avoid high-risk operations—night patrols, for example—and how to reduce weapons fire that brought down on them enemy counterfire.

Field officers worked to minimize the resort to frontal attacks and to employ them only after overwhelming applications of artillery and airpower against opposing positions.[97]

Fatalism was a refuge, but as a mental persuasion easing slightly battle's pressure on the soldier rather than a set of convictions by which soldiers guided their important actions. The surrender of hope might have brought great relief, but few GIs could capitulate. They told themselves that fate determined deaths, that they themselves were doomed, that they had nothing more to lose and thus need not destroy themselves with worry, but they continued to take every precaution possible. Fatalism was a trick that the soldier, in his quest for self-protection, played on himself.

Each method of coping helped a bit, but neither singly nor in concert could they succeed in shielding soldiers from battle's unrelenting shocks or in arresting the deterioration of those subjected to prolonged combat. Among American soldiers, there were very few resignations from the human club. To remain alive in battle was to continue to suffer hurt.

3 FIGHTING THE GERMANS
The War of Rules

When, in November 1942, American ground forces entered World War II against Germany with landings on North African shores at Casablanca and Oran, they entered upon a campaign whose contours had been set by German and British combat in 1940–41. It was a conflict characterized by relative restraint and by adherence to rules, a pattern with which the Americans quickly aligned themselves.

German and British soldiers had of course fought one another before, twenty-four years earlier in World War I, and thirty months before in the German lightning offensive through Western Europe. That subsequent combat could be cautiously circumscribed may seem curious. The blitzkrieg of May and June 1940 had been catastrophic to the cause of the Allies, its results the ruination of the French Army and the expulsion from the continent of the British Expeditionary Force. It was true that older German military personnel, veterans of World War I, had demonstrated no desire to disturb that fundamental consideration for the enemy characteristic of 1914–18, and that numerous German soldiers thought in 1940 that theirs had been a chivalrous campaign at whose climax their high command had permitted the British to escape from Dunkirk rather than destroy an already-defeated foe. Still, fighting in 1940 had offered signs that this war would reach to new levels of brutality. German SS *(Schutzstaffel)* units had massacred at least one hundred British prisoners of war. Luftwaffe aircraft had machine-gunned columns of refugees fleeing the German advance. German bomber assaults during the Battle of Britain had cost the lives of at least thirty thousand British civilians. Thus there were grounds to believe that British forces subsequently dispatched to North Africa would arrive intent on vengeance.[1]

A campaign of bitterness, however, never developed. At the conclusion in May 1943, each side agreed that the other had fought temperately and decently. The most famous of the war's correspondents, Ernie Pyle, assured his millions of American readers that there the Germans had fought "a pretty clean war." The German Panzer leader Hans von Luck called it the "always fair war," and when, years later, the German radio-television network ORTF produced a film on the campaign, its title was *The War Without Hate*.[2]

For such moderation, the setting—the great North African desert—was in important ways responsible.

It was an arena unusual in its isolation from other, more important theaters of combat and from civilian societies. Neither side felt itself engaged in a desperate defense of homeland; neither side was concerned that there lay the critical theater of the war. Battlefields distant from developed areas, moreover, meant that the crucial battles would not focus on cities; they would not be fought through the ruins of streets, houses, and shops. So, while civilians were spared the destructiveness of battle, soldiers were relieved of the unnerving complications of combat in the midst of a civilian population, painful entanglements of the sort that would soon appear in European campaigns—the grenade thrown at a sudden movement, blowing the leg from a ten-year-old boy; the shot snapped off as a door began to open, striking a farmwife in the chest. North African combat required neither side to give much thought to civilians. The *fellahin* (Arabic-speaking peasantry) ordinarily did not care who won, and even the British, who persistently suspected that local Arabs were pro-German, knew that they would remain passive.[3]

Equally as important was the setting's vastness. The desert's spaces seemed empty and endless. By itself, the occupation of those voids meant nothing to either army. Seldom were soldiers persuaded that territory had to be seized or defended at all costs. Indeed, so vacant seemed those spaces and so limitless their distances that the desert appeared to dwarf and to intimidate the human actors who trod it. Soldiers frequently likened its sands to the waters of the sea and felt no more control of them than of the tides. None were at home in the desert. One British officer described his "overwhelming sense of personal minuteness." Eighth Army soldier Robert Crawford was convinced that the Italians were so frightened of the desert that it destroyed their morale; that the Germans disliked it and, in it, were never quite sure of themselves; that his British comrades came to it worriedly and timorously. No soldiers in this campaign suffered the debilitating conviction that those on the other side possessed a congenial relationship with the terrain.[4]

Combatants did suffer, however, an acute fear of becoming lost in those great tracts. H. P. Samwell, a British officer with the Eighth Army, endured "dreadful dreams" in which "that terror of being alone in the desert came over me." When a company on one of his flanks moved ahead without informing him and another company was late in coming up to take position on his other flank, though he remained surrounded by his own men, he recoiled from "a nauseating wave of terror . . . at the thought of being all alone."[5]

With the desert bearing equally on both sides and often seeming more malevolent than the human foe, each side could sometimes think of the other as a cordial force in alliance against the desert. A limited comradeship, based on common dangers, fears, and hardships, became possible, and from such foundation Britons and Germans arrived at a series of understandings.

Prior to the battle of El Alamein, Samwell thought of the day's schedule almost as if it were a minuet danced with the Germans. His men rose before dawn and "stood to" against the possibility of an enemy attack at first light. A return to sleep often followed. A short time later, the Germans sent over a few shells, and British artillery replied with an equal number. That exchange completed, soldiers on both sides, though often within sight of enemy observers, emerged from their holes to brew tea and coffee and to eat breakfast. Under the terms of the gentleman's agreement in effect during certain periods, hostilities were suspended for the day at five o'clock each afternoon, in order that units might establish their night laagers and there find some slight semblance of home in food, drink, and companionship.[6]

Other terms were equally capacious. British and German supply columns, coming upon one another in the desert, often withheld fire and simply went about their missions. Both sides respected the Red Cross, and doctors ordinarily took good care of the other side's wounded. That widespread concern for the fate of individuals lost in a menacing terrain led to regular radio contact five minutes after the halt of the day's fighting. "Do you have one of our patrols?" "Yes. . . . All of them are unhurt and send greetings to their [families] and friends." Von Luck was pleased that a Canadian pilot about to attack a German radio van signaled its operator to leave immediately. Capitulations were arranged with ease and with safety. When, after Von Luck's return to Germany, his battalion surrendered to the British, the victors were gracious. "It is an honor for us to capture [such a unit]. Please keep your pistol. Is there anything we can do for you?"[7]

The treatment of prisoners was the most considerate of the war. A British officer who had imagined the enemy as glowering SS troopers found that the German prisoners he came upon did not look at all fearsome. And by that time he was anxious that they receive food and good care, for British prisoners, he had heard from escapees, were well treated by the enemy. So he and his men exchanged British bully beef for German chocolate, and both groups stood, eating and talking, measuring hostility by at first debating the merits of British and German aircraft and then, reassured, moving to show off family photographs.[8]

Dramatic fluctuations in the theater's military situation enabled prisoners on both sides to retain sufficient heart to foster light-spirited relationships. German POWs often chided the British that they would soon become prisoners of the Afrika Korps, and the British chaffed back. Not all British soldiers approved of persiflage with the Germans ("I wish you would shut up. It is a damned disgrace being so pally with a filthy Boche"), but relationships between German and British enlisted men nevertheless became so amiable that the British high command decided it necessary to issue strict orders against fraternization.[9]

Desert terrain was open terrain, a circumstance of prodigious military and psychological significance. No factor was more influential than the desert's ability to permit antagonists to see one another often without bestowing on either side the capacity to kill at close range from concealment.

British and American soldiers disliked intensely certain modes of combat. Sniping was a widely despised practice. The use of booby traps, too, was sure to intensify bitterness. Similarly, close-quarters fighting was likely to become combat of a most vicious sort. In the desert, however, with few places for marksmen to hide, there was very little sniping. With few structures, booby traps were denied their usual lodgement. With high visibility, opposing forces found it difficult to surprise and rapidly bring one another within killing range.[10]

The openness of the terrain also accentuated contrasts between the living and the dead. Crumpled bodies stood out starkly, importuning each side, prodding their disposal, and in the process often advancing a respect for enemy dead. Captain Strome Galloway, a Canadian seconded to the London Irish Rifles, remembered that English soldiers took just as much care in fashioning crosses for dead Germans as for dead comrades.[11]

The desert's effect on the war waged across its surface was, as Alan Moorehead recognized, "antiseptic." Numerous British soldiers described desert fighting as "clean." With front lines anchored only until mobile warfare resumed, possessions beyond the minimum required to sustain oneself in combat became burdensome. Paired with the poverty of the land, this fact meant that looting would play little role in the campaign. In fact, insisted a young British replacement officer, Neil McCallum, there was none—except for the rifling of enemy depots and of POWs' useful possessions. The great distances between battlefields and cities also made for a self-sustaining clarity of outlook. Cairo, so far away, appeared a Sodom set against what seemed to combat soldiers the moral simplicity and transparency of the desert. All of this prodded participants toward an asceticism; in Moorehead's words, an "enforced monasticism" that helped to make the campaign "a soldiers' tournament in empty space."[12]

Moorehead's choice of the term "tournament" suggested how cultural values on both sides abetted a relatively moderate combat. North African conditions nurtured the British upper-class inclination, a survivor even of World War I's horrific trench warfare, to view war in the imagery of the game. Samwell likened the North African campaign to a hard-fought football (soccer) match. William Dreux recalled that his Scots commando instructors had made war seem a game: "The Jerries had a team and we had a team." Mark Henniker, a captain in the Engineers, found compelling the similarities between battle and fox hunting. The British commanding officer, General Bernard Montgomery, invoked "the rules of the game we are playing with the Germans." "You play so much better," he urged, "when you know the rules." For them all, war was comprehended as a game in which the best team won. Others who did not share this perspective and found its similes pernicious underscored its influence by the vehemence of their denunciations. A German Jew fighting with the Allies suggested sardonically that the British thought it "more sporting" to give an advantage to the other side.[13]

American soldiers, at the least, found such metaphorical constructs compatible with their own understanding of war. Brigadier General Theodore Roosevelt, Jr., said of his men in North Africa that they treated war "like a football game." More pertinent to most Americans, however, was the prewar and early war ideal of sportsmanship, a concept related to British games notions but more diffuse. At its core was a fundamental dedication to the conviction that fairness should govern relationships involving the individual, combat not excepted.[14]

Within this context, Afrika Korps commander Erwin Rommel became a figure critical to both British and American soldiers. His military skill was widely admired—especially by the British, who frequently suffered its sting. Some British rank-and-file were convinced that Rommel could "outsmart our own generals anytime," and many came to identify with him in quite remarkable degree, as, for example, "a cunning bastard [who] was one of us." More important, all saluted his courtesy to prisoners, his gallantry, his equitableness. "He fought hard, he fought fair." He was "a tough opponent, but . . . one who played fair."[15]

German thought accorded war a seriousness far beyond British and American conceptions. To many Germans, it had the quality and the force of a powerful natural phenomenon or an activity in which they, by virtue of the human condition, were destined to participate. To regard it as the English and Americans did they thought frivolous. There was, nonetheless, a set of German values that did contribute to the same result, moderation in battle. The British affinity for sporting imagery and the American penchant for individualized fairness conjoined harmoniously with the German inclination to formalism. A German officer in North Africa spoke for many of his countrymen: "We pride ourselves on behaving correctly."[16]

There was thus a powerful sense between opponents that they understood one another and that the atmosphere of battle to which all sides contributed would remain one of mutual respect and "fair play."[17]

When American forces arrived, they evinced no desire to depart from the understandings earlier arrived at by Britons and Germans. Nor did the latter find any reason to treat American adversaries differently than they dealt with the British. The Germans counted their new opponents, as they had the British, as a civilized, even "almost a supercivilized," people. Again, each side was willing to trust the other in critical categories of battlefield comportment. American army nurse Theresa Archard described her unit's willingness to group its medical tents, display a Red Cross, and worry no more about German respect for the installation. She and those around her had "infinite faith in the integrity of the Germans as far as the Geneva Pact was concerned. . . ." German and American medics often worked together to save the wounded of both sides. Seldom did German or American troops in North Africa kill those whom they captured.[18]

American combat soldiers, knowing little of the SS and nothing of *Einsatzgruppen* extermination squads, listened sympathetically as German prisoners of war explained that they could not believe stories of atrocities committed by their countrymen in Poland and Russia. The Americans were favorably impressed and remained persuaded that such tales were untruths or exaggerations. They had little difficulty accepting the British notion that the Germans concentrated their "thugs and perverts" in special units and used them apart from regular army formations of "decent fighting men." It was a distinction that no Russian would have entertained for a moment; but in North Africa, given the conditions of combat and the absence of SS units, it appeared a defensible proposition. So American soldiers fought German soldiers without hatred or even much moral indignation, at least until their subsequent European encounters with slave labor and concentration camps. Theodore Roosevelt, Jr., caught best what feeling there was: "Our men don't take to this 'bitter hate' business. . . . [They] will fight like the devil, but when battle's over, it's over. [And then] let's all get drunk together. They gave the prisoners candy and cigarettes and roared with laughter." And again, one whose background excluded him from this perspective was puzzled: an Austrian-born GI could only express his vexation that fellow American soldiers had "no particular feeling for fighting the Germans."[19]

None of the conditions here described guaranteed that North African warfare would not descend to bitterness. No agreements were more difficult to maintain than those that evolved in battle, and violations were of persistent concern to both sides throughout the campaign. Within both armies were individuals and units dedicated to a warfare more terroristic than that upheld by the consensus. The Goums, Algerian and Moroccan tribesmen fighting for the Allies, frequently returned from combat brandishing the severed heads of German and Italian soldiers. Reprimanded, they agreed to settle for ears as proof of their prowess and to accept fifty cents in compensation for each. One of their "tricks," by report, was to find two German soldiers asleep, to cut the head from one and leave the other undisturbed. (American soldiers, watching the Goums at work in Africa and later in Italy, were unimpressed, concluding that they were far more adept at grisly pranks, rape, and pillage than in extended combat.) A more elaborate variant practiced by a Gurkha patrol, reported Neil McCallum, was to slit the throats of four sleeping Germans, leaving the fifth untouched. Such "dirty players" were used willingly enough as a way of weakening enemy morale. When the Germans protested these actions as violating all understandings, they were assured that such practices were and would remain exceptional, the work of "less civilized" peoples. At one point Rommel complained of atrocities committed upon German prisoners; they were attributed to New Zealand aboriginal troops: "That's the Maoris."[20]

In their turn the Germans received heated objections to the behavior of some of their subsidiary forces. The British at times accused the Italians of treating disgracefully numbers of British wounded, of torturing prisoners of war, and of acting treacherously on the battlefield, even to the point of planting bombs on British wounded.[21]

Nor were the actions of the principals themselves always impeccable. The Germans, from the start of the war and in every theater, were inclined to what Ernie Pyle called "scores of crafty, brutal little tricks." During the climactic Tunisian campaign, a German platoon waved a white flag and marched toward the British soldiers waiting to receive its surrender—only to suddenly drop to the ground and open fire. A little less unsettling than this clear and iniquitous violation were issues of constant fragility. Crews attempted to escape from tanks that shellfire had set afire by "bailing out" and running. Were they to be shot down or allowed to make it away? In such matters, the French campaign had generally upheld forbearance. There the Germans, whose superior tactics had destroyed so much of the opposition's armored forces, were inclined to sustain what one of their officers, Alexander Stahlberg, called "an unwritten law not to fire." Sometimes, however, in more evenly fought North African tank battles, combat passions incited German tankers to machine-gun British crews, and, just as often, the reverse.[22]

Because there were frequent rules violations, each side had to find ways both to police its own ranks and to ensure the other side's continued adherence. Rommel, at some risk to himself, ignored Adolf Hitler's order to execute all captured paratroopers and commandos, even after capturing a British commando squad sent to assassinate him. Both sides had to educate to the rules of North African combat new arrivals transferred from other, quite different fronts. On one occasion British enlisted men brought the force of their disapproval to bear on a new officer who relished shooting up the bodies of Germans killed earlier, a practice that the men insisted was a desecration. German soldiers had less success in restraining a recently arrived officer who insisted on capturing a British truck thirty minutes after the appointed cessation of the day's hostilities, but here equilibrium was restored by the immediate riposte of the British: they seized *two* German lorries. Often, such corrective measures involved sufficient escalation that the enemy could not ignore the losses incumbent on his own actions but falling short of losses severe enough to require another round of retaliation.[23]

Such rebukes usually accomplished their purpose. Rules violations remained exceptional—and generally unacceptable—because powerful amelioristic forces rooted in battlefield terrain and cultural propinquity continued to ensure that assumptions of the enemy's treachery never became entrenched. With both sides enforcing restraint, a balance could be maintained within a structure of rules. North Africa remained a campaign without hatred.

———————

It is difficult to imagine a contrast greater than that between North African warfare and the campaign that the Germans waged simultaneously on the Eastern Front, one of the most unremitting harshness.

What ultimately shaped the fighting there was the Germans' dedication to racial views of their eastern opponents very different from their estimation of their British and American adversaries. Adolf Hitler, characterizing Russians, other Slavs, and Jews as people of inherently inferior but very dangerous dispositions, insisted on the necessity of a life-and-death struggle against the *Untermenschen* of the East. His war against them rapidly transformed itself into a crusade of extermination.[24]

There was at the outset no complete commitment to the Führer's ideological struggle. When, prior to the invasion, he ordered that all Communist Party commissars found within Red Army ranks be executed on the spot, SS units obeyed without hesitation, but numbers of Wehrmacht commanders blocked or hampered enforcement of Hitler's directive. In Alexander Stahlberg's regiment, the lieutenant colonel, as required, told his officers of the order—and then repeated the provisions of the Hague Convention, reminded his audience that Germany had bound itself to those terms, and threatened to court-martial any German soldier who abused a prisoner of war. Tension on this issue persisted within and between many commands, with local responses ranging from complete compliance to complete contravention.[25]

Strain also appeared around the operations of the *Einsatzgruppen,* the execution squads that became, with the extermination camps, the ultimate embodiment of Hitler's ideological warfare. They began their work in occupied Poland, moving from town to town and systematically murdering Jews, local officials, teachers, doctors, clergy, and others. As they extended their activity to the Soviet Union, and its scale drastically increased, they more often required the cooperation of regular army units. At the outset, Wehrmacht commanders sometimes proffered, sometimes withheld that aid.

The ranks were similarly divided. Many German soldiers entered Russia convinced that they would become there, as they had thought themselves elsewhere in Europe, a force for good. German superintendence would revive other economies as Hitler had rejuvenated Germany's. The German presence would bring jobs, improvements, culture. And German soldiers saw in the enlistment of other Europeans in their ranks—there were SS units composed of French, Belgians, Dutch, Danes, etc.—confirmation that others saw them as they saw themselves: as conquerors, yes, but as liberators rather than oppressors.[26]

Those thoroughly imbued with Nazi ideology were uninterested in notions of a potentially beneficial German presence and found in Russians precisely the people they had expected to find. To them, Russian villages seemed unredeemably primitive, the villagers hopelessly brutish. The peasants, German soldiers wrote home, urinated in front of their huts and used their own spit to wash themselves. "[T]hese Russians can't be people any more," decided an SS private; "they must be immune to any sort of feelings now." But those many German soldiers still open to observation found surprises. Numbers of Russians seemed intelligent and even technically gifted, more highly educated, cleaner, more moral, and more pious than expected. Much that they saw—new schools, for example—did not "fit into the frame of the Russia that has been depicted to [us]." The welcome accorded German forces in parts of the Soviet Union reinforced such receptivity. Some peoples—Ukrainians, Cossacks, others with aspirations for independence from Moscow—greeted the invaders with bread and salt, or strawberries and milk, in gratitude for their deliverance from Stalin's control. Peasants with undiminished memories of the forced collectivization of farms, the liquidation of the kulaks, and the closure of the churches were also favorably disposed. Significant numbers volunteered to work with the Germans against the Soviets. These forces, whose sensitive use would have confronted Moscow with regional civil wars almost as menacing as the foreign invasion, were never effectively mobilized or employed because Nazi ideology could not accommodate distinction among components of broad and, by definition, utterly vile racial groupings.[27]

The range of contradictory German actions was stupefying. Some German units simply shot down all Russian soldiers attempting to give up. Others, willing to accept surrenders, found among their captives numbers ready to join in military action against that Red Army of which they had so recently been a part. A German army surgeon described a Russian soldier who surrendered to a German unit and then remained with it, in faithful service, for four years. Of such materials, the Germans ultimately formed the Vlasov Army, whose troops, Russian ex-prisoners of war, served the Wehrmacht almost to the end of the war. At the same time, however, other Russian POWs were so starved and mistreated that as many as three million may have perished in German hands. A Wehrmacht soldier might thus see at the front

Russians fighting with and for the Germans, might see from the window of his leave train compounds in which Russian prisoners of war were dying by the thousands, and might see at home Russian "volunteer" or "guest" workers being treated decently—or being worked to their deaths.[28]

The Russian response to German actions, drawing both on aroused local reaction in occupied territory and on strong direction from Moscow, was to resort to a partisan warfare that mobilized civilians, including numbers of young people. Guerrillas fought as spies, saboteurs, and snipers. They seized opportunities ranging from the killing of German soldiers separated from their units to attacks on rear-echelon installations. The military effects of their activities were not at first significant, but the psychological consequences were profound. Those German soldiers who had come to Russia already won to Hitlerism found in guerrilla warfare a final confirmation of its depiction of their enemies. More important, those Germans who had regarded Russians more openly now came to view their continuing, irregular resistance as a treachery that impelled them to widen their definition of the enemy—from uniformed Russian soldiers to Russian civilians who engaged in partisan activity, and then, because it proved impossible to distinguish guerrilla and non-guerilla civilians, to all Russians. The result was a gathering of German soldier opinion around the central tenet of Hitlerian ideology: the condemnation of whole peoples. "*All* Russians are guilty," concluded German troopers.[29]

There followed a war that rapidly descended to the uttermost barbarity. Stung by partisan activity, the Germans adopted draconian countermeasures, with results that German soldiers' letters leave in no doubt. Were two German sentries shot? Execute one hundred Russians. Was a German officer killed by partisans? Execute three hundred Jews. Was a village discovered to be hiding a dozen Russian soldiers? Seal one hundred peasants inside their huts and set them afire. Was the schoolteacher found with a radio capable of receiving Moscow broadcasts? Shoot him and his family. Groups of vaguely suspect women were driven across ground known to have been mined by the Red Army. Some of those believed to be connected with specific partisan incidents were hanged heads-down. A Wehrmacht soldier wrote in his diary that he had just participated in the executions of fifty women and children, and a field policeman in his, that he had had thirty Russian youngsters killed that day. Thus the Germans produced much death, much rage, much bitterness—and more guerrillas.[30]

Action and reaction, reprisal and counter-reprisal lost all touch with measured response and merged in an accelerating escalation of rancor and a raging resolve to exact vengeance. As German soldiers decided that all Russians were "animals," Russians concluded that they were fighting "beasts." War on the Eastern Front became a *guerre à outrance*.[31]

The North African war and the Eastern Front war did not coalesce as they moved on different axes to meet in the German homeland. The Germans continued to fight both types of war; against them, the Soviets fought their kind of war and the Americans and the British theirs. Collisions between the two wars were rare, but when they occurred, as they did with the transfer of SS divisions from Russia to the Western Front, the consequences, though grave, could be constrained in ways preventing a fusing of patterns.

In Italy following the building of an Anglo-American foothold in Sicily, the Western Allies and the Germans extended to the European continent the fundamental precepts of the North African war. The momentum of established assumptions favored the transfer, yet the transition was strained. The terrain, the relationship between soldiers and civilians, the strategic stake— all were different from those of North Africa.

As one would expect, the British were most aware of the change. The intensity of the fighting in Sicily surprised H. P. Samwell. No longer, he decided, could campaigning be likened to the playing of an intensely contested football match. Efforts to "preserve the decencies," he noted, dwindled. Attitudes seemed to harden. Puzzled, Samwell traced the shift to the presence of "a different type of German altogether." Alan Moorehead agreed. In reports that Germans had burned Italian villages and shot down villagers, he found evidence of a new and icy German personality given to implacable calculation. "Many of us had only known the German army in Africa, where the war had been reduced to a straight military contest between the forces in the field. In general the Germans had behaved very well. . . . But now something quite different was happening behind the German lines . . . [N]ow for the first time in our experience they were killing civilians for no military advantage. . . ."

In reality, a new situation was altering people's behavior rather than new people altering the situation. Italy brought the war menacingly closer to the German homeland. Different natural and social terrains lent themselves to new battle techniques, signaling, for example, that the Allies would suffer serious losses from German booby traps hidden in fruit trees and in houses. Combat in built-up areas brought home an awareness that fights would no longer exclude civilians. It was in the Italian village of Pietramellara that Peter Cochrane of the Queen's Own Cameron Highlanders "realized with a jolt that this was a different kind of war, one which involved civilians. In the desert and in Eritrea, the fighting went on without damaging anyone but soldiers; all the battles were in terrain that nobody had tried to inhabit: war was idiocy, but it was self-contained. But here were poor folk whose houses had been smashed, their belongings destroyed, fields unsown and animals killed; every family had suffered death and injury, the children were in rags and evidently half starving. War wasn't merely idiotic, it was wicked and cruel."[32]

Events, too, conspired to alter the conditions of warfare. Following the Badoglio coup, the ouster of Mussolini, and the negotiation of a leaky Italian armistice with the Allies, German soldiers suddenly found themselves fighting among a civil population whose loyalty was no longer assured. Some units of the Italian Army changed sides and immediately entered combat against the Germans. Some Italian civilians sought out opportunities to kill German soldiers. Repaying what they considered turncoat treachery, the Germans everywhere left behind booby traps, time bombs, and other infernal devices, the results of which were most spectacularly demonstrated in the mammoth explosion that destroyed the Naples Post Office. In the minds of many British and American soldiers, such methods pointed the way to a more remorseless combat.

In the end, despite such strains, the framework of warfare constructed in North Africa did prove transferable to Italy and, with the Normandy invasion, to Western Europe. In the campaign across France one could see most clearly the stresses that threatened to bring down the structure of rules and the accommodations that soldiers were prepared to make to preserve it.

American and German soldiers in France assumed that their clashes were subject to regulation. "We . . . fought," said Harold Leinbaugh "by rules of a sort." More important, soldiers on both sides—and their high commands—acknowledged that their enemies were fighting in accordance with those rules. They constituted a system of restraints that was subjected to constant challenge and that struggled daily to adapt to the stresses imposed on it. There were times when it was not at all certain that such a system would endure.[33]

At its center stood two of the most pervasive fears of the combat soldier: that he would be wounded, would remain alone and unaided, and would die a forlorn and solitary death; and that, if taken by the enemy, he would be killed rather than held captive, or that, if made prisoner, he would be treated with cruelty.

From the infantryman's perspective, any set of rules would have to begin with the care of the wounded.

For such a purpose, a formal structure was already in place. The Geneva Convention of 1864, as amended in 1906 and 1929, required belligerent nations to ensure that all wounded received humane and equal treatment. To enable armies to meet that charge, it followed that those who provided that care should themselves be safeguarded: medical personnel and chaplains were to be protected from harm, were to be left free to perform their duties, and, if captured, were to be returned to their own side as quickly as possible. Their auxiliaries—ambulances, military hospitals, etc.—were also to remain immune from attack.

How the system was intended to work, and how the foot soldier hoped it would work, was best illustrated by the successful medical truce.

During one of the 28th Division's assaults on the German town of Schmidt in November 1944, American troops were caught by enemy fire and two wounded GIs were left hanging in the barbed wire. Amid heavy shelling, a private in the American lines, Harold Sheffer, began waving a white handkerchief and then dared to stand upright. The Germans halted their fire, and one of their officers, moving forward to meet the American, agreed to allow the recovery of the wounded. Soldiers on both sides stood up in their holes, stretched to relieve cramped muscles, and then, as the truce ended with the evacuation of the injured, returned to earth and to the battle.[34]

In another instance whose circumstances did not permit so formal an arrangement, a member of a patrol along the river Roer was wounded and left lying helpless on the bank in advance of the American lines. "Pulling on his Red Cross bib, Doc stood in the open to make sure the Germans spotted him. He then walked slowly toward the river." The medic, while able to bandage the soldier's wound and to ease his pain with morphine, realized that he would be unable to carry him to safety, so he returned alone, retrieved a wheelbarrow, and started back. "Men yelled across the river to the Germans, 'Okay, hold it, hold it,' and the Germans hollered back, 'Okay.' . . ." Though the rescue "proceeded in agonizingly slow motion" and one German rifleman continued to fire, Doc was finally able to propel his makeshift ambulance the quarter of a mile to safety. "As he finally pushed the wheelbarrow into an alley behind a ruined house . . . a cheer went up from every man in K Company."[35]

Help came not only during truces and not only from American aidmen. Allied soldiers reported many instances in which German doctors ventured out to bring in American or British wounded, and German stretcher bearers, fallen temporarily into Allied hands, sometimes volunteered to retrieve their wounded enemies from beneath German artillery fire. In special situations, across-the-lines aid received the blessing of the opposed military commands. During the battle for Arnhem, the British suffered high casualties and quickly exhausted their resources when medical re-supply by air failed. German and Allied medical personnel thereupon formed joint teams to treat the casualties. And as the situation continued to deteriorate, the Germans granted a truce in which *they* assumed the custody and the care of the British wounded.[36]

With medical personnel willing to treat enemy soldiers and sometimes even to attempt their rescue under fire, there developed accommodations that neither side wished to publicize at home. In rapidly shifting combat situations, there was often insufficient time for aid stations to pack up and withdraw with their own forces. On one such occasion, an American medic was startled by a knock on the aid-station door. A group of German soldiers, with great civility, informed those within that they were prisoners. Did the Americans have any weapons? Told that they did not, the Germans accepted that response on faith. Did the Americans have rations? Enough for a day. Very well, we shall bring rations—and we shall send German medics as well. Later, as the Germans prepared to move on, they posted a guard to ensure that other advancing units would not interfere with the station's operation. The Americans responded in a similar spirit of trust and goodwill: when they discovered that one of their number did possess a weapon, a .45 pistol, they turned it over to the German guard.[37]

As hospitable as they might be to their "guests," both sides made efforts to return captured medics and chaplains to their compatriots as soon as conditions permitted. Shortly after the 9th Infantry Division crossed the Rhine at Remagen,

> Three of us were selected to make a jeep patrol to check a bridge about two miles away. We went to a nearby farmhouse and . . . the farmer . . . said the bridge was there the last he knew. . . . We . . . moved cautiously through the heavy woods . . . [and] found the bridge intact and returned to the farmhouse. While [there], we spotted a German soldier in the woods and when we ordered him to come to the house, we discovered he was a medical officer. He told us there were more in the woods and they had two trucks, but were out of gas. Our jeep driver made a special trip for gas and when all of them came out there were 43 including several nurses. At last report, our regiment had returned them to the Germans because of the German shortage of medics.[38]

In the course of such a return in the opposite direction, a German soldier halted an American medical jeep and warned its riders that the road ahead had just been mined.[39]

During heavy fighting in Normandy, an American outpost was "startled to see a German medic climb nonchalantly over a hedgerow and make his way calmly across the field. . . . He wore the fore-and-aft garment common to all German medical personnel, a white smock bearing a very large Red Cross. Furthermore, he seemed to have complete confidence in the immunity it was supposed to give him." The German, a captain, saluted stiffly and handed to an American sergeant a note requesting a truce enabling both sides to retrieve their wounded and dead. The American high command agreed, and during the next two hours its medics found an infantryman who, though without food, water, or medical aid for two days, still had a chance of survival.[40]

Based on such experiences, the American combat soldier assumed the existence of a set of rules and found in the efforts of both sides to observe those rules a welcome message: that he might reasonably expect that when injured, he would receive help; that his enemies would not view his incapacitation simply as an invitation to finish him off; that if American aid could not reach him, he might still expect assistance from enemy medical personnel; and that the quality of that care would not fall much below that which the Germans provided their own wounded. No suppositions did more to determine the relationship between combatants.

Still, such assumptions were always fragile. Private Harold Sheffer's medical truce took place as described, but it must not, in its seemingly simple adherence to the provisions of Geneva, be taken to constitute common experience. There were occasional near-perfect rulebook cases, but World War II combat was not a game and its regulations were hopelessly deficient. Decisions to observe the rules, no matter how frequently made, were seldom simple ones. Action in compliance with the rules was rarely advanced because it constituted the path of least resistance; far more often the momentum of combat favored inaction. The soldier had to exert himself to abide by the rules, and that was to enter upon processes that were complex, messy, hazardous, and costly.

Seldom was there a negotiated or tacit medical truce whose course did not demonstrate the frailty of the rules. Soldiers in positions a bit distant from the immediate sector often continued to fire. And if problems of communication and coordination with those nearby were difficult, those with rear areas frequently proved impossible. Front-line soldiers agreeing to hold their fire could not speak for those on their flanks, for their superiors, or for their supporting artillery units. Medics quickly learned that the truce was no rules-manual exercise.

In severe fighting around Vossenack, southwest of Cologne, in November 1944, a German counterattack sent units of the 28th Infantry Division into a headlong retreat that left in its wake numerous American wounded. Their regimental surgeon, Major Albert Berndt, mindful that headquarters had refused him permission to ask the Germans for a truce but wishing to evacuate his casualties, decided to proceed on his own. With a German-speaking medical clerk walking beside him, white flag in hand, he set out to find the nearest Germans. A Wehrmacht lieutenant, courteous and without inclination either to threaten or to search the Americans, agreed to let Berndt evacuate the wounded from his aid station. The German added, however, that he had "no way to communicate with . . . his own superiors or with nearby artillery batteries. The heavy snow might obscure Red Cross markings, causing distant gun batteries to fire upon [the] convoy." Berndt decided to accept the risks.

When the wounded had been loaded, three vehicles set off for the point at which they were to meet ambulances from the American lines. At that site the Germans had gathered additional American wounded, whom they covered with German raincoats and blankets, but that activity had drawn the attention of another German unit, headed by a captain who knew nothing of Berndt's agreement with the lieutenant. The captain was determined to make prisoners of war of all lightly wounded Americans, so his men carefully checked the casualties and demanded to inspect the Red Cross credentials of medics, who were by then wary and worried. Soon an argument erupted over the German's new insistence that, because surrounded American combat units in the vicinity would soon need medical attention and the Germans were short of doctors, two American battalion surgeons would have to remain behind. Berndt objected and "after much prayer, anxiety and four hours," prevailed; the German captain and his men departed.

Later, however, as Berndt sought a truce extension from him, he met yet another demand: that no more American wounded be evacuated until all American combat soldiers in the area had surrendered. Impossible, replied Berndt. At that point, bittersweet fortune produced an artillery barrage that interrupted debate and forced both sides to flee. The Americans next turned to a German medical officer; he wished to pick up his own dead, and in return for American cooperation was willing to authorize the resumption of the evacuation. Soon, however, all parties realized that theirs was a truce only between medics: American artillery refused to recognize it and opened fire. Medics on both sides continued their work, and at last all medical personnel, along with the wounded and dead, were within their own lines.[41]

Stray small-arms fire; truce-time fire heavy enough to provoke a firefight; an unknowing or uncooperative artillery unit; a misunderstanding; an error in translation; momentary stubbornness on one or both sides—there were myriad ways in which the lives of medics and their charges could be rendered forfeit.

A persistent problem was that of deciphering the other side's motivation. Occasional battle encounters left no room for doubt: an American wounded by German fire

> kept calling for someone to help him. Isn't anybody going to take care of me? he was saying . . . and then he'd cry. [Medic] Pico . . . couldn't stand it. . . . He grabbed a Red Cross flag and ran across the snow waving it. There was no mistaking what he was doing. He was kneeling by the wounded man; he had just given him a shot and was putting on a dressing when the machine gun cut him in two. The German was clearly having a lot of fun because he kept on firing long bursts into the wounded man and into Pico, keeping the bodies jumping and spreading red all over the snow. He'd used the wounded man for bait, an old SS trick.[42]

But relatively few incidents offered such unambiguous markings.

American aidmen frequently found themselves the targets of sniper fire. Were German marksmen targeting medics or, at that distance, were they unable to distinguish Red Cross armbands? German soldiers were in that house ahead, marked with a Red Cross. Were they unhurt and thus active combatants? Were they exhausted and perhaps seeking safety while awaiting an opportunity to surrender? Were they wounded or sick? What danger *did* they pose? Was the installation itself an actual medical facility, or was the flag simply a German ruse? And if artillery were called down to destroy a fraudulent aid station, what would be the result? Would the Germans grant by their silence that they had been caught in a deception or would they respond with an angry and perhaps costly retaliation against an American medical facility? Such situations demanded snap judgments while withholding any way to gain command of the many elements at play.

Specialized knowledge was often a requisite. All understood that medics, in return for the protection theoretically accorded them, undertook not to act as combatants. American medics thus carried neither pistols nor rifles.

German aidmen, however, often carried Lugers or P-38s, weapons that technically rendered them legitimate targets of American fire. So it was important to know the limited purpose to which those special, shiny pistols were put. An American medic watched one of his German counterparts examine a wounded landser, shake his head, draw his pistol, and shoot the man. ("What a method of mercy!" thought the American.) Even when understood, the practice itself could create further complications. When German medics who shot comrades to relieve them of irremediable misery extended the practice to wounded Allied soldiers, how were Americans to react? Were such killings acts of mercy based on authoritative decisions that the wounds were unsurvivable? Or would they raise the cry, "They're shooting our wounded!" and be cast as German atrocities demanding vengeance?[43]

The second personal fear pressing on the combat soldier contemplated another quandary of helplessness, one no more welcome than the wounding: whether, if caught by the enemy, he would be shot down rather than taken alive, and whether, if made a prisoner, he would be severely mistreated.

Again, a formal structure provided only partial reassurance. The Hague conferences of 1899 and 1907, expanded by the Geneva agreement of 1929, had produced a code that addressed imprisonment but not capture. It required that belligerents furnish full information about prisoners taken, provide housing in sanitary quarters, and offer sufficient wholesome food and adequate medical attention. Prisoners of war were not to be compelled to do work that was excessive, dangerous, or of a military character; for their legitimate labor they were to be paid on a scale varying with rank. They were also to be allowed to send letters and to receive letters and parcels. But there was no provision requiring armies to accept the surrender of enemy soldiers, a practice spottily sanctioned by custom since the seventeenth century. Fortunately for World War II GIs and landsers, both the U.S. Army and the Wehrmacht established as policy the acceptance of enemy soldiers' surrender—if those yielding were German or American rather than Japanese or Russian. When enemy soldiers found in a Dutch house anxiously asked their captors if they would be shot when the GIs moved on, PFC Frederick Becker replied—and firmly believed—that "Such things aren't done in the American Army." Another American foot soldier put it more tentatively, and realistically: "Dead prisoners was not policy." But the weight of consensus among American soldiers in Italy and Western Europe fell heavily in favor of taking and sparing prisoners.[44]

Soldiers on both sides recognized how the system was meant to work. A soldier desiring to give up would display some touch of white—a cloth, sheeting, a paper, a handkerchief. That would cause those on the other side to cease firing. The soldier would then advance toward his enemies, unarmed and with hands raised above his head, until met and taken into custody. He would be searched and perhaps interrogated, but he would be moved expeditiously to the rear and transported to a POW camp far removed from the battle zone. There he would be interned, and treated decently, until the end of hostilities.

Again, however, the formal structure bore only a distant relationship to the actualities of the battlefield. Soldiers, whatever their instruction in and receptivity to the restraints of international law and army policy, immediately discovered that even full compliance would not suffice to regulate combat between Americans and Germans; important elements of cultural dissonance complicated their relationship. Combat soldiers on both sides came to realize that certain of their own practices, though violating no formal precept, so antagonized their opponents that, if left unregulated, might endanger the whole structure of agreement. Each side, in short, had to learn something of the other side's cultural peculiarities and to accommodate them within a set of informal battlefield rules it imposed on itself.

Of those borne in on American soldiers, one of the most important, had it been codified, would have read: Do not be caught in possession of items of German manufacture, especially those of army issue. Discovering such articles in American pockets or packs, German captors construed them as evidence that their possessors had killed their original German owners. It was a logic hardly unassailable. Seldom did soldiers engrossed in killing the enemy have the time or inclination for scrounging. Those who later did so ordinarily rifled the bodies of soldiers killed by others. Many such items, moreover, were obtained at second or third hand, by barter or purchase. The Germans nevertheless acted on their conclusion. Often they immediately shot GIs captured with German souvenirs. Platoon leader Howard Randall knew of an instance in which a captured American soldier, searched by the Germans and found to be holding a German watch, was killed, his body cut open, and the watch sewn inside. On other occasions, Germans wishing to advertise their outraged feelings shot the GIs caught with forbidden articles, slashed warning Xs across their chests, and placed the offending objects at the intersection of the lines.[45]

American combat soldiers had no difficulty deciphering the message. Never be captured with souvenirs, warned Irgang. If you are found in possession of a P-38, Leinbaugh told his company, the Germans will shoot you. In a patrol action, an American platoon leader simultaneously fired at approaching Germans and threw away German watches. Caught in a skirmish, Leinbaugh suddenly realized that the pack he was carrying contained a German blanket and that he could not jettison it; he would, he concluded, have to "fight to the end."[46]

In an important index of the rapport between the two sides, American soldiers accepted the German prohibition, however unfounded its basic assumption; adjusted their behavior to accommodate it; and did *not* retaliate in kind. When GIs noticed that a newly captured German was wearing U.S. Army combat boots, they forced him to take them off and to walk through the snow in stockinged feet. When American paratroops of the 82d Division discovered that a captive landser wore American paratrooper boots, they were angry, but the question they pondered was, "Did that Kraut take those boots off one of our dead buddies?" rather than, "Did he kill one of our buddies and take his boots?" The American guard struck the German with his rifle and kicked at the boots. The German quickly removed them, but several Americans who remained unappeased ordered him to take off his pants. "He can march to the rear both bare footed and bare assed." More discussion followed—the guard proposed to shoot off the German's penis, one "no damn Kraut deserves"—but that caused the German "to dance and squirm and plead for mercy," and he was marched to the rear, pants on, boots off. A capital offense on the German side was seldom perceived so on the Anglo-American side.[47]

There were, however, other enemy practices that incensed American soldiers no less than American acquisitions inflamed German soldiers. The one that figured most prominently in the American mind required Germans to heed a rule that might have been phrased: Do not continue to fire on advancing Americans until the last moment and then attempt to surrender.

At the heart of this clash was the enemy's dedication to formalism, often defined by Germans as the fulfillment of the demands of honor, and by Americans as a series of silly gestures utterly at odds with the practicalities of the situation at hand. In their defense of one of the Metz forts, the Germans insisted on a token bombing before they would agree to surrender. The Americans obliged with "four fair-sized bombs," and a white flag appeared. Near the French village of Tal-ar-Groas, Paul Boesch thought it strange that those Germans opposite his position who had fought all night to regain the hill would suddenly send a representative to negotiate their own surrender but would agree to capitulate only after they had been brought again under enemy fire. That, they were convinced, would remove any imputation of desertion and would solidly cast them as surrendered combatants. An American lieutenant shrugged and fired a single shot in the air; forty Germans, happy that honor had been satisfied by that token duress, then marched out and into captivity. Though often willing to accede, American soldiers continued to express scorn for such formulaic and highly symbolic solutions.[48]

The immediate problem derived from the fact that the Wehrmacht forbade its soldiers to surrender while their ammunition remained unexpended. Accordingly, they strove to perform as required, even when that meant continuing to fire long after the hopelessness of the military outcome had become patent. As, however, the last shot satisfied the essential condition, they were instantly freed to down their weapons and raise their hands. They regarded themselves as instantaneously transported from a state of combat to a state of non-hostility. Advancing Americans were seldom able to duplicate the switch, and battle emotion that could not be quickly extinguished was in fact heightened by what GIs were convinced was the Germans' determination to fight to the last, despite the obviousness of the military verdict on the encounter. Perseverant fighting had for the Americans only one meaning: a German desire, divorced from all other considerations, simply to kill as many Americans as possible.

Moving toward the Vosges Mountains, Private Norman Adolph's L Company, 397th Infantry Regiment, 100th Division assaulted a hill held by the Germans, and following two artillery barrages and three failed assaults, took it: "The bastards shoot and kill as long as they can, and then they bring out their white flags and surrender." Airborne trooper Kurt Gabel was a part of his platoon's assault on a group of Belgian farmhouses occupied by the Germans: "'Let's go!' I heard the lieutenant's voice, and it sounded like a jump command . . . In a wave . . . came the chilling yell of 'Geronimo-o-o! Geronimo-o-o!' over and over. . . . From the holes in the embankment the Germans . . . tried to burrow out and lift their hands at the same time. For three or four . . . it was too late. Troopers, still yelling, were thrusting bayonets into them, shooting, and yelling again. 'Stupid Krauts,' I thought, 'why did they wait so long?'" "Even in hopeless situations," reported Joseph Shomon, who saw many bodies as the commander of a graves registration unit, "the Germans would usually fight to the last, refusing to surrender. [Then] when their ammunition was gone, they were ready to give up and ask for mercy [but because] many American lives had been lost in this delay, our troops often killed the Germans. . . ."[49]

Individual Germans to whom GIs thought they could trace specific American deaths often provoked similarly lethal reactions. Just after his unit crossed the Rhine, Frank Irgang watched American soldiers beat to death with his own weapon a persistent German machine gunner who "was known to have inflicted several casualties upon us." In such situations, executions were frequent—but not inevitable. Charles MacDonald's company of the 23d Infantry Regiment was furious at German soldiers who had killed four Americans and then surrendered. Following heated debate ("We oughta take every one of the bastards and cut their nuts right out!"), the Germans were compelled to remain for a time in the open, exposed to their own machine-gun fire.[50]

It was unlikely that earlier surrenders would have safeguarded many more sniper lives, but other Germans were able to learn saving lessons. James Fry, an American regimental commander, encountered German artillery crews who had grasped that "American troops acting on their own initiative frequently elected not to accept the surrender of men who used their guns to the last second"; the artillerists had decided to ignore their orders because they "preferred to live."[51]

Another zone of conflict involved German behavior that infuriated Americans by evoking the characteristics of the Hollywood Nazi. Germans who, in surrendering, exhibited what their captors thought of as arrogance or any swaggering concern for distinctions of class, caste, or rank risked violent reactions.

Friction here often focused on the actual manner of offering or accepting surrender. Under the terms of the Geneva Convention, no surrendering officer could be forced to treat with a representative of the other side more than two ranks below his own. And because Germans maintained that the higher the enemy's rank, the less disgraceful the surrender to him, it was a provision German officers frequently invoked. That, coupled with the way in which it was often done, grievously offended low-ranking American soldiers' sense of their own dignity as individuals. Continued insistence on the punctilio of rank and on the special treatment due to officers intensified—and provided accessible German targets for—grievances that many American soldiers thought inflicted on them daily by their own Army.[52]

At Normandy, a sergeant in the 29th Division found a German field-grade officer hiding in a hayloft. The officer insisted that "he would not surrender to a simple soldier; he demanded that [the sergeant and his men] produce an officer. That would be fine, said Sergeant Ogden. But they would have to disarm him first." The German gave over his pistol and then an eighteen-inch knife, presenting the latter by its carved ivory handle. The sergeant immediately reversed the direction of movement, driving the knife

into the officer's body to its hilt. "He had a very startled look on his face."
Luftwaffe pilots had an especially strong sense of their prerogatives. One, a
colonel, refused to submit to any American not of his rank. With no American colonel in the vicinity, the men summoned a lieutenant, who, when the
German remained insistent, promptly "shot him down." Another pilot
pressed for special treatment, emphasizing his demand by pointing frequently to the medals on his chest. "*Ich bin Offizier.*" "I don't give a shit if
you're Baron Von Richtofen. Get your ass out of here." "*Ich bin Offizier.*"
The American lieutenant thereupon lost his temper and brought the butt of
his pistol down on the German's head. "For Christ sake! What kind of war is
this when a goddamn enemy prisoner of war can harass a Company Commander? Get this son of a bitch out of here or he's going to be a dead pilot."
Perhaps embarrassed by his tantrum and by his own invocation of rank, the
lieutenant felt it important to add, in mitigation of his action, "Any other
Army commander might have shot him between the eyes." In the last days of
the war an American patrol escorting a German general back to its lines
came on a half-track whose driver was willing to carry them. "Get in" said
the sergeant to the general. "I am a general officer," he replied. "I will ride in
front"—only to be immediately and roughly flung into the back, perhaps
without realizing how lightly he had escaped.[53]

Arrogance in particular incited GI anger. It summoned stereotypical images of stiff, correct, bemonocled, tight-lipped, or condescendingly amused
Prussians—reminders of what American soldiers had earlier been told they
were fighting against but had seldom found in German field soldiers. Encountering haughty German commanders, James Fry was sometimes able to
confine his reaction to angry words: "I am not at all interested in cooperation
or mutual understanding. You are the defeated; we are the victors. Bear that
in mind and conduct yourselves accordingly." At other times restraint failed
him. "I stepped through a doorway, pistol in hand, to encounter a couple
dozen enemy who had obviously agreed to surrender. The decision had
probably not been left entirely to the commander, for . . . he stood alone, a
tall and disdainful individual. There was a half sneer on his face as he looked
me straight in the eye and lifted a bottle . . . to take a drink. His expression
changed as the barrel of my Luger smashed the bottle against his face."[54]

German enlisted men occasionally demonstrated the same arrogant formalism. When a GI of the 9th Infantry Division asked a prisoner to give up
his watch, the German protested that "according to the rules of the Geneva
Convention" he was not required to do so. (He was right: under Hague-
Geneva principles, personal belongings, except arms and ammunition, were

to remain the prisoner's private property.) When, however, the American insisted, "the German took off his watch and stomped on it." The American shot him dead.[55]

For Germans whose reactions proved irritating rather than infuriating, a favorite antidote was the top of a C-ration can painted with an "R." German prisoners curious to know why they had been ordered to wear it on their backs were told that it designated those who were scheduled to be turned over to the Russians. There was no further annoyance.[56]

There was another precept that the Germans learned would sometimes determine their survival: Never avow to Americans your devotion to the Führer. Often, in a test designed to detect the most fanatical of the enemy, captured German soldiers, particularly SS, were asked about Hitler, and those who acknowledged loyalty were killed. "We are fighting SS troops today, Hitler's bad boys," reported Orval Faubus on December 4, 1944; "[Company] K had ten [POWs]. . . . Four said . . . 'Heil Hitler.' So only six ever got back to [the regimental POW] point."[57]

Medic Frank Irgang watched as an American lieutenant questioned a newly captured German first sergeant—"but he would give no information. 'I am fighting for my country!' he screamed. 'I love my country, and I love my leader!' 'Who is your leader?' asked the lieutenant. 'Adolf Hitler—yet,' he answered. . . . 'Take him away, Smoky.' The pair hardly had disappeared into the bushes, when we heard the chatter of a grease gun. . . . 'What happened, Smoky?' . . . 'He tried to escape.' We all knew differently, but it was better to get rid of the fanatics than to have our sons over here in another twenty-five years."[58]

Even without the question put, those Germans who continued to use the Nazi salute or to insert "Heil Hitler!" in their answers to field interrogators' questions placed themselves in jeopardy.

Combatants had to learn the precepts to be drawn from the cultural propensities of those on the other side, for these, no less than the Geneva rules, disposed of soldiers' fates.

Combat soldiers knew how much they had at stake in preserving a system of rules: dramatically enhanced odds that they would survive a wound or capture by the enemy. No one knew better what a *guerre à outrance* would cost them—and yet their reactions to battle cast them only sometimes as upholders of the rules and almost as often as violators. Set against their strong impulse to maintain moderation was an array of forces limiting the soldiers' ability—and desire—to restrain themselves. At issue were the conditions of combat, and whether, how often, with what intensity, and for how long they would overthrow the American combat soldier's ordinary image of the enemy.

The fundamental American view of the German soldier encompassed a measure of sympathy. As one infantryman in the 94th Division put it: "[Most] of us were innocent victims of a brutal war. I had known the Germans in Brittany. The average German soldier had been sold a God and Country message by his family and Führer. Or maybe he simply fought to protect his family from a concentration camp. Either way, he was a victim." An artilleryman attached to the 4th Infantry Division said: "We recognized that we were in a war, but we recognized that [German soldiers] came from families like we came from families and that they had loved ones and they were good guys and they were bad guys. . . . Personally, I had no malice at any time toward the Germans." A combat photographer: "[The] average German soldier was just a young man who was drafted." A nineteen-year-old American rifleman: "They were exactly our age. [They] were boys like us." A medic with the 101st Airborne: "The Wehrmacht soldiers were ordinary guys. . . ." Most Americans agreed with Keith Douglas that these enemies could reasonably be thought of as "decent fighting men."[59]

But developments within combat often made it impossible to hold to such views.

In Europe, the Germans intensified their resort to the "tricks" that GIs had first encountered in North Africa. They relished artifice and at first used such tricks to gain a minor tactical advantage; then more systematically to induce Americans to use ineffectively their far greater numbers of weapons; and finally, with increasing frequency and desperation, to slow the Allied advance on the homeland.

American soldiers found no fault with dummy gun emplacements along the Normandy coast; or fake splashes, in simulation of American shellings, designed to throw off Allied naval fire; or the various stratagems—such as Germans pretending to speak from Allied spotter aircraft—aimed at luring American artillery into bombarding American rather than German units. Here the enemy broke no rules. And when in one sector the Germans began firing daily mortar barrages of eighteen shells and, after those opposite had become habituated to the pattern, suddenly added rounds ("[T]hose last three . . . blew the ass off more than one of our guys because we weren't expecting them"), the GIs only lamented that they had been outwitted. More difficult to abide were deceptions that the Germans made an integral part of their final offensive in the West, the Ardennes attack of December 1944. They dropped 150 paratroopers wearing American uniforms and dog tags. They sent forward groups of soldiers, some organized as assassination squads, who spoke English, rode in American vehicles, and dressed as Americans. Front-line GIs were not mollified that under the rules such Germans subjected themselves to charges of spying and that a number of those apprehended were executed. Notwithstanding the Americans' occasional disguise of their own tanks as Panzers and the use of German-speaking GIs to further the deception—one such effort attempted to seize a bridge across the Rhine at Oberkassel—the conviction grew that the Germans' "crafty, brutal little tricks" were becoming bigger, more brutal, and no less crafty.[60]

The Americans also regarded mines and booby traps as falling within the category of dirty tricks, in part perhaps because they themselves used so few of them. With American armies advancing, such weapons remained prime instruments of German defenders grudging every inch of withdrawal. Their use in Italy and Western Europe was more extensive, more sophisticated, and more deadly than earlier. In North Africa, minefields had been positioned to deny enemy forces access to certain areas or to funnel tanks and trucks into pathways sighted by artillery; but in Europe the Germans, abandoning the straightaway laying of minefields, used far more antipersonnel mines than vehicle mines and planted them far more dexterously. Writers Shelagh and Denis Whitaker cited cases in which a few mines were left visible to draw Americans upon those thoroughly hidden. Compounding the American soldier's problem were German technological improvements. When Schumines and the even newer glass and plastic models could not be detected by conventional sweep equipment, frustration soared. When mines were located only as their detonations cost limbs and lives, or Germans stole back to plant mines in areas from which they had retreated, they seemed to mock the boundary between zones of safety and of danger. Infantrymen were angry that with mines the enemy again extended mutilation and death far from his presence.[61]

Soldiers further anathematized the mine because its blast most often came from the underside, striking them where they thought themselves most vulnerable. A soldier in the vehicle just ahead of Richard Tobin's was emasculated, and many American combat soldiers agreed with the correspondent's conclusion—that mines, used with "German thoroughness and inhumanity," were Hitler's "most formidable weapon."[62]

As the mine engendered bitterness, the booby trap compounded it. The mine made it unsafe to step; the booby trap made it perilous to step and to touch. The Germans converted to conveyers of death "fence posts, teacups, doorbells, jackknives, purses, drawers, light switches, automobile starters, window curtains, inkwells, fountain pens, logs . . . , boxes . . . , pieces of food, souvenirs, 'discarded' German booty, clothing, tools, strings, wires, electric-light bulbs, horns, bells, bottles of wine (corked), water faucets, door handles [and] about anything else that might be picked up by an inquisitive or relaxed conqueror." Often they wired pictures of Adolf Hitler that they knew Americans would be eager to tear from the walls of barracks, homes, and public buildings. Another contrivance joined three rifle rounds with a pressure plate. Stepped on, it detonated into the crotch of the passing soldier—"the nutcracker," GIs called it.[63]

Particularly offensive was the Germans' occasional practice of booby-trapping the dead. The use of mines, however one-sided, violated no agreement, and at least a few Americans ignored their comrades' conviction of its sneakiness to argue that mines were, like artillery barrages, a necessary cost of war, but no one believed that wiring the dead was other than intolerable. "This was sickening," said Major Joseph Shomon of booby traps placed on enemy bodies. "Our men hated such a despicable trick." Still more degraded was the use of American dead, a practice GIs thought meant to kill medics on whom their own lives might depend. A variant—booby-trapping American graves—aimed to kill the noncombatants of the graves registration units. The ultimate debasement was the Germans' use of unconscious American wounded, who were wired so that aidmen or comrades coming to their assistance would die with them in the explosion.[64]

It became clear that not even the provision of medical services, though of central concern to soldiers on both sides, could be kept sacrosanct in a war fought as fiercely as this one. Sometimes, the Germans used medical vehicles to surmount a local crisis—e.g., by transporting badly needed supplies of ammunition—or to gain an immediate tactical advantage by surprising their opponents. In Normandy, GIs were startled to see German troops leap from a Red Cross convoy and open fire. Even at Arnhem, with its high order of medical cooperation across the lines, on at least one occasion Germans emerged from ambulances shooting. Comparable was the occasional use of an aid station as a combat position. At a Roer crossing, Americans suddenly found themselves under fire from an enemy machine-gun nest installed in a Red Cross shelter. The Germans may have calculated that normal trust heightened the probability that such unexpected tactics would work, and were thus powerfully tempted to employ them in situations they regarded as critical.[65]

Just as serious a threat to cooperation were German attempts to turn the
medical truce to military advantage. During heavy fighting near Brest, the
Germans sought a truce to evacuate their wounded and dead, then used it to
infiltrate troops behind two companies of the U.S. 28th Infantry, a ruse that
enabled them "to capture or kill all the men in one quick blow." In Holland,
airborne captain Robert Phillips was certain that one of the Germans circulating with medical personnel during a truce was an NCO sent forward to
study the American position. GIs sometimes suspected that German doctors
aided their artillery to pinpoint American strongpoints, and they complained that a medical truce was a likely prelude to a shelling. In Normandy,
a company of the 29th Division was hit by a powerful mortar and artillery
barrage, under whose cover charging German infantry cut off two platoons
and sent the others into flight. Later, a prisoner attached to a German headquarters company related that "the whole attack was a direct result of the
visit of the medical officer two days before, when [a] truce had been requested and granted." "If this were true," declared an American line officer,
"the battalion had paid a terrible price to save the life of that one American
[we] had got out of the orchard alive [as a result of the truce]."[66]

Because few practices were more important to German and
American infantrymen than the regulated surrender, one of the tricks most
threatening to the battlefield equilibrium was the counterfeit capitulation.

Here was a subterfuge employed with greater frequency in Europe than
in North Africa. Occasionally, German soldiers approached American positions, and when within range shifted smoothly from arms locked behind
their heads to arms flinging potato-masher grenades drawn from behind
their backs. In a variant, Germans emerged from their position seemingly intent on surrender, but at a signal dropped to the ground and opened fire.
Again, a German officer advanced waving a white cloth and then shot his
would-be captor with a pistol hidden in his other hand. German paratroopers introduced still another variant: When GIs emerged from cover to accept
the enemy's surrender, a hidden machine gun opened fire on them.[67]

In problematic medical-truce and surrender situations, the American
soldier's immediate assumption was German treachery; his immediate reaction anger; and his immediate inclination retaliation. It did not always require behavior contrary to the rules to provoke such reactions. Enemy
snipers, for example, remained anathema. While their work—shooting from
cover those often unsuspecting—was prohibited by none of the rules, it still
became the target of the harshest stricture. As Ernie Pyle wrote from France

in June 1944, "there is something sneaking about [sniping] that outrages the American sense of fairness." In North Africa, there had been few snipers; in Europe, they seemed to be everywhere. "Snipers," snapped Whiting, "how they were hated by . . . Allied soldiers!"[68]

Sniper activity often led Americans, from squad to division, to reprisals that were themselves gross violations of the rules. When a member of Lester Atwell's company was shot through the head by a sniper, those who captured the German were excited: "They got him! They got the sniper who killed the guy." A lieutenant with "large, solid fists" first administered "a sound beating." Then the sniper was dragged from the house, marched out of town, and ordered by the general to dig his own grave; he toppled into it as he was shot. Historian David Irving reported that during the campaign in Sicily, an Army captain ordered forty-three captured snipers lined up against a barn and machine-gunned. The 1st Infantry Division, after suffering heavy casualties on Omaha Beach, "refused on principle to take snipers prisoner when they surrendered [after] having taken their toll in blood." GIs often identified snipers as members of German "suicide squads," thus obviating surrender by establishing (almost always falsely) the enemy's determination to die. Snipers were often made the exception to every precept of sympathetic treatment.[69]

American animosity against sniping had a curiously contradictory quality: the practice was reprehensible only when carried on by the enemy. Few GIs had sniper scopes, but there did arrive from time to time opportunities for carefully aimed fire indistinguishable from sniping. Paratrooper Ross Carter described one such occasion: "[Our] boys, lying in their foxholes, could see Nazis slinking through the orchards and fields which lay across the road. They picked them off coolly, unhurriedly, deliberately. Berkely shot one to pieces with an automatic rifle; tobacco-chewing Wild Bill McMurtry sniped purposefully and spat at random; Casey said nothing but drilled any head that he spied; Duquesne smoked cigarettes while he and Gruening railroaded round after round at unwary enemies." Carter reported no sense of the unseemly. And then there were the designated American snipers. "The reaction to snipers," Atwell realized, "was both understandable and a puzzle. We had snipers of our own, skilled soldiers, picked for their intelligence and keen eyesight. . . . It always struck me as odd: the enemy snipers were unspeakable villains; our own were heroes."[70]

Another mark of the propensity to associate "unfair" practices with special-purpose soldiers rather than with the commonality of the enemy's soldiery, this time with greater justification, was the Americans' standing grudge against the SS. Extending Eastern Front methods to the West—there was no discernible relaxation of zealotry because Americans and British were less repugnant ideologically than Russians and Poles—the SS fought fiercely and unforgivingly. In actions opening the Normandy invasion, American paratroopers suffered their first encounter with SS iron-handedness, and later at Bayeux the 12th SS Panzer Division shot down forty British and Canadian prisoners of war. In the minds of Allied soldiers, all SS quickly became authors of atrocities.[71]

GIs placed SS troops in a category of their own. Thus, many of those characterizations of German soldiers as "boys like us" immediately proceeded to exclude the SS. "The Wehrmacht soldiers were ordinary guys, but the SS troops were something else. They gave no quarter. . . ." "The SS . . . were the elite. They were so brainwashed they were impossible to reason with. Those people made me angry. . . ." "And these SS troops were so brazen. They acted as though nothing could hurt them. And they sneered at you. They acted the super race. I've had a couple of experiences where I came very close to shooting somebody."[72]

It seemed inevitable that in the fighting in the West, SS and American paratroop units would develop a special antagonism. Both organizations indoctrinated members far more rigorously than did regular army units, with the SS using racial identity to anchor its instruction, and the paratroops, less directly, employing notions of a superior masculinity. Each inculcated in its units a bumptious pride in their elite status and a no-quarter warrior spirit. Both accentuated the heinousness of the enemy and the dedication that would be necessary to overcome him. It was thus a paratroop colonel, commanding officer of a regiment that had made three combat jumps in North Africa, who, in setting out for his men "lessons I had learned," reached for an extreme characterization rare in units of the U.S. Army: "[F]orget good sportsmanship on the battlefield. War is not a refereed football game but the dirtiest game yet devised by human minds. And, if for one moment you feel soft towards that Nazi shooting at you, remember he's trying to kill you and, if he had the chance, he'd drive your dad into slavery, cut your mother's throat, and rape your wife, sister, sweetheart or daughter. You'll get no quarter from him. Give him none!"[73]

American paratroopers seemed to bear the brunt of German fierceness—and they struck back hard. In Sicily, two of them were captured in their chutes, tied to trees, doused with gasoline, set afire, and left "as flaming torches." Their comrades were unforgiving: "Those two burnt, charred bodies symbolized the raw, naked brutal force we would have to overcome to win the war. We never forgot them." In France, Frank Irgang "came upon a sickening sight. Several paratroopers were hanging in the trees. . . . Those . . . high [up] were literally riddled with bullet holes, while those . . . lower had been subjected to a merciless bayoneting. The intestines of some hung to the ground, while others had been completely disemboweled. A few had been disrobed, and portions of their bodies were missing. . . ." Irgang "burned inside, glowing for revenge." Para Donald Burgett noticed American dead "all lying face up. Then the weak feeling came back in my stomach and . . . I wished I were somewhere else. For they had their pants pulled down and their manhood had either been shot or cut completely away, leaving nothing but blood-caked, gaping wounds in their crotches. The way they were lying, shoulder to shoulder, made this look like anything but an act of war."[74]

In Normandy, when the advance of Burgett's regiment of the 101st Airborne was held up by two German machine guns and several attempts to break through failed, "Red Knight and Brennenstool routed the prisoners out of the stables, lined them up . . . in a column of twos and, counting cadence, marched them down the hill toward the machine guns. They were hoping the enemy wouldn't fire on their own, but it didn't make any difference to the men on the machine guns, and they opened up, drilling holes in their own comrades in trying to hit the American troopers. The prisoners started screaming, '*Nicht schiessen*' (Don't shoot!), and leaped headfirst for the ditch, and possible escape, so we opened up on them too. The poor bastards were caught in a murderous cross fire, and before the shooting stopped they were all dead."[75]

Airborne soldiers were involved more frequently than infantrymen in the execution of SS adversaries. As the battle for Munich ended, cameraman Walter Rosenblum watched as paras placed SS defenders against a wall and then "shot 'em all." GIs were sometimes aware that numbers of young French, Belgians, and Dutch were fighting in the ranks of the SS; their role as renegades, traitors to the Allied cause, was another inducement to withhold mercy.[76]

In a sense, the ferocity of special units served to uphold the structure of rules, for it focused GIs' attention on the violations of the SS and thus cast into exonerating relief the violations of Wehrmacht units. Danger, however, lay in the driving force to retaliate. When elite forces wished to strike back at the transgressions of enemy elite units, seldom did they discriminate between targets. Angry avengers went for any enemy at hand. American paras hit at Wehrmacht as well as SS, SS at American infantrymen as well as paratroopers. They thus threatened, through spillings over of savagery, to induce a generalized descent to the level of their own combat.

German weapons whose use American soldiers regarded as dastardly; dirty tricks; the presence of certain units that GIs regarded as ruthless and unworthy of civilized treatment—all jeopardized the system. But not one of these destabilizing elements, or any combination, did more to overthrow the rules than did the ordinary week-by-week processes of the war itself, especially those that inured the soldier to battle, diminished the soldier's sense of his own power, and assuaged the soldier's grief at the loss of his friends.

Soldiers suffering battle strain, feeling unable to tolerate repeated assaults on their nerves and seeking refuge in emotional withdrawal, moved through stages denominated earlier: numbing, toughening, coarsening, and brutalization. It was in the third stage that the process began to pose problems for the war of rules; enemy personnel became the first targets of a new callousness.

Artillery observer Bradford Perkins saw an American sergeant kill two wounded Germans in a nearby foxhole simply because their moans bothered him.[77]

When two GIs on the Italian front, smoking cigarettes near the body of a German soldier whose head was hidden in a doorway but whose hobnailed boots extended into the street, were asked what had happened, one of them replied, "Oh him? Son of a bitch kept lagging behind the others when we brought them in. We got tired of hurrying him up all the time."[78]

Also in Italy, correspondent Eric Sevareid was talking with a lieutenant just back for a reconnaissance mission when "a pink-cheeked private" reported: "Lieutenant, sir, pardon me. I can't find my officer. We've got some civilians in a house back there. What shall we do with them, sir?" Snapped back the lieutenant: "If you can spare a guard send them back. If you can't, why, shoot 'em in the back. That's what we always did in my outfit. Don't take no nonsense from 'em." Sevareid decided that he had listened to an "order to commit mass murder" and concluded that "I could never bring myself to write or speak with indignation of the Germans' violations of the 'rules of warfare.'"[79]

Similarly corrosive was the nature of the ordinary surrender process. For the fighting man to determine whether an enemy soldier wanted to surrender to him or was still intent on killing him was a matter of great delicacy and difficulty—so much so that others almost never attempted to gainsay a comrade's judgment. The decision, wrote Lester Atwell, "seemed to depend on the individual . . . soldiers and on how they felt at that particular moment. . . . [Some] would let wounded or surrendering Germans through; others mowed them down."[80]

Photographer-writer Carl Mydans described surrender from the perspective of the submitting soldier: "One of [his] most harrowing experiences . . . comes . . . between the time it takes him to raise his arms . . . and the moment he has completed the trip . . . rearward and is delivered alive [to] higher authority. This does not guarantee him life. But it guarantees him that much life. For he has just passed [beyond] the point where the law of war makes killing right. . . ." Simultaneously, on the other side, the potential captor was presented with the slenderest of distinctions: between the seeming impossibility of taking prisoners during battle versus the possibility of doing so, between the killing of enemy combatants and the sparing of prisoners. In no more than instants the mind had to flash between these sets of alternatives in "that terrifying zone of anarchy where," as Mydans confirmed, "men . . . brutal with the impulses of battle . . . decide the law for themselves."[81]

There were in soldier accounts inklings that decisions to kill enemies who might otherwise have been taken prisoner were sometimes the work of soldiers who had come to believe themselves the pawns of distant, powerful forces working toward their own destruction and who longed to reassert their ability to make autonomous and consequential judgments. To refuse to heed those hands in the air, to shoot, to determine irrevocably the fate of another was a combat soldier's avowal that he could still control matters of utmost importance. In the last stage of the battle for the Rhine, two dazed and weary German soldiers approached a roadblock in order to surrender. An American—a glider pilot—moved forward to take them prisoner, but the NCO in charge of the position, a sergeant of the 194th Infantry Regiment, spoke out: "We aren't taking prisoners." The Germans were told to walk away down the road and, with their backs to the Americans, were shot down.[82]

Still another pattern of thought disposed soldiers to punish the enemy rather than to accept his submission. The GI deciding how to receive an approaching adversary knew that the German entreating his mercy may have been, only moments before, intent on killing him. He was aware, too, that if he granted mercy, the enemy would soon go off to hot food, warm shelter, and care of at least a basic level, all of which would likely continue to be denied the GI. With the captor's emotions recently raw with fear and certain to be so again soon, he found troubling the thought that his "victory"—at least over that particular German—would have no consequence for himself save to extend his personal jeopardy, while the enemy's "defeat" would carry the captive to that personal survival so desired by the captor. Who had "won"? As a prisoner, the German might even, as his captor so desperately wished for himself, go to the United States. When a Wehrmacht officer unwisely ex-

pressed the hope that he would be sent to America, infantryman Orval
Faubus became furious: "Almost all of them hope to go to the States. The
bastards have been fighting to destroy our way of life, our kindness, our generosity, our willingness to forgive, and have criticized us for those qualities.
Yet they are the first to take advantage of them . . . like a heartless criminal
who gives no mercy in the commission of his crimes but is the first to cry
pitifully for mercy when he is caught. The Germans have shown no mercy to
those they have conquered. I hope the guilty scoundrels get none when they
are finally finished."[83]

Prospective prisoners did not improve their positions by making visible
the transformation of their own feelings. Grady Arrington recorded the
anger with which he and his comrades reacted to the "gay spirit" of German
POWs: they hated them "passionately." Indeed, Germans who realized that
they were not to be shot but escorted away from the front sometimes endangered themselves by premature celebration. When, in a Sicilian town, four
landsers emerged from a cellar with their hands up and an American soldier
raised his tommy gun to cover them, one of the Germans cried out, *"Nicht,
nicht!"* "We're not going to shoot you," replied Sergeant Sheehan, the squad
leader. But the German held out his hands and spoke again, *"Nicht."* "For
God's sake," said Sheehan, *"nicht."* "The German understood and tried to
smile, but nothing came out. Sheehan motioned them down the road and
they shuffled off, followed by the soldier with the tommy gun." A short time
later, when the squad returned to its jeeps, "we found the prisoners sitting on
the bank of the road, surrounded by the drivers. . . . The prisoners seemed
happier now and were smoking American cigarettes. . . . They smiled at us
when we came up. Sheehan said, 'Smile, you sons of bitches.' . . . 'I'd like to
shoot the four of them,' one of our men said. I think that was what we all felt
. . . [but] there was only the impotent hatred . . . [so] all we did was look at
them. Finally we put them into our four jeeps, one man into each. Then the
rest of us climbed in and we drove slowly back down the road."[84]

With longing, envy, and fear just beneath their anger, many GIs insisted
that American treatment of prisoners of war was "too good."[85]

Although of widely varying effect, another phenomenon—the private
revenge campaign following a comrade's death—also had frequent impact
on regulated warfare. When his best friend was cut down by machine-gun
fire just as he rose to accept a German surrender ("They're waving a handkerchief. I'll go get 'em"), Audie Murphy charged up the hill to destroy several
German positions, including the one from which Brandon was shot. Such
incidents served to intensify local combat without further repercussion, but

others as aggrieved as Audie Murphy often struck out in ways that did not confine their retribution to combatants. In Harold Leinbaugh's company, a soldier "whose best friend had just been killed took revenge on four prisoners. He said they had jumped him and tried to escape. . . ." Not long after, Leinbaugh watched a tanker whose buddies had just been killed shoot down two German prisoners of war. Near the end of the war, an American captain, the commander of a rifle company, learned that shell fragments had blinded his brother. Tears streaming, he shouted for his driver and ordered him to drive to a wooded area. Once there, the captain "started shouting for any Germans . . . to come out with their hands up and surrender to him." When seven emerged, they were lined up and searched; then the captain "backed up several paces, calmly raised his pistol higher and shot each German in the head in rapid succession. . . . The next two registered horror. . . . The last three . . . were hit in the back of the head as they turned and started to run." After the driver had doubled over and vomited, the captain "drove like a wild man from the scene of his massacre."[86]

And the impulse to exact vengeance could return long after the first convulsions of feeling had passed. Grady Arrington described a battle scene in Germany near the Weid River:

> All along the small winding road, in and out among the brush, lay dead and wounded Krauts. As Tilson and I came upon a third wounded man, he opened his eyes and began begging for mercy. Tilson glanced angrily in my direction and snapped, "Shoot him[, Arrington] . . . Hell, he's about to die; he needs to get outa the misery. I already killed two to your none!" The Kraut seemed to know every word the Sergeant spoke and started pleading for his life with all the strength he could muster. Certainly, it did not occur to me then that to take that life would be cruel and unforgivable. I could only see Dodson, Bain, Jennings and the others who had passed from this scene of inhumanity. Filled with a hate that only a man who has killed or seen his closest buddies killed can know, I raised the rifle butt to the crevice between my shoulder and collarbone and pulled the trigger. The Jerry writhed to silence.

Later, in contemplating the case of a lieutenant who had accepted the surrender of a German, sent him toward the rear, and then shot him, Arrington insisted that it too compelled all others to ask: "Have I ever experienced the slaughter of friends?"[87]

But at issue here is neither the moral liability of soldiers' impulsive destruction of the enemy closest at hand nor the greater burden of using a dead comrade simply as pretext ("The Nazi bastards tried to escape, and I had to shoot them. I think they're the ones who killed Boda, anyway"). It is rather the ability of such episodes to endanger the counterpoise of combat. Masayo Umezawa Duus recounted an incident in France's Vosges Mountains that, because it occurred within easy sight of enemy troops and involved medical personnel, would almost certainly beget a retribution payable in other Americans' lives. "Once when a [medical] cease-fire order came, and the white gunsmoke had cleared, the men saw a German medic kneeling to tend a wounded comrade. To judge from his insignia, the fallen German was an officer. Suddenly one of the Japanese American soldiers began to yell. 'You did a fine job, you son of a bitch! You son of a bitch, you murdered my buddies!'" And with that he sent forward "a hail of bullets [that] riddled the wounded officer and the unarmed medic."[88]

Even when the enemy's battlefield behavior was "correct," when there were no SS or snipers present, when "dirty tricks" were not at issue, the reactions of American soldiers to injured or capitulating Germans—variously based in soldier fear, callousness, anger, and envy—still imperiled the battlefield's status quo.

Serving as a counterforce in support of regulated combat was the ordinary soldier's conviction that rules violations constituted not only, for some, severe moral lapses, but, less abstractly, incitements to enemy retribution that might cost many of them their own lives. GIs thus often acted to moderate vengefulness and to mitigate eruptions of the no-quarter spirit.

Occasionally, combat soldiers worked to temper the harshness of their own officers. When their commander, a captain, refused the request of Atwell and others in the company that he see to the care of German wounded in their custody, the men stopped a truck and negotiated the Germans' transportation to treatment in the rear. Later, when three German snipers, somehow in the company of a colonel, wounded two Americans, they were immediately flushed from hiding: "Jeez, we sprayed the place, and then the sonsabitches come out with their hands up." The colonel, wounded, asked for water, but as Atwell was drawing him a cup, an American captain barked, "Don't give that son of a bitch anything!" Connecting the colonel with the snipers, the captain was determined to deny him mercy. Moments later, the captain, maneuvering to speak privately with Atwell, asked him with feigned casualness, "Do *you* think we ought to turn him in?" Atwell, realizing that the officer wished to kill the German, played the innocent: "Why, we've got to turn him in. What else could we do with him?" The captain, failing to secure the support he sought, had to content himself with another cursing of the prisoner, who was then transported—alive—to regimental headquarters.[89]

In combat, comrades often required more forceful interventions—to ward off, for example, the results of their sudden rages. During severe fighting near Mt. Belvedere, John Bassett's platoon "walked up on a large pile of frozen American corpses that had been gathered for identification and . . . burial. A single Kraut stood nearby with his hands clasped tight over his black helmet. [My foxhole buddy Luca] Luhaink suddenly stepped towards him with his M-1 thrust out—'See! See! You goddamned Kraut, what you did?' It was close. We grabbed Luhaink and pushed up the gun. He was very mad, but allowed us to bring him back to his senses in time."[90]

One of Leinbaugh's most conscientious NCOs ("always the good sergeant") spent much of each night checking positions. "When I was making my rounds . . . I found our dead-end guy trying to rape this German broad. The mother and father were right there in the goddam house. I was ready to shoot him right there on the spot." Sergeant Pope may have intervened from some sense of fundamental decency, but likely there was as well a practical resolve to permit nothing that would, by menacing families, needlessly intensify the battle-emotion of German soldiers in the vicinity.[91]

Sometimes intervention came too late to prevent a breach but in time to confine it and make its recurrence less likely. When, in a newly taken French town, members of Leinbaugh's company had completed their emplacement, they "walked to a house and finished the food left on the table by German soldiers. Two very young dead Germans were [found] stuffed in a woodbox. . . . The next morning Clayton Shepherd noticed one of the dead youngsters had a gold ring on his finger. An hour later someone had cut off the youngster's finger. The ring was missing. Shepherd shook his head; he couldn't believe it. . . . 'Now ain't this a damn thing.'"[92]

That malefactor escaped detection, but word of the men's reaction may have deterred him, for it was not he who was responsible for the next episode. "In Cierreux a German paratrooper lay frozen in front of our [command post] and one of the new replacements who had worked in a mortuary cut off his finger to get a gold ring. J. B. Cole tracked down the culprit and our new man was warned that he would be court-martialed or shot if he ever pulled another stunt like that." Such a threat—less one of institutional punishment (almost always a bluff when invoked by enlisted men) than of isolation from one's fellows, *the* vehicle of intimidation—was sure to be effective.[93]

Soldiers rarely turned in members of their own units who had killed prisoners; the claims of comradeship prevailed. But the terms of comradeship, as demonstrated above, allowed for confrontation, especially when the survival of the group appeared at issue. Atwell described an incident occurring near the war's end as his unit faced composite German detachments of Hitler Youth and regular army troops, all under the command of the SS.

> Lieutenant Serletis returned, smiling widely, his eyes alight. "Boy, oh boy," he said with a laugh, . . . "the line-company boys are sure gettin' tough. They just took about sixteen Jerry prisoners out in the woods, right out there, and shot 'em down. Killed every fuckin' one of 'em. They're not taking any shit from *no* one."
>
> We stared at him.
>
> "But that's murder!" Warren Troy pointed out.
>
> "Murder?"
>
> "Simple, cold-blooded murder, that's all it is." . . . Lieutenant Serletis scratched his head. "The boys are pretty pissed off," he said tentatively.
>
> "I don't give a damn what they are, anyone who'd do that is a murderer." . . .
>
> Phil, Preacher and I agreed with Warren, and at this Lieutenant Serletis became more and more confused.
>
> "Well, *gee*, I don't know . . . It's different for them: they're under a strain." . . .
>
> "Who did the murdering?"
>
> "Well, C Company guys, and some tankers, and—" He named a new aid man at C Company.
>
> "Damned brave of them," I said, "shooting down a bunch of unarmed high-school boys."
>
> "Well, it's—it's the war. You know how it is. If you were there, you'd—"
>
> "No, I don't think so. Not even if I were there."[94]

The pattern was, at every level, the same: alternating enforcement and violation, often by the same parties. At the top, the raw reality was that it was not in the interest of either high command that prisoner prescripts be strictly obeyed. Neither wished to make surrender to the enemy too easy or too safe or too certain. If it were, too many of the soldiers on one's own side might decamp. In April 1945, Atwell's outfit overtook a German unit that had captured a number of its men a month before. "It irritated me that I could not speak to any of the recaptured men. All of them were held separate and questioned by our G-2 upon their return, and, we heard, so favorable toward the Germans were their reports that they could not be united with their companies, but instead they were to be shipped to Paris and from there rushed home, to be released from the Army." "Sure," Atwell heard from those with him, "[otherwise] it would break down the fighting morale." One of the guys said the German guys were friendly—[and] just like us."[95]

Alert to the problem that, in Lieutenant John Toole's words, "Every soldier has at one time or another thought of surrender . . . ," high commands tried to lower the perceived odds by raising dark fears of what awaited those who attempted to surrender. Troops persuaded that the enemy shot down those with lifted hands or brutalized those in POW camps would, it was assumed, continue to fight with fervor. It was the stand of men like Frank Irgang—". . . I made up my mind to fight this war with all the skill and cunning I could master. I would never be taken prisoner. The captured soldiers that we found with bullet holes in their heads and necks were too grim a reminder of a prisoner's fate. I would fight to the finish"—that Army leaders hoped would dominate soldier opinion. The obstacle here was that however heinous those arriving from stateside training camps thought the enemy, their experience at the front only rarely led to Irgang's conclusion. Ironically, one side's mistreatment of, and especially atrocities against, prospective or actual prisoners of war served a useful and necessary purpose of the other side's high command.[96]

At the same time, however, neither military establishment wished to make impossible the surrender of enemy soldiers to its own units; were it so, enemy soldiers would have no option but to fight to the end, exacting a higher toll of friendly forces. So American and German military leaderships were compelled to undertake a difficult balancing act: to depict the enemy as so ruthless and abusive of prisoners that their own soldiers would be deterred from attempts to surrender—while not so merciless that their own soldiers would conclude that enemy soldiers deserved no opportunity to surrender. It was hard to determine where, between rulebook care on one side and liquidation on the other, such a poise could be achieved, and whether, if it were, it could be maintained amid the constant fluctuation of battlefield conditions. In such circumstances, it was no surprise that the American high command labored in ways that sometimes upheld and sometimes undermined warfare by the rules.

There is ample evidence that just prior to the Normandy invasion, high-ranking American officers ordered that no prisoners be taken. In the foreground were concerns that every man ashore would be required as a fighter and that no stockades would be available; in the background was the conviction, shared by Franklin D. Roosevelt and Dwight Eisenhower, that American soldiers felt an insufficient hatred of the German enemy. The provenance and compass of such orders were unclear, but they seem to have originated no lower than the division level. General Maxwell Taylor, commander of the 101st Airborne, told paratroopers loading for their night drop into France that they were to fight with knives until daylight, "and don't take any prisoners." Just prior to departure, a company commander repeated the instruction: "No prisoners. We are not taking any prisoners." John Slaughter, a staff sergeant in one of the four American divisions to assault the Omaha and Utah beaches, the 29th, reported that "On D-Day we were instructed not to take prisoners."[97]

Here played out one of those episodes in which the actions of those at the lowest level worked to police those at the highest. One would have thought that, of all the American forces, the airborne would have been most inclined to respond as ordered: their fervor for combat and antipathy against the enemy exceeded the infantry's; they prided themselves on their discipline; their sector—behind enemy lines—provided no inducement to take opponents into custody. Yet the very company reminded not to take prisoners did so in its first fight. Even in a charge down a trench, firing rifles and throwing grenades, the paras spared and made captive two wounded German machine gunners. Totals for their first encounter were fifteen Germans killed—and twelve taken prisoner. Germans at Normandy were so little afraid of on-the-spot executions that significant numbers remained behind to surrender when their own forces retreated. There was evidence of some but not many killings prompted by the no-prisoner order; in general, initial treatment had about it a harshness quickly ameliorated by contacts with helpless Germans.[98]

On other occasions, the Allied command worked to uphold a rulebook war. It did so with one eye on its own units—its concern was that atrocities were prejudicial to troop discipline—and with the other eye on the enemy's units—its worry here being that widespread violations might bring down the whole structure of understanding with the Germans. One of its enforcement activities was the occasional punishment of American soldiers who killed rather than captured no longer belligerent enemies.

A controversial episode, a massacre of German prisoners of war near Tambach in southwestern Germany, revealed both the command structure's effort to curb gratuitous violence and its limits in so doing. The killings came to light when, a week later, the division commander, General Purvis,* "was . . . chewin' the ass off the Artillery colonel about the conduct of his

---

*Atwell's account employed pseudonyms.

men, accusin' them of [all] the stealin' and rape committed by the entire division. . . ." Exasperated, the colonel burst out in retaliation that "at least his men weren't cold-blooded murderers. . . ." The general demanded an explanation, and when the colonel told him to "look into what happened at Tambach," he began an inquiry.

Battalion tipped the implicated company to the schedule of the divisional Inspector General (IG) and his investigators. Its senior lieutenant, Ward MacKenzie, knew that the killings, which had sickened him, had been led by a subordinate: "It was that damned Lieutenant Morse makin' a big grandstan' play." Just prior to the IG's arrival, however, he and Morse coordinated their cover stories, and at a hastily called formation, MacKenzie "told the men that they remembered nothing that happened at Tambach. They saw nothing, they knew nothing. Not a damn thing. Then I dismissed them an' everything was as usual when the IG an' his party drove up." The IG called a formation "that no man could miss," announced his investigation, and described the questions each man would be asked. The company was then divided into fives, each group separated from the others. An officer held a Bible open and swore the men to truthfulness. " 'Did you *see* any German prisoners killed at Tambach? Do you *know* any man who killed any German prisoners at Tambach?' The answers came back from man after man. 'No, sir.' 'No, sir.' . . . 'All right, the next five men.' "

Nevertheless, the investigation continued, and when several days later Lieutenant Morse was to be flown back to the United States on a rare furlough ("The thing was obviously rigged. . . ."), IG agents stopped his jeep en route to the airport and told him, falsely, that MacKenzie had just confessed. Panicking, Morse "broke down an' spilled the whole thing." At the trial, MacKenzie, who continued to deny involvement or knowledge ("I repudiated everything Morse said"), collapsed on the stand and while recovering from an emergency appendectomy thought of an escape from his apparently hopeless situation: "If this works, I'm out!" He had recalled that near Metz, General Purvis had ordered the shooting of a German sniper known to have killed an American medic. A friend of MacKenzie, a first sergeant who had witnessed the Metz incident, then drafted an account and induced fifteen of his men to affix their own signatures in corroboration. When the trial resumed, that statement was given General Purvis, "with the suggestion that his action . . . with the sniper . . . had been taken as an example . . . by the men of the . . . Division." The general immediately halted the proceedings and closed the matter by transferring both defendants and their defense counsel to other divisions. Morse had saved himself by catching the command structure in its dual role, acting as field soldiers acted, both as upholders and violators of the rules supposed to govern combat with the Germans.[99]

Similarly, a sergeant charged with killing thirty-six POWs in Italy and a captain accused of machine-gunning forty-three others based their defense on a claim that, in his speech to their division just prior to the invasion of Italy, General George Patton had given an order to kill prisoners. Patton denied any such command, and the men were convicted—but returned without punishment to their units.[100]

In many of the episodes described above officers were the transgressors, but they too had an important simultaneous role as sustainers of the system. Infantry officers often policed medical truces and exerted themselves to prevent the destruction of the other side's ambulances and medical posts. Many artillery officers impressed on their men the consideration to be extended to open cities and civilian hospitals. And often officer reactions proved decisive in determining whether prisoners were spared or slain. On Christmas Day 1943, a unit of 82d Division paratroopers lost a comrade in Italy. "A Krauthead rose up from behind [the pillbox] and shot the Master Termite full of holes." "We mourned him with aching, hating hearts. He was one of those great, original characters that command love and devotion." After the battle, "Four prisoners came carrying the Master in a shelter half and put him down at our feet. A hole was above his left eye, one in his throat and several in his stomach and chest. We stared down at his blank eyes fixed on us, fingered our guns, and looked at the Krautheads and then at the colonel." But the colonel shook his head—and the men swallowed their hatred. On the German side, when at Normandy two landsers captured Father Sampson, a chaplain in the 101st Airborne, and immediately stood him up against a wall, it was an enemy officer, firing his pistol in the air and angrily chastising the soldiers, who saved his life.[101]

One would think that aidmen, with lives so vulnerable and so quickly forfeit to rules violations, would always act to strengthen compliance; but in reality there was no level at which the tensions of the dual role played out more poignantly.

American medical personnel seemed continually engaged in policing those on their own side. Knowing that their lives depended each day on the Germans' willingness to observe the rules, they tried to fend off enemy retaliations by keeping American fighting men within the canons of combat.

Maintaining the neutrality of the aid station required constant vigilance:

to persuade soldiers to check their arms outside ("Can't bring weapons inside a medic's tent; against the Geneva Convention rules"); to keep combat personnel from congregating or even refreshing themselves within; to ensure that weapons emplacements were sufficiently far away that the enemy would not target the station. The situation could not often have been worse than that of Captain Paschal Linguiti's battalion aid station in Kommersheldt in early November 1944, where "confusion, ignorance, and contempt" gave rise to multiple violations—five feet off was an artillery observer; ten yards away was an 81-mm mortar; at the same distance in another direction was a machine-gun site; twenty-five yards to the rear were two parked tanks, all inviting German fire. Fearful that the combat arms endangered both the wounded and those caring for them, Linguiti sent off his assistants to appeal, cajole, and threaten. (Often, when others failed, chaplains were able to persuade weapons crews to move on.)[102]

Most aid workers strove to provide medical care for enemy wounded equivalent to that afforded injured Americans. "We treat [wounded Jerries] just as though they belonged to us. . . ." "We had a mixture of patients now, German and Italian prisoners along with our own boys, seriously wounded and getting the same heroic treatment." And though no one undertook to guarantee that care of the enemy would be delivered in a gentle, comradely spirit, the doctors' attention alone often brought them into collision with many front-line soldiers who objected to their "coddling" of the enemy. Here, as everywhere, medical personnel were required to perform balancing acts of great delicacy.[103]

As aidmen were toiling to uphold—and to hold others to—the rules, however, they found themselves struggling against intense pressure to violate those rules. Long before combat, soldiers in training had chided medics for failing to join in their bellicosity. "In the States Jeff had been the butt of endless jokes. He was called a 'pill roller,' a 'shanker mechanic,' and a 'corn surgeon.' It was all in good fun, but to Jeff, it hurt." When infantryman Keith Winston recognized his "horror of killing and . . . weakness at the sight of blood" and, half-contradictorily, resolved to apply for training as a medic, the captain who interviewed him asked: "Do you hate [seeing] even German blood?" Winston's reply—"Just as much as any other"—brought an ostentatiously martial retort: "I'd like to bathe in [German blood]." Then the captain moved pointedly to his conclusion: "Oh, you don't like to see Germans killed!" "If it meant saving the lives of our boys—yes," Winston answered, "but I don't want to do it, and furthermore, I'm not asking for any special privilege. I want to fight, but in the way I'm most capable—

and not with a gun." The captain, though he "burned" with anger, passed him.[104]

Medics who in training had to fend off jokes about their skill in draining boils and blisters found that their very different services in combat brought immediate regard. As Jeff's platoon of the 36th Armored Infantry Regiment saw its first combat, shrapnel from a German shell sliced through a soldier's face. He shrieked and pleaded for assistance. The riflemen sought cover, but the medic ran to him through artillery and machine-gun fire; Jeff became "the most respected man in the platoon." Yet few medics could forget that many had challenged their aggressiveness and might continue to equate a careful observance of the rules with an unjustifiable sympathy for the enemy.[105]

Far more powerful in pushing medics toward belligerency were the cumulative effects of daily battle. In chastising an aidman who had spoken in friendly fashion with a wounded German sniper, Keith Winston had complained that "This Medic was merely acting like many others not within gunshot range. . . ." But most medics did become targets, and frequently so. And with each close call the aidman was less likely to believe that the enemy fire was not deliberate; with every concussion of German bullets on the ambulance, he inclined more to believe that the Germans were targeting medical personnel. Some enemy transgressions were known to have been purposeful: "A litter party . . . plainly marked with white patches and red crosses on helmets and arm bands, had gone out earlier, only to come under heavy German fire. The Germans had killed one of the medics." If some were intentional, why not all? Such questions drew medics deeper into combat.[106]

Often the first step was to arm oneself. As combat doctor Klaus Huebner of the 88th Division lost confidence in his armband's ability to protect him, he picked up and began to wear a pistol. One of his friends, a medical sergeant, began carrying an M-1 rifle. Neither wished to become a combatant, but with death passing so close, they could no longer bear their feelings of helplessness; being without some means of protecting themselves had become intolerable. A wounded American paratrooper who was being evacuated in a Red Cross jeep noticed that its medic-driver had placed two grenades in his shirt pocket, and he understood that the medic had come to feel just as he did. They had both seen medical jeeps shot to pieces; neither wished "to go down without a fighting chance."[107]

Aidmen were next tempted to use weapons to advance their work. Frank Irgang, finding himself without litter-bearers and with only an hour to evacuate three seriously wounded Americans, decided to use German prisoners. He approached an infantry lieutenant and asked for a pistol, "to keep the prisoners under control." The officer hesitated—"You'd get in trouble for having it, and I'd get in trouble for letting you take it"—and then reluctantly handed over a Luger. "I suggest that you keep it under cover, especially when you are in view of the enemy. . . . Remember, I did not give it to you. You found it on the brick." "I won't forget," Irgang assured him. (These pressures were equally at play on the German side. In several instances German medics used their mercy pistols to compel captured Americans to carry German wounded to safety.)[108]

Some aidmen subsequently used their weapons to save infantry comrades from enemy action. When they realized that soldiers' lives were in balance, medics in those split seconds of danger sometimes chose to open fire, reacting as fellow countrymen rather than as aidmen. A rationale stood ready at hand: If it is my job to save American lives, can it violate my duty to prevent actions that will inflict death on Americans within my care?

The final step, taken by only a few, was one that propelled the medic to believe himself almost indistinguishable from a combatant. The cumulative effects of combat took their toll on Keith Winston. The uncertainties of so many situations, the multiple and repeated risks, the harrowing escapes cost him all faith in the rules. The notion that he was not supposed to be shot at, he decided, had become laughable. American medical personnel near Falaise in northwest France agreed it was with good reason that combat GIs had begun to call the large red crosses on medics' helmets "aiming stakes." Medics who shared such conclusions often became vulnerable to battle emotion and lost all ability to remain detached from the struggle around them. Frank Irgang became the fiercest of warriors. As he grew convinced that the Germans meant to fire on aidmen—and to kill prisoners—he yielded to a full-fledged hatred of the enemy. His conception of the conflict came to rely on notions increasingly ruthless and cataclysmic: the war, he decided, was a fight to the finish, to be won by Americans proving themselves the dirtiest fighters and relishing every dead German as a step toward victory. He acted on his conclusion: on the battlefield he shot down two German soldiers. "It gnawed at my very soul, but now I was a seasoned killer."[109]

Again, some medical personnel on the other side were yielding to the same pressures. In the Rhineland, British soldiers of a Wiltshire regiment took prisoner a German medical officer whom they saw firing his revolver and whose ambulance, they discovered, was loaded with ammunition.[110]

Warrior-medics did not, however, throw off entirely the behavior expected of corpsmen. Frank Irgang, understandably, continued to observe rules that served his survival: "I've got to stay alone [on the battlefield], or I'll get bumped off. The only person I can be seen with is someone [wounded or in some other way] knocked out of action." But, peculiarly, he also persisted in sometimes heeding rules that ran counter to his new bellicosity. As he watched an American infantryman crawling from yard to yard toward a fence, he caught sight of a landser approaching from the opposite side: "I wished to cry out and warn my brother-in-arms, but I could not."[111]

In the end, medics on both sides joined American and German combat soldiers, though in sporadic and circumscribed patterns, in both respecting and violating the rules—observing some more than others, seldom following any with full faithfulness, contending throughout with combat tensions pulling them sometimes toward compliance, sometimes toward infringement, but threatening, as the war advanced, a bellicosity less and less constrained.

As breaches became more numerous and severe, however, the reactions of the side suffering the harm remained limited, seldom becoming fuel for further escalations.

Officials on both sides sometimes went to extremes to explain enemy actions in ways consonant with the rules. When an aircraft bombed a clearly marked hospital-ship off Naples, an American Fifth Army general declared that because the Germans—witness their ordinary respect for Red Cross markers—possessed loftier motives than those of the Soviets, the misdeed must have been the work of a Russian pilot flying a German plane![112]

Sometimes the culpable side itself moved to repair matters in ways that forestalled reprisal. During the campaign in Germany in November 1944, an enemy patrol attacked a group of American medics, wounding two. Approaching, the Germans expressed regret, explaining to the shocked aidmen that they had thought to strike against "infantrymen" and in the dark had failed to see the Red Cross bands on their sleeves. This battlefield apology for a mistake had counterparts on every level, not excepting the high command. When in 1945 a train carrying German prisoners of war reached its destination and 130 of them were discovered to have suffocated in jam-packed boxcars without adequate ventilation, General Dwight Eisenhower expressed regret to the German high command via the American legation in Berne. He had ordered the Inspector General to open a full investigation, and he promised the enemy that "If it is found that United States personnel were guilty of negligence, appropriate action will be taken. . . . The Supreme Commander profoundly regrets this incident and has taken steps to prevent its recurrence."[113]

But some enemy transgressions that could be neither forgiven nor explained away engendered an anger that clamored to be vented. "Two can play that way." "We got to give those bastards a taste of their own medicine." In December 1944, as the enemy's Ardennes offensive pushed back Allied forces, the Germans reoccupied a number of Belgian towns. In Trois-Points, an American combat engineer reported, they "gathered all of the people left in the town into the cellar of one of the houses and there they proceeded to punish them for befriending the Americans"—a massacre of women, children, and men. The dead included three affable women who had lived near the American motor pool; one of them, pregnant, "had been cut open and left to die." Two small children had had their heads smashed. Men had been dismembered and shot. After American tanks recaptured Trois-Points, some of the hundreds of GIs who had viewed the carnage rounded up German prisoners, then marched them to the cellar, "forced [them] to view the awful scene in it," marched them into the woods and shot them.[114]

What was surprising, given the frequency and seriousness of the provocation, was that retaliatory emotion did not escape restraint. It was as if some element of calculation remained in place. The optimum action was understood to be one that, while punishing the enemy, was sufficient to deter a repetition of the offending conduct, without going so far as to provoke a counterreprisal. Enlisted men did seem inclined to maintain a system of equilibrium with enemy enlisted men, and retaliations remained bounded, in rough proportion to the offense.

Near Falaise, infiltrating SS troops captured five members of the 103d Tank Destroyer Battalion. Although one escaped, the other four were found shot through the head, hands tied behind their backs. Americans took no prisoners *in that sector on that day.* When, early in the war, SS troops overran D Company of a British battalion and a counterattack caught enemy soldiers "smashing in the heads of [British] wounded and prisoners with pick-axes," battalion replacements were thenceforth instructed, "We will have no mercy on them." But not all German soldiers, nor even all SS. The word came down: "Never take prisoners in the Langemarck Division!" When medic Frank Irgang sought German prisoners to carry his wounded, a GI told him that though some were being held in a nearby basement, there were not many. "Haven't taken many lately. We're not fighting that kind of war *right now.*" In mid-September 1943, as paratroopers of the 82d Airborne Division were emplaning for a drop on Paestum in southwestern Italy, a flushed colonel, the regimental commander, stopped his jeep at every aircraft and shouted to his soldiers, "Men, it's open season on Krautheads. You know what to do!" In fact, "open season" never arrived on the Mediterranean or Western European fronts.115

Still, the great danger in early 1945 was that the American soldiers, increasingly angry that Germans continued to fight when the military verdict seemed obvious, and the German soldiers, increasingly frustrated by their inability to protect their home territory, would set in motion a dynamic that would move beyond their intention or control. As Alan Moorehead observed, savagery fed on savagery; in the last months of the war there was always a danger that some severe violation would trigger runaway reactions and counteractions summoning to Western Europe the patterns of the Pacific and the Eastern Front, and quickly barbarize the campaign.116

Of all the events in the European theater, the one posing the greatest risk was the Malmédy massacre of December 17, 1944.

In the early stages of the Ardennes offensive, Colonel Jochen Peiper's battle group of the 1st SS Panzer Division surprised a truck convoy of the American 7th Armored Division, destroying it and taking approximately 150 prisoners. As Edwin Hoyt has noted, "The Germans were in a hurry; their object was to drive through the American lines, not shepherd prisoners." The POWs were herded together in a field near Malmédy, searched, and ordered to stand with their hands over their heads. The Germans made no effort to separate medical personnel and combat soldiers; indeed, the signal shot was aimed by a German officer, standing in an open command car, at a medical officer. Tank machine guns then opened fire, traversing prisoner ranks. Infantry circulated, administering coups with bullets and butts. One hundred and seven Americans died; forty-three, feigning death, were able to escape, only a quarter of them without wounds.117

To many GIs, Malmédy was a decisive event. Later, during their trial, SS defendants would argue that it was unexceptional, that what they had done was of a piece with American directives at Normandy; but in late 1944, American combat soldiers proclaimed it an outrage impossible to justify. Said Harold Leinbaugh: "If K Company's reaction to the atrocity was typical, the Germans had committed their worst mistake of the war on the Western Front. We had fought by rules. . . . In the heat of battle, prisoners were sometimes killed. We knew that. But this was mass murder, and the SS was going to have to pay and pay heavily." Among his men, however, were those who would not seek targets of vengeance only among the SS. Said Clayton Shepherd, "When Leinbaugh told us about the massacre, everybody got pissed off. I just wanted to get down to Belgium and start killing *Germans*." Henry Giles's wife reported that Malmédy sealed in the minds of her husband and his comrades "a deep hatred of the enemy"; that they thereafter fought "savagely and bitterly."[118]

Many Americans would not be satisfied until they had participated in, or witnessed, retributive actions. It was fortunate for the formal structure that GIs could often be appeased by operations that, however intensified, remained within the rules. Only a few days later Lavender's unit was gratified to call down artillery on an entire battalion of Germans and to watch its utter annihilation. Pergrin's combat engineers helped to retrieve the Malmédy dead from beneath eighteen inches of snow. As they dug, "military policemen marched a group of about fifty German prisoners through the adjacent Five Points crossroads. All work in the killing field ceased and a great wave of hatred rose from our ranks and reached out to the passing Germans. It is a wonder that none of our troops opened fire." But soon Pergrin, too, witnessed a cathartic act of revenge. He and a comrade spotted on a river road "a lengthy German column, complete with horse-drawn artillery. . . ." The subsequent barrage, intense and prolonged, destroyed many "countrymen of the scum who had murdered my countrymen in the field below Five Points." Some infantry units retaliated directly. At least two regimental orders directed that no further German prisoners be taken. Accounts make clear that a number of units applied a no-mercy policy, but it, and the pulverization of retreating German formations, appear rather quickly to have assuaged GI wrath ("[The] Americans took . . . few prisoners during the next few days"). Within a week the *status quo ante* was again the reality on most battlefields.[119]

Combat left a few Americans with an enduring ferocity. Audie Murphy learned early on, he reported, that "The only safe Germans are dead ones." In a Normandy assault, a paratrooper in the 506th Regiment, 101st Airborne Division, stopped long enough to bayonet each of four wounded German soldiers because "I'm not going to leave one of them behind to play possum and shoot me in the back." Grady Arrington, too, was convinced that "even a wounded Kraut was a dangerous one; if [a] wounded [German] were allowed to remain alive and await medical units, it was not uncommon for him to turn on us and unload his rifle. Those men wounded worst were often the most vicious; they knew they were going to die, and vengeance was their only hope." Implicit was the conviction that the enemy was a fanatic driven by his determination to kill Americans, but rarely was that of a scope sufficient to degrade combat behavior.[120]

Paratrooper Donald Burgett, sighting a German soldier crossing an opening at the edge of a ruined Norman farmhouse, shot him. "He went down hard and rolled over on a small pile of bricks; then, lying on his back, he dug his heels into the ground and twitched for several minutes. Finally, taking a deep breath, he arched his back up until only his shoulders and heels were touching the ground, then collapsed. I could have put another bullet into him, but somehow I was fascinated and watched him in his losing battle for life." Burgett remained under cover.

> Every once in a while I would glance at the dead man, and I suddenly noticed his long blond hair. GIs were never allowed to have hair that long, and it agitated me in a strange way that I can't explain. Deep inside, something primitive stirred within me, and I thought of the muskrats and other game I had skinned for their pelts. Then the whole thing became clear to me. I wanted that scalp.
>
> Nerves quivered throughout the entire length of my body and my hands became cold and sweaty as I slid over the top of the hedge and started crawling toward him. Thoughts of how I would salt and stretch the scalp on a small willow limb filled my mind. I could carry it inside my shirt. And how nice it would look hanging on my living-room wall after the war was over. The prize was nearly within my reach when rifle fire opened up on me, and I was forced to run like hell and dive behind the . . . hedgerow. Two more times I tried to reach him, but each time was driven back. . . . Finally I decided to forget the whole damned thing. . . .121

But only a minuscule number of GIs in Europe succumbed to perversities on a par with Burgett's. Indeed, Arrington was far more representative, not so much in imputing furor and malignity to German wounded, but in those more moderate views he held simultaneously. The American soldier "can fight his way through hell like a raving maniac," he said, but always "emerges from that hell to retrieve his sense of benevolence and generosity. . . ." And when his buddy Robertson, to avenge the death of a friend, wished to kill a wounded German soldier they had found hiding in the cellar of his father's house, Arrington argued against it. He bowed slightly to vengeance: Left alone, the German would, he was sure, die slowly and painfully of his wounds. But Arrington returned to "benevolence and generosity," summoning an across-the-lines comradeship: "Hell, Robertson, he's only a soldier like you and me. . . . [He] fought because he had to." They departed without killing the landser.122

The narrow amplitude of soldier opinion, with the point of balance remaining at relative moderation, revealed itself in several ways.

There were limits to the GI's ability to find gratification even in the most justifiable vengeance. The utter destruction of that German column soon became repugnant to Pergrin. He was "stunned by the ferocity of the death struggle and sickened by the carnage." Leinbaugh, too, found that a deadly artillery bombardment not only satiated his desire to avenge Malmédy but restored his sense of sympathy for the enemy: "The cries for help from wounded and dying Germans carried clearly to our lines. We admitted to ourselves that we were sorry for the poor bastards up there in the pocket."[123]

In an episode near Bastogne during the Battle of the Bulge, members of the 513th Parachute Infantry Regiment, advancing with walking fire, captured more than twenty Germans. Just as Kurt Gabel, a German-speaking American, completed his interrogation of one of the prisoners, the eruption of machine-gun fire drew his lieutenant's attention: "Well, look! That Kraut bastard is firing on the medics!" Gabel watched as a figure wearing a Red Cross armband and kneeling next to a fallen soldier rose from the field and was immediately knocked over by a burst of fire. A rifleman jumped from cover to aid the wounded medic, but was himself shot through the arm. Two other troopers, "crazed by an unspeakable rage," leapt up, with one screaming, "You goddamn bastards! They [American aidmen] were trying to get *your* wounded, too!" The German machine gun, so expertly camouflaged that its location could not be detected, drove them back to cover. The lieutenant despaired of retrieving the wounded: "We can't get to them." "Yes, we can," said Gabel. "What you got in mind?" asked the platoon sergeant. "Well, we'll just take the Kraut prisoners and line 'em up between the [machine gun] and the wounded. Simple." "Can't do that," came the lieutenant's reply. "That's about as far against the Geneva Conventions as you can go." The sergeant disagreed: "Geneva Conventions shit, sir. What do you suppose that bastard over there is doing to the Geneva Conventions when he shoots at medics and wounded?" "Go!" said the lieutenant.

So Gabel ordered the prisoners to rise, to fall in, to face right, and to set off across the field at route step. ("I had suddenly turned into a German NCO.") He explained the problem of the machine-gun; pointed out that they were covered by American guns, including his own Thompson submachine gun; threatened that if one of them ran or took cover, all of them would be shot to pieces; and promised that if they followed instructions, "we would all be safely back in a few minutes." Seeing the approaching line, the German machine-gunner loosed "two short, tentative bursts," but the prisoners waved their arms and shouted, *"Nicht schiessen, Helmuth. Wir sind's. Nicht schiessen!"* and the firing ceased. As the prisoners moved forward to place themselves between the fallen soldiers and the German line, GIs scrambled from cover to carry the wounded to safety. Then Gabel ordered an about-face and walked the prisoners through the American position. Meriting special regard is that the Americans, even in their high anger, had rescued German wounded as well as their own. "Get the Germans, too," the lieutenant had shouted out. It was an unconsciously conciliatory gesture, a signal establishing the limits to which these American soldiers would reach in an instance of blatant disregard for the rules and an acknowledgment that in combat against the Germans they found few situations irreparable.[124]

At every moment of day and night, the rules, major and minor, formal and informal, were violated. "[S]omebody," Audie Murphy said in words much more nonchalant than he felt, "is always forgetting the rule book." Soldiers daily infringed some of its provisions and for short periods many of its provisions, but frequent violations and frequent retaliations never conjoined to impart momentum to a downward cycle capable of sustaining itself. Remarkably, the canons of combat—constantly threatened, constantly renegotiated—remained in place on May 8, 1945.[125]

Karl von Clausewitz, the nineteenth-century Prussian military philosopher, believed that implicit in war was a limitlessness, a steady thrust toward moral extremities propelled by the opposing sides' reciprocal actions and continuous escalations. So it proved during World War II on the Eastern Front and in the Pacific; but not in combat between Germans and Americans in Western Europe.[126]

4 FIGHTING THE JAPANESE
War Unrestrained

American soldiers, as they collided with the forces of Japan in the Philippines, foresaw a war like that their compatriots would wage in North Africa and Western Europe. They accepted the importance of rules, both because they had been instructed in the Geneva agreements and because they assumed that rules maximized their own chances of survival. With each side willing to accept and yield prisoners, capture would not become a death sentence. Medical personnel on both sides, offered protection as they treated wounded soldiers, would ensure that combatants were not denied life-saving ministration.

Japan, however, retained the military initiative throughout the first six months of the war, a period that determined the terms of encounter. In the end, the power of the Japanese to defeat General Douglas MacArthur's Filipino and American soldiery also proved the power to establish the patterns of battlefield contact; indeed, to fix how the war in the Pacific would be fought. Americans expected to fight their kind of war; on Bataan, the Japanese imposed on their enemies the war they intended to fight.

By March 1942, the issue of surrender, however reluctantly admitted, was a major American concern. The Filamerican army had been in retreat since its first clash with Japanese invasion units; it was powerless to reverse the military balance without massive aid, promised but undeliverable, from the United States; and it was running out of space. The question had become how long it could hold out—before surrendering.

To Americans contemplating capitulation, it seemed reasonable that Japanese incarceration, while promising no ease, would offer a basic consideration. On this point the historical record was reassuring. During the Russo-Japanese War of 1904–5, the Imperial Japanese Army ordered that prisoners of war "shall be treated with a spirit of goodwill and shall never be subjected to cruelties or humiliation," and there was overwhelming evidence of compliance. Toward war's end, an authority on international law wrote that he could not refrain "from paying a tribute to Japan for the way in which she has observed the rules of International Law in her present conflict [and for] her chivalrous treatment of her wounded and prisoner enemies. . . ." Japanese soldiers, by report, brought to wounded Russians cigarettes and wine drawn from "their [own] scanty rations."[1]

When a tsarist colonel became one of the 700,000 Russians held prisoner in Japan, his wife was allowed to visit him in the prison hospital at Matsuyama. "It is not my idea of a prison at all," declared Elizabeth Scidmore. "Surely there is the fullest liberty within the barracks. There are no fetters, no restrictions. Everything is . . . simple . . . and clean. . . . The prisoners' lot could not well be a happier one, and I . . . would less willingly be a prisoner of war in some places I can think of in Russia." First escape attempts—Elizabeth Scidmore condemned them as "such childish foolishness"—drew confinement to the compound, i.e., curtailment of shopping trips to town and visits to the mineral baths. Another try brought six months in a cell. "Vladimir says it is unaccountable that the Japanese did not shoot [a recaptured prisoner] at this second attempt. In any other army, it is the rule." Russian officers who had been captured in the field and then released to return home, and who had instead re-entered combat in blatant violation of their *parole d'honneur* and been retaken by the Japanese, were treated no differently than other prisoners. Thus the Japanese soldier of 1904–5 was plausibly viewed, in the words of Susie and Meirion Harries, as "magnanimous—generous in his respect for brave enemies and chivalrous in his treatment of their casualties."[2]

This pattern held during and beyond World War I. Observers commended the care afforded the Kaiser's soldiers swept up during the Japanese occupation of Germany's Pacific colonies. During the 1920 Siberian intervention, a British captain in Vladivostok came upon a camp filled with Austrians and Turks. "Poor devils! Think of still being prisoners after all these years. Am told that a number of them have gone off their heads as a result of their long imprisonment. However, the Japanese are caring for them now and seem to be treating them very well." During the hostilities that erupted between Russian and Japanese forces in 1939, *Life* magazine reported that, with Japanese medical and supply systems superior to those of the Soviets, "Neutral observers believe that the Russian prisoners in Manchukuo are getting better treatment than the Japanese prisoners in Outer Mongolia. . . ."[3]

Early in World War II the Japanese offered assurances that they would continue such practices. The 1904 instruction remained in force. Japan had been party to the Hague Convention of 1907 and was still bound by its provisions. Although no formal ratification had followed the Japanese delegation's endorsement of the Geneva Convention of 1929, when in early 1942 Britain and the United States reiterated their intention to fulfill its requirements and requested Japan's adherence, Foreign Minister Shigenori Togo pledged that his nation would apply the convention, *"mutatis mutandis,"** to all British and American prisoners. Concurrently, Emperor Hirohito ordered his soldiers to treat POWs as "unfortunate individuals" whose situation merited "the utmost benevolence and kindness," and field commanders seemed determined to give effect to the emperor's words. As he urged surrender on the British in Singapore, Lieutenant General Tomoyuki Yamashita cited the "spirit of . . . Japanese chivalry" and the "many sincere respects" due his beleaguered enemies. On March 8, 1942, the senior Japanese Army officer on Java agreed to insert in the document governing the capitulation of the Dutch East Indies a passage "promising to adhere to the Geneva Convention rules for proper treatment of prisoners of war."[4]

In his turn, Lieutenant General Masaharu Homma, Japan's commander in the Philippines, directed that captives be treated "in a friendly spirit." On Bataan, a newly commissioned American second lieutenant, Harley Hieb, noted carefully the Japanese promises held out by radio and loudspeaker: confinement in accord with Geneva precepts, then release and return home in "only a matter of months." Japanese aircraft dropped copies of a letter addressed to MacArthur's successor, Lieutenant General Jonathan Wainwright. "In accordance with the humanitarian principles of 'Bushido,' the code of the Japanese warrior," it urged "honorable surrender" to halt "needless bloodshed." "International Law will be strictly adhered to by the Imperial Japanese Forces, and your Excellency and those under your command will be treated accordingly. The joy . . . of those whose lives will be saved and the delight and

---

*after necessary changes

relief of their dear ones . . . would be beyond . . . expression. . . ." "Your worries are over," Homma told the only American prisoner with whom he spoke. "Japan treats her prisoners well. You may even see my country in cherry blossom time and that is a beautiful sight."[5]

Despite episodes on Bataan battlefields that confused and troubled frontline soldiers, most Americans continued to count on the enemy's promises. The governing expectation was that, beyond formal obligation, American stalwartness in defense of the Philippines would earn Japanese respect for those who survived to surrender. Hong Kong had resisted the invader for eighteen days. The Dutch East Indies succumbed, without a major land battle, in fifty-eight days. From Japanese landings to the surrender of Singapore, the British in Malaya held off the enemy for seventy days. The Philippines campaign, from first incursion on December 8, 1941, to Corregidor's capitulation on May 6, 1942, required 150 days, three times the number that Tokyo had allotted Homma. Surely, American soldiers persuaded themselves, the Japanese would honor those whose battlefield performance met, indeed clearly exceeded, the demands of duty.[6]

Just as Bataan's surrender became imminent, an American captain, Manny Lawton, discussed the issue with members of the Filipino infantry battalion he served as adviser. "What do you think they will do to us, sir?" asked a corporal. "It may not be too bad, Bautista. There are rules of international law [regarding] prisoners of war, you know." A Filipino lieutenant, however, was incredulous. "What do they care about rules? Those Japanese are uncivilized. What about the way they abused people at Singapore and [in] China?" Lawton lost little equanimity: "Yes, we have heard of atrocities, but we don't know for sure. Maybe since we gave them a good fight they will have more respect for us." When an American company commander, as skeptical of Japanese pledges as the Filipino lieutenant, pondered fleeing to the hills and fighting on as a guerrilla, he was dissuaded by his division commander, who assured him that his worries were baseless. The Japanese, said Brigadier General Maxon Lough, would abide by Geneva and treat their prisoners decently.[7]

Similarly, Americans believed at the outset of the Philippines campaign that the Japanese would observe restraints devised to preserve the lives of the wounded. The Japanese had proved "chivalrous" in the care of enemy casualties during 1904–5. Accompanying *Life*'s report of the Japanese-Russian clash of August 1939 was a photograph of a wounded Soviet flier carefully bandaged by his Japanese captors. Accounts of Japanese operations in China continued to concentrate on the harm done civilians, with almost no suggestion that

Japanese soldiers killed enemy wounded or refused to observe distinctions between opponents-in-arms and non-combatant medical personnel.[8]

On Bataan, the Imperial Army began to force on its American
antagonists an unwelcome battlefield education in the Japanese way of war.

Japanese forces demonstrated a mixed inclination to make prisoners of
those whom their advance overran. "When the Japs captured Filipino[s],"
Colonel Paul Thompson determined, ". . . they stripped them naked and sent
them to the rear without any guard. They did not take individual American
prisoners, though they did apparently send some groups of captured Americans to the rear. Where a single American fought until surrounded he wasn't
given any chance to give up." The impact on front-line Americans was formidable: the Japanese were killing GIs taken alone or in twos and threes but they
also made such deaths excruciating and exerted no effort to hide their handi-
work. John Coleman, an Air Corps captain reassigned to infantry when his
squadron was destroyed, awoke one morning to a report that a twelve-man
enemy patrol approaching his position was "torturing . . . Americans to death
where they caught one or two by themselves." And it was not by seizing prisoners that Japanese infiltrators marked their success in penetrating opposing
lines. "An American soldier was found with his hands and feet cut off, bayonets driven into his stomach." Another reassigned airman, Samuel Grashio,
reported that it became "commonplace to find the bodies of one's comrades,
tightly bound, obviously tortured, disemboweled, with their severed genitals
stuffed in their mouths." The word passed quickly in the immediate vicinity
of such discoveries, but amid the desperation and disarray of the American
stand, reports went unwritten or unheeded or uncompiled. Those who saw
dead, disfigured comrades were not slow to draw new conclusions—
"[B]ecause I was an American," reckoned Harley Hieb, "I knew if I were to be
caught alone, I would be bayoneted or shot"—but many others heard what
seemed no more than rumor, and continued to assume that the enemy were
holding, and treating reasonably, those Americans they captured.[9]

In their battlefield operations, the Japanese did not, as Americans inclined
to do, distinguish between enemies still combatant, no longer combatant, and
officially non-combatant. In the war's early stage, few Americans realized how
differently they and the Japanese appraised the incapacitated soldier. Only extensive contact would reveal that the enemy often regarded his own wounded or
otherwise impaired soldiers as little better than wastage, assets expended beyond
reclamation. "The Japanese had little time," noticed George Gray, an American
civilian imprisoned in the Philippines, "even for [their own] troops wounded in

action. . . ." (The Imperial Army assigned to each infantry company one medic, the Americans three.) When, in early July 1944, American authorities decided to send fifty of the most severely injured enemy prisoners taken on Saipan to hospitals in Hawaii, a Japanese medical officer questioned Marine general Holland Smith. Why were the Americans acting in such a way? Those soldiers— "blind, legless, broken-backed"—were "useless." Smith turned the query on his interrogator: What would the Japanese do in such a situation? "Very easy in the Japanese army. We would leave them a hand grenade apiece, and if they didn't use the grenades, it would be a simple matter to slit their jugular veins." Even ordinary ailments were thought shameful. Within Gray's internment camp, "it was not unusual for the American hospital staff to treat guards who were afraid to admit illness or injury to their own medical staff."[10]

Later in the war, Allied soldiers found numerous jarring instances in which the Japanese abandoned men too weak to keep up the pace of retreats, or, with seeming indifference, left their dead lying on battlefields. Particularly repugnant to Americans ("a sight I shall never forget, a vision of horror beyond the powers of Edgar Allan Poe") were situations in which hospital patients, confronting the approach of American units and unwilling or unable to commit suicide, were killed by other Japanese.[11]

With such views of their own wounded, the Japanese were not inclined to special measures to preserve the enemy's wounded. In the course of Guam's capitulation, a Japanese doctor surveying American wounded spotted a sailor whose feet had been "pulverized by machine-gun fire," and kicked both feet. On Bataan, helpless American infantrymen were targets no less than the able-bodied. "Erroneous information that the [Japanese] roadblock was cleared resulted in the dispatch rearward of a truck packed with fourteen wounded. The truck, marked with a large red cross, was ambushed. Only two men escaped. . . ." Again, news of a departure from American expectations circulated rapidly. During the final retreat, a rout in many units, those under John Coleman's command were near collapse: "Our men are worn out and cannot carry the wounded any farther. We will have to lay them beside the trail." To relinquish comrades, though always distasteful, was admissible if soldiers thought they could count on the other side's medics to save American lives. Here, however, a wounded lieutenant's experience had run beyond Coleman's. "I can't live much longer. I am losing too much blood. Please do not put me out near the trail. The Japs are cutting the bodies to pieces and stomping those [wounded] the Americans leave [there]." Coleman placed the dead deep in the bush; his men continued to carry the wounded.[12]

Japanese reasoning also precluded, it would become clear, any allowance for those attempting to aid fallen soldiers. In this category, as in many others, suspicions of the enemy developed on Bataan became indictments of the enemy six months later on Guadalcanal. Marine officer Frank Hough described the Japanese soldier in the South Pacific as one who "would as soon kill a chaplain administering the last rites to the dying as he would an active enemy. Nothing delighted him more than killing our wounded lying helpless between the lines, unless it was killing the doctors and hospital corpsmen who went out to attend them." That medics were not armed—"not at the beginning, anyway"—was important, thought Hough, because it *drew* the Japanese to attack them. Aidman Robert Thobaben, when accompanying patrols on Peleliu, carried a carbine: "I never did have a red cross painted on my helmet. I thought . . . that . . . was insane. It . . . was only a target." In enemy eyes, Americans came to believe, no one still alive was *hors de combat*.[13]

Because the Japanese understood their enemy far better than the Americans did theirs, the Japanese were able to exploit on the battlefield American proclivities to aid wounded soldiers. On Bataan's Abucay Line, a Japanese soldier, feigning death, waited for a Philippine Scout to come out to bandage a badly wounded Japanese nearby, then shot him dead. The Marine commander on Guadalcanal protested to Washington that Japanese wounded "wait until men come up to examine them . . . and blow themselves and the other fellow to death with a . . . grenade." Japanese soldiers, Eugene Sledge recalled, pretended to be wounded, called out for American corpsmen, then drove their knives into the medics who responded. During a raid on Florida Island, one eighteen-year-old Marine "tried to help a wounded Nip officer get to his feet inside one of those caves. The Nip shoved a . . . grenade into the kid's stomach and both of them were blown up." The enemy's resort to such stratagems multiplied until American soldiers and Marines became alert to them. Raider commander Evans Carlson explained why his battalion took no prisoners during its foray behind enemy lines on Guadalcanal: "[We] had already learned our lesson. We lost half of our corpsmen trying to help their wounded." In the Okinawa campaign, Sledge and his friends were no longer easy to surprise.

[We] found this emaciated Japanese in [a] bunk of what may have been a field hospital. . . . About ninety pounds. Pitiful. This buddy of mine picked him up and carried him out. Laid him . . . in the mud. There was no other place to put him. We were sittin' on our helmets waitin' for the . . . corpsman to check him out. He was very docile. Suddenly he pulled a . . . grenade out of his G-string. . . .

He was gonna make hamburger of me and my buddy and himself. I yelled, "Look out!" So my buddy said, "You son of a bitch, if that's how you feel about it—" He pulled out his .45 and shot him right between the eyes.[14]

As Americans initially anticipated that they would surrender to the Japanese without forfeiting their lives, so they expected to reciprocate, to accept the surrender of the emperor's soldiers. In reality, grounds for confidence here were far less substantial than those underlying their supposition that the Japanese would safeguard American prisoners. If there was some flexibility in the Japanese treatment of those they captured, there was none in the prohibition against the Japanese themselves becoming prisoners.

Few Americans appreciated how heavily Japanese culture bore down on surrender and, scarcely less, on capture. Imperial Navy combat pilot Masatake Okumiya, however, knew how "startlingly different" were Japanese values from those of the Yankee enemy: ". . . the Japanese people would not recognize existence as a prisoner of war." As Hiroo Onoda of the Imperial Japanese Army prepared to depart for service in the Philippines—he would hold out there until 1974!—his mother presented him with her grandmother's dagger: "If you are taken captive use this to kill yourself." Those at home, imbued by government, school, and state religion with the traditional precept that Japanese warriors do not surrender, and assured throughout the war that *no* Japanese were being held prisoner, endorsed severe sanctions against any who might yield.[15]

To surrender, then, was to estrange oneself from family, community, military comrades. As a Japanese soldier explained to the Americans with whom he had agreed to work on Guam, "When a Japanese surrenders . . . he commits dishonor. One must forget him completely. His wife and his poor mother and children erase him from their memories. There is no memorial placed for him. It is not that he is dead. It is that he never existed." The name of the prisoner was to be stricken from the register of his village or ward. Criminal sanctions ranged from confiscation of all property to lengthy imprisonment and even to death. (On Bataan, a new POW, Air Corps sergeant Bob Reynolds, watched in astonishment as the Imperial Japanese Army regained custody of some of its soldiers captured by the Americans: they were marched to a clearing, offered a cigarette, shot, and left unburied.) Captives were living dead, their pasts expunged, their futures dissolved; there would be for them nothing of the paradise promised those who lost their lives on the battlefield, no immortalization of their souls among the spirits of the warrior dead at the Yasukuni Shrine.[16]

Americans were amazed by the force of will revealed in the Japanese resolve to die rather than surrender. Survivors of sinkings often swam *away* from enemy rescuers. When the submarine *Sterlet* sank an enemy vessel, surfaced, sighted thirty Japanese clinging to flotsam, and attempted to take a prisoner, the Japanese "declined en masse." An American flotilla, Seaman James Fahey recounted,

> . . . came across a raft with four live Japs in it. Admiral Merrill sent word . . . to pick them up. As the destroyer *Spence* came close . . . the Japs opened up [on it] with a machine gun. . . . The . . . officer then put the gun in each man's mouth and fired, blowing out the back of each man's skull. . . . The officer was the last to die. He also blew his brains out. . . . All the bodies . . . disappeared in the water. There was nothing left but blood and an empty raft.

Early in 1945, two senior Japanese naval officers posted to Germany received orders to return home; they took passage on a German U-boat that failed to keep its Indian Ocean rendezvous with one of Japan's subs. Later, in the Gulf of Mexico, the German vessel became disabled and, hoisting the white flag, was intercepted by an American patrol. Without incident, the U-boat captain and crew passed into captivity; the Japanese, found dead, had taken poison. And Japanese pilots, Zero ace Saburo Sakai explained, had long resisted parachutes; when finally ordered to wear them, they left them unbuckled because their presence might otherwise have suggested "a willingness to be captured. . . . No fighter pilot of any courage would ever permit himself to be captured. . . . It was completely unthinkable."[17]

On Bataan, this obduracy still lay beyond American comprehension. On January 22, 1942, the Japanese landed six hundred men at Quinauan Point far behind American lines, instigating two weeks of severe fighting that cost five hundred Filamerican casualties. Finally, on February 4, assaults overran the Japanese and drove the survivors into a cliffside cave whose mouth was lapped by the sea. Wainwright, confident that enemy troops recognized the hopelessness of their position, ordered up loudspeakers to invite them to act accordingly. To his surprise: silence. "They refused to surrender. When this was reported to me, it was hard to believe. I ordered another proffer of honorable surrender, but the trapped Japs fired on troops who brought the offer." (Four days earlier, one of MacArthur's communiqués had reported that those Japanese had been "glad to surrender.") Finally, engineers lowered a fifty-pound box of dynamite and "blew the place to pieces. There were no survivors. It had at last dawned on me, as it was to dawn on so many commanders who followed me in the Pacific War, that the Jap usually prefers death to surrender." "The old rules of war began to undergo a swift change in me."[18]

Again, as long as Americans remained oblivious to their opponents' fundamental assumptions, the Japanese were able to exploit their awareness of American assumptions—here with false surrenders. In both the Malayan and the Filipino campaigns, *Life* correspondent Cecil Brown reported, small groups of Japanese moved forward until they encountered patrols whose vigilance they then lulled by raising white flags—only to bring up their weapons and open fire point-blank. At Longoskawayan Point, Bataan, two Marines died when they stepped from cover to accept the submission ("Me surrender. Me surrender") of a Japanese feigning capitulation. A story that Americans subsequently carried with them to every atoll "concerned Japs who surrendered in pairs. Just as they reached the Americans, one man would fall on his hands and knees, revealing a light machine gun strapped to his back. His companion would man it quickly, shooting down the startled Americans."[19]

The Japanese introduced other stratagems that violated no rules but still seemed to Americans "unfair," or worse, charged with treachery. In the air, Japanese planes machine-gunned First Lieutenant Marshall Anderson ("one of our best and most respected pilots") as his parachute drifted down from his burning P-40; on the ground, American soldiers cursed and shook their fists skyward. Japanese soldiers often used English to lure Americans with familiar commands or entreaties; cries in simulation of wounded GIs ("Corpsman! Corpsman!") sometimes brought medical personnel within the sights of Japanese weapons. Booby traps placed on their own and American dead targeted both infantrymen and medics. Infiltration tactics—the surprise descent on the American foxhole, the gashed throat, the disappearance into the dark—seemed equally deceitful. ("This kind of infiltration," estimated researcher-writer Donald Young, ". . . was responsible for over one-third of all front-line . . . casualties . . . on Bataan.") The most portentous artifice was the death pose. "To our cost," wrote Captain William Dyess of combat on Bataan, "we became acquainted with their strategy of playing dead until an American column had crept past them. Then the supposed corpses would rise up and shoot the Americans in the back." By mid-1942, American front-line soldiers and Marines had evidence to conclude, as Susie and Meirion Harries would write, that to the enemy "Any ploy was acceptable . . . in a war to the death."[20]

From repeated surprises, the defenders of Bataan began to grasp the sense of an unbridgeable gap between their overturned expectations and the actuality of Japanese conduct in battle. They were puzzled and ultimately incensed by the disparity and its costs. "Many of our troops get killed learning [the] tricks [of the Japanese]."[21]

On their side, the Japanese would prove more unbending in their attitudes toward the enemy in this war than in their earlier Russian conflict.

Americans failed to grasp that the Japanese placed the treatment of prisoners within the realm of national policy rather than moral commitment. In 1905 the Japanese government had been determined to impress world powers with the nation's Westernized achievement—military, industrial, even behavioral. In contrast, the policy matrix of World War II was one of anger against the Western powers and fierce determination to oust them from their Asian and Pacific outposts. Any impetus toward respect, emulation, and alignment had flown. Defiance dominated, so considerations of statecraft no longer prompted government efforts to suppress the contempt reserved for those who allowed themselves to be taken prisoner. When Death March survivors staggered into Camp O'Donnell on Luzon, its Japanese commandant's first words were that Caucasians "had been enemies of the Oriental for 100 years and would always be enemies," and that "Americans were dogs, that they'd always been dogs and that they were going to be treated like dogs." "You think you are the lucky ones. Your comrades died on Bataan. Those comrades are the lucky ones."[22]

All remaining flexibility disappeared with the determination of Tokyo leaders to persuade Japanese soldiers that the enemy were blood-sotted killers. The high command advised its troops on Guadalcanal that "The Americans on this island are not ordinary troops, but Marines, a special force recruited from jails and insane asylums for blood lust. There is no honorable death [for] prisoners; their arms are cut off, they are staked on the airfield and run over by steamrollers." No gentler was the imagery of the enemy pressed upon Okinawans. "We knew that if we were captured we'd be chopped to pieces," said Shigeaki Kinjō, a village boy in 1945. "They'd cut off our noses [and] our ears, chop off our fingers, and then run over our bodies with their tanks. Women would be raped." He and a brother, in prelude to their own anticipated suicide, used stones to kill their own mother, sisters, and younger brother. "That's why we were committing suicide, to avoid capture by the enemy." When student nurse Kikuko Miyagi, in hiding, heard American voices urging surrender and promising care, she "thought we were hearing . . . demons. From the time we'd been children, we'd . . . been educated to hate them. They would strip the girls naked and do with them whatever they wanted, then run over them with tanks. We really believed that. Not only us girls. Mothers, grandfathers, grandmothers, all were cowering at the voice[s] of the devils."[23]

The Japanese soldier required no great leap of mind to believe that the Americans would treat their captives mercilessly; he knew how unsparingly his side dealt with prisoners. China veterans described to civilians on the island of Zamani what they had done at Nanking; proposed that "The Americans naturally will do the same things"; and urged that they kill their children "and die by your own hand [rather] than be shamed and abused, disgraced and raped."[24]

Although many of the patterns of Japanese culture would remain beyond their ken, American fighting men who contested the enemy's invasion of the Philippines thought of themselves as engaged in a process of learning, learning about the Japanese, and using newly acquired knowledge to inform their reactions to the unexpected. Their search, perplexing and often dismaying, was for new comprehension, not some easy elicitation from current events of corroboration that Japanese actions were, as long expected, heinous. Jonathan Wainwright spoke of his "search for the suddenly revealed evil spirit of the Japs. . . ."[25]

Indeed, American commanders complained that their soldiers lacked the animosity that the war required. Colonel Milton Hill, the inspector general of U.S. Army Forces in the Far East, who was ordered to Australia just before Corregidor's capitulation, wrote soon afterwards that the American soldier did not

> . . . have much honest hate for the . . . Jap until some of his comrades have been killed by the enemy, or until he himself has been made to suffer at the enemy's hands. This was true right on Bataan. . . . But the Jap hates the American with a downright hate that carries him through in battles to success or death. And we could do with more of a similar individual fighting spirit. On Bataan our troops soon learned the usual lesson of battle . . . kill or be killed . . . but by no means all of them gained the spirit that goes beyond it—the belief in the heart of every man that he must kill the enemy, and the feeling that he *wants* to kill him to the extreme of his own fighting ability.[26]

In light of the ferocity that would soon command every aspect of the American-Japanese encounter, the open, roseate quality of early American views may come as a surprise. Lieutenant Juanita Redmond, the Army nurse, gave passing thought to the possibility that Japanese bombs might strike her hospital on Bataan—but only by accident or miscalculation. It was unnecessary to consider enemy intentions: "[We] didn't think of their *trying* to hit the hospital." On March 30, 1942, bombs slammed into the doctors' hut, set fire to several outbuildings, and killed several Americans. Immediately, however, enemy voices spoke reassurance. Over a Manila radio station the Japanese command broadcast apologies for the attack, assurances that it had been an accident, promises that it would not recur. Japanese prisoners receiving care in the hospital echoed that message; Japanese pilots, they insisted, had been instructed not even to overfly the facility. Redmond was relieved: "We really believed it must have been a mistake; you get used to thinking the Red Cross sign marks a sanctuary, inviolable even by the vilest enemy." Still, to ensure that identification was unmistakable, additional red crosses were "strewn over the grounds." Doctors and nurses began to take their rest breaks lying on the banners; "[We] found ourselves remaining close to that insignia of safety on our off-duty hours." Redmond and her colleagues thus extended to the Japanese the same confidence that Nurse Archard would offer the Germans in North Africa—but with very different results.

On Easter Monday, the shout "Planes overhead!" aroused no alarm—until bombs exploded at the hospital entrance. A second wave of aircraft destroyed doctors' and nurses' quarters, and a third sent down direct hits on the wards. "There were mangled bodies under the ruins; a blood-stained hand stuck up through a pile of scrap; arms and legs had been ripped off and flung among the rubbish. . . . One of the few corpsmen who had survived unhurt climbed a tree to bring down a body blown into the top branches." More than one hundred were killed or re-wounded. Only sixty-five of the hospital's 1,600 beds remained intact.

This time Juanita Redmond did not look back. Now the matter was "clear and simple in my . . . mind."

> That night we stayed in our foxholes. I didn't sleep. . . . We were like hunted animals, waiting for the kill, almost hoping it would happen quickly so that the torment of waiting would end. But stronger than that was anger; anger and hate and a hot desire to fight back, to avenge our dead. What kind of human beings would deliberately bomb a hospital, defenseless, openly marked for what it was, filled with the wounded and the sick? . . . The only answer I found . . . [was that this] isn't a war in which anybody—*anybody*—is let off. . . . An enemy that will bomb hospitals . . . isn't an enemy you can ever come to terms with. . . . The war must end without compromise.[27]

A similar sequence of events had occurred earlier on Wake Island. On December 9, 1941, the Japanese launched their second air assault on the tiny atoll, with twenty-seven bombers creating results described by Marine officer Walter Bayler:

> Worst of all in point of horror, the Naval hospital had been bombed and several patients killed. That was the crowning infamy. We no longer questioned the accuracy of Japanese bombardiers[, not] after the demonstration [of precision aiming] they gave us the first day. Now it was clear . . . they had deliberately bombed the hospital where they knew their shrapnel would find a concentration of wounded men helpless in bed, unable to run for shelter. . . .[28]

Some American front-line soldiers, correctly gauging the rigidity of the enemy's unwillingness to surrender and their resistance to Americans doing so, threw off all tentativeness during the Bataan campaign. Sidney Stewart's unit found one of its men with all his limbs severed and his torso perforated by bayonet thrusts. "We found the body lying there in the sun as the Nips had left it. We knew they weren't taking any prisoners." Stephen Mellnik, a coast-artillery lieutenant seconded to command a Philippine Scouts battery, realized that his troops had "developed a special hatred for the enemy. Though they condemned the infiltrators' after-dark throat-cutting as murder, they understood the reasons that prompted such actions. But they could not rationalize the enemy's practice of executing prisoners and mutilating their bodies. . . . Cruelty and sadism were not unknown to Filipinos, but the Japanese brand made them vomit." To those artillerymen, combat had become "a 'no-holds-barred' . . . war in which one killed to survive."[29]

But once again, battle commanders were engrossed in holding their lines, rear-echelon commanders in improvising support and supply for underarmed and underfed soldiers. No one had time to write or read reports. Japanese rules violations reached many simply as stories in the wind. Others with more authoritative information, anticipating their own surrender to the Japanese, chose to discount reports revealing malice on the part of their prospective captors. This impulse to denial revealed itself in an episode that occurred after Bataan's surrender. Just as the Death March began on April 9, 1942, the Japanese ordered the American adjutant of a medical battalion to drive a truck back to his hospital. When he returned, he told his fellow captives what he had seen: Japanese guards bayoneting exhausted POWs, shooting down parched prisoners who had merely broken ranks to secure a drink of water. Captain Paul Ashton described his comrades' reaction: "We could not believe these fabrications and accused him of deliberately destroying the morale of the listeners. We drove him, a Major, from the area as a willful troublemaker." Within days, numbers of these Americans would wish that they had fought to the death rather than surrendered.[30]

The capitulation of the Filamerican army and the incarceration of its members did not, however, suppress for long the crystallization of a new consensus regarding Japanese practices. Some Americans, escaping captivity, made it all the way to Australia; others joined guerrilla groups in radio contact with MacArthur's headquarters in Brisbane, via Darwin. Later, submarines carrying in weapons and supplies for the guerrillas brought out their accounts of Japanese depredations. Civilian internees exchanged for Japanese citizens held in the United States returned home in August 1942 with reports of the enemy's harshness. And the Australians were not slow to make public their own experience of Japanese fierceness, one whose pattern was identical with that of Bataan: sick and wounded butchered, prisoners bayoneted, no effort at concealment. (In New Guinea, the Japanese placarded dead Australian prisoners: "It took them a long time to die.") Although Washington withheld the true harshness of the Death March from the American public until early February 1944, it became as early as mid-1942 a war cry in United States training camps, and, within a year, the focus of a film shown to all draftees.[31]

Still, it required the Guadalcanal campaign of August 7, 1942–February 8, 1943, to fix in American combatants the state of mind that would sustain almost to the war's end the pattern of warfare in the Pacific.

The Marines' landing drove into flight the six-hundred-man Japanese garrison. In the next days a number of "sad-looking characters," hungry and dispirited, emerged from the jungle and entered American custody. The distinction between those who surrendered, Korean airfield construction workers, and those who had not, Japanese soldiers, did not impress Marine commanders as forcefully as it should have done. Thus, when a patrol probing the reassembly of Japanese units near Matanikau village returned with a prisoner, a Japanese sailor who told of a contingent of soldiers unable to maintain itself and disposed to give up, his story roused no more than passing caution. The 1st Marine Division's intelligence officer, Lieutenant Colonel Frank Goettge, linked this information with another report, the sighting of a white flag, and was eager to seize the unfolding opportunity. Quickly he won approval to lead a patrol of four officers (including a surgeon and an interpreter) and twenty-one men to gather in the prisoners.

Landing from a Higgins boat on a beach identified by the informant, the Goettge patrol walked into a withering fire that killed Goettge and the Japanese sailor. Captain Wilfred Ringer, succeeding to the command of a desperate defense, sent one Marine, and soon another, to summon help. At dawn, with almost every Marine dead or wounded, the Japanese moved forward. One defender, still with strength to swim away, looked back to see "the glint of swords or bayonets as the Japanese hacked to death" his helpless comrades. Although details of the calamity remained in dispute and any conspiratorial connection between the sailor and the enemy force seemed increasingly unlikely, Americans almost to a man were convinced that the Goettge patrol had been tricked, and that in its fate lay a decisive illustration of the Japanese strategy to resort first to treachery and then to cruelty.[32]

The Goettge incident again illuminated the ragged pace at which Americans had abandoned their assumptions about the way the war would be waged. The division commander, Lieutenant General Alexander Vandegrift, had accepted Goettge's report that "hundreds of Japanese troops were roaming the jungle west of us ready to surrender." Disabused, he wrote the next day to the commandant of the Marine Corps to report, in astonished tones, that he had just discovered Jonathan Wainwright's conclusion of six months earlier: "I have never heard or read of this kind of fighting. These people refuse to surrender." Faster-moving combat Marines, however, derided their leaders' gullibility.[33]

From their opening glimpse of the sailor, "the first live Jap we had seen at close quarters," Grady Gallant and his friends were suspicious. "He must have wanted to get caught." "They don't just give up." "Maybe he'll tell 'em [Marine intelligence] something." "Probably a bunch of lies." Gallant was already persuaded that "You couldn't trust a Jap." When officers, in expectation that thirty to fifty Japanese would enter American lines with their captors, cautioned Gallant's squad to hold its fire, "It didn't make sense to us, but orders were orders." Told of the patrol's destruction, Gallant and his comrades did not doubt that the enemy answerable for this "first mass killing of Marines on Guadalcanal" had simply lain in ambush "waiting for the innocent to follow the Judas goat to death." And they were shocked—but no longer by Japanese actions. "Shocked because we had fallen for such an obvious trap; shocked because headquarters had believed anything a Jap had to say; shocked and angry and sickened because the Japanese had been able to kill so many and suffer no deaths in return." They wished they had killed the sailor. "The Japanese, we knew, preferred death to surrender; we wondered why this simple fact had not presented itself to the minds of those at headquarters." No revelation to them, the doom of Goettge and his men.[34]

The Japanese persisted in, and even stepped up, battlefield practices American soldiers regarded as heinous. Bataan's pattern reappeared in all Pacific-Asian theaters in all phases of the war. One of Merrill's Marauders, Bill Hoover, could not forget that in Burma, "We'd come along and find some of the guys who'd been captured. They'd be staked or strapped down, and [the Japanese] would rub some honey and food . . . on them, around their mouth and eyes, and their eyes were forced open, and they were just laid out and left in the sun, with the bugs crawling all over them." At other times, Americans would come upon prisoners whose hands and limbs the Japanese had severed and then reassembled, "laid out in the shape of a man." "[The Japanese] make sure it was right there out in the open where you could see it." On Bougainville, reports that the enemy were "cutting up captives and throwing the pieces back to Yank foxholes" gnawed at GIs. On Kwajalein, "One night an American was captured on reconnaissance forward of our front lines. The Japs took him into their pillbox and mercilessly butchered him, then threw his body outside." On Iwo Jima, in February 1945, Americans seized by Japanese were still being "gutted." Such acts, targeting soldiers almost within view of their comrades, provoked reactions more profound and enduring than far more comprehensive cruelties committed by other enemies against non-Americans remote from the sphere of American soldiers' immediate, compelling concerns.[35]

Hatred of the Japanese now suffused the American forces. A sign above a Guadalcanal road exhorted passers-by:

> Kill the Bastards!
> Down this road marched one of the regiments
> of the United States Army
> Knights serving the Queen
> of Battles.
> Twenty of their wounded in litters were
> bayoneted, shot and clubbed
> by the Yellow Bellies.
> Kill the Bastards!

On December 7, 1942, in remembrance of Pearl Harbor, artillerymen opened a day-long bombardment of the Japanese; the "First Anniversary Hate Shoot," they called it. Correspondent John Hersey noticed that Americans at Guadalcanal, timing the explosions of grenades they had thrown, counted, "One-dead-Jap, two-dead-Japs . . . ," while GIs fighting Germans marked off, "One-thousand-one, one-thousand-two. . . ."[36]

American soldiers soon denounced as futile any attempt to bring the enemy around to their own precepts. The Japanese, said Marine major Frank

Hough, "had showed us the way [and] there was nothing for it but to play the game the way they wanted it played." Writer William Martin Camp limned Marines' reaction to the shooting down of sixty Japanese soldiers caught unawares while relaxing on a beach: "Sure, it [was] cold-blooded murder, but those yellow bastards had it coming to 'em. . . . By any other standard, ours was a cruel triumph. But by [the Japs'] own standards, it was a complete and total victory: brutal, heartless and quick, without a chance for defense. We were now playing the game by their rules." Actually, most Marines took exception to that final formulation, for few American fighting men believed that they were exchanging their rules for the enemy's; to their minds, the Japanese heeded *no* rules. Hough saw in the enemy's conduct a "complete lack of inhibiting battle ethics, as defined by modern civilization and the precepts of the Geneva Convention."[37]

The absence of rules made senseless any effort even to negotiate with the enemy. With no common foundation, probings for mutually acceptable battlefield terms like those of the European theater would accomplish nothing. After Guadalcanal, no one deliberated medical truces—or, indeed, any communication with the enemy. The Japanese, Americans became convinced, had dedicated themselves to killing every GI and Marine, and had avidly subordinated every other consideration to that goal. Grady Gallant and his friends "could never understand [the Japs'] zeal to die, their willingness to bayonet the wounded, their eagerness to be so wasteful of life. . . . We had no intention of negotiating with them. We knew we could make them more thoroughly peaceful, less gluttonous for the world that was not theirs and more pliable to reason by literally beating hell out of them. We were determined to do this."[38]

Here disappeared any chance that close contact with opponents might attenuate animosity, as it often did in Western Europe, when helpless and hurting prisoners gave a human character to the enemy. Americans coming upon even genuinely enfeebled prisoners began to resist all feelings of sympathy. On Cape Gloucester, GI Sy Kahn first saw the enemy at close range. "So these pitiful prisoners were the vaunted 'Sons of Heaven,' the supermen who were going to exterminate the white race. They didn't look very super then." "There were two prisoners, and a more miserable sight I've hardly seen. . . . One looked on the verge of dying from starvation. He . . . trembled, his eyes sunk far into his head, his cheekbones a sharp outline against his pasty flesh. Both . . . were so weak they immediately sank to the ground upon disembarking from the LCM. . . ." Only for an instant, however, did Sy Kahn soften: "I felt sorry for them, until I remembered the fellows they may have killed, and how easily it could have been me." And then he grew angry that captivity would relieve their distress. "Little did they know what good food and hospitalization awaited them in Australia even though our [POWs] are atrociously treated by the Japs."[39]

Americans believed that both they and the Japanese realized where a war without rules would carry them. The Japanese soldier feigning injury and then setting himself to kill those who came to help him understood, and did not care, in Kenneth Davis's description, "that this would mean not only the loss of his own life but . . . the lives of future wounded Japanese who might otherwise have been saved." In telling Marine commandant Holcomb that "These people refuse to surrender," Vandegrift sped to his conclusion: "You can readily see the answer . . . war without quarter."[40]

Integral to the evolution of American reactions on Bataan and on Guadalcanal was a complicated, multifaceted transformation of attitudes toward the Japanese as a people. Propelled by the view that the Japanese, in their zeal to destroy both Americans and themselves, had abandoned the value of life, American soldiers came to consider infinitely killable an enemy believed to lack fundamental human attributes. Successive stages in the dehumanization of the Japanese traced a series of culture-bound propositions that consecutively diminished the adversary.

"Nobody can understand the Japs."

Americans, led by those who became prisoners of war, first decided that the Japanese were incomprehensible. On the Death March, thirsty POWs rushed an artesian spring, the sentry laughing at their scramble. "The first five of us drank our fill, and when the sixth man began drinking the guard suddenly pushed his bayonet down into the man's neck and back." Why? When parched prisoners came on a carabao (water buffalo) wallow coated with green scum, their guard laughed and waved them to it, but while they were drinking, the shouts of an oncoming officer sent them running back into the column; then, "with a big broad smile on his face," the Japanese ordered a search of the ranks for all who had water spots on their uniforms. Perhaps forty prisoners were lined up and shot. Why? Sometimes English-speaking officers did respond to prisoner puzzlement—"Why are you doing this to us?"—but their answers—"To teach you the humility appropriate to captives and the discipline suitable to soldiers. . . ." "Because so many of our soldiers died fighting against you"—rarely connected with American expectations. Who could understand these people?[41]

Those who escaped captivity reported a phenomenon, evident above, as mystifying as Japanese harshness, the enemy's propensity to abuse prisoners while wreathed in smiles and laughter. Nipponese soldiers chortled as they leaned from their trucks to strike plodding prisoners with staves, rifle butts, and bayonets. Guards held up before famished captives their own steaming sausages and rice—and grinned. Japanese crewmen hailed a POW survivor of a sinking ship to climb the ladder of their rescue vessel and then, just as he reached the deck, threw him back into the sea, "laughing as if it were [a] joke." No less disconcerting were smiles and other expressions that, to Americans, signified amiability but now appeared as preambles to punishment. A Japanese officer, with courtesy and seeming sympathy, offered a cigarette to each prisoner, but "After we had finished smoking . . . he proceeded to beat the living hell out of us." Who could understand these people?[42]

As a preliminary reckoning, the resort to Japanese inscrutability helped to alleviate bewilderment and to simplify the image of the enemy, for it relieved Americans of further effort to comprehend the incomprehensible and left them free to measure Japanese behavior exclusively by their own yardstick. Any Japanese "kindness," they concluded, was likely to conceal a lethal trap. Seeming considerateness simply screened enemy trickery, treachery, and even sadism. Whether in prison stockade or on the battlefield, the Japanese could not be trusted.

No Japanese—for in the Pacific, seen through American eyes—all enemy were alike. Soldiers and Marines never met Japanese who offered the ministrations of sympathetic German soldiers or surgeons; indeed, all Japanese seemed dedicated solely to killing them. And behind Japan's soldiery seemed to stand a nation of identical resolve. During the war, "One hundred million [people], one mind" was the favored slogan of the Tokyo government. "We shall never cease fire til our enemies cease to be!" became the national war cry for Army Memorial Day, 1943. The *kamikaze* ("divine wind") phenomenon of late 1944–45 and Tokyo's late war attempts to present—and prepare—the populace as a "special [i.e., suicide] attack force" all appeared as logical extensions of a profound commitment. Americans interned in Asia and then returned home aboard the liner *Gripsholm* in mid-October 1942 thought it essential that their compatriots understand this iron resolve: "Practically every Japanese is 100 percent behind the crusade . . . they are carrying on. . . . Only . . . complete defeat can ever [break down their idea of a divine origin and a divine mission]. . . . [They] have a singleness of purpose which as yet we cannot match." Twenty months later, a War Department poll of fighting units revealed that Pacific soldiers were almost twice as likely as European theater soldiers to believe it necessary to "wipe out" the enemy nation.[43]

"The Japs are crazy!"

Here the point of departure was the American conviction that the Japanese cared nothing for human existence. "Those ———— ———— Japs," railed a Marine on Guadalcanal, "they're crazy. They don't think anything of human life. Plain crazy, sick in the head, that's all." Crewmen assailed as "crazy sons o' bitches" the Japanese pilots who dove upon their vessels. And if the failure to value life was evidence of derangement, the absence of any fear of death was conclusive.[44]

More ominous but more intriguing to Americans was the conviction that soldiers unafraid of dying were afraid of nothing. Here, ordinarily enclosed within denunciations of the Japanese as demented, lay an authentic respect for Japanese fearlessness. Combat troops told Seaman James Fahey that "[The] Japs are as tough and fierce as they come; the Jap is not afraid to die. . . ." Later, Fahey found an object lesson as he watched his vessel's heavy guns pound Japanese pillboxes on Bougainville: "Those Japs have plenty of guts; they are not afraid of anything." When, on Okinawa, the Japanese withheld their fire until the Marines were ashore, a young rifleman new to combat suggested, "'Maybe we got the Japs scared.' Everybody laughed. 'The Japs just don't get scared,' somebody told him. 'You'll see.'" P-40 pilot Robert Scott "once saw . . . fear" in the face of a Japanese flyer he was about to shoot down over China; he employed that experience repeatedly to bring relief to the younger airmen of his squadron: "it always made them feel better to know that the Japs were afraid. . . ." Marine Russell Davis remembered lying in a clearing on Peleliu, pondering his own and his opponents' fear: "I didn't believe the Japs were scared. Until I had personal friends among the Japanese after the war, I didn't believe that Japanese even felt fear." To Americans arriving in combat, the prospect of death in battle seemed the ultimate fear; few considered that enemy soldiers too suffered fright at the likelihood of their own deaths but might subordinate that fear to others felt even more powerfully—the fear of failure, the fear of isolation from fellow Japanese.[45]

Bravery and fearlessness were traits Americans ordinarily admired, but here they heavily discounted them as built upon irrationality. "Wherever they have fought in this war," Marine sergeant Herman Kogan believed, "the Japs have shown an amazing aptitude for the queer and fantastic." They "staged solemn funeral processions in the midst of hot battles" and "danced wildly atop ridges while exposed to American fire." On Guam, a group of shirtless Japanese "paraded solemnly in single file in front of the Marine line. Then they moved forward again. They executed this step several times before they were shot down." A single Japanese appeared on a crest and shouted to the Marines below, "One, two, three, you can't catch me!" On Cape Gloucester, enemy attackers roared, "Gimme back my hill! Gimme back my hill!" and, "To hell with Babe Ruth! To hell with Babe Ruth!" In almost every campaign there arose from the Japanese "shrieks and bloodcurdling yells from the darkness of the jungles"—"crazy howls," Kogan called them. So ingrained became the conviction of Japanese lunacy that Ernie Pyle illustrated the enemy's "silliness" with the report of a lone Japanese in the Marianas who appeared one evening before an unarmed American officer sitting on an outdoor box toilet, laid down his rifle, and knelt in submission. He explained that for two weeks he had, with what now appears utter reasonableness, been searching for an American who would not shoot him down on sight. But perhaps by that point in the war comprehensible Japanese action no longer seemed possible.[46]

Enemy tactics seemed to confirm mental aberration. Exhibit number one was the banzai charge. At first, some apprehension hovered over the prospect of close-quarters combat. Marines who had observed Japanese training during tours of duty in China circulated on Bataan disturbing reports. "[The] Japanese infantryman was trained in jiu-jitsu," a system of hand-to-hand fighting employing surprise—notably a frightening *"Kee-yi"* cry—and body leverage to defeat heavier and stronger opponents. "The Japanese used to boast that if an American and a Japanese infantryman were advancing . . . with fixed bayonets . . . the Japanese would always win, because, just before making a mighty lunge with his bayonet, the Jap would utter this terrifying 'kee-yi' and paralyze his American opponent, delivering the death blow to his heart before he could fully recover from the shock." Heightening the sense of intimidation on Guadalcanal was the recent record—"For nine months, Allied units had sometimes bolted to the rear abandoning duty and dignity when confronted by shrieking Japanese infantry. . . ."—and the realization that Nipponese soldiers were far more willing than Americans to risk, and sacrifice, their lives to inflict casualties on their enemies. But the banzai charge, when it came on Guadalcanal, impressed Americans only at first with its menace and then, lastingly, with its madness.[47]

In the Battle of the Tenaru, Colonel Kiyoano Ichiki sent 1,200 veteran soldiers—"clean, well dressed and splendidly equipped"—lunging toward two reinforced Marine regiments, perhaps 4,500 men. The Japanese did not bring up their artillery or call on nearby naval vessels for supporting fire; in charge upon charge, they hurled themselves against dug-in Americans. Survivors did not withdraw but awaited the daylight's lethal pounding by American artillery and aircraft. Colonel Ichiki burned his regiment's colors and sent a bullet through his own head. Forty-four defenders died; no more than a handful of attackers lived. Frank Hough declared the banzai charge "plain silly." It may have won battles in China and the Dutch East Indies, GI John George calculated, but it thereafter lost the war for Japan. The charging soldier "makes a big target . . . and usually announces his exact location . . . with a lot of loud yelling. The poorest shot can mow him down with ease, even with a bolt action rifle. With a semi- or full-automatic weapon you can stop a banzai charge with usually negligible casualties on your own side. A hundred Japs to one Yank was not an infrequent ratio." On Guadalcanal, the banzai charge "became the very symbol of Japanese stupidity."[48]

Later banzai assaults introduced elements that further dispelled American fear—and correspondingly heightened American disgust. Saipan's, on July 7, 1944, was the greatest of the war, sweeping up the three thousand remaining members of the Japanese garrison:

> Behind the enemy assault formations moved a weird, almost unbelievable procession: the lame, the halt and the blind, literally. The sick and wounded from the hospitals had come forth to die. Bandage-swathed men, amputees, men on crutches, walking wounded helping each other along. Some were armed, some carried only a bayonet lashed to a long pole or a few grenades, many had no weapons of any sort. . . . The carnage [was] ghastly beyond belief. Burial parties needed days to deal with the . . . dead. . . . One single space about an acre in extent was entirely covered with them.

Hough's conclusion was again disdainful: "As regards its only conceivable object, suicide, General Saito's banzai had been an unqualified success." Such charges "never in the course of the entire war achieved any results of importance. . . ." Marine lieutenant general Holland Smith so agreed that he began to welcome Japanese attacks: "This is generally when we break their backs." Fighters in the field came to regard the banzai charge, said Merrill Twining, the 1st Marine Division's assistant operations officer, "as a sure sign of American victory."[49]

What most astonished Americans was the seeming willingness of the Japanese to eliminate *themselves* as military factors, to subtract themselves from the equation of force that determined battle verdicts. On Bataan's

Quinauan Point, Dyess and his men suddenly heard "above the noise of the gunfire . . . shrieks and high-pitched yelling. Scores of Japs were tearing their uniforms and leaping off the cliffs." Soon the beach below was "littered with bodies." On Kwajalein, five Japanese officers rushed an American tank and flailed its armored plate with their swords until astonished crewmen killed them. On Guam, three Japanese, occupying a Marine emplacement whose machine-gun crew they had killed, found it difficult to reverse the weapon to bear on the next American position. "Finally the Japs tried to lift the entire gun on its mount and turn the whole thing. A Marine . . . blasted them with his BAR. . . . Two of them fell over the bodies of the Marine crew. [The] third pulled out a grenade and, holding it to his head, blew himself up."[50]

On an Okinawan beach, as Marines moved to trap a group of seven Japanese, its officer gave "emphatic orders" that drove his men to extend their necks to receive the slashing strokes of his sword; when all were dead, he took to the water and defiantly beat his sword against the surf until the approaching Americans shot him down. "What code," Ernie Pyle wondered, "led the officer to kill his own men rather than let them fight to the death...?" A Marine sentry guarding a command post atop a ridge on one of the Marianas islands heard a noise and fired a shot into the darkness below. There followed a large explosion: a Japanese soldier had held a grenade to his chest. Again Pyle was puzzled: "Why he did that, instead of tossing it up over the bluff and getting himself a half dozen Americans is beyond an American's comprehension."[51]

Anton Myrer depicted young Marines grappling with the fate of a wounded Japanese soldier who had just blown himself up.

> *Woodruff:* "Jesus, I couldn't do that. Jesus."
> *O'Neill:* "You think that took guts?"
> *Woodruff:* "Sure I do. . . ."
> *O'Neill:* "The hell it did. He just couldn't stand the gaff. They do it every time they get in a squeeze."
> *Derekman:* "What the hell. . . . He was [a goner], anyway. We'd have got him: he probably knew it."
> *O'Neill:* "Okay—but he knew where *we* were by then, too. Why didn't he give you that grenade? What's so rugged about blowing your own guts out when you know you're going to go anyway? Why not at least take two or three with you on the way down? Son of a bitch took the easy way out—"
> *Woodruff:* "I don't rightly know. I just wouldn't have the guts to do that. I know I wouldn't. . . ."

As the war proceeded, Americans increasingly regarded such incidents as exemplifying weakness rather than strength. A suitably climactic event occurred on Okinawa when, in a rare instance of a Pacific theater truce, the Japanese asked Americans to hold their fire, not to save the lives of the wounded but to allow Japanese officers "time to commit suicide according to traditional ritual." What people would go so far as to do its enemies' job for them? "These Nips are nuts!"—a dismissal rather than an explanation—seemed to cover it all.[52]

"The Japs aren't human."

The inexplicability of Japanese behavior in tandem with the conviction of the enemy's singular cruelty led to another verdict: that the Japanese lacked all humanity.

The first to reach this judgment were prisoners of war. As soldiers on Bataan gathered at Mariveles to surrender, the victors found on one private a small amount of Japanese money, "positive proof"—to captors but not to captives—"that he had either killed or robbed a Jap or both." The American was executed with a saber. John Emerick stared at the headless body and thought, "Oh Christ, we are really in trouble. These people aren't human." Later, in Japan, forced to mine coal in freezing weather without protective clothing, Emerick returned to the refrain: "Those sons of bitches. They aren't human. Nobody can tell me they're human." To fighting men too, Japanese cruelty signaled an absence of humanness. Marine Raider Mario Sabatelli was wounded in wild combat on Tulagi. "I guess I passed out a couple of times, but I'd come to and fight . . . to stay conscious because I knew what the Japs do to the wounded. They just aren't human." William Camp's protagonist, in the moment before he opened fire on those sixty Japanese resting on the beach, pondered what he was about to do: "I felt my stomach . . . cave in a little, and I got weak between the shoulder blades. [But] I couldn't feel sorry for them. I remembered everything I had ever heard or ever seen about them. I couldn't think of them as human beings with hearts and minds and feelings and loved ones. To me they were the demons who had killed in cold blood and raped and robbed and tortured." Private Henry DeBoer, Jr., a Marine BAR gunner on Tulagi, explained that "they weren't anything human, as far as we were concerned. Every time I pumped a bullet into a Jap, I had the feeling I was getting rid of something unclean."[53]

John Hersey was "surprised" and somewhat disoriented to find "intimations of humanity"—a flag inscribed lovingly by friends, a snapshot of a girl—

on the bodies of dead Japanese. "What do you think about the enemy as people?" was the question put to Herman Steenstra, a radio-section sergeant in the 32d Division. "Never thought of them as people," he replied. Home-front war posters represented both European and Asian enemies as murderers and rapists. However harsh the depiction of the Germans—often as sharp-beaked, monocled, ugly Nazi executioners—they retained human form. The Japanese became smiling, brutal rat and monkey men.[54]

"The Japs are animals."

Denials that the enemy were human injected the problem of an alternative imagery: If they were not people, what were they?

"Though the Japanese possessed considerable cleverness," in Grady Gallant's sardonic estimation, "the average Nip could not be classified as an intellectual. He was more of an animal." Marine general Holland Smith believed that Japanese soldiers "were taught to live and die like animals." From Guadalcanal, John Hersey sent home a précis of Marine opinion: the Leathernecks wished that "we were fighting against Germans. They are human beings, like us. But the Japs are like animals. Against them you have to learn a whole new set of physical reactions. You have to get used to their animal stubbornness and tenacity." The United States, Hersey concluded, would win only when Americans "sacrificed as bitterly as our animal adversary seems willing to." Elsewhere, he described from his imagination a Japanese mortar squad in action:

> After each report [the officer] would bark out brief orders. A swarm of intelligent little animals would fuss around each tube, changing the angle a hair, turning the aim a trifle. Then the officer would shout to stand by. Some of the animals would step back; one or two at each tube would put their fingers in their ears. Then one . . . would reach out over the mouth of each tube. . . .[55]

Even their accomplishments tied the Japanese to an animal existence. The Japanese soldier, after allowance for a smaller average physique, sustained himself on far less food than GIs consumed. "He seemed to eat almost nothing and yet fight like an animal, or rather like the whole animal kingdom compressed into a nearly human frame." Japanese forces resisted the American invasion of every atoll with a fierceness seldom equaled. "If we try to take island by island it will take years to beat the Japs because they are like animals and you have to go into or blow them out of every foxhole, lime cave, or coconut tree and kill them all. . . ."[56]

Infantryman Ken Curley was skeptical that the American public understood the enemy's animal nature. "It's just difficult to explain to anyone else . . . that these people, these Japs, are just animals." On the other hand, Sherwood Moran, one of the Navy's specialists in Japanese culture and language, had no such doubt. At war's end he saw, with sadness, much evidence that would have delighted Curley that his compatriots at home envisaged Germans as "simply misguided human beings, susceptible of re-education, while the Japanese were animals to whom decent behavior could not be taught. . . ."[57]

American soldiers took up a variety of discrete animal images—"the Japanese . . . in all things like to move as a pack, as a swarm of bees"; ". . . the Jap . . . at night . . . fights like a jackal"; "The Japs are lice"; etc.—but the most frequent invocation of an individual species was of monkeys. "They ain't nothing but a bunch of monkeys." "In the Pacific," Pyle reported, "the Marines have an expression of their own for the Japs. They called them 'Japes,' which is a combination of 'Jap' and 'ape.'" On Wake Island, Marines cheering the repulse of the enemy's first thrust from the sea "decided that the little bucktoothed monkey people would think two times or three before they came back. . . ." As a composite Army unit moved forward into dense jungle on Bataan, a private asked William Dyess, "Cap'n, how will we tell which are Japs and which are monkeys?" Before Dyess could reply, a sergeant answered for him, "Just kill 'em all, son. We can eat the ones that ain't got uniforms on." Caught up in the frenzy of night battle on Guadalcanal, Marine sergeant Al Schmid taunted the Japanese to renew their assault on his machine-gun emplacement: "Come on, you yellow monkeys, come and get it!" Jerry Angel, a replacement first lieutenant in the 32d Division during its return to the Philippines, was asked what he thought of the enemy as people: "Monkey men!" At a Los Angeles press conference, Admiral William "Bull" Halsey, naval air strategist and commander of several Pacific fleets, spoke of the Japanese as the "little yellow monkeys."[58]

Almost as prevalent were allusions to the enemy as rats. Japanese, said Al Schmid, "always looked slinky to me. Those slanty eyes they had would always get to me. They just reminded me of some dirty little rat." GIs with whom Pyle spoke perceived enemy soldiers as "slippery" and "rat-like." The Japanese as rat, like the Japanese as maniac and the Japanese as monkey, transited from war front to home front, becoming a staple of both media and playground exchange. Ron Veenker, who grew up during the war in a small South Dakota community, remembered that "if we wanted to be in big trouble, we'd get angry and call the other kid a dirty Jap rat. That was the filthiest thing you could say."[59]

Other figures combined stereotypical characterizations. "Mad dogs" drew on the Japanese as lunatics and as animals; Hersey's "a swarm of intelligent little animals" on the Japanese as of small stature, a constantly repeated reference, and as animals; "a gang of silly, teethy, grinning apes" and "smirking Nipponese apes" on the Japanese as both sadists and simians.[60]

"The Japs are jungle animals."

Key to the way that monkey-ape imagery dominated the idiom was its connection with what Americans regarded as the Pacific theater's dominant terrain feature: the jungle. They assumed that they as a people were temperamentally at odds, and the Japanese in harmony, with jungle existence.

To Americans, the jungle conjured darkness and danger, stealth and predation; it was forbidding, even impenetrable. "There was a long line of jungle about a hundred and fifty yards from the bivouac," wrote James Jones of Guadalcanal. "Off through the coconut trees and through the steaming, chill curtain of tropical rain it looked more like a massive wall than anything else. Dense, solid . . . up [its] steep green slope one could climb, to walk over the top on a surface at least as solid as the wet earth on which [we] stood." Those compelled to breach this mass found there no fit place for Americans. A sense of the sinister hovered over the jungle. "[It] loomed there," Jones went on, "alien, supremely confident . . . a fact of nature . . . ominous to the human ego."[61]

The desert's "antiseptic effect" and "enforced monasticism" seemed to spur the spirit upward, toward worthiness; the jungle's impulse was atavistic, pressing one into relapse. "Whatever else you could call this teeming verdure," said Jones, "you certainly could not call it civilized. And as civilized men, it made [members of the unit] fearful. The toughest barroom brawler among them was fearful." Some American soldiers, as Hersey observed, suffered "a curious psychological quirk"—a debilitating sensation of being trapped first within the jungle and then within a war with no exit or end. "Looking across the African desert, standing on an open hill in . . . Italy and looking down onto an open plain, men can see the avenue ahead. But in the encircling, limitless jungle there seems no way out, no end." On Guadalcanal, "the Americans tended to stick to the grassy heights. . . ." "These open spaces were our natural terrain. They were American. . . ."[62]

The average Marine's antipathy to the jungle, and to its topography's moral dimensions, was, as Kenneth Davis learned, profound.

[Fighting erupts] so fast, without warning! But then it always does in the jungle—the stinking jungle. God, how he hates this closed-in, stealthy, dirty kind of fighting in a terrain where there is no freedom of movement and practically zero visibility! . . . Here all is cramped, narrow, turned in upon itself; an inward-spiraling darkness. Here a man hasn't a chance to brace himself against shock, no time to choose between different . . . responses to fatal challenges, and the decision goes not to the fairest and bravest and strongest but to the liar, the sneak, the cheat.[63]

The jungle, then, offered vantage to the enemy, not alone because it was inimical to the American spirit but because it perfectly fit the Japanese. "They take to the jungle," Hersey held, "as if they had been bred there. . . ." Yes, the open spaces were American, but "the jungle was Jap. . . . Each side derived certain advantages from following its bent. On the ridges, the Americans could dominate the jungle with their fire-power, and they could see what was going on. In the jungle, the Japs could hide themselves in ambush, and they could lead the Americans into easy traps." Kenneth Davis, too, underscored the enemy's tactical ascendancy in the jungle. Guadalcanal was "Jap kind of fighting in Jap kind of country—gloomy, tricky, full of sickness and a sudden stab-in-the-dark kind of death. . . . The fact [is] that the Jap prefers this terrain to any other. . . ." Aboard troopships bound for Guadalcanal, American briefing officers read to enlisted men from manuals outlining the startling success of Lieutenant General Tomoyuki Yamashita's forces in descending the Malay peninsula to seize Singapore, and then pronounced the Japanese soldier "the greatest jungle fighter in the world." Army sergeant Myles Babcock was convinced: "We cannot compete with Japs in jungle conditions. Truly a white man's graveyard."[64]

Americans so discomfited by the jungle easily connected it and its animals with the enemy. That the Japanese chose dark forests over open spaces was, Kenneth Davis posited, "one of the elements of [the Marine's] belief that the enemy, after all, isn't truly human but a furtive jungle animal. A reptile, say. A poisonous reptile." In May 1942, correspondent Cecil Brown, reviewing enemy infiltration and envelopment tactics that had attained so much in Malaya, Burma, Java, and the Philippines, wrote that Japanese soldiers "climbed trees like monkeys and even swung on jungle vines like Tarzans in order to get around the enemy." The monkey-Japanese effortlessly clambering up trunks, the reptile-Japanese slithering silently through the brush—these became soldier and Marine articles of faith. No more difficult was the transition from Guadalcanal and New Guinea jungles to Pacific atolls, from rain forests to caves and caverns and other underground bastions, from images of the enemy as animals that fought by slinking and climbing to those that dug—"squirming into the sand" . . . "burrowing like rats in holes and in piles of rubbish."[65]

The scarcity of visible enemy reinforced the sense of animal adversaries. Set against sightings in North Africa and Western Europe, those in the Pacific were sparse. That the Japanese were invisible, insisted infantryman Douglas Valentine, was "the scariest part of the fighting in New Guinea." Soldiers at Buna, *Life* reported, "sometimes . . . would go for days without seeing a living Jap." Sergeant Asa Bordages described the frustration of Marine assaults across Suicide Creek on Cape Gloucester: "[The attackers] would be hit and pull back, and then [other] detachments would push across the creek at other points. They'd be blasted by invisible machine guns, and leave a few more Marines dead in the brush as they fell back across the creek. Then they'd do it all over again. . . . You don't know where the enemy is. His pillboxes are so camouflaged that you can usually find them only when they fire on you." Four times those in PFC Calvin King's platoon crossed the run, four times enemy fire forced them back; "not until the last time did they see a Jap." Jack Charles was with the Marines on Bougainville: "Though we spent over a month [there], engaging the enemy in several fire fights while on patrol and on line . . . I can honestly say few, if any of us, ever saw a Japanese. The jungle was that thick." On Iwo Jima, noted Albert Hemingway, "Few, if any, Japanese were seen. . . . While the assault troops were attacking one fortification, the Japanese could scamper [through their intricate cave and tunnel system] and fire on them from the rear. It was a case of one army entirely above ground and the other below." Front-line Marines who caught sight of one of the few prisoners "would stop and gawk. It was the first time [that some] had seen a live Japanese since landing on Iwo Jima."[66]

Enemy "invisibility" lent itself to animal imagery—species elusive, predacious, menacing—and to other vocabulary of its own, one of specters. The Japanese "were like phantoms slipping silently in between the trees, living in the shadows. . . ." "This enemy was . . . quiet as a ghost. . . ." Ernie Pyle combined both sets of figures when he reported from the Marianas in late February 1945 his partial recovery from "that creepy feeling that fighting Japs is like fighting snakes or ghosts."[67]

The ultimate effects of all this imagery were mixed. To envisage the enemy as an animal somewhat diminished his capacity in contention with human beings but sometimes seemed to enhance the danger he posed. More debilitating, notably in the first stages of warfare against the Japanese, was the accompanying conviction that the enemy was at one with the environment being contested, that the Japanese had merged with the jungle jointly to victimize American soldiers. During battle on Bataan, an American sergeant fighting with the Philippine Scouts became convinced that "the goddamn jungle had even gone over to the Japs' side." "The work, the jungle, the mud, the Japs," said Army private James Johns, fighting on Guadalcanal, "it all comes together to make one bad nightmare."[68]

The emergence of these views distilled the Pacific campaign to a warfare of far greater simplicity than that waged in Western Europe: no rules complicated the encounter with the enemy, no respect inhibited action against him. By the end of 1942 the uncertainties and ambiguities had disappeared, leaving behind an intense, unmixed antagonism. The Pacific conflict had reduced itself to war's fundamentals: killing and dying. In the minds of American soldiers and Marines, their role was to kill Japanese; the role of the Japanese was to die. Accordingly, those in the Pacific regularly voiced their intentions in ways expressed by European GIs only in the hours following friends' deaths in battle. A Polish American PFC on Tarawa said of his Japanese enemies, "I just want to kill them all—that's all." John Ciardi told Studs Terkel, "I did want every Japanese dead. . . . We were there to eliminate them." As early as the Marine landing on Florida Island in late August 1942, Private Henry DeBoer registered the new consensus: "By this time we all had the same feeling about Japs. We just wanted to kill them." As the invasion force approached Peleliu, a Marine first sergeant said to his men, in the low key of a necessity accepted, "We'll have to kill every little yellow bastard there."[69]

Obliteration of the enemy had become the sole means to the nation's victory over Japan and to the Pacific soldier's personal survival. By contrast, there persisted in Europe a sense of complementary routes to the same goals. Killing every enemy soldier seemed unnecessary. Victory could be achieved and deaths minimized by expelling German forces from the territory they had seized and by continuing to push them into Germany until, with the Russians pressing on them from the east, the enemy surrendered. The destruction of German soldiers was a function not of an Allied conviction that all must be killed but of the recognition that losses of a certain scale would be necessary to break down their ability to resist being pushed back. Indeed, the faster they retreated, the less became the necessity to kill those who remained. Defeat of the enemy did not become synonymous with destruction of the enemy.

One sees again the centrality of both topography and the antagonists' attitudes toward surrender. The way to Tokyo was not the road to Berlin. The Japanese neither could nor would be pushed back. The loss of naval supremacy diminished drastically their ability to evacuate Pacific garrisons, just as the growing threat to the home islands stiffened them against the abandonment of any piece of their protective barrier. "Japs do not leave any place they hold," declared General W. E. Lynd. "They don't go away." Islands had to be seized and those on them who would neither leave nor surrender had to be destroyed. "You just kill them," said Lynd. No one in the war zone or at home had an alternative approach to offer. The American commander in China and Burma, Joseph "Vinegar Joe" Stilwell, would not allow his economic and psychological war experts to demonstrate their effectiveness by adducing evidence of declining Japanese resources or morale; they "had to prove their worth in body counts." "[The] only way to beat [this] enemy," Stilwell was sure, "was to kill him. . . ." At home, *Life* published a photograph of a Japanese soldier incinerated by an American flamethrower, the "most cruel and terrifying weapon ever developed. . . . But so long as the Jap refuses to come out of his holes and keeps killing, this is the only way."[70]

On Guadalcanal, Merrill Twining came upon a suspicious Japanese "body." Approaching from the rear and seeing no wounds, he and the corpsman accompanying him kicked away the enemy's weapon and began to tie him up; suddenly the Japanese soldier rose up, "broke away and ran to recover his rifle." In a sentence that might have served as the watchword of Americans throughout the Pacific theater, Twining closed his story: "There was only one thing for me to do."[71]

No one distilled the situation more casually, or chillingly, than Grady Gallant: to Marines, "War was killing. Seeking out the enemy and killing. Killing without mercy. Killing for God and country. It was something like being a Boy Scout. You camped out. You killed for God and country. There was no plan to die."[72]

To the degree that GIs and Marines were given to contemplate enemy reactions to this austere and primal warfare, they at first thought that the Japanese would fulfill their role—dying—with indifference. "To them," said Twining, "their death did not seem to matter." Soon, however, Americans told one another that the enemy *wanted* to die. They fought not to win or even to survive but to die—and not only willingly but happily. Americans, Gallant observed, "were men who planned to live and to live and to live," whereas "The Japanese wished to die for the Emperor," so Marines would

". . . help [them] die." "It was the only gentlemanly thing to do." Official Japanese declarations occasionally gave credence to such ideas.[73]

In its issue of November 1, 1943, *Life* published prints of the Kabuki dramatization of Japan's most celebrated vendetta: In 1701, the Forty-Seven Rōnin, samurai retainers who vowed vengeance against a lord who had forced their own feudal master to commit suicide following an indiscretion, killed him and then themselves. *Life* found in the play's immense popularity "the very essence of Japan"—"the bloodthirsty character of our enemy. . . . Their military behavior in this war has revealed a cold-blooded ruthlessness, not only toward their enemy but also toward themselves, that has shocked us." The article provoked a reply from Radio Tokyo: "The magazine *Life* takes up *The Vendetta of 47 Rōnin* as an illustration of the Japanese outlook on life which culminates in the act of taking one's own life for the cause. The only reason for which . . . Japanese men chose that manner of death on Attu and [in the] Gilbert[s] was the happiness and satisfaction they could derive from it. . . . It is a pity that this sense of moral happiness and satisfaction is lacking in those American fighting men who meet with death in this war." American soldiers thought it bizarre that anyone would find fulfillment in death, but they also found in the enemy's ability to do so a way to ease their own passage from "Thou shall not kill" of their 1930s youth to "You just kill them" of the mid-war years. The Japanese, foxhole banter insisted, desired to die.[74]

Without a consensus establishing limits, without the restraint of rules, battlefield behavior on both sides spun into a downward cycle.

By American reckoning, the Japanese descent came earlier and dipped deeper than the conduct of GIs and Marines. Here, one should not overlook the degree to which the China war had contributed to the barbarization of Japan's military. Army doctors killed Chinese prisoners in order to practice surgical techniques and to extract from internal organs microbes with which to culture plague for use in bacteriological warfare.[75]

In Tsingtao, at the end of the war, U.S. Army language officer Donald Keene's interviews with Koreans in Japanese service confirmed *Life*'s report of eight years earlier that Japanese units had regularly employed executions of Chinese civilians (called "communists," "criminals," or "bandits") to harden the "fighting spirit" of soldier and sailor trainees. "Why did you order your men to bayonet the Chinese?" Lieutenant Mochihara: "I thought it would be good practice for the younger men." Captain Okabe: "We expected an American landing. . . . Our naval troops here were mostly young boys with no knowledge of war and no particular feeling of combat spirit.

Something had to be done to ready [them] for the battles in which they were soon to engage." "About half [of the sailors] didn't seem to want to take part in the bayoneting," Mochihara explained, "but naturally no one complained. Every man took his turn." Some prisoners were denied food and water in order to contract and harden their livers, which were cut out immediately following the killings and prepared for consumption. "Every month from five to twenty persons were executed to keep up the supply of liver," a Korean policeman in Japanese employ told Keene. "It was supposed to be good for all ailments. The officers, particularly the high-ranking ones, regularly took this medicine." Keene, a critic of his own country's ignorance of Japanese culture, thought at first that his informants were joking, but when investigation corroborated both practices, he was shaken: "It is sordid brutality—worse, utter degeneracy."[76]

In Burma, Colonel Masanobu Tsuji and members of his staff ate the liver of a British or American pilot. "The more we consume the more we shall be inspired by a hostile spirit towards the enemy."[77]

In the Pacific, the impulse to kill oneself degenerated into the killing of other Japanese. Some doctors took the lives of their patients and some soldiers those of their civilian compatriots. In the mass suicide at Marpi Point on Saipan, soldiers pushed from clifftops civilians who evinced any hesitation. When a family of five walked into the ocean planning to drown themselves but then returned to shore, a Japanese soldier shot the mother and father but missed another Japanese woman who ran from her hiding place to sweep up the three children. Worse, "aiding" others to die metamorphosed on Saipan, Tinian, and Okinawa into spectacular outbursts of anger expressed in destructive frenzy. On Okinawa, survivors of the 32d Army raped and murdered large numbers of civilians.[78]

The Pacific War's most severe slide into savagery, in tragic echo of Nanking, came at Manila on February 17–March 3, 1945, during the American reconquest of the Philippines. Admiral Sanji Iwabuchi, ignoring the orders of his superior, Lieutenant General Tomoyuki Yamashita, to retreat from the city, imposed on his own 20,000 sailors and marines and on an infantry rearguard of 1,600 his resolve to fight to the end—and to carry with them into death as many enemy as possible, American soldiers *and* Filipino civilians. As Lawrence Taylor reconstructed what happened, "Iwabuchi issued . . . orders to . . . lay waste to the city! The men were instructed that they were to die for the emperor but that their deaths should be paid for in enemy lives. Beer, *sake,* and wine from Manila's shops were distributed to the men, and within hours [Iwabuchi's] force was a raging, drunken mob." The result was an "intoxicated fury of revenge and despair . . . an orgy of burning, shooting, raping, and torture" that, before advancing Americans killed the last Japanese, consumed the lives of almost sixty thousand Filipinos, including babies, young girls, old women, and hospital patients. The Manila massacre, Taylor concluded, was "one of the most tragic and heinous incidents in the annals of 'civilized' warfare."[79]

American combatants were not immune to the corroding impulses provided room for expression by the boundlessness of the Pacific War.

Nanking was a case not of common soldiers gone berserk but of high-command intent. Admiral Iwabuchi incited what happened in Manila. The point of departure for American actions violating the other war's rules, however, was far less often direction from above. An exception, one standing alone in its remove from the combat-zone dynamic here described, was the U.S. Navy's decision, immediately after the attack on Pearl Harbor, to wage unrestricted submarine warfare and thus to sink Japanese fishing, merchant, and passenger vessels. The most conspicuous battlefield exception, one implicating the chain of command at least as high as theater headquarters, was the use of asphyxial gases against Japanese soldiers—and island civilians—in Okinawa's caves. A student nurse, Kikuko Miyagi, was with a group in which two teachers and three fifteen-year-old students lost their lives. "The way they died! Their bodies swelled up and turned purple. There were no injuries. It was like they suffocated to death. They thrashed about so much we had to tie up their arms and legs like the soldiers with brain fever." In a nearby cavern, forty-six out of fifty-one people who had hidden died in the same way.[80]

But American barbarousness did not often derive from command design. That was the point Donald Keene tried to make in postwar conversations with Japanese acquaintances.

> When I speak of the terrible things that the Japanese have done, I am not saying that individual Americans are not capable of acts of wickedness themselves. . . . If you want to know if Americans haven't done the same things of which I have accused the Japanese, I will say that they have indeed committed some of those atrocities, but always individually and not as part of an organized program of immorality. There is no parallel to the savagery shown by the mass of Japanese soldiers at Nanking or at various other places in China. . . .[81]

The dominant pattern was one in which the initiative appeared at the level of individual Americans, sometimes moved out to permeate large units, but just as often encountered wide variation in soldiers' susceptibility to participation. Few, however, failed to acquiesce. Conduct regarded as deviant in France, though not often ordered by Pacific commanders, was licensed by those in authority whose views of the enemy remained obdurate. "The only good Jap," said Admiral William Halsey for publication, "is a Jap who's been dead six months." "When we get through with them, the Japanese language will be spoken only in hell." Command officers ignored and field officers condoned much that elsewhere they would have moved against. GIs and Marines who had reservations about battlefield practices seldom found a unit consensus willing to draw lines and to chastise those who stepped beyond.[82]

Hot-anger vengeance killings continued against the Japanese as against the Germans. Marines on Cape Gloucester, after finding comrades trussed and bayoneted, closed in on the enemy unit they held responsible; from it came running a group of Japanese nurses, their breasts exposed "to show they were females," but the Marines, as they told Sy Kahn, "cut them down unmercifully." Peculiar to the Pacific, however, were actions that had been adopted as essential to survival, and then became so ingrained that they persisted where survival was no longer at stake.[83]

The early conclusion that it was necessary to kill all enemy because the Japanese became prisoners only to kill more Americans developed such momentum that it left behind the connection between what was done and why it had to be done; it was automatically assumed that every Japanese threatened American lives, any evidence to the contrary notwithstanding. "Possum Patrols" riddled all enemy within reach, the wounded with the impostors. Actually taking prisoners, once the attempt to do so had been expunged from what Americans construed as the flow of battle, became most difficult, requiring sharp, laborious breaks with established practice. Some exerted themselves only halfheartedly. On Okinawa, Nisei language officers were surprised when a Marine unit requested their assistance for the interrogation of several Japanese prisoners. "You know the Marines. They fight their way in, and they fight their way out. Taking prisoners only slows them down." Four interpreters succeeded in making their way to the rear sector where the Japanese were held, but its personnel—cooks, clerks, medics, etc.—had just been brought under fire by Japanese snipers. "You can guess what happened to the POWs. We never got any." Some made it a point not to try. The members of Company I, 184th Regiment, 7th Division, shared an understanding that no Japanese would be captured, and the unit completed five island campaigns before it took a prisoner—"the secret pride of our Company," as rifleman Joseph Routledge described its record.[84]

As the killing of all Japanese became habitual, so did it seem to become casual. When a Japanese soldier, one of three trapped by Marines, spoke out in English, pleading that he had a wife and three children, a Leatherneck shot him down and quipped, "Now he has a widow and three orphans." During fighting near Munda, three Japanese, jarred from a coconut tree, lay on the ground "dazed but alive." A Marine of long service, glancing at his captain as he said, "This is the way we used to do it in Nicaragua," drove his knife into the throat of one, then into the chest of the second, and finally, while suppressing the third's strugglings, into the man's abdomen, as if his actions were but demonstrations of a long-ago bush war.[85]

But beneath an offhand style, anger at the enemy continued to intensify the violence. "I got so tired of seein' guys get hit and banged up," said Marine Eugene Sledge, "the more I felt like takin' it out on the Japanese. The feeling grew and grew. . . . We had orders not to kill the wounded," Sledge added, "to try to take prisoners. . . . But the feeling was strong. . . ." In some so strong that killing owed much more to murderousness than to necessity. From a PT boat exploring coves on New Britain's Arawe Peninsula, a Japanese American language officer called out into the night in Japanese urging enemy soldiers to surrender. When voices responded, crewmen fastening on the sound opened fire with the vessel's two .50-caliber machine guns. Sy Kahn heard that members of the 41st Division, "living up to its reputation as the 'bloody butchers,'" had come upon a Japanese hospital on Biak and killed everyone in it. Private Watson confided in Arthur Miller that on New Georgia, "It stopped being a question of saving yourself from being killed. You didn't want to shoot Japs any more. More and more you found men creeping up on Japs and choking them to death when they could have shot them."[86]

John McCormick has suggested that, among Marines, combat as it evolved in the Pacific became a mode of warfare suitable to those on both sides. The Marines' analysis began as did every other: "The Japs aren't going to give up. . . . It ain't smart to try to talk them into giving up. All you're going to get is a .31-caliber bullet in the head or a grenade fragment in your guts." But these Marines did more than accommodate to the Japanese terms: they embraced them. They professed their respect for the enemy's war as "a war waged without mercy, a war in which those who surrendered were executed by their captors as spineless cowards and traitors to their own cause. . . ." "The Japs shouldn't surrender to us, and we shouldn't surrender to them."

In Europe a German machine gunner kills ten of our men and when things get hot for him he hangs up a white flag and comes out with his hands up. Even though the son of a bitch is a member of the Nazi party and has killed . . . your best friend, you're supposed to pat him on the head, hand him a ration of Texas steak, and give him a free ride to a stockade way out of range of his own artillery. Next thing you know he's in Louisiana cutting cane or in Illinois picking sweet corn. Then when the war is over, he applies for American citizenship, grabs our own girls, has a family, and enjoys the beer. All the time your friends are six feet under and missing all the fun.

But "In the kind of war we're fighting with the Japs, there's no favoritism. Everyone gets what he's got coming to him. . . . In fact, the whole psychology of the Pacific War allowed a perfect objectivity to those in the act of shooting down Japanese soldiers in a banzai charge or pouring high-octane gasoline into a Jap tunnel and tossing in a lighted match." To other Americans, it was "the dirty war"; to these Marines, it was "the simple war." Without the "distractions of things like pity or Geneva conventions," it enabled the Marines to reach to the warrior ideal, as men who "neither liked nor hated the Japanese" but who destroyed them "without anger or mercy" in "the sacrament of killing." The Pacific War was, in sum, "the right kind of war."[87]

But if killing could conceivably be a sacrament, rites often surrounding it in the Pacific—notably the degradation visited on the bodies of dead Japanese—profaned all ritual. During a lull on Peleliu, Sledge remembered, "the men stripped . . . the enemy dead [of] souvenirs. This was a gruesome business. . . . Helmet headbands were checked for flags, packs and pockets were emptied. . . . The men gloated over, compared and often swapped their prizes. It was . . . brutal, ghastly . . . and was carried out with that particular savagery that characterized the struggle between the Marines and the Japanese. It wasn't simply souvenir hunting or looting the enemy dead; it was more like Indian warriors taking scalps."[88]

Incursions on Japanese corpses reached further. "[G]old teeth," said Sledge, "were extracted." On Tulagi, as a Raider platoon sergeant went from body to body, a Marine captain objected—on grounds no broader than personal hygiene: "How in the name of heaven can you put your hand into a stinking Jap's mouth?" The sergeant waved his bag of gold teeth and shouted over that "he could sell them for a lot of money." Some used pliers; some used knives. "I've seen guys shoot Japanese wounded when it really was not necessary and knock gold teeth out of their mouths . . . ," Sledge reported. "What you did is you took your K-bar [a seven-inch fighting knife] [and] you extracted gold teeth by putting the tip of the blade on the tooth of the dead Japanese—I've seen guys do it to wounded ones—and hit the hilt . . . to knock the tooth loose." Some smashed the jaws of the dead with their rifle butts until the inlays broke free.[89]

The significance of such marauding lay less in the numbers of Americans engaged—most never pulled teeth—than in the climate of acquiescence reaching from enlisted men well into the command structure. Some might call the extractors "ghouls," but censure never crystallized as it did against rendings of German bodies. Tooth-wrenchings became another side of war to which soldiers inured themselves. On New Britain, a group of Marines "pushed down a broad trail and soon came upon a [Japanese] camp that held a scattering of bare skeletons. It was the beginning of an eerie patrol. A little farther on we came to a camp with two or three hundred skeletons, all bare. There was nothing of value present except the gold teeth in some of the skulls, and we began collecting these. Every half-mile or so along the trail we came to another camp with such skeletons. . . ."[90]

If the profit motive at least played about the extraction of teeth, another impulse informed the widespread disfigurement of Japanese bodies. At Arawe, language officers placed a badly wounded prisoner of war aboard a PT boat bound for New Guinea. "When he got there, he had no ears." A Japanese soldier who succeeded in surrendering on Iwo Jima told interrogators "how he had watched from hiding as U.S. Marines slashed the ears off corpses. . . ." On Attu, Donald Keene saw enemy corpses whose ears had been cut away. In a grotesque inversion, Japanese body parts became prized souvenirs, preferred trophies of the war coveted for a time from war front to home front. "Before I left ship," Keene wrote a friend, "a regular-Navy lieutenant commander begged me to get him a pair of ['Jap'] ears. . . . 'I promised my boy before I left Honolulu that I'd get him a pair. When [I was] off Guadalcanal in my destroyer, I saw a great big 'Jap,' must have been one of the Imperial Marines, floating in the water, but we were going too fast to stop. Damn! They would have made me a fine pair of ears. You'll get me one, though, won't you?'"[91]

Skulls commanded equal interest. On New Britain, Sy Kahn recorded in his diary that "one of the truck drivers has a Jap skull on the cab of his truck." Keene was sure that possessors of such prizes "did not cut the head off the body of a Japanese and then wait for it to reach a suitable condition. . . . It was quite possibly not a Japanese soldier's skull after all, but just one . . . picked up. . . ." But Keene was not entirely correct. At Cape Gloucester, New Britain, four members of the 495th Port Battalion went ". . . into Jap territory to see what they could see. . . . They came across two dead Japs in a foxhole that the maggots were using for stamping grounds. Later they found another that was half-buried face down to the waist, with legs sticking up. They dug him up. Jack wanted a Jap skull, so he hacked away the head. Rouse drove a bayonet through the skull just for practice. The hacked head didn't come off cleanly, leaving the lower jaw torn off. The head smelled so badly that they discarded it after taking its three gold teeth." Kahn himself found acquisition easier. Returning from the ruins of a Japanese encampment, he found in the jungle "a Jap skull" that moved him to meditate on its tenant.

> I keep thinking about [him]. Here was a living man only a few days ago. Perhaps he was an unwilling Jap soldier; perhaps he was educated, wise, had a wife and children. He might have been a good man, or he might have been one of the rapists of China, or an invader of the Philippines; he might have ended many American lives. . . . When I look [at the skull], I think about him, but I feel no pity. Have not our own men been blasted before my eyes, and might not my end be the same yet . . . ?

Sy Kahn washed the skull in the surf and decided to use it as a candleholder. "We have named him Charlie."[92]

Servicemen mailed home a variety of body parts, to mixed reception: initial enthusiasm soon infiltrated by disquietude. A store in Jackson, Mississippi, displayed in its window the skull of a Japanese soldier who had died on Guadalcanal, but when local opinion coalesced to conclude that such booty "overstepped the bounds," the proprietor removed it. *Life*'s May 22, 1944, issue published as its Picture of the Week the photograph of an Arizona war worker, a well-dressed and well-groomed woman, writing her Navy boyfriend a thank-you note for the gift that she was regarding appreciatively: a skull autographed by the lieutenant and thirteen of his friends, inscribed "This is a good Jap—a dead one picked up on the New Guinea beach" and named "Tojo" by its new owner. Four of five letters subsequently printed by *Life* denounced the undertaking on grounds moral ("revolting and horrible") and tactical ("an opportunity for potent anti-Allied propaganda"). One writer asked readers to imagine their reaction if an American skull had appeared in Japan, and another simply declared that the lieutenant's head was as empty as his gift.[93]

The American armed forces, as *Life* pointed out, "disapprove strongly of this sort of thing"; high-command directives had forbidden soldiers to take body parts. Still, no home-front consensus emerged. When *Life* earlier published a full-page picture of a Japanese skull propped by GIs against a burned-out enemy tank on Guadalcanal, a reader denounced it as "the most uncivilized, repulsive, morbid, barbarous [fourteen like adjectives followed]" of "all the pictures that have appeared in your heretofore fine magazine. . . ." Another subscriber warned that "The cruelty of war is no excuse for sadism," and asked, "Are we cannibals or headhunters to display the foe's skull . . . ?"— to which an Army corporal still in training replied that "for the duration" he would be both. These tensions were largely absent in the Pacific. A war-zone consensus existed, but it was not that at which Washington pronouncements aimed. Censors continued to find fingers being mailed home as souvenirs.[94]

The cycle of battlefield action and counteraction that dissolved so many ordinary restraints did not develop its powerful momentum free of all resistance. A minor counterweight was the antagonism front-line soldiers directed at what they castigated as rear-echelon bravado. Support soldiers, they insisted, had not earned combat trophies. In the campaign to retake Corregidor in mid-February 1945, Harry Akune parachuted onto the island; later, just as the fighting ended, he noticed a visiting "American Navy man" about to cut the ears from a prisoner and stopped him with a shout: "Go get some from a *fighting* Japanese!"[95]

A far more important check at the front itself was the apprehension of at least some fighting men that combat was degrading them. One day on Peleliu a friend offered to show Eugene Sledge "a unique souvenir," a hand he had severed from a Japanese corpse and then shriveled. Sledge gasped, "Have you gone Asiatic? You know you can't keep that thing. Some officer'll put you on report sure as hell." "Aw, Sledgehammer, nobody'll say anything. . . . [Nobody] says anything about the guys collecting gold teeth, do they?" "Maybe so, but it's just the idea of a human hand. Bury it." Here his friend's demeanor darkened: "How many Marines you reckon that hand pulled the trigger on?" The impasse broke only with the arrival of other platoon members who shared Sledge's view. "I don't want you going aboard ship with me if you got that thing. It gives me the creeps." "You dumb jerk, throw that thing away. . . ." Reluctantly, the collector "flung his unique souvenir among the rocks," and Sledge was left to ponder what had happened. "Although I didn't collect gold teeth, I had gotten used to the idea, but somehow a hand seemed to be going too far. The war had gotten to my friend; he had lost (briefly, I hoped) all his sensitivity. . . . I shuddered to think that I might do the same thing if the war went on and on." But such a local consensus was uncommon and interventions to impose it were scarcer still. Among Americans fighting in the Pacific there was no agreement on the outer limits of battlefield behavior.[96]

Callousness and barbarousness worked to debase American participants in the warfare of the Pacific. On Okinawa, American BAR fire blew away the top of a Japanese machine gunner's head, leaving the body sitting upright and exposed to the rain. Sledge, with a group of Marines resting after battle, noticed "this buddy of mine just flippin' chunks of coral into the skull. . . . Every time he'd get one in there, it'd splash. It reminded me of a child throwin' pebbles into a puddle. . . . There was nothing malicious in his action. This was just a mild-mannered kid who was now a twentieth-century savage." Sledge might have reserved that epithet for those who had already moved beyond callousness to barbarousness. Mac, said Sledge, "was a decent, clean-cut man," who during a patrol on Okinawa carefully positioned himself *vis-à-vis* the body of a Japanese soldier whose pants had been pulled below his knees. "After getting just the right angle, Mac took careful aim and squeezed off a couple of rounds. . . . [He] was trying . . . to blast off the head of the corpse's penis. He succeeded [and] he exulted. . . ."[97]

Whether the descent carried soldiers to utter insensitivity or beyond to brutalization, the price that warfare against the Japanese exacted of the individual was high. Whatever the provocation, to dehumanize the enemy had placed American soldiers on the path to their own dehumanization. A few realized it in 1944–45; most years later.

"We had all become hardened," Sledge acknowledged. "We were out there, human beings, the most highly developed form of life on earth, fighting each other like wild animals." "It was so savage. We *were* savages."[98]

Bill Hoover remembered the rage he had felt at the Japanese who had so cruelly killed captured Marauders. "How, how, how could anybody be so inhuman?" And then, thinking again, he added: "But after a while, you're just inhuman yourself."[99]

5 DISCIPLINE
Not the American Way

American soldiers shared the common supposition that for the war to be won, many would have to do as they were told. They accepted the necessity of a basic martial discipline and of their subordination, as individuals, to the cause of success in combat. But they came to denounce scathingly the ethos of command; the orders it engendered often seemed less intent on enhancing their effectiveness as fighting men than on humiliating them as enlisted men. Beneath their ostensible submission there developed a resistance to military discipline that became a fundamental feature of the soldiers' experience in World War II—and a source of their further isolation.

The way to ensure that soldiers surmounted the stresses of battle, the U.S. Army leadership assumed from the outset, was to build an organization that rigidly prescribed the place and practice of each of its members. With hierarchy assigning positions and regulations dictating actions both binding and barred, the high command aimed to make each soldier, in the phrase of sociologist Samuel Stouffer, "an integral part of a vast system of discipline and coordination." The results were expected to yield an operation largely automatic on two levels. The structure itself would function on the battlefield independently of other influences: "Army organization is devised to work even when personal ties cannot be depended on. . . ." And the individual soldier too would respond from repetition and habituation, his training impelling what Old Sarge called "instant and involuntary obedience." Repeated drilling and tight garrison control, reinforced by stringent sanctions, would inure the soldier to his station, and his subsequent internalization of Army discipline—with the individual conscience forbidding disobedience "even when there is no likelihood of detection by either superiors or fellows"—would hold him to that station. It was to be a military whose officers would know the orders necessary to wage war and whose privates would, without question or evasion, obey those commands. Here was a vision like that of professional European armies whose recruits brought to military service far higher respect for authority and much greater willingness to defer to it than did young Americans.[1]

The military's awareness that the American individualistic ethic did not lend itself to easy subordination led it to design basic training as "intensive shock treatment" rendering the trainee "helplessly insecure in the bewildering newness and complexity of his environment." A regime in turn intimidating, exhausting, and overpowering would shear from soldiers their idiosyncrasy and contrariness. Individuals had to be broken to powerlessness in order that their collectivity, their units, might become powerful. "They tear you down," said Louis Orlin of his basic training at Fort Benning, "knock all the civilian out of you." "When you first enter the [Marine] Corps," wrote Art Buchwald, "their only goal is to reduce you to a stuttering, blubbering bowl of bread pudding. . . . The purpose . . . is to break you down, and then rebuild you into the person the Marine Corps wants. . . ." The erasure of individuality would create a malleability to discipline; repetitive actions would instill that automatic response for which the services strove.[2]

Training then was to be the process in which the soldier would learn, through forced subordination, that the individual was unimportant relative to the organization and would be persuaded, through daily chastening, that indiscipline would bring down on him penalties that ranged from annoying to life-altering. One of basic's first lectures, on hygiene and morals, emphasized that, beyond the physical effects rendered so repulsive in the training film, the Army would court-martial any soldier who contracted venereal disease. Keith Winston and his fellow trainees also received four talks on the consequences of going absent without leave: "First, a dishonorable discharge, then imprisonment from one to twenty-five years—or even life. Army law even permits death." "[The] ghost of that yellow ticket," warned Old Sarge, "would haunt any soldier discharged dishonorably." (Ironically, the rise in the military's prestige as a result of its accomplishment in World War II did give the dishonorable discharge a bite, a power to penalize in the civilian sector, that it utterly lacked prior to the war.)[3]

Time would reveal that instructors wildly exaggerated the penalties that the Army itself was prepared to impose, but outsize punishments seemed at first to make credible the most dire threats. When a private unthinkingly flipped a cigarette stub to the ground, his sergeant upbraided him and ordered that he give the butt "a decent burial"—in a hole to be dug six feet deep. When Private Robert Neimeyer neglected to button up his shirt, he was sent to scrub barracks steps for a week—with a toothbrush. Training cadres found it simpler to punish soldiers for failures to conform than to commend superior performance, easier to try to stamp on individuality than to bend it to team effort.[4]

Soldiers took exception to NCO attempts to subordinate them and compel receptivity to discipline, especially to that range of practices GIs called "Mickey Mouse" or "Chicken Shit": saluting, the manual of arms, close-order drill, spit-and-polish grooming, inspections, policing trash. The men soon decided that the punishments administered to them were, like so much of the language directed at them, excessive. As intended, they did not forget their chastisements, but memory spurred anger, seldom resolve to perfect their behavior. Outraged friends of the trainee who dug his cigarette's grave succeeded in pushing the sergeant into the hole, then making their escape. Years after the war Neimeyer remained choleric over the toothbrush episode; "asshole" remained his term for his tormentor. Many so resented their superiors' imposition of Mickey Mouse, and the image of the soldier it conveyed, that it seemed to justify broadening indiscipline into a continuous covert resistance. Sergeant Myles Standish Babcock decided that

> Much army time is devoted to useless construction, useless training and jobs that verge on the idiotic. The theory behind these practices is inspired by the belief that an idle soldier is a troublemaker. On details such as these, goldbricking becomes an art. Appearing busy when idle, swinging quickly into activity at the approach of a brass hat, launching into an educational lecture only when an officer comes within earshot. . . .

Soldiers thought these reasonable responses to unreasonable orders.[5]

After basic training, soldiers confronted a series of reinforcing institutional inequalities that they were not for an instant persuaded bore any significant connection with combat.

One that enlisted men suffered for short durations but inflicted grave damage on their relationship with officers was the matter of shipboard accommodation. NCOs, plying ridicule and contempt, had riveted privates' attention during basic training; officers, though occasionally intervening, often remained just beyond focus. To Carl Becker, "the captain or colonel (I forget his rank) commanding the battalion" was not one of those who "gave shape" to the lives of trainees: ". . . he was a wraithlike figure . . . an anonymous man to us; seldom did we see or hear him. Really commanding us was the first sergeant"—at whose every appearance Becker "shuddered and stiffened." An even greater font of fear, indeed of "immediate terror," was another cadreman—Sergeant Billy Ray Bass, "Sergeant Bastard," whose "every word . . . dripped with sarcasm." With such characters commanding their actions and monopolizing their thoughts, trainees developed little sense of how officers functioned as a group—until they were transported overseas.[6]

Shipping out made manifest the break with home and often signaled the approach of battle. At this juncture of considerable vulnerability, young soldiers would have welcomed officers' expressions of support, indeed any mutuality. Instead, strict separation seemed designed to seal off enlisted men from any sympathetic contact with their officers. On a transport bound for the central Pacific, the troops were ordered to run through repeated abandon-ship drills and then, while "hot, sweaty, bruised, and ill-tempered," commanded by the captain, "cool, clean, well-dressed, and smiling," to scour the ship. "A clean ship," he spouted, "is a happy ship." Private Robert Thobaben recoiled: "it was at that moment that the glaring gap between officers and enlisted men, between equality and inequality, was driven home to me in a lesson I shall never forget. It was *we* and *they*. It was an unbridgeable gulf. It was human estrangement, alienation and isolation, in its most exacerbated form."[7]

Quartering arrangements disgusted most of the passengers. The enlisted men, said Keith Winston, were "herded like cattle" into fetid, stifling holds "so crowded you can't move without bumping into some soldier." But "Don't get the idea . . . the ship is small." The ratio of officers to men in Winston's 100th Division, bound for Europe, was 1:17, but aboard ship fully half the space was reserved for those with commissions. Officers had private dining rooms and lounges, while soldiers, Winston complained, could find no place to sit and write a letter. More injurious was most officers' reaction to the situation, a determination to keep "officers' country" free of GI intrusion. "Don't you know enlisted men aren't allowed on the boat deck?" cut short many soldier explorations for more space. "Where we can go, and where we can't go," Winston observed, "seem to be of paramount concern to the officers."[8]

The ensuing tension did not escape Richard Tobin, correspondent for the *New York Herald Tribune*. Traveling on a converted passenger liner, he noticed that members of a company assigned to sleep on the floor of the ship's cinema had to remove themselves and all their gear between sunrise and 10:00 p.m. so that officers could use the space as a lounge. "The GIs involved are as close to mutiny as they'll ever be. . . . One young soldier, in tears, keeps telling his mates that he will not be surprised if his own first lieutenant, whom he hasn't seen below decks since the trip began, becomes an early casualty in the invasion fighting."[9]

Officers' access to liquor ("the officers play poker for big stakes and drink Old Fitzgerald in the fan-cooled officers' country") gave rise to a problem far broader and more enduring than shipboard space. Officers' clubs served liquor; enlisted men's facilities were restricted to 3.2 beer. Even in the field, officers were offered opportunity to buy a monthly liquor allotment of at least two bottles; combat soldiers, though recipients of occasional beer distributions, ordinarily sought heavier spirits either via the black market—Myles Babcock reported that in the Pacific, soldiers paid $45 for a quart of the brand purchased by officers for $1.50—or via the covert, local, often amateur manufacture of swipe, concoctions sometimes rendered ruinous by the use of methyl alcohol or other toxic substances. Such blatant discrimination first surprised and then angered the enlisted men. Why, on one side of a wall, should privates be confined to purchasing bottles of beer, while on the other officers downed glasses of whiskey? And these disparities seemed to compound themselves in the combat zone. Three months after the invasion of Bougainville, Babcock and his friends remained "on the outer rim of defense"; while they still "suffered and flirted with death," officers within the "quite livable" inner perimeter read books in their libraries—and drank liquor in their clubs.[10]

Segregated facilities were of course ubiquitous. At Ulithi, enlisted men were restricted to one end of the island set aside for recreation. On the Riviera, officers took rest leaves in one city, the men in another. At Papua New Guinea, Frank Mathias complained, "Military police guarded on a beautiful beach for 'officers and gentlemen' [while] enlisted men swam on a beach featuring rip tides, rocks, and encroaching jungle." Just granted respite from the fighting on Okinawa and heavy with the consciousness that "very few familiar faces were left," Eugene Sledge and a fellow Marine stumbled upon a wood and entered to eat their rations. It delighted them. "We walked into a completely untouched scene that resembled a natural park in a botanical garden: low graceful pines cast dense shade, and ferns and moss grew on the rocks and banks. It was cool, and the odor of fresh pine filled the air. Miraculously, it bore not a single sign of war. 'Boy, this is beautiful, isn't it, Sledge-hammer?'" As the two friends eased into relaxation "for the first time in months," an NCO's bark broke their repose: "OK, you guys. Move out. Move! Move! Outa here." "Is the company moving out already?" "No, it isn't, but you guys are." "Why?" "Because this is off limits to enlisted men." He pointed to a group of officers munching rations as they sauntered into the sanctuary. "But we aren't in the way." "Move out and follow orders." Such episodes propelled one of Bill Mauldin's most celebrated cartoons: Two officers stand on a mountain crest as the sun, playing against the clouds, sends shafts of light streaming toward the peaks and valleys before them. Says one to the other, "Beautiful view! Is there one for the enlisted men?"[11]

Another grievance focused on the unequal provision of entertainment opportunities. In the combat zone it was almost an article of faith that famous-name shows would not venture close enough to perform for front-line troops. And informal possibilities seemed no better. Even at the end of the war, in Germany on July 5, 1945, Ralph "Zig" Boroughs of the 508th Paratroop Infantry found scant improvement. "We are posted around homes of Generals and around several officers clubs, swimming parks, etc. It lowers the morale of the boys to see the officers with so much entertainment when we have none. Mainly the boys steal the officers' liquor and get drunk. . . ."[12]

In this regard medic Tsuchida felt that his own front-line unit had been unusually fortunate: "Even had a USO show come up here to 'entertain' us. . . . And then we had a Red Cross Clubmobile come by with coffee and donuts." Gratifying as those occasions were, however, they immediately led him to an irate reprise of another of the combat soldier's complaints: officers' monopolization of women. "If the enlisted men tried to talk to the girls the officers would give them . . . a 'Scram, buddy' and take over like big operators. And that's the way it was, a bunch of EM standing around with mouths open, watching the conversation go back and forth between the RC girls and the officers. . . . But that's the way it always is. Do you think we could get near these movie actresses? Hell no, it's always the officers mess or club that they see."[13]

Soldiers trained their anger on their superiors and, quite unfairly, on the women themselves. Nurses, enlisted men believed, had been granted commissions so that their status would trigger non-fraternization regulations and thus ensure the continuation of male officer control of their company. Just as infuriating was the high command's own *sotto voce* rationale for the situation, that it was the duty of gentlemen-officers to "protect" women from enlisted personnel. At Espíritu Santo in the New Hebrides, Babcock thought he saw where such glaring class partiality led: officers flaunted their nurse "courtesans" within easy view of "sex-starved soldiers who haven't spoken to white women for over a year." "Most nurses," he was convinced, "become degenerate in the Tropics."[14]

The core of the privates' complaint in the Pacific was the denial of contact (north of New Zealand and Australia) with white women; in Europe, it was the enforced distance between themselves and "nice" women. The Army's sequestration of women within the officers' sphere, Zig Boroughs fumed, blocked privates from all access to high society. More realistically, Grady Arrington lamented that he and his friends were denied entrée to all social sectors save the lowest: "Why does a soldier get himself all mixed up with a bunch of whores? Why can't he meet the right people? Why does he try to make every skirt he . . . meets?" It was not, soldiers argued, that they were crude or predatory, but that officers blocked their every approach to people with whom soldiers might have acted differently.[15]

Food had first become a source of dissatisfaction on those transports sailing for the war zones. En route to North Africa, Robert Welker and his friends ate twice a day, standing up; officers ate three times, seated. The soldiers' food was substandard and so scanty that they were constantly hungry. On the *Aquitania,* Wayne Weber discovered the disparity between enlisted and officer mess: "[The] officers were eating much better food, [though] we were all crossing [the Atlantic] for the same purpose." Soldiers thereafter assumed that anywhere they came upon separate messes—i.e., everywhere except at the front—officers would receive superior food, a grievance throughout the war. In Germany, almost four months after the final gunfire, Ben Tumey set down in his diary: "The food is worse than bad and not enough to keep a man going. The officers get the best; the men get what is left. A few days ago we had a chicken dinner. Some of us, who remember the good old days and Southern fried chicken, watched the chickens being brought in. Our mouths were watering for a drumstick or breast. At noon what a letdown. On the officers' table were all the choice pieces. . . . In the chow line were wings, backs, and necks."[16]

Soldiers were repeatedly reminded that shipboard segregation had only anticipated the array of separate, unequal facilities that they encountered in the field. Grady Gallant was one of many Marines who found offensive the imposition of hierarchy on a universal function; he was angry that officers used private-stall privies and NCOs sat on boards with holes cut in them while privates were left to straddle slit trenches. In Holland, Zig Boroughs's paratroop section was ordered to erect a tent twenty-five feet long and fifteen feet high so that:

. . . the officers could shit in style. [We] also prepared the conveniences . . . dig-
ging the trenches and erecting the boxes over the trenches, each with two holes
. . . standard equipment for high-ranking field officers. After the officers' latrine
was prepared with the sweat and labor and oaths of the enlisted men, my normally happy disposition was rankled every time I had to lower my pants over a
straddle trench in the rain and the mud.

And again the willingness of some officers to push their advantage even beyond obvious privilege sharpened the soldier's antagonism. A Mauldin drawing caught two officers using the EM latrine rather than walking five
hundred yards through the rainy night to the officers' privy: "Whistle if you
see anybody coming." The fact that in some units it was a court-martial offense for an enlisted man to use a toilet reserved for officers did nothing to
enhance tolerance of officers' encroachment.[17]

Differential treatment galled again in the censorship of correspondence.
Privates' letters had to be read and passed by a company officer; officers' letters were cleared by other officers, often without a reading. An additional security provision stipulated that base censors check every third or fourth
officer letter, but this step, when not neglected entirely, seldom discom-
moded the writers. Here, as in all of these privileged relationships, a number
of officers sympathized with the men's irritation and rued their own role.
Reading his Marines' mail made Captain Garrett Graham feel as if he were a
Peeping Tom. Some worked to repress their reservations by performing the
task as conscientiously as possible. Paul Boesch was tempted to regale fellow
officers with stories drawn from his soldiers' letters, but in the end he "never
divulged the contents of any letter, no matter how trivial it might seem. . . ."
Other officers reacted to their soldiers' prose with a disgust that bespoke class
bias and reinforced their conviction that social distance had to be maintained. Marine aviator Samuel Hynes found in his men's letters "clumsy expressions of affection and preposterous lies about their military exploits."
Often in the evening the officer assigned as censor "would begin to laugh:
'Hey, listen to this guy,' and he'd read out some mechanic's fancy, addressed
to his wife, of what he'd do to and with her when he got home. It . . . was astonishing . . . that there were marriages . . . in which sexual relations were apparently conducted with such violent and inventive enthusiasm." Still, "we
expected that sort of thing from the enlisted men."[18]

True, soldiers could occasionally find in the system some marginal benefit—the welcome intervention of an officer who pointed out to the private
sending off love letters to two women that he had inserted both in the wrong

envelopes; the opportunity to include in letters home "ironic references" meant to malign the censor or other officers; etc. But most soldiers continued to damn censorship as an intrusion upon their individuality, a violation of their fundamental rights, or both.[19]

When Samuel Hynes said that the forthrightness of sailor letters "seemed pornographic to middle-class young men" like himself and his fellow officers, he touched unknowingly on a phenomenon that further separated enlisted personnel from all officers except those few closest to them in battle: the leveling down of the values that dominated the ranks. In fact, those of middle-class background always constituted a strong component within World War II units. Harold Leinbaugh's army company—ranging from Harvard and Yale graduates and ASTP "Whiz kids" with IQs above 120 to illiterates, beyond the conspicuous absence of African Americans "an authentic melting pot"— was close to the mean. "What a mix!" exclaimed David Pergrin of his combat engineers battalion; "We had . . . born gentlemen and youngsters from the wrong side of every situation our society fostered. There were thinkers and men who rarely imagined beyond the next meal. . . . There were men capable of committing unimaginable crimes, and men capable of bringing such moral outcasts back within the sphere of humanity. . . . We had strong men, weak men, rough men, and soft men." Middle-class soldiers may have held certain advantages—aspiration, articulateness, savoir faire—but they did not press them, and their values played no prominent role in the ranks.[20]

Indeed, for several reasons, they quickly moved to adopt styles associated with values far less genteel. It began with the intimidation of Regular Army drill instructors; to become coarse in the midst of coarseness was to take on a protective coloration. It took no more than a day of basic training to comprehend that military life accorded no premium to intelligence. "The first thing the Army teaches you," Henry Giles realized, "is if you've got any brains it's best to keep it to yourself. You get along better if you play it strictly G.I." To stand out was to invite hammering down. Middle-class soldiers, moreover, believed that earthier values might serve to accelerate the toughening process preparing them for combat. Finally, their disgust with rank and its prerogatives created its own gravitation away from bourgeois officer-corps values and toward those, however crude, in whose contrast they might find some solidarity with like-minded others.[21]

Anton Myrer described a young Marine of elite background who, believing himself the victim of officer privilege, renounced family advantage. Once he realized that the platoon's "inarticulate ragamuffins were somehow bound up with his emotions, indissolubly welded to his heart with bands of steel,"

"Harvard wit" no longer titillated, and tastes previously thought impeccable became affected and alien. Soldiers in the Pacific, Sy Kahn remarked, all eventually came to heavy smoking, heavy drinking, and the heavy use of foul language. Thus, as Lester Atwell put it, many "boys of good background" submerged themselves and "became indistinguishable" from their fellow dirt soldiers.[22]

However roughened, enlisted men were no less sensitive to unequal treatment. On Guadalcanal, the arrival of Japanese bombers caught Marine Robert Leckie out in the open. He ran from foxhole to foxhole; all were occupied. "At last I came to the officers' shelter dug in the hillside. With [bomb] fragments falling around me in a chilling fugue, I swept back the burlap over the entrance and gazed into the unblinking formidable glass eye of Captain High-Hips. What disdain! It was as though the holder of a coach ticket had sought to enter a parlor car! His hostility was as curt as a slap in the face. . . . I muttered an apology and . . . retired to . . . the rain of shrapnel. . . ." "In that moment I hated High-Hips and all his class." Keith Winston responded angrily to an episode at Camp Blanding, Florida, in mid-1944.

> We'd been working hard in the hot sun for 3 solid hours, and finally [been] given a rest. When we started to drink from our canteens, the water was literally [so] hot . . . very few boys could take it. However, set aside in a shady spot were three 5-gallon cans of cool water for the officers. The guys saw this and about a dozen went over and filled their canteens. When the Captain discovered it he questioned the men but no one would admit to their 'guilt.' He turned blue with anger and ordered us all to walk back in the hot sun—a distance of 7 miles—even though we were slated for a truck ride back.

Here was "another taste of the Captain's ruthlessness."[23]

Whether inequities were major or minor, soldiers read into them a heavy significance. On the last day of the war in Europe, Ben Tumey was in no mood to celebrate: transfer to the Pacific campaign, he guessed, loomed just ahead. What did draw emotion was of a different order: "We moved yesterday into [old construction] barracks. . . . The concrete was hard to sleep on last night, but it is not as bad as the cold and ice that we have often had to sleep in. The only real sad thing about it was the fact that the officers have a nice house and beds. Are they better than we?" Here was the combat soldier's *cri de coeur* throughout the war: "Are they better than we?" The officer corps, Tumey was convinced, constantly transgressed fundamental precepts of the social contract—by impugning his dignity and autonomy, by raising over him others of no perceptible merit, by violating his sense of his own personhood. There was even an awareness of a spiritual breach. If they had thought in Hawthornian imagery, soldiers would have convicted officers of trespass against the souls of others.[24]

Their anger at the denial of their equivalence with all other men was profound, whether directed at institutional insults—e.g., the Army's injunction against recruits talking with officers; the "Officers Only" signs in hotel bars—or at personal slights—e.g., some officers' habit of heeding only rank. "Many officers never recognize anything unless it is pinned on [the] shoulders." Lester Atwell bridled every time he chanced to meet officers for whom he had worked and they passed by with no sign of recognition. More aggravating were officers who exerted themselves to maintain and even reinforce the official distance separating them from the men. One of Sergeant George Baker's most applauded comic strips placed Sad Sack at the officers club, waiting tables. As he served, he overheard the story with which one officer regaled another. He smiled and then joined their laughter. The officers, however, noting his reaction, became stiff with anger and shouted him into silence. Subservience restored, they returned to their chartered joviality.[25]

Among the worst indignities, more hurtful than disregard of the soldier's existence or reminders of the soldier's official subordination, was an expectation that privates would render to officers any personal service.

In December 1944 Corporal Rev Ehrgott landed in southern France with the 70th Division. "[W]hen we got to the front and the 1st Sgt. told me my lieutenant wanted me to lay out and roll up his bedroll for sleeping, my response was that I was not Lt. Zahora's servant, and [I] refused to do it. I could tell that the 1st Sgt. liked my reply and I was not gigged for it."[26]

"It is a citizen army," declared Bill Mauldin, "and it has in its enlisted ranks many men who in civil life were not accustomed to being directed to the back door and the servant quarters. To taking orders, yes; but to taking indignities, no." But soldiers came to believe that officers intended many of their orders explicitly to inflict indignities. In December 1944, just prior to a mountain unit's departure for combat in Italy, the men were commanded to "Drop your pants and bend over." Thomas Noonan pushed aside explanations of a search for hemorrhoids; he knew the purpose of the examination: "in reality to humble the individual soldier." With little difficulty, then, soldiers grew to expect the worst of the officer corps. Its members' first impulse, apparently, was to serve themselves.[27]

Officers distributed to Marines about to embark from Guadalcanal the Christmas packages that had arrived from home, but they then ordered that the riflemen carry aboard ship only packs and weapons. Each officer, however, was permitted a sea bag, an item ordinarily issued only to enlisted personnel. These ploys, Robert Leckie was certain, the officers had devised to "satisfy their covetousness by forbidding us things rightfully ours, and then take them up themselves, much as politicians use the courts to gain their ends." So, to frustrate officer acquisitiveness, ". . . we devoured what we could of these Christmas gifts from home, and threw the rest away." Soldiers could not trust their officers.[28]

A Mauldin cartoon presented two officers who, arriving at a house, decided to dispossess four privates who were busily cleaning and refurbishing what they assumed were their new quarters. Seating himself outside, one officer suggested to the other that they wait until the enlisted men completed their repair of the stove; *then* they would post their "Officers' Quarters" sign and pitch the privates out.[29]

In the experience of some soldiers, however, Mauldin here understated the problem. Prior to its movement overseas, Floyd Mauk's ammunition company was confined to dingy quarters, devoid of recreational opportunities, in Romulus, New York. "We borrowed, begged and stole enough lumber, chairs, tables, books and magazines to fix up a [club] room. Working nights, Sundays, and off hours, we soon completed it. We decided to celebrate the opening . . . with a beer party the following night. Everyone was in high spirits. . . ." But at dinner that evening the men were ordered to remain in place until dismissed. Comprehension dawned as they looked from mess-hall windows across to the club room. "There we could see five officers, drinking whiskey, eating sandwiches, kissing and fondling five women, scantily dressed or nearly nude." At 10:00 p.m. the enlisted men were released, with orders to clean up the club room and to prepare for movement by rail to the port of embarkation at 4:00 a.m. the next morning. The episode left 180 men with what Mauk described as "enduring hurt"—unsurprisingly, for it combined officer control of women and liquor; duplicity; violations of fundamental fairness; smugness in superior rank; and a clear intent to humiliate common soldiers. Had all officers acted like those in Company U, 4th Battalion, 301st Ordnance Regiment, the U.S. Army might have found itself simultaneously battling Axis powers and risings within its own ranks.[30]

The men frequently assumed that the commission was an immediately corrupting influence. When a unit member named Ziegler received a battlefield commission, Atwell was among those who congratulated him: "Nice goin', boy." But when they next saw him in the company of other officers, Ziegler would not come over to say hello or shake hands. "Boy, it don't take 'em long, does it?" "Americans usually go mad," wrote one disgusted soldier,

John Horne Burns, "when by direction of the President of the United States they put a piece of metal on their collars. They don't know whether they're the Lone Ranger, Jesus Christ or Ivanhoe." Keith Winston thought that the brass were ". . . treated like gods . . . through [enforced homage]. 'Yes, sir,' 'No, sir'— saluted under compulsion. One word from their 'godly' mouths is law, regardless of reason or logic," so ". . . their rank goes to their head and suddenly they feel a power and authority they never dreamed possible—and many are merciless in their use of it." If that were so, for soldiers to play by the book became futile. Sad Sack's preparation for an inspection was herculean, with his clean-up leaving the barracks spotless, but then the inspecting officer, spying an unbuttoned pocket, gigged him and sent him off to KP. Victimization by officers intent on flaunting their prerogatives was virtually inevitable.[31]

James Jones insisted, with good cause, that among combat soldiers, "There was a lot more bitterness in World War II than historians allow." He had first in mind fighting soldiers' consciousness of their own expendability: "basically the men were bitter at getting their asses shot off." But equally unacknowledged and almost as rancorous was soldier sentiment against those who sent them toward battle, humiliated them en route, and then (with some exceptions) failed to go with them to the juncture with ultimate danger.[32]

Perhaps the most embittered were soldiers convinced that the brass sought to build careers atop the corpses of the men. On this issue, the soldier-writers were unsparing. Irwin Shaw's Captain Colclough, in addressing his troops, indicted himself: "When this battle is over I expect to be promoted to Major. And you men are going to get that promotion for me. . . . This Company is going to kill more Krauts than any other Company in the Division and I'm going to make Major by July fourth, and if that means we're going to have more casualties than anybody else, all I can say is: see the Chaplain." One of James Jones's commanders, just promoted to brigadier general, introduces his successor: "You men got this star for me! Now I want you to go out and get one for Colonel Grubbe, too!" The memoir literature offers few examples of such blatant ruthlessness, but it does substantiate an extensive late-war suspicion that promotions at and above the regimental level hinged on aggressive accomplishment—and thus on the shedding of soldiers' blood. "He's another one of those goddam officers," ran one of the darkest apprehensions on the line, "who wants to get us all killed."[33]

As the war unfolded and combat soldiers' sense of separation solidified, they increasingly alluded to officers in caste and class terms. Caste's connotation

of hereditary disconnection hardly squared with the men's notion that officers had been much like themselves until twisted by commissions, but no
matter; talk of Brahmins and untouchables fit their feelings. GI Walter
Gustafson warned that the first thing the draftee would learn was that "He is
completely at the mercy of the . . . men . . . above him in the military hierarchy, the Army caste system." In New Guinea, Robert Leckie claimed to have
discovered a way of measuring the progress of battles—by noting officers'
eating arrangements. As long as there remained any danger that the Japanese
would defeat the Marines, officers were willing to "pig it with the men," but
as soon as victory was assured, the officers mess reappeared and "caste was restored." Some soldiers decided that because officers had set themselves up as
a "different caste [they] ought to stay there." In December 1944, Corporal
Rev Ehrgott's unit moved by train from Marseilles to the front. "Our 21-
year-old lieutenant was with us in the [boxcar], the longest and closest he's
ever been with his men, such is the caste system, and when he reminisced
that all he had known so far in life was college and Army, he got no response
at all because it was too late in the game to start getting chummy, and I for
one wasn't gonna buddy up to this 21-year-old 90-day wonder."[34]

Enlisted men also routinely referred to officers as a separate class. Leckie
hissed his hatred for Captain High-Hips and "all his class." In fact, foot soldiers were as little interested in explorations of class as of caste; the former,
with its Marxist associations, and the latter, with its taint of foreignness,
served not as tools of serious analysis but as imprecations against relationships they found oppressive. Indeed, they employed the terms interchange-
ably. Ben Culwell, who joined the Navy to escape the Army draft but still
found himself "writhing in violent resentment against the military system
and the under-caste niche in which I had been placed," skipped easily from
caste to class: "[I was] fresh from American boyhood [and Navy service] was
my first real contact with caste. I was the lower class, and the class line then
seemed as insurmountable as the color line. Every instinct in me rebelled."[35]

Equally loose was soldiers' appropriation of the war's ideological cause,
the defense of democracy against fascism. Enlisted men rarely inclined to vi-
sionary speculation. They had countless reasons to recognize that the term
"democratic Army" was an oxymoron, and they spent no energy in seeking
to democratize the military. After the war, a group of wounded combat veterans remained doubtful "that the American people should or could reshape
the internal policies of their armed forces in a democratic direction." Nor
did soldiers worry much about the "fascism" of the U.S. Army as it was later
described by Norman Mailer, Malcolm Lowry, and Paul Fussell, among oth-

ers; they felt no concern for its possible infection of the larger polity. But "democracy," as a concept beyond contamination, could be invoked to commend practices of which soldiers approved.[36]

When Private Wayne Weber was appointed a major's secretary, he was invited to join the headquarters mess. Eating as a group, he reflected appreciatively, was the "one and only democratic set-up" he encountered in the Army. When Keith Winston wrote that "The Captain and Lt. are decent, democratic guys," he intended just what other GIs meant when they said that reserve officers were far more democratic than West Point graduates— that they were as friendly, fair, and flexible as the circumstances of war allowed, that they didn't "go around pulling rank." And predictably, soldiers cited democratic values to indict officers for their violations of equitable practice. "Last night," Ben Tumey flared, "the soldiers were given about one swallow of schnapps apiece. I know for a fact that the officers had two bottles apiece. Is this democracy?"[37]

What, then, did combat soldiers want? They accepted, as noted, that the winning of battles and thus of the war necessitated hierarchical organization: Some would give orders, others would have to follow them. No special strain was expected to surround the latter experience; the Great Depression had taught daily lessons in subordination. What they desired was not a standing equivalent to that of officers but acknowledgment of an equivalent worth. They saw no reason why submission to discipline had to manifest itself as officer superiority and soldier inferiority. In northern Italy, on April 15, 1945, rifleman John Bassett added an entry in his war journal: "We were eating our K rations when Captain Bucher came by. 'Be ready to move out at 7 a.m. . . . ,' and he kept going. I hated him with a sullen passive energy that I could not understand. He had disciplined me in Camp Swift after I ran away from a barracks cleaning detail and played the piano for the GIs on a Sunday afternoon at the service club. I don't know how he had hurt me—except that he had *humiliated* me." What the soldier wanted was the end of Chicken Shit, the abuse of rank and privilege wielded so as to confirm his inferiority; an end to indignity.[38]

There was here the potential for a divisiveness that might have hobbled the efforts of the United States to defeat the armies of its enemies. Five factors, however, worked to hold such contention within the bounds of restraint: the bent of some officers to introduce local accommodations into the system; the attractions of promotion; the diminution of Chicken Shit in combat; the fact that the line separating Americans in battle did not fall so as to place all officers on one side and all enlisted personnel on the other; and the inclination of some combat soldiers to think of their own officers in ways at odds with their view of the officer corps.

A modest ameliorative influence was the willingness of some officers to relinquish certain of the privileges the system bestowed or to relieve some of the burdens it imposed. Aboard a transport sailing for North Africa, the considerateness of officers dissolved some of Sergeant Don Robinson's resentment:

> We walked the deck to try to find a place to sit down. There wasn't any. It took two hours and a half to get into the ship's store. "Officers' Country," where enlisted men were not permitted, took up the promenade and boat decks. There wasn't a shady place to read, and the holds were hot in the daytime. But the troubles soon were soothed. The officers gave up all their "country" except their staterooms and half the promenade deck. As this gave us much more room for lounging, the ship didn't seem crowded.

In Luxembourg, Lieutenant Paul Boesch purchased all the liquor that the Army allowed, but not for his own consolation. "Since I didn't drink, I could have sold my ration at an astronomical profit, but there was much more satisfaction in dividing it free among the men of the platoon." Charles MacDonald received a monthly allotment of a quart of scotch, a pint of gin, one to two bottles of Cognac, a bottle of Cointreau and another of Champagne; but he regarded his purchases as "far from personal items. The bottles were passed among all the men of the platoons until they were exhausted. . . ." So prevalent was the practice within his combat sphere that he mistakenly thought it universal and "wondered at letters to the editor in the *Stars and Stripes* complaining about officers getting whiskey rations when enlisted men did not." Sergeant Henry Giles received a rare exemption from censorship regulations. "[The lieutenant] called me in one day and told me he was putting me on my honor. He had never had to censor out a word. He said I could write more freely and personally now . . . for he wouldn't be reading my letters any more." Officers making such gestures had to be careful whom they benefited, for to appear to play favorites would only add partiality to the indictment against them. Still, these uncountable local accommodations salved soldiers' indignation and brought them closer to officers willing to foster any equivalent treatment.[39]

Privates' surprising aspirations for promotion also exerted some moderating effect. "To be an officer," declared Grady Arrington, "is the one hope of all enlisted men, even though many openly say they would not accept a commission if offered." There was exaggeration in his opening assertion but also a kernel of substance. David Breger, who drew the "Private Breger" cartoons, was actually Lieutenant Breger. Nor did Bill Mauldin place himself beyond ambition. Though General George Patton charged that his drawings were designed to "incite a goddamn mutiny," Mauldin pleaded that "No matter what Patton thought, I never disliked officers. If I'd had my druthers, I'd probably have been a smart-ass little lieutenant. I'd have gone to OCS or something. . . ."[40]

The men seldom discussed such inclinations among themselves, as if the bent for promotion laid bare some disloyalty, so no consensus emerged in explanation of its appearance. For some, the commission represented an escape from harassment and humiliation. Robert Welker agreed to the great leap, from sergeant to second lieutenant. "Once across the line . . . I had seen my last training film, had done my last close-order drill, had stood my last inspection, had queued up the last time for eating and dishwashing or being paid or seeing a movie. I had submitted my mail for the last time to a stranger for his censoring. Except for certain formal occasions, and certain feeble-witted proud colonels, I had saluted my last superior." "Decent victuals" would replace soldier "swill," and a single room would supply "the convenience associated with individuality and privacy." "I was out from under," he rejoiced; "I was no longer one of the vulnerable." Others found intolerable those demonstrations of officer superiority and sought commissions to prove that they were no less worthy. William Owens left behind comrades "who knew . . . that I could never invite them to the officers' club for a drink" because there he found, as anticipated, that "officers who for almost a year had observed the distinction of rank between us now slapped me on the shoulder and bought the drinks." A major, grasping his hand, said with ardor, "By God, you made it." A few smarted for a sphere less limited than that of the enlisted man: "I would like to be an officer, of course, because I feel I can do more as an officer. . . ."[41]

Most compelling was the pressure to fulfill what soldiers felt were the ambitions the homefolks held for them. "Do the best you can" was one of the American social ethic's most powerful injunctions, and soldiers had no way except rising rank to signal success in their efforts. A Stein and Brown cartoon caught Private Finch at home for the furlough following basic training. "Why aren't you an officer?" his wife demanded. "You're just as good as they are. I feel ashamed to be seen on the street with a miserable private." Girlfriends, too, Private Gene Gach confirmed, pressed privates to "better" themselves. In James Jones's *From Here to Eternity,* a Honolulu prostitute rejected bugler Robert E. Lee Prewitt's proposal; there was, she decided, not enough respectability in NCO rank. A Breger cartoon featured enlisted men lined up on an English street, awaiting their turn to be photographed with their heads inserted above an officer cut-out: "Send Home a Picture of YOURSELF as an OFFICER! 3 prints . . . £1."[42]

Many combat soldiers remained outwardly immovable in their opposition to promotions, sometimes even to NCO appointments, arguing that one was compromised both in striving for rank ("brown-nosing") and in securing it (becoming "one of the phonies"). They were, however, caught between their convictions—that no differences in intelligence or talent divided officers and men, that because luck determined promotion, any preferment was insignificant—and their own often concealed strivings. John Mc-Cormick explored the strain. When Marine private Faltynski moved up to squad leader, the old-timers "did not welcome the change. There was no way, we were convinced, that the old easy sense of equality could be maintained, especially now that our longtime friend would be required to spend part of each day in the company of sergeants, officers and other despots who were constantly plotting new strategies against us. It was almost as bad as having a buddy fall to a sniper's bullet."[43]

Faltynski, however, felt no need for circumspection. "Our friend . . . couldn't wait to get hold of needle and thread to put the damned stripes of authority on his arm. You wait long enough and you find out what a guy is really like underneath his sixteen coats of base paint." Squad members ragged Faltynski that he was "selling his soul to the high brass." "There goes another one of the good guys." "Goddammit! I ain't goin' nowhere. I'm still right here where I've always been." "But not for long. Not for very damned long. You've all seen it happen a hundred times. A good buddy . . . gets three stripes on his sleeve, and in no time at all he starts acting like a lieutenant or captain or major." "Yeah, and we all know what bastards they are." "The whole episode," concluded McCormick, ". . . was the sort of hazing every newly appointed squad leader could expect from old friends; but beneath the clowning there was an undercurrent of resentment and maybe some envy. Our good friend would be giving us orders now."[44]

Amidst these tensions, two verities—that privates had known, and once liked and trusted, some of those who had climbed the ranks, and that few had not imagined themselves in officer uniform—muted some of the stridency of soldiers' hostility to their superiors.

More powerful in restraining malice was the slackening of formal discipline in battle, a phenomenon that sundry observers found striking. Samuel Stouffer and his colleagues reported that combat "fostered a closer solidarity between officers and enlisted men than was usual in the rest of the Army. . . . Formalities were largely abandoned. . . ." A junior officer, Ralph Ingersoll, discerned "an easy democracy" in the way his company's officers and men ate and slept together in forward areas. Eugene Sledge noted that during the fighting, relations between Marine riflemen and their officers were "all buddy-buddy. . . ."[45]

Combat conditions did conduce to closer affiliation. The harshness of the battlefield worked toward a parity of subsistence, while the danger of death placed a premium on cooperation. "Out there [in the Pacific]," Watson told Arthur Miller, "[officers] wear the same uniforms we do and you call them by their first name. Bars don't mean one little damned thing. . . ." Actually, such modifications owed much to the new, large, lethal significance of bars as an objective of enemy fire. With German and Japanese snipers targeting officers, survival required the elimination of all ensigns of rank: officer insignia; uniform variations; salutes; conversational references to titles that might be overheard; differences in weaponry. Finally, the shocks and costs of battle often scrambled hierarchical roles. When, during heavy fighting on Peleliu, exhaustion pared down Russell Davis's Marine company, "the 'duty' fell on those who would take it. Rank meant nothing. Privates, who had something left, led sergeants who didn't have it any more, but who would follow, even if they wouldn't order other men to." Battle deaths compelled surviving riflemen to take up NCO functions and sergeants officer functions. Some privates saw in such fluidity, beyond the exactions of battle, a model for the relationships they desired in training, in garrison, everywhere in the military. In battle, said Corporal Rev Ehrgott of the 96th Division, "we were all in it together, and the dogface, with his limited future, got respect."[46]

Gratifying as soldiers found these developments, even amid the violence of battle the tension between these men and their officers did not disappear. Facing destruction, they were sharply sensitive to any intimation that officers' lives possessed a value higher than their own, and when provoked they used the comparative informality of the combat zone to sharpen their resistance. As Ehrgott knew, "There were things you could do in combat, and say, that you couldn't get away with in training. . . ." A battalion commander on the European front complained to a sergeant that an assault had not gone forward on schedule: "For Christ sakes, Pope, it's after eight and you haven't . . ." Pope cut off the colonel: "What's the big fucking rush? Where the fuck you think you are at, Louisiana on maneuvers? This ain't maneuvers, this is real shit, and I'm going out there, not you." In execution of an order that the 506th Regiment of the 101st Airborne Division attack up and over Normandy hedgerows twelve feet high, an officer shouted at the men, "Get going. Get moving over the top. Hurry up," and then, riveting a private struggling with his climb, he added with even sharper edge, "Get going there." Reaching the top, Donald Burgett looked back and retorted, "Don't worry, joker. I'm ahead of you [and] so is everyone else. Get your ass up here and go with us." Enlisted men felt that in exposing themselves to death, they acquired an authority to resist the authority of those who ordinarily remained at a safe remove.[47]

In the new dispensation created by combat, the men insisted not only that officers who issued fateful orders know what it was to risk their own lives but that they give proof of their ability to lead and thus validate their claim to command. Infantrymen barely in control of their feelings were alert to officers unable to govern their own—and justifiably so: soldiers' lives were at stake. Company officers had no choice but to accede to the test; their preparation—and privileges—had been premised on their capacity for leadership, and here was the accounting. For no one was this more difficult than for the replacement officer. Combat immediately demonstrated the sway of experience. Surviving GIs possessed it; he did not. But he was nonetheless responsible for leading them in battle, and, when behind the lines, for their continuing training, both according to precepts that had been rendered obsolete by that experience he had yet to acquire. He would, moreover, be judged against a ghost, the officer whose place he had taken. The men may or may not have liked their defunct superior, but a singular fact dominated their memory of him: that the dead man had gone where the men believed he ought to have been—with them, in jeopardy. To the replacement officer, Laurence Critchell explained, "It quickly becomes obvious . . . that only a baptism of fire will unite him with his men, and in occasional moments of bitterness he is apt to feel that only his own death in combat will raise him to the stature of the man he has replaced."[48]

There thus proceeded beneath a surface of regulation relationships a grim audition. John Toole's took place amid conditions that could not have been worse. Arriving on the Vosges front in mid-October 1944, he was ordered to assume command of an infantry platoon while it was trying to fend off a German attack. He crawled into a foxhole containing two GIs, one with a bullet through his forehead and the other, Private John Orr, with an inhospitable temper. "Who the hell are you?" "I'm your platoon leader." "Shit! Another 90-day wonder!" While greeting Toole, Orr repeatedly raised his rifle, rested its barrel on the edge of the hole, and, without raising his head to fix a target, pulled the trigger. "Why don't you aim your rifle?" "You damn fool! You think I want a hole in my head like Davis there?" Why don't you fire *your* carbine? You ain't doin' anything else." Toole began to fight, Orr-fashion, but he could not shake himself from his daze. "I am so terrorized and confused that I don't have the slightest idea what to do or how to conduct myself. . . . I've never had an enlisted man talk to an officer like Orr talks to me."

Suddenly, compounding Toole's confusion, Orr blurted, "Listen, Lieutenant. We gotta get out of here or we'll all be corpses." "We can't do that. It would be an unauthorized withdrawal." "Are you crazy or something?" Orr flung back as he bolted, "I'm gettin' out of here."

Finally, a sergeant, the acting platoon leader, discovered Toole and, evincing respect no greater than Orr's, began issuing orders: "Listen, Lieutenant, we can't hold these holes. We gotta get out of here. You stay here and see that these boys pull out one at a time. No panic. Understand?"

Though the withdrawal was completed successfully, it left Toole too agitated to sleep: "I think of all the rules of the Infantry School at Ft. Benning which we had violated. We had dug in on the reverse slope of a hill. We conducted an unauthorized withdrawal. An enlisted man had deliberately disobeyed the orders of a commissioned officer. A Sergeant gives orders to a Lieutenant. Is this the way it's really supposed to be?" Three days later, his feelings still smarted—"The situation in my platoon is completely haywire. I'm taking orders from enlisted men and it should be the reverse. . . . They are very cavalier about their treatment of junior officers with no experience"—but he recognized what he had to do: "these . . . are probably the most experienced and battle-tried men in the U.S. Army. . . . I absolutely must behave in such a manner as to gain their respect."[49]

Such officers developed methods of leadership different from those taught at Fort Benning. They had known at OCS that they would face a test, but mistakenly assumed that the outcome would hinge on their professional proficiency and especially on their bravery. Yes, the men welcomed competence, but the suppleness to respond to combat's surprises far outweighed foreknowledge, and even then "knowing his stuff" was not enough to make for successful leadership. Like most officers, battalion commander Glover Johns thought that he "must prove himself—especially his courage—to every man in the outfit. . . ." Privates, however, were leery of warrior valor; zeal often killed their superiors—and the soldiers whom officers' boldness exposed. Courage was important principally as it contributed to leadership's essential quality, as replacement lieutenant Charles MacDonald overheard in a shower. "What's he like?" "He's damn young, but he doesn't seem scared to come around and see you once [in] a while, no matter where the hell you are. He seems to care what happens to you." "Caring" was not a matter of sentiment. It was the officer's solicitude to hold casualties to the minimum—and, as his earnest to the men, his unwillingness to order them to do that which he would not do. Here was the assurance both that he would not risk needlessly the lives of others and that he regarded the existences of the men as no less valuable than his own. This tacit recognition of soldiers as equivalent persons was the key requisite of leadership in the field.[50]

In the course of the Normandy campaign, Colonel Robert Sink concluded that troops sighted on a river's far bank were British; his men insisted they were German. "Well, I've got to see for myself," he decided, and crossed with a patrol, all of whose members soon had to swim back under heavy fire. "Goddammit, I could have sworn there were British over there, and I was going to shake [Field Marshal Montgomery's] hand." Pondering the fiasco, the men neither damned the colonel for professional ineptness nor praised him for fearlessness. "You've got to hand it to Colonel Sink though. Most commanders . . . *send* a patrol out to find out what they want to know. Colonel Bob won't ask a man to do something he wouldn't do himself. You don't mind going out for someone like that, even getting shot at a little, if it's necessary."[51]

Establishing even a semblance of equivalence required great tact, for soldiers never failed to detect and despise the false "we." Robert Welker remembered with disdain one officer whose invocation of parity in training never rose above sham: "Now this is an informal group here, we're all in the same Army, and I want anyone with any kind of complaint to speak right up. . . . Speak up, men. . . . [F]orget that you're a soldier and I'm, well, a major. Forget that I'm an officer at all! Just come over to battalion headquarters and talk to me, man to man!" During the Italian campaign, John Bassett sprinted all-out to cross open space splattered by German machine-gun bullets, and once safe, collapsed in exhaustion. Suddenly, hovering above him, was Lieutenant Colonel Shelor, standing next to his jeep. "Get up, soldier." "Yessir." "Son, we've got these bastards on the run. Do not doubt that we will be victorious." In the Pacific, a colonel offered Russell Davis a lift from the hospital back to the front lines. "Hit?" "Just in the leg. There was no sense hanging around back there." "Attaboy." (Here Davis began to register his inward reactions.) "The quicker we get in there, the quicker we get it done and get out. Right?" ("Yeah, if we get out at all.") "You won't have to be out there much longer, son." ("It only takes a second to get hit good.") "We're going to bust right through them." ("So are *we*.") "Once this rain stops, we'll. . . ." ("This rain will never stop.")[52]

Effective officers eschewed invoking rank in attempts to engender affinity in the men; indeed, they minimized all resort to rank. "Our C.O.," testified PFC Keith Winston, "is an example of what I call a real officer. One who says little or nothing, always trying in his quiet way to make things more comfortable for his men." The Army, thought Winston, invested its officers with such power that "it takes a real man not to take advantage of the situation." Men in all the services often conferred authority on those officers who seemed most willing to renounce their authority. On Saipan, John Ciardi worried that the B-17 guns that "keep us all alive" had become dangerously fouled. "[Bombardier officer] Grow—to whose eternal credit be it said that he pays no attention whatever to rank—immediately pitched in and helped us, and knowing nothing about the guns just took orders and worked. It's a good man that doesn't need brass to make him feel whole and right." Seaman James Fahey's day of drudgery, carrying 135-pound shells the length of the vessel, 607 feet, under a "head-sapping sun," was unexpectedly eased; "Even some of the officers helped. It makes you forget the heavy work that you are doing when you see the officers pitch in. . . . To see an officer work with the crew is great for morale. The men will respect him and naturally go out of their way to help [him]."[53]

Some of those officers who worked to surmount mistrust—by their concern for the men's welfare, by sharing the men's conditions—did achieve a rapport at odds with ordinary soldiers' attitudes towards superiors. Walter Gustafson, the private who complained that Army posts at home "reeked of caste," felt his own spirit injured by soldiers' inferior status, and doubted that officers qualified as "ordinary human beings," ultimately discovered exceptions. "I don't have much pity or sympathy or regard for overbearing, tyrannical officers, but there are many good fellows who are officers—Captain Friel, our C.O., for instance. He is one of the best. And so is Lt. Hirschhorn." Ben Tumey, amid a litany of complaint, paused in his arraignment. "There are some swell officers. [The] Lt. . . . is one of them. He is brave . . . yet kind and sympathetic. The battery would do its best for him in any undertaking." Commando Kelly liked two lieutenants. One "saw to it that all of his men were fed before he ate," and the other "was friendly . . . and was willing to talk things over with the old-timers . . . before he'd try them."[54]

Bill Mauldin's portrayal of company officers often contrasted with that of majors, colonels, and generals, especially when the former joined GIs in their victimization by the latter. A cartoon depicted a soldier and his lieutenant, equally bedraggled, seeking respite in a rear-area town. From their jeep, they survey the Officers' Bar, posted to prohibit all except base and staff officers, and the Soldiers' Club, where an MP stands ready to enforce the ties-required dress code. "Th' hell with it, sir. Let's go back to th' front." Mauldin applauded company officers who shared, and accepted equably, the leveling conditions of combat. Willie, drinking and playing poker with Joe and their unkempt lieutenant in a sandbagged emplacement surrounded by mud, asks: "By the way, what wuz them changes you wuz gonna make when you took over last month, sir?"[55]

The outcome, set in motion by this war-zone tendency to generate closer relationships between company officers and their subordinates, and then propelled forward by those officers' vulnerability to the same death-dealing conditions confronting the men, was a shift in the way company officers envisioned themselves *vis-à-vis* those both below and above them. The decisive division had previously been that between officers and men; now, in combat, lieutenants no longer identified their own interests first with those of the high command, but instead found some common cause with the ranks. No one caught this transition better than combat surgeon Brendan Phibbs in his "vision of modern war." Battle, he wrote, brought

> . . . sudden, shattering loneliness [to] men dumped in the enemy's face, men until minutes before controlled by godlike figures who fed, drilled, clothed them, moved them to the edge of danger and then left. Godlike figures suddenly shrunken to tiny voices, electronic dwarfs calling from the other side of the universe. . . .
>
> [And] it seems the gods didn't know what the hell they were talking about. Decisions [are] now up to lieutenants, sergeants, privates, organizing confusion, calling for artillery fire, siting machine guns, building defenses. . . . The battle-field has stepped in and is shaping the battalion's actions; colonels and generals may as well bay their orders to the moon.

Combat thus advanced, at least temporarily, a new alignment of company officers and soldiers.[56]

These developments did restrain soldiers' inclination to convert antagonism to action, but field relationships worked no fundamental change. Rapport between some men and some company officers was real, but it seldom lost its tentative cast. Until the American advance drove into Germany, Grady Arrington and his platoon mates found no cause for complaint against Lieutenant Carnes, the last of the company's six original officers. Then, in a town just secured, he gruffly "routed" them from the house into which they had just settled. There was reason to consider whether combat had pushed the lieutenant beyond his limits—the men had realized since crossing the Weid river that Carnes was "not the same leader"—but instead they reacted as if they had long expected a reversion to type: ". . . just like a damn officer—pulling his rank every time he gets a chance!" Soldier endorsements were provisional, with trust reliant on the officer's most recent action. As Watson posed the critical issue, "If [an officer] leads a platoon through one day he's OK and the men'll do absolutely anything in the world for him. But if he gets his men butchered the next day he's through and they know it."[57]

And even the most sympathetic relations, when able to survive combat stints, were unlikely to outlast the relief that followed. Yes, as Sledge had said, officers might be "buddy-buddy" in battle, but as soon as the unit withdrew, he added, they start "getting chicken again and throwing the crap around." Any soldiers confident of their accord with superiors were likely to be stunned that front-line camaraderie could so quickly give way to rear-echelon impersonality. "The officers are alright in combat but why"—a staff sergeant wondered—"do they have to treat us as complete strangers afterwards? After all, we all go through the hell together." Others like Ben Tumey, with hopes never high, saw officers' reversion to aloofness simply as the function of return to areas where there was no "danger of getting a slug in their backs." Commanders pleaded that a tightening was essential to re-establish requisite levels of discipline. Lieutenant Colonel Glover Johns praised drill's restorative powers; it enabled the men "to see the team in close formation again." But the men noticed how much smaller was the formation and suspected that the reimposition of formal discipline owed as much to the determination of officers, who had discovered in battle how little they controlled, to reassert sway—if not over events, then over the men.[58]

In the end, though rapport with company officers helped to contain front-line friction, divisiveness remained sufficiently sharp to render it the defining quality of the soldiers' relationship to the officer corps. And this played out in an opposition, passive and active, that reached to the edges of a guerrilla resistance.

Pranks at first harmless could turn menacing. Soldiers decided that salutes angering officers were not wasted motion after all. They could cause annoyance by holding their salutes until inattentive or otherwise occupied superiors returned them. ("I have all night. I'll wait the fool out.") Unpopular officers could be saluted to vexation. Noticing the approach of enlisted men, a company executive officer recognized their tactic: "They'd line up a few paces apart to make me salute over and over." During a nighttime training march in the English countryside just prior to D-Day, a dash of malice passed into a paratroop private's use of his ability to imitate voices. When the men found that wire fences made for tough travel, he duplicated the inflections of the battalion executive officer, Major Horton. "Captain Sobel, what's the holdup?" "The barbed wire." "Cut those fences!" "Yes, sir." The next morning, with cows wandering Wiltshire, farmers furious, and the colonel vindictive, the captain explained that he had obeyed the orders of a superior officer—who for several days had been off in London on leave. Much rougher was the mischief when the same unit incorporated in a field exercise casualties simulated to provide practice for the medics. One of those designated for the role was the same Captain Sobel, "a petty tyrant." The medics thereupon placed him under an authentic anesthetic, made an incision as if for an appendectomy, sewed it up, bandaged the captain—and disappeared.[59]

Threats of violence were hardly exceptional. By its intimations of homicide, a group of Marines on Guadalcanal seemed only to flirt with force. "We used to carry our .45s tied on a string around our waists, like a gang of cowpunchers. We'd walk along and when we'd meet some guys from our own outfit we'd say, 'Halt, pardner, and draw your weapon,' and then we'd pull our guns. The lieutenant would yell, 'Cut that out. Do you want to kill somebody?' And we'd laugh and say, 'Sure we want to kill somebody.'" The lieutenant was left to assess their intent—and their target. Drawing closer to violence, and courting an outburst, were members of the 506th Parachute Infantry Regiment determined to punish once again the "sour and sadistic" Sobel. As the company moved through a combat range firing live ammunition at pop-up targets, "More than one shot was aimed from the rear and side to crack by close to Sobel's head. He'd flop down, . . . bounce around and shout something, and jump up again. There was much laughing and gesturing from the men. I can't believe that Sobel thought what was happening was accidental, but maybe he did." The men maintained a lottery (actually, a dare they flung at themselves) keyed on "whoever gets Sobel"; clearly, they were competing to miss by the narrowest margin.[60]

Violence moved closer, within clear intent, when in North Africa unwise commanders scheduled training exercises that pitted officers against the men, thus offering paratroops of the 509th Regiment risk-free opportunities to chastise their superiors.

> The officers dug in on a hillside . . . armed with Very [flare] pistols. The enlisted men attacked them, armed with concussion grenades. Nearly every enlisted man would have given a lot to sock it to his company commander for all the "wrongs" done him in the service.

>Private Doyle was particularly eager to "get" his commander, Capt. Caspar
>Curtis. . . . He had the pin pulled from his concussion grenade and was about to
>lob it [into Curtis's foxhole]. That would make up for a lot of things that had
>happened in the past. Then one of the officers fired a Very pistol at someone
>else. The red flare caromed off a rock, and socko—hit the car of the Fifth Army
>inspector general. . . . [He] . . . got out, and began delivering unshirted hell to
>all concerned. The exercise came to an abrupt end. What a time Private Doyle
>had getting the pin back into that concussion grenade.

Most resorts to force bespoke revenge for specific actions by officers. But here
soldiers began to take action from a generalized and enduring sense of insult.[61]

The impulse to escalation did not stop at threats or at acts reaching to the
edge of force. Some enlisted men inflicted physical damage on their officers.
Soldiers in Germany, angered by unceasing guard duty and officialdom's failure to open to them any recreational opportunities, blamed their officers:
"[One] of the boys in my squad beat up a 1st Lt., a Major" and several of their
sycophants, chauffeurs and orderlies. "He got away with it too."[62]

Seldom did the desire to avenge wrongs or slights suffered at the hands
of officers result in death. A different matter, however, was the necessity to
restrain or cast off officers who, the men felt, threatened their lives in combat. Soldiers often placed in jeopardy those whose intentions seemed sure to
shorten, beyond battle's own odds, the men's chances of survival. Enlisted
men sometimes prompted fate—and the enemy's snipers—by saluting an officer on the front line. During the Ardennes campaign, a replacement officer,
Lieutenant Galicki, joined Kurt Gabel's paratroop unit. ("'Stay seated, men.'
That is what he said! We looked at one another to be sure we heard right.")
"Is there any action?" asked Galicki. ("The word 'action' sounded odd.") No.
"Well, what do you *do* here? . . . Combat patrols?" No. "You mean you don't
go out and harass the Krauts? . . . Doesn't sound like the airborne I know!"
No audition was necessary. The men knew their area to be under enemy observation and as a precaution ordinarily went for food in twos or threes,
groups too small to attract artillery. Now one of the men, Otto, heartily
waved Galicki into the chowline, and six others followed. Otto knew from
experience how long the Germans required to transmit sighting reports and
execute fire commands; at his signal the group burst apart, the men sprinting
for foxholes and leaving Galicki to welcome alone the explosions of two 88
shells. They blew his messkit from his hands and sent him slithering along
the ground, snatching at safety. "It was the last time," reported a para, "I ever
saw that lieutenant."[63]

The murder of officers was not a matter soldiers often wrote about or discussed. Threats were frequent; their execution was not. Most of those who served in World War II had no contact with, or perhaps even knowledge of, officer homicides. Robert Lekachman, a clerk in an Army unit that saw heavy fighting on Guam, in the Philippines, and on Okinawa, told Studs Terkel that he had heard of "no fragging of unpopular officers" in the Pacific. Still, although its extent is lost to history, it did occur. A replacement officer immediately aroused animosity in Douglas Valentine, a GI fighting on New Guinea. Lieutenant Silverman issued orders peremptorily and by the book. "Charley and I stared up in disbelief." He demanded that Valentine remove from his uniform a cross-swords patch acquired in Moresby in trade for a Japanese flag. While Charley muttered, "Asshole officer," Valentine replied, "Sure, right away, sir," but did nothing to comply. "Silverman was one of those typical 'ninety-day wonders' whose only concern was appearing like a 2nd lieutenant in complete control of the situation. He had been somebody's aide down on the beach . . . when he was sent up to the line, and he hadn't wised up at all since then. We had already written him off." He was a "quester for glory."

> All along the line we had lost as many men to our "questers for glory"—bad officers like Silverman who were quite willing to sacrifice a few GIs for the sake of their own advancement—as we had to the Japanese. Don't get me wrong; most of our officers were a minor nuisance we had learned to ignore rather than getting into the inevitable hassle, and we were able to forgive them in their fear and stupidity. But we could never forgive our "questers," and we developed an uncontrollable hostility toward *them*. Now, if a "ninety-day wonder" needlessly sent GIs to their death, he paid with his life. It was that simple. The company sergeant got him out behind a tree, and that was the end of it.[64]

Valentine's seeming casualness should not obscure what the slender evidence suggests, that when officer killings occurred, the men were themselves in the throes of breakdown. Valentine described the state of his platoon:

> The gradual disintegration of our unit, coupled with the loss of our comrades and the insanity of our surroundings, had a profound numbing effect on each and every one of us. . . .
>
> There was no semblance of order, only a sense of flux. . . . We saw men wandering aimlessly in a trance, mute, unable to mutter above a whisper, or men so badly shell-shocked that their hands had to be pried from their rifles. Men simply disappeared. . . . [D]eath could surface anytime, anywhere. There was so

much madness going on, such a feeling of distance from everyone and every-thing, that we stopped making judgments about anyone's behavior. Surviving became our one and only concern.[65]

With stakes so high, the struggle over discipline inevitably permeated the patterns of day-after-day combat. There it incorporated that fragile reori-entation of those platoon leaders and company commanders drawn closer to soldiers and their sufferings than OCS training had contemplated.

The Army charged commanders both with looking after their men and with achieving the military goals specified in orders. When the second mission inevitably proved incompatible with the first, officers were absolved if they limited as much as possible the loss of American lives. This they could do, as the social philosopher Michael Walzer pointed out, by ceasing to pursue victo-ries more costly than they were worth and by breaking off engagements that were unwinnable. But the privates had seldom trusted those placed over them to make such fateful calculations, and now, with their own survival so starkly at issue, company officers often demonstrated misgivings that echoed those of the men. Embattled lieutenants and captains realized that for the good officer, satisfying high-command precepts often courted suicide; that their fates rested more than they had anticipated on the actions of their men; and that, when pulled between those above and below, small tilts downward might better their odds. In these circumstances company officers often proved little more in-clined to heed distant authority than did those in the ranks.[66]

Here officers at odds with their superiors deployed a variety of tactics. They impeded insupportable orders by expressing reservations, suggesting modifications, "correcting" information. Near Samrée, Leinbaugh and an-other company commander thought their men too exhausted to continue an advance. "Neither . . . was challenging the Army's authority; they were just arguing the facts." Did the colonel know that the men's weapons were frozen? That the units were at less than half strength? Now that he knew, surely. . . . Such approaches occasionally succeeded; orders were sometimes changed. In the Huertgen Forest, the colonel listened to George Wilson's al-ternative scheme of attack and, when others intervened to support it, agreed. During the same campaign, a major argued so persuasively that not only was an attack order rescinded but his soldiers were relieved by fresh troops.[67]

Where such overtures failed, other means were at hand. An officer insist-ing on making a personal inspection of the terrain could cloak delay in con-scientiousness. Literalness, too, sometimes offered a refuge. "Do we own that barn, Lieutenant?" John Toole's regimental commander asked him. "No, sir, we do not." "Don't you think we ought to own it?" "Yes, I guess so, sir." But "He has not given me a direct order . . . so I don't do anything. . . ." Orders that could be neither modified nor deflected might still be discharged on field officers' terms. Timing—the execution of directives sooner or later, in daylight or darkness—they knew to be critical. Said Paul Boesch, "It was my job to carry out orders, not to dispute the judgment of those above me. But I knew that in the deep dugout which Battalion occupied nobody had any real knowledge of whether it was sunrise or sunset or high noon."[68]

Distance offered officers additional opportunities to insulate themselves against insupportable orders. The voice on the telephone insisted on a movement that Boesch believed invited disaster:

"Lieutenant Boesch. . . . Lieutenant Boesch. Can you hear me, Lieutenant Boesch?"

I listened and I could hear, but I could not bring myself to press the butterfly switch [that] would allow me to answer. "Lieutenant Boesch. . . . Can you hear me, Lieutenant Boesch?"

I sat there, staring into the growing daylight.

The voice finally gave up.

Amid costly and complex battle in the Vosges, Captain Young Oak Kim of the 442d Infantry received a call from a rear-echelon communications officer. "There's someone who wants to talk to you." "Who?" "Guess." Recognizing the next voice as that of the 36th Division's commanding officer, Kim immediately yanked out the only remaining connection. "I guess the last line got blown up," he remarked to the curious lieutenant colonel standing at his shoulder. The frequency of failure might have led one to conclude that American radios and field telephones were the war's worst-designed equipment.[69]

Once again, however, the common interests of the officers and men proved insufficient to dispel all of the infantryman's resistance to his immediate superiors. Predictably, soldiers supported their officers' opposition to operations likely to be expensive of GI lives. Kurt Gabel, who as a young boy had watched admiringly the parades of the "perfectly drilled" Hitler Jugend and had later left a Los Angeles Boy Scout troop in indignation at its want of a comparable discipline, discovered that as a paratrooper obedience no longer enthralled him: he praised his captain and lieutenant as men "furiously intolerant of anything that expended valuable blood or energy to no purpose." But neither he nor his comrades were ordinarily willing to delegate to officers the sole determination of purpose. True, there was at their level little latitude to negotiate orders, but they were not without methods.[70]

Sometimes officers given to dangerous orders could be stifled at the outset. Don Lavender, foot soldier in the 9th Division, recalled that on a patrol just across the Rhine a new lieutenant "attempted to show his influence [and] get [the] attention of the men" by positioning his fingers in his mouth and producing a piercing whistle. "It broke the silence of the forest like the blast of a German mortar and the men [by their conspicuous contempt] left no question about the folly of his action." Thereafter, the lieutenant followed along, deferring to the lead of the platoon sergeant.[71]

And just as lieutenants probed the resolve of their regimental commanders, soldiers continued to test their lieutenants. In a clash on Okinawa, both parties left open routes of retreat. When muddled American machine gunners opened fire on Marines, Russell Davis's platoon leader turned to him: "Davis, you're well known to the whole battalion. Crawl forward and tell them who we are." Davis crept from protective coral—into a new burst of fire. "Stand up," ordered the lieutenant. "Drop dead, Lieutenant," Davis shot back. "If you want to do this, come on out here." Soon his shouts persuaded the gunners that no enemy were nearby, and all relaxed—until the lieutenant summoned Davis and, before the men, said to him, "Davis, I know there was a lot of excitement out there, but at one point it almost sounded as if you told me to drop dead. I'm sure we all must have misheard you." Davis, realizing the lieutenant's concern to re-establish his authority, knew both how to accept the proffered escape and how to avoid, via extravagance, any loss of personal standing. "Lieutenant, there is no officer or enlisted man in this regiment or division for whom I wish a longer or more happy life than you, sir. I respect you, admire you, even love . . ." "All right, Davis, we don't need any speech. I was just checking."[72]

Orders undeflectable and unalterable might still be sabotaged. Told near Saint-Lô to take out a night patrol, Lieutenant George Wilson objected, but, as he expected, "Colonel Walker would accept no excuses." With two of his squads, twenty-four men, gathered around, Wilson was explaining the mission when a voice broke from the darkness: "Lieutenant, what are the consequences if I refuse to go on this patrol?" And another: "I don't give a damn what the consequences are. I'm not going!" Wilson, unintimidated, replied that he didn't like the orders either, but he had been directed to lead "this damned patrol" and he and they "were all going like it or not." The patrol set out in a single column difficult to maintain and guide on so dark a night. Soon, a soldier emitted a cough that demonstrated an instantly contagious character, spreading up and down the line. "I bawled the men out because of the danger their noise put us in, but I couldn't see them in the blackness, and it all seemed so futile." Wilson decided on the spot that his orders *were* impossible. He abandoned all thought of a combat patrol; selected five men, leaving the others behind; and pushed on as a reconnaissance patrol. He later steeled himself against Walker's fury, but the colonel "never mentioned it at all."[73]

When the men were beyond oversight, it was often possible to falsify compliance. John Roche, an NCO in the 88th Division, reported of his experience in Italy that "More often than not I led a patrol to the assigned objective. When this was impossible, I 'faked it.'" To be sure, company officers were sometimes co-conspirators. When Captain Winters, in combat with his paratroop unit near Haguenau, in Holland, concluded that a patrol ordered by the colonel would be suicidal, he told the men to stay still. "The patrol could report in the morning that it had gotten across the river and into German lines but had been unable to get a live prisoner." At other times, combat infantrymen did not scruple to deceive their own officers. On the eve of an attack in Alsace, Lieutenant Paul Fussell

> . . . got an order from Battalion . . . to send out a patrol . . . to see how deep the river was between our position and the Germans'. So I sent out my best sergeant and three or four . . . men . . . and they went out for a couple of hours and reported that the river was nine inches deep and was very easy to cross without any . . . bridging equipment.
>
> I sent the news back to Battalion. All right . . . the attack . . . was not terribly successful[;] they did achieve their mission, but with many casualties. After the war I was in a German town and I found this sergeant and we were very friendly and we drank some beer together, and he said, "You know, I want to ask you something. You know that night you sent us out, do you really think we went down to that river?" And I said, "Yes, I did. I really did." He said, "But of course we didn't. We . . . were scared to death. We went down from the house about fifty yards, we lay in the grass for about two hours, we all agreed on the story about the river, and we came back and made the report."

The sergeant's confession convinced Fussell "that a lot more is going on in the Army than you think," and that such episodes occurred "much more often . . . than most people are aware."[74]

Even in the face of the GI conviction that soldiers were punished more often and more onerously than officers guilty of the same infractions, defiance of orders was not infrequent. When during fighting in the Vosges engineers positioned a minefield incorrectly, at the cost of an American tank and its crew, Sergeant Foreman of Toole's platoon refused an order to retrieve the shattered vehicle: "I'll pound your fucking rock at Leavenworth before I go down there again!" His superiors found him not responsible for his revolt; he was "at the end of his rope." Charges went unfiled, as they often did, in surrender to several pressures. A pattern of courts-martial, mid-level commanders feared, would make unmistakable to higher echelons that they had been unable to enforce discipline in their units. Prosecutions, moreover, further aggravated relationships with the men.

Finally, there was simply too much insubordination to be suppressed by formal process. Discipline at the front, Sergeant John Roche insisted, "cannot be strict or harsh"; any rigorous enforcement "would lead to gross insubordination or mutiny" and courts-martial prosecutions for those offenses, and for desertion, "would have left no fighters at the front. (Even I allowed my orders to be ignored.)" True, there remained at the disposal of company officers wide-ranging informal punishments—offenders could be listed as company "troublemakers," removed from the unit's rotation lottery, deprived of leave, assigned to the most perilous missions—but these, because they both threatened unit working relationships and courted retaliation, had to be used so sparingly that they generated little deterrence.[75]

Assertive individualism led Americans in two directions, one brilliantly beneficial to the war effort, the other very expensive of soldiers' lives. It underwrote men's confidence in reaching beyond assigned stations, in asserting initiatives (more in matters of logistics and weaponry than in tactics), and in bringing to those efforts a high inventiveness. GIs convinced that their officers were no better than they did not hesitate to assume officer functions. In mid-1994, General George Patton called upon his engineers to rebuild seven bridges between Saint-Lô and Le Mans to enable ammunition trains to pass over them in 48 hours. "I was there at one bridge," began a major.

> It was pretty bad. One edge of it had been blown into the stream and some ranking brass looked it over and said it couldn't be done. But there was a master sergeant who used to be a bridge designer and he got together with some noncoms and figured out how it could be finished in time. It looked kinda impossible to me, mostly because they didn't have enough of the right equipment. But goddam if they didn't do it. It was finished in forty-seven hours.[76]

The Americans' struggle to break beyond the Normandy perimeter, "Operation Cobra," succeeded where Montgomery's Operation Epsom failed—in part because they had produced, in the historian Max Hastings's term, a "secret weapon": the "Rhinos," steel tusks fixed to the fronts of their tanks and capable of uprooting the Norman hedgerows that had hitherto stalled the Allied advance. The idea had been born of a "bull session" in the 2d Armored Division's 102d Cavalry Reconnaissance unit. "Why don't we get some saw teeth," wondered a Tennessee soldier named Roberts, "and put them on the front of the tank and cut through these hedges?" Though some laughed, Sergeant Curtis Culin saw the possibilities; he salvaged the steel of German beach obstacles, directed the fashioning of tusks, arranged the demonstrations that convinced first the tankers and then General Omar Bradley. "It is difficult," Hastings believed, "to overstate the importance of the 'Rhinos,' . . . for they restored battlefield maneuverability to Bradley's armor. Henceforth, while the German tanks remained restricted to the roads, the Shermans [outflanked] them across country." Seldom in other armies was change effected in such a manner.[77]

The GI frame of mind seemed to lend itself to the retrieval of disadvantageous situations—from the acknowledgement that a weapon was failing its primary purpose, followed by fashioning an alternative solution to the problem *and* an alternative use for the superseded weapon, to determining what was wrong with a vehicle and fixing it. "[Soldiers] *knew,* their *hands* knew," said Eric Sevareid, and in their ". . . world of the knowing hands," no reserve, no deference prevented GIs from using them. Winston Churchill would later praise "the inventive genius of the [American] citizen-soldier" as the marvel of the U.S. Army during World War II.[78]

Underlying the resolve to "do the job" was the conviction that individuals, wherever placed, were of consequence—even in war. Marine William Manchester held, at least until the atomic bomb fell on Hiroshima, that "In my war a single fighter with one rifle could make a difference, however infinitesimal, in the struggle against the Axis." In July 1943 an Air Force sergeant in North Africa wrote reassuringly to his sister that "on the whole, this war is being run like clockwork with the pleasing results you read about in the newspaper. But behind all these successes, major or minor, the underlying factor is an individual's bravery and guts. One person can provide the spark that causes an Army to do unheard-of things." Those thus convinced saw corroboration in reports from Normandy, that the actions of forty-seven men on Omaha Beach had converted the landings from calamity to success, and from the Bulge, that small numbers of GIs without orders or information had held their roadblocks and brought thrusting German armored columns to a standstill. "It was this desperate resistance by isolated Americans . . . ," concluded Alan Moorehead, "this and nothing else, which saved Belgium and Holland from being overrun." True, those American soldiers whose combat experience was most prolonged often counted among their losses this faith in the efficacy of individuals; but not far behind the lines it persisted, advantageously.[79]

The war, however, also bared other manifestations of individualism whose consequences were grievous. Especially costly was the propensity of Americans, in struggling to survive drastic pressures, to rely mainly on themselves; in ignoring or clashing with their own organization, they evaded its dictates but denied themselves its protections.

The Japanese subjected American and British prisoners to far more pitiless treatment than did the Germans. By their responses, American POWs in the Pacific impaired group cohesion. Indeed, at certain junctures such cohesion disappeared, often where it was needed most.

Imprisonment weakened further the American soldier's willingness to be bound by formal authority. Capture the men regarded as a leveling influence; it revoked officer authority to command others. "[A]nybody that was captured was like a chicken with his head cut off," declared one POW private, Victor Mapes. "How is he going to give you orders?" Ben Waldron, the coast artilleryman, described his incarceration on Corregidor: "No one paid any attention to the officers, who had no say whatsoever now that they were prisoners. I remember actually hearing privates cussing out colonels." Discipline was "unheard of."[80]

When the Japanese, impatient with what looked like anarchy and anxious to secure a level of POW organization that would relieve them of the camps' internal administration, empowered senior American officers, the first results ranged from minor to cosmetic; in fact, the privates' resentment rose another notch when (as Geneva prescribed) the captors exempted officers from work assignments. Nor did anyone fare much better when the Japanese chose to ignore American ranks. The commandant of Camp Fukuoka, Japan, angry that there was so little order at meals and so much theft of food, appointed as mess officer a U.S. Navy lieutenant who, in moving to solve the problems with which he was charged, gained more influence than the senior American officer. To his solutions, however, he brought the tactics of a mobster. He recruited a goon squad that beat POWs jumping the line. He turned over to the enemy three prisoners caught stealing food. The Japanese starved the first, beat the second, bayoneted the third; all died. To present to detested captors at least the appearance of a united front, Americans attempted to maintain a surface of respect for officers. Given the mistrust just beneath, they often failed.[81]

Authentic leadership, when it appeared, was likely to be improvisatory and grounded in force of character rather than rank. In Java's Bicycle Camp, a Marine first sergeant, H. H. Dupler, exhorted his fellow POWs: "Gotta stay fit, men. Any day, now, our guys'll hit the beach out there. And by gawd we better be ready." He "started leading us in close-order drills, marching us back and forth across the dirt parade ground. . . . Had anyone else tried to instigate such a thing, we would have told him to forget it. But we were eager to please Dupler." Amid panic in the hold of a Japanese ship, one Frank Bridget, not the senior officer, mounted the ladder and "began to exercise command." He ". . . shouted at first until men began to hear him [and then] spoke soothingly and calmly. . . ." Most officers felt compelled to consider first the threat to their own survival. Captain Benson Guyton worried that he should be "doing something for the men," but he knew that the exercise of command posed a problem: unless he earned the respect of the men, they would ignore him, but to win them over required interventions with the Japanese sure to result, at minimum, in beatings, no small consideration to those already dangerously weakened by mistreatment and malnutrition. And always, thought Guyton, the enlisted men were so foolishly stubborn. "Salute the [Japanese] bastards!" he angrily advised them. "It won't hurt you. Why get beat for something as stupid as not saluting?"[82]

Thus, although most enlisted prisoners knew at least one officer whom they liked, they became ever more disdainful of officers as a group. "Trouble with officers at [Luzon's Camp] O'Donnell"—here PFC Jack Brady looked upon officers just as officers like Benson Guyton viewed privates—"was not unusual. The one thing that just really bothered me more than anything else was the absolute lack of control anyone had over them. And they apparently couldn't control themselves." When bananas appeared in the officers' mess but not in the hospital, "A large number of enlisted people began to take things into their own hands." Threats—"They were going to kill the officers responsible"—halted the diversion. Officers who invoked rank to try to cut into the water line were "told where to go and fast." On a labor detail far from camp, a lieutenant annoyed the men by "trying to pull his rank on us." "We had Sandy [a sergeant] ship his ass back to Cabanatuan." But when the officer persisted, "He got knocked right out through the side of a grass shack. . . ." In attempting to form work parties, "Some stupid officers . . . would stand out in front and bleat orders, while the men laughed at them and did what they pleased." In 1945, at the hour of their liberation, several prisoners in Japan's Omine Machi Camp ran over to Jerome McDavitt, jolting him with their first words, "Captain, sir, . . ." "You know," he told them, "that's the first time you've referred to me as 'sir' in three and a half years."[83]

In prison camp or on prison ship, then, as Victor Mapes recognized, "An officer's rank didn't mean anything. We knew we were on our own"—and thus often pitted against other Americans.[84]

At camps in the Philippines, the Japanese often required American prisoners to guard the compound's interior as their own sentries paced the perimeter at night: "if anyone escaped, those on guard would be shot. . . ." In Cabanatuan Camp, an American sentinel intercepted two Army lieutenant colonels and a Navy lieutenant breaking out through a drainage ditch. He hissed that they must return to the barracks. They demanded that he help them. He argued that the responsibility he bore was to himself and the other prisoners. (The Japanese divided POWs into groups of ten "Brother's Keeper" or "Blood Brothers" squads, whose remaining members would be executed if any escaped.) Whispered debate deteriorated into blows. Other prisoners arrived to subdue the three men and hustle them into the American guardhouse, but a struggle erupted, so shrill that it brought the Japanese. They beat the three officers into unconsciousness, staked them at the front gate, and compelled passing Filipinos to club them; left them there through thirty-five hours of sunglare, darkness, and even a typhoon; then beheaded one, shot the second, and bayoneted the third.[85]

No prisoner ordeal was crueler than that of the "death ships" employed in transporting POWs to Japan, Formosa, and Manchuria. On the worst of these passages, American organization shattered. No voyage created greater agony than the Philippines–Japan transit of the *Oryoku Maru* in December 1944. At Manila, 1,631 POWs were herded into holds still foul with the horse urine and manure of the vessel's previous passengers. Ventilation, food, and water were hopelessly deficient; suffocation, hunger, and thirst brought on panic. "The prisoners were screaming," Sidney Stewart recounted, "crying for air and begging for water. Their cries were like those of tortured animals. By now the screams . . . were maddened screams. Sometimes I heard hysterical laughing, like that of a crazy woman, high-pitched and broken with sobs. The men began . . . fighting. They tore at each other. . . . Their screams of terror and their laughter were terrible things." As some sank down and died, those still upright stood on bodies. "Men were choking each other. Then the awful truth dawned on me as I looked at a body lying beneath me. . . . His throat had been cut and the blood was being drunk." Stewart watched as a father and son, West Point graduates, grappled: "The son was killing his father. I could see the look in the father's eyes . . . compassion and pity for the son who was a maniac." In that moment Stewart began to distrust even his closest comrade: "Could [Rass] do a thing like that to me?"[86]

John Emerick, who survived a thirty-two-day voyage to Japan in a similar hulk, later realized that "Your mind just couldn't comprehend how bad things were." "Cannibalism, the works. You would fight your best friend for his water or his food. It was survival of the fittest"—or the least restrained. On another crossing, Sergeant Forrest Knox could not forget, some men came to fear that the bedlam would provoke the Japanese to cover the hatch and thus cut off the last of the air drifting down to the hold, so they beat and strangled those around them who would not or could not stop screaming and wailing. "If they howled, they died." Knox, meanwhile, wrestled a terror of his own, a terrible fright that the man who stole his canteen would refuse to return it: "I was going to do my best to kill him. . . . [On] this ship, in this place, there was no mercy."[87]

Relentless as was the behavior of Japanese captors, it did not dictate that their captives' reactions should be fragmenting and isolating.

The British determination to maintain cohesiveness despite imprisonment contrasted sharply with the American experience. In Changi prison camp, Singapore, British officers remained firmly in control—to the astonishment of a GI held there: "Their enlisted men . . . took orders as if there had been no surrender. . . . We Americans could barely believe our eyes. . . . British soldiers stand at attention and salute their own officers, the officers actually prancing around expecting it." Regulations were circulated and enforced. British Army Sikhs rather than Japanese sentries policed the camp and confined violators. Camp committees controlled by officers oversaw all escape plans, assigned preparatory roles, and determined final participants. Officers retained almost all their prerogatives. Tempering dire but inescapable circumstances with familiar organization, the British sustained pride, organized large-scale education and recreation programs, and maintained a comradeship far broader than the Americans' three or four-man survival groups, thus minimizing conflict with the Japanese and predaciousness among themselves.[88]

Yet most GIs liked little that they saw in the British compounds. Frank Fujita, captured on Java and transported to Changi, first recoiled from what most angered him in the U.S. Army: the discrepancy in conditions between officers and men. While privates struggled under "starving conditions,"

> . . . just across the fence . . . was a large palatial manor that a bunch of British officers occupied. They lived . . . in splendor and had their . . . soldier servants to do their bidding. They were well-dressed, well-fed and swaggered about with their little riding crops as if they were royalty and answered to no one. Their lawn was immaculate, the hedges were neatly trimmed, and in their front yard

were two big trees . . . full of . . . mangos. To us starving men, the sight was more than we could cope with, and several of us went over the fence and began to knock fruit from the trees and stuff our shirts full. The British officers came running out ordering us to stop stealing "[His] Majesty's fruit!" We knew damn well that the [King] was not eating this fruit, but that those well-fed, pompous stuffed shirts were.

When the British command tripled the guard to fend off American raids on supply carts returning daily from Singapore with officers' food purchases, and then decided to limit South African Red Cross food parcels to Empire troops, Fujita developed "a genuine dislike for the Englishmen."[89]

Americans often concluded that the British system smacked of a "deal" between the Japanese and the British brass, negotiated at the expense of the other ranks. To their protests against officers' easier lives, GIs added another category of complaint: excessive cooperation with the enemy. Fujita objected to the use of Sikhs as police ("It made me angry to see these guards in the employ of the Japanese"), freeing up enemy soldiers, he assumed, for combat operations. PFC Michael McMullen began his captivity in a Philippines camp whose American prisoners had saluted the Japanese but had somehow held the line against bowing; transferred to Omine Machi in Japan, where the British were "breaking their backs bowing to the Japanese," he and other Yank resisters were beaten. When the British refused to reconsider their practice, Americans argued with them and with those of their own who had begun to bow. Finally, the Japanese found it essential to separate British and American prisoners. In Omuta Camp, Americans negotiated with their captors a coal-mining quota, but arriving British POWs exceeded it. The Japanese then began clubbing underachieving Americans, who in turn "beat the hell" out of any British they could catch. J. J. Carter was one of many Yanks perplexed by the *Bridge on the River Kwai* syndrome: "I'd been with these Limeys [at Aomori Camp in Japan]. They had this achieving thing. It was as if some of them felt they almost owed the Japanese something. I never could understand it."[90]

At Omori Camp, when a building caught fire, the Japanese peremptorily ordered a bucket brigade.

> The English jumped right in and started helping the Japs put out the fire. That was on one side of the building. On the other side, we Americans discovered a big stack of lumber and, since we couldn't see any reason not to, we began tossing the lumber into the fire. When the British found out what we'd done they got upset. We were upset with them. . . . We couldn't see them helping to put

the fire out. Of course, when the Japs caught us, they too were a little upset. They cut our rations. And the British ration. That's another reason why the British were so unhappy.[91]

A few Americans, however, noticed other aspects of British behavior—that some of their officers, for example, were willing to place themselves between the Japanese and British other ranks, deflecting punishments to themselves, urging and sometimes wringing concessions from their captors, compelling enemy acknowledgment of their leadership (and thus drawing from their own privates renewed sanction for their authority and prerogatives). Knox, angry that American officers at Cabanatuan did no work, complained further that "if they went on a work detail, they just stood around and did nothing to try and protect a man." At Niigata Camp, PFC William Wallace realized both that some jobs were easy, others killing, and that American officers "never suggested to the Japanese that the jobs be [rotated]." In the Mukden camp, PFC Robert Brown "never once saw one of my American officers try to defend anybody [but] I saw the British officer go over to the Japs and raise hell with them. He got knocked on his butt, but he got up and started all over again." Also at Mukden, American non-commissioned POWs, irate that their officers were stealing their food and possessions while they were off toiling, put an end to their losses by persuading the Japanese to remove American officers from kitchen and bakery jobs and to confine them to their barracks during working hours.[92]

Granted that at the time of their surrender British units retained a higher order of cohesion and British soldiers a higher state of health than their American allies on Bataan and Corregidor, the subsequent resilience of British discipline was nonetheless impressive. The chain of command carried on, intact, even amid such demonic inflictions as the Siam-Burma Railroad construction and the hell-ship voyages. A British flight lieutenant, W. M. Blackwood, described a passage of 67 days survived by 325 out of 630 prisoners, when, encircled by "scenes of indescribable horror," orderlies continued to remove bodies and padres to read out the burial service. Commanders insisted on access to senior Japanese officers in order to make representations and voice protests. In the holds, spacing schemes permitted some to sleep because others stood, confident of their turn to lie down. When one hell-ship sank (the Japanese did not mark prisoner transports; American torpedoes and bombs destroyed at least fifteen of them), the British "formed into queues and climbed out in perfect order." Seldom did they surrender to bedlam. In the

hold of that vessel on which GI prisoners took the lives of howling compatriots, Knox remembered, were "about fifty English troops who had survived the
building of [the] railroad in Burma. They were put right in the center, under
the hatch, and during the entire voyage not one of them died."[93]

The Yanks spurned all notions of untraversable social distances separating officers and men, dismissed suggestions of higher capabilities inhering in
superiors, derided Tommies' obedience to orders, and detested that officer
noblesse oblige indistinguishable, in GI eyes, from arrogance. ("We all felt
they were in no position to brag," Knox declared, "since they had nowhere
near put up the fight we had. We found them insufferable.") But the British
contract—the willingness of many officers to accept service to the men as an
indissoluble component of leadership, the willingness of the men to defer to
rank, its orders and its prerogatives—served soldiers well when, in one of the
war's sternest ordeals, survival often hinged on the preservation of military
cohesiveness. And it was here, for GI prisoners of war, that the cost of American convictions came due.[94]

    Two lines of development, very different in form but both linked
to the Marines, aimed to break beyond the U.S. Army pattern of relationships and to fortify discipline by fostering a sense of equivalence between the
men and their officers.

Marine basic training was more rigorous—and harsher—than the
Army's, but with quite different results. Recruits who passed through it
seemed to emerge with considerable martial spirit and with little of that
alienation from their branch so conspicuous in Army inductees.

The effort to neutralize personality, to suppress individual assertion, and
to create receptivity to commands was more resolute at Parris Island than at
Fort Knox, and Marine instructors simultaneously strove more strenuously
than their Army counterparts to connect Chicken Shit and combat—with
indelible results. While cleaning a latrine, a group of recruits obeyed an order
to wash their hands in the toilets. The instructor next demanded to know
whether they would drink that water. "Yes, sir." Then came the usual reversal
of direction designed to sharpen receptivity by sowing confusion and intensifying vulnerability—"Do you run around drinking out of toilets?"—as prelude first to the prime prescript—"You obey orders. . . . It doesn't matter if
you like it or not. It ain't yours to think"—and then the linkage with combat—"One of them damned Japs or Germans might make you drink out of a
toilet. You would be insulted and do somethin' foolish, an' get shot. . . . You
got to be able to take cussin' an' insults. . . ."[95]

Many trainees agreed with their sergeants that harshness was salutary. When a private's underwear, displayed for inspection, turned up dingy and wrinkled, and he was remanded to the brig for three days on bread and water, Gallant's reaction was not indignant, rebellious, or cynical; in the episode he found "a good warning and example for us." When drill instructors resorted to collective punishment—the offending recruit was made to watch as the platoon was double-timed to exhaustion—the reaction was just as the high command wished: trainee ire targeted the transgressor. The men, warned Gallant, forgave only the first time. For Marines, basic ended more frequently than for infantrymen with a sense of accomplishment—a sense that their sweat, exhaustion, and compliance had won them admission to a select company. Grady Gallant was rhapsodic: "By now we had been convinced the Marine Corps was the great fighting unit of the world. We respected the Marine Corps, revered it, and were absolutely loyal to it."[96]

Here the Marines drew, with great effectiveness, on special advantages: They invoked the mystique of the Corps as an elite force, repeatedly reminding recruits that they were volunteers (as all were until 1943), and they inculcated pride by appealing both to an unequaled masculine toughness and to the Corps's superior standing with the American public. And a final factor in particular helped to reconcile individuals to the demands of the organization: the Marines' effort to narrow social distances between officers and men.

Trainees heard each day "Every Marine is a rifleman" and "Every Marine is a combat Marine." Elite units elsewhere had similar policies—in the 86th Infantry of the Army's 10th Mountain Division, "No matter what job or rank, you took part in the Regiment's operations"; Airborne divisions were proud that jump school suspended rank, that officers (including generals) and men entered battle in identical fashion—but no other organization matched the Corps' stress on equivalence. Not all Marines entered battle, but there was an impetus for officers to engage combat more directly, to lead more aggressively than did infantry captains and majors. Most Marines saw the slogans converted into actuality.[97]

Correspondent Richard Tregaskis found in Marine captain Harold Torgeson "the outstanding hero" on Tulagi. His modus operandi was "to tie thirty sticks of dynamite together, run to the cave mouth while four of his men covered it with rifles and submachine guns, light the fuse, shove the TNT in amongst the Japs and run like hell." Torgeson "blasted more than fifty Jap caves with [his] home-made dynamite bombs." In the same campaign, under Japanese fire so heavy that it forced Marines to abandon their advance, Major Kenneth Bailey crawled to the cave shielding the enemy emplacement and kicked rocks away from the entry until he was shot in the leg. On Bougainville, Captain Gordon Warner instructed his men to direct their fire to pin down Japanese in a machine-gun nest; he then filled his helmet with grenades, circled alone behind the enemy position, and blew it up, losing a leg in the clash. On Okinawa, Major Henry Courtney revived an assault stalled by gunfire. "Who's coming with me?" he asked, and began to climb Sugar Loaf. The citation accompanying his posthumous Medal of Honor described the next moments: ". . . he pushed ahead with unrelenting aggressiveness, hurling grenades into cave openings . . . with devastating effect." In fighting on Guadalcanal, 23 percent of the enlisted men in "Chesty" Puller's battalion became casualties—and 50 percent of the officers.[98]

In and beyond battle, a number of Marine officers made it a point of pride to claim fewer of the prerogatives of rank than their Army opposites. Captain Garrett Graham, with the swell of forgoing an entitlement, wrote that "[A] Marine officer does not have a body servant. He fends for himself." Officers, Graham added as an example, did their own wash. Senior officers stressed the duty of company officers to look after the needs of their men. While at the construction site of a new training camp in the United States, Gallant was impressed that within two weeks all enlisted men's tents had wooden floors, for "the officers were told they could not have floors until the men did." In North Carolina, in his talk to the battalion's officers, "Chesty" Puller added a directive: "One more thing. Wherever we are at chow time, the privates will be fed first. Then the noncoms, and the officers last of all." Puller subsequently came upon a private ordered to salute over and over because he had failed to acknowledge a passing second lieutenant. Summoning the lieutenant, Puller reminded him that officers must return every salute: "[Now] let me see you get to it, and do your share." Enlisted Marines, like Army privates, welcomed all gestures mitigating separation and responded appreciatively. On a Sunday morning in the Pacific, a Marine visited the cemetery on a recently won atoll. "I walked between the rows of white crosses, straight in their long lines and evenly spaced. The paint was fresh and white, the names plain-lettered. Here a major, there a private, all quietly resting."[99]

Strikingly, these efforts did not ward off the rapid war-zone migration of Marine rank-and-file attitudes toward those of the GIs. As a young British lieutenant had learned in African and Italian campaigns, "[T]rust depends on a man's knowing that his commander thinks of him as a person and therefore treats him fairly, and looks after him . . . as well as conditions permit." American soldiers were alert to officers' fulfillment of the first prescription;

without that, the second remained no more than an excursion into paternalism—and here, once more, there was trouble in many matters of inequitable treatment.[100]

Captain Garrett Graham sensed that aboard his transport to the Pacific, the men, angered by the great divide in the ship's accommodations, were growing "sullen and resentful." He expected trouble—"After all, Americans are not accustomed to such a pushing around when they feel there is no necessity for it"—and trouble arrived forthwith. The men laughed at a shipboard sentry who ordered them to pick up their trash; they would not accept direction from one of their own no matter how anointed by the command structure. And the sentry, rather than brave ridicule deriding traitorousness to comrades, began to ignore officer instructions. Another sentry also retreated, taking to his bunk when his feet started to hurt; and a third suspended his rounds to join a crap game, thus losing five days and all nourishment save bread and water. Soon the whole ship seemed rife with insubordination, neglect of duty, petty theft, illicit smoking. The brig overflowed. Graham tried a final time to bridge the gap that he watched widen. "We're the same kind of guys you are," he assured a private. "We've just got different jobs, that's all." "I guess you are, sir," came the cutting reply, "but I never thought of it that way."[101]

Nor did the Marine officer's sense of obligation to his men's welfare always lift him above class attitudes patronizing or demeaning of privates. A platoon leader, David Brown, explained in a letter home that "After a day attending to the needs and troubles of each man, then [censoring] their letters at night, there is little time or spirit left for the recreation which educated persons need to keep the mind alive and keen." At the same time, he added, the enlisted men played cards, wrote letters, and went to the movies; "They have an unlimited capacity for dreaming, or for idling, or for inventing hobbies, or trifling amusements, just as children have these qualities. Such are the blessings of those not deeply concerned over knowledge, or destiny, or freedom, but content to live with what they have at hand. . . ." In the end, Marine riflemen felt no less powerfully than GIs the social divide and the antagonisms it engendered.[102]

Gallant recounted an episode eloquent of the way Marine attitudes evolved. As units training to land on Guadalcanal stood off the Fijis, with enlisted Marines lining the rails of their transport, a Higgins boat pulled alongside and a Marine lieutenant, "laden with combat gear," began to descend the cargo net hanging over the side of the transport. Suddenly, he lost his grip and plummeted into the sea. "Well, I'll be damned! He fell in."

"Wonder if he'll drown." "That pack ought to take him right on down. . . . But he's supposed to know how to get out of it under water. I wonder if he can." "Where is he?" "Under water." "There he is!" "Ain't he wet, though?" Again the officer sank—and recovered. "I don't think he'll make it." "Oh, hell yes, he will. We ain't lost an officer yet." "Well, you wan' to bet?" "Bet on what? They ain't goin' to let him drown." A Marine captain appeared and demanded, "What's goin' on here?" A private explained. "Great God! Why hasn't a man gone over the side to help this officer?" No reply. The captain rapidly ordered a sergeant, "Get some men down there at once, by God!" Marines began descending the net. "Damnit, why didn't you men move out when this man fell?" "It just happened, sir. Just happened, like that. We were stunned." "Why . . . why . . . by God, he could have been killed . . . damnit! Next time, you people move out on the double and lend a hand immediately . . . by God . . . damnit . . . why, damnit!" Several men, reaching the lieutenant, finally pulled him to safety.[103]

No organization pushed further toward equivalence than Carlson's Raiders, an elite within the Marine elite.

Evans Fordyce Carlson, a career officer, had served extensively in China (1927–29, 1933–35, 1937–39) and while there had found inspiration in Mao Tse-tung's Eighth Route Army, notably its relationships between officers and men stressing mutual respect under the rubric "Gung Ho" (Working in Harmony). Around this concept Carlson was determined to construct the Raider battalion he won authorization to organize in February 1942. Three thousand Marines volunteered for the unit's one thousand places. Carlson decreed the abolition of such officer privileges as separate messes and clubs. Saluting became a rarity. Distinctions between officers and men—in uniforms, equipment, living conditions—diminished dramatically. Carlson slept on his tent floor, made his own fire, policed his own quarters, waited with others in chow lines, completed marches with the men. He pledged to the Raiders that he and his officers would "live as you live; work as you work; eat as you eat; fight as you fight. We give up all our privileges cheerfully and willingly."[104]

At the heart of Carlson's vision lay the rejection of imposed discipline and its replacement by collective, cooperative problem solving—in other words, American teamwork. In his view, officers were to earn their status by demonstrating superior ability, knowledge, and character; but even success here would not empower Raider officers to impose discipline as did even unproven officers elsewhere in the services. Carlson called for the restraint of rank. No one was to devise directives to increase an officer's "comfort, convenience [or] security." All orders were to meet tests of essentiality and justice; officers were "never [to] order a man to do anything they're not willing and able to do themselves."[105]

Carlson encouraged enlisted men to speak out: "You can say what you think about anyone—officers and yours truly included." He summoned them to discussions of the issues underlying the war, and he opened to debate the weaknesses of the Raiders' first combat performance, the generally successful raid on Makin. He experimented, playfully, with enlisted men's common tribunals as an alternative military justice system. ("If you tell me to shoot him, I'll shoot him.") He promised the men that he would remain accessible to all of them. He fostered the use of first names, convinced that the American military, in mistaking informality for indiscipline, had succeeded only in linking its discipline with the humiliation of the individual.[106]

Carlson's experiment bore bitter fruit. Marines trained in a system whose central doctrines held them incapable of self-discipline and who were by 1942–43 inured to estrangement and resistance seized the latitude offered them as an unexpected weapon with which to wage their struggle. As Michael Blankfort described their reaction, "old habits of thought" reasserted themselves: "Slowly, almost without willing it, men began to take advantage, to see how much they could get away with." And officers able to demonstrate no qualifications higher than their men's "began to use their rank as a decisive argument." The men in turn became derisive of Gung Ho. Carlson, moreover, had miscalculated. There appeared little foundation for his position that the privates wished and needed to comprehend the political issues undergirding the war, notwithstanding such Friday Night Forums as one at which four Marines debated "The Kind of Social Order We Want after the War." Equally at odds with the assumptions of coarsened combatants was Carlson's Christian idealism, notably his conviction that unselfish behavior brought divine protection to those who practiced it. Of greatest moment, however, was the displeasure of the Marine high command. At home the Raiders received much publicity, too extensive, too complimentary. In the closing stages of the Guadalcanal campaign, unsubstantiated reports appeared suggesting a degradation of the unit's fighting capacity; to the contrary, there was much evidence for the opposite. Carlson's Raiders, operating for a month on their own, had traversed 150 miles of jungle behind enemy lines, had killed 700 Japanese at the cost of 17 of their own, and had, most remarkably, suffered only one case of neuropsychiatric collapse. Nevertheless, Carlson was "promoted" beyond field command, and Gung Ho abruptly expired. His successor immediately re-established formal channels and rigid officer-men relationships, restoring the Raiders to what they called "a Chicken Shit outfit."[107]

Evans Fordyce Carlson had extended greater trust to enlisted men than any other command figure of the war. In the midst of conflict, he had pursued a military discipline "based on knowledge and reason." "It's yours to reason why," he told Marine privates. "In a democracy, men must [always] be thinking human beings, not puppets." They had not always been able to return his trust, but some of the men were aware of what they had lost, an experiment tempering hierarchy with teamwork and offering them uncommon respect. Combat correspondent James Lucas was with the Raiders when, on their return from a training exercise, they learned of Carlson's promotion: "Tragedy awaited us. . . . I stumbled with them up the beach, tears in their eyes, and heard them curse the fate that had robbed them of their old man. I sat in their tents and heard them cry like babies."[108]

Bill Mauldin, who passed every minute in the European theater, still saw from a distance that "of the brass, only Eisenhower and Carlson had the respect of the GI."[109]

The close of fighting against the Germans on May 8 and against the Japanese on August 15, 1945, exposed for a final time how little the American military drew on internalized discipline that their training had been expected to inculcate.

V-E celebrations commonly moved beyond control, first in rear areas where support personnel, unlike front-line soldiers, had no difficulty in grasping that the war could actually end—and without taking their lives. Many rear-echelon troops, Major Joe Shomon reported, broke out and began firing weapons, including antiaircraft guns; threw grenades; and started fires. A number of celebrants were killed, many wounded. "It was a mad, dangerous night. Control was completely absent, except for a few companies."[110]

Leinbaugh's line company soon celebrated in like craze. Drunken GIs used their weapons to create a Fourth of July sky, and thereafter few semblances of discipline survived. "Sergeant Olson, if you want my goddam boots shined you'll have to shine them yourself." Officers continued to post guard-duty rosters, but soldiers seldom appeared. One of Leinbaugh's men took a young German woman to his barracks bed—after promoting her brother to guard and assigning him to walk the perimeter. The only American diligence was that of a few sentinels whom the men set out to warn of any officer's approach.[111]

Lieutenant John Toole received orders to escort across Europe to a replacement center in Mannheim a contingent of 220 enlisted men scheduled to return to their units. When their train passed through Paris, "fully one-third of them [took] off for the delights of the city." With the train halted temporarily in a freight yard, those who remained entertained themselves by throwing rocks at nearby cars loaded with U.S. Army vehicles and applauding those whose aim was sufficiently steady to smash windshields. Toole threatened to turn them over to MPs; they mimicked his words. They were "absolutely impossible to control. Their war is over and they don't give a shit for officers, commands, or any of the other trappings of the military." In Mannheim, Toole delivered to authorities one-third of his original charges, and he did not much care. As early as Paris, he had decided that he would not concern himself with deserters, for "I feel like taking off myself."[112]

Orval Faubus, with the 75th Division in Rheims, also noticed how epidemic became disaffection. "Everybody was bitching"—including doctors, Red Cross representatives, and even chaplains. A priest starkly refused to write one more letter to the parents of Catholic soldiers lost to accidents or suicide. As for the fighting men, "Those who had been most responsible soldiers during combat in the finest American Army ever put together, now declined, and often refused, to accept any responsibility or to perform properly any assigned duty." Officers were "frightened at the possible consequences." The "one all-consuming desire" was to go home at once; but as soon as soldiers moved even the smallest step beyond that stunned relief that they had survived war against the Germans, they collided with their government's intention to commit them to the war against the Japanese. "[The] average soldier," Shomon judged, ". . . was now completely disillusioned after having fought one war, escaping with his life, and was now being sent to another, perhaps yet more horrible." When a colonel told him that the 3d Division, then in Europe, was scheduled to invade Kyushu in November, John Toole had no idea how he would escape, but he was certain that he "absolutely [could not] go through with it." Chaplain Morris Kertzer watched an Army transport draw away from a Marseilles wharf bound for the Pacific: "The men were not happy. They had been separated from their families for months, some for years. . . . If ever I saw mass misery it was there on Pier F." Theirs was the misery not of sullenness but of rebellion. Americans were fortunate that the Pacific conflict ended only ninety-nine days after the European War. Had peace not brought an end to the transfer of forces between theaters, the government's efforts would have provoked indiscipline of unprecedented scale.[113]

In the Pacific, as earlier in Europe, enlisted men demonstrated in their celebrations that they had not confined their antagonism to the battlefield. On August 15, 1945, at Escolta in the Philippines—as many yelled, cried, laughed, drank, danced, and embraced—"Sailors stripped off their middies and threw them to Filipino girls. Soldiers ripped off buttons and chevrons in a rush for civilian anonymity." A story seeming to circulate everywhere among combat Marines held that just prior to Japan's capitulation, as a colonel climbed into his jeep, the sergeant standing at attention administered a powerful kick to the buttocks. A PFC, observing the sergeant's feat from a foxhole, ran up and added a kick of his own. In subsequent proceedings the sergeant explained that the colonel had trod on his toes, galling a tender corn, and that his foot had simply shot out reflexively. The private, on the other hand, pleaded: "I ain't got no excuse. Hell, I thought the war was over!"[114]

When transportation limitations delayed until spring 1946 the departure for home of many units, discipline often dissolved. In Europe, Orval Faubus described "open and defiant demonstrations" and a fractiousness so intense that hand grenades pitched into officers' bedrooms late at night caused casualties. In early March, an illegal protest meeting drew twenty thousand choleric American servicemen to Rizal Stadium in Manila: ". . . none of us gave a good goddamn about 'winning the peace.' We just wanted to go home." On R. E. Lee's last night on Guam, his cards-loving commanding officer was, as usual, awaiting Lee's arrival. Prodded by several drinks to a conviction that integrity insisted on candor, Lee rounded on his superior: "Is this why you [tried to keep] me on board, so you'll have somebody to play acey-deucey with for the next two goddam months? . . . I just want you to know, I loathe [this kind of life], I really loathe it. . . . You're just taking it out on me because I'm not Regular Navy and don't want to be, and trying to see how much shit I'll put up with, and I'm here to tell you, sir! that I've just about had enough!" Robert Welker and his soldier friends settled for a calmer way to write *finis* to their military careers. On the day of their discharge from the United States Army—with high ritual—they committed every extra uniform item to the trash can. Once home, Welker discovered delicious pleasure in his freedom to wear no hat at all.[115]

After World War II, the Luftwaffe squadron commander Johannes Steinhoff contemplated a wartime episode: Angered by a signal from Reichsmarschall Göring that cast contempt on all German pilots fighting over Sicily, Steinhoff had nevertheless pledged to his own general, with a "Yes, sir," that he would press forward no objection to a baseless and blatant insult.

> In this answer lay that trust in one's superior—a whole attitude towards life—which had been instilled into us, into our fathers and into their fathers before them. For us soldiers it had hitherto been the only right attitude, indeed the only conceivable one. The obedience practiced for centuries by the German soldier had always presupposed an unshakeable trust that the orders he received would be sensible orders and that the high command would search their hearts very carefully before sacrificing whole formations. And the many who were sacrificed died in the certainty that this was so.[116]

The worth of discipline in and of itself; obedience as the indispensable standard; trust in one's superiors, and high confidence that their commands welded intelligence, courage, and true concern for the lives of soldiers—these were not the values that infused American society. In World War II, its young men resisted a system of military discipline that had been designed as if they were.

6

THE APPEALS OF BATTLE
Spectacle, Danger, Destruction

In 1959, J. Glenn Gray, a professor of philosophy at Colorado College, published *The Warriors*, a remarkable book of "reflections on men in battle" drawn from his experience of World War II. It languished for several years, but then, catapulted by high praise from Hannah Arendt, developed a large and devoted following. Though its discussion of war was multifaceted, the book's principal accomplishment was to establish a framework within which many soldiers, scholars, and others concerned with conflict have come to discuss combat's most engrossing aspects. Most striking was Gray's formulation of three universal "enduring appeals of battle"—the delight in seeing; the delight in comradeship; and the delight in destruction. Gray found "the secret attractions of war" in war as spectacle, in our love of looking with what the Bible renders as "the lust of the eye"; in war as communal experience forging bonds of the highest emotion between men; and in war as demolition, as "the rage to destroy." A fourth element, a delight in danger described by Hannah Arendt as "the poignancy and intensity of life in the face of death," was interwoven in Gray's discussion of the other three; it deserves to be drawn out and is described here as well. (Comradeship is considered separately in chapter 7.)[1]

In these conceptions, J. Glenn Gray recognized and described emotional reactions that seemed to reach to the core of the battlefield experience.

"The wine of danger-emotion"

It seems paradoxical that soldiers wishing above all not to die should respond in any favorable way to the jeopardy in which battle placed them, and yet GIs could draw from their own peril a sense of excitement and intensity. There was an attraction in "risking all." "It was," said James Jones, "like facing God. Or gambling with Luck [or] taking a dare from the Universe." An American naval officer in the Pacific, so embarrassed by his insight that he derided it as a "Solemn Pronouncement," realized that he had "learned this much, at any rate, even if I never get back, that . . . it is death which is the intoxication, the intensifier [that] explains the war." Charles Cawthon, as an infantry officer in France, discovered in the presence of death an "intensified life force" that concentrated itself in "a hard, bright flame to survive." Correspondent Eric Sevareid limned a classic depiction of the delight in danger as soldiers prepared to cross the river Rhine:

> At the outer edge of the village I stood beside a Commando major and watched the assault troops take formation. . . . They marched in line right before us, some of their faces blackened with soot so that the whites of their eyes seemed abnormally clear. . . . Now and then [the major] reached out and touched a passing soldier; just touched him, saying nothing. . . . The major would suddenly start away, walking a few paces beside one of the men. Then he would come back to me and after a few moments of watching would start away beside another man. I thought he was speaking to them now. He did this several times. . . . I knew suddenly that I was looking into his open heart and that I understood how he felt. The war had become his very life; these men were all his world. Here with them under the dark moon, in the middle of the hellish noise, in this moment when his comrades prepared to challenge the unknown, he was intensely alive. Elsewhere, he was half-dead. And, I thought, there will be many like this man, many who will remain but half-alive when all this is ended.[2]

Such feelings reached beyond the battlefronts to civilians living in distant war zones, though with attenuated force. As it was put by Christabel Bielenberg, an Englishwoman who married a Hamburg lawyer and remained in Germany throughout the war: "Living close to death I knew to be heightened living." The British writer Vera Brittain, recalling her experience in a World War I hospital station twenty miles behind the lines, felt "the intense sharpening of all the senses, the vitalizing consciousness of common peril for a common end."[3]

Soldiers often experienced this heightened life force as exhilaration. It came to Cawthon as a "surge." To one of James Jones's soldiers it was, in the vulgate, more electrifying "than all the hunting, gambling and fucking he had ever done all rolled together." Correspondent Jack Belden, plunging toward the Sicilian shore in an assault boat, realized that "All my senses were now altered to the straining point. A flush of thrill and excitement shot through me like flame. It was wonderful. It was exhilarating." Invasion landings, firefights, air raids, and other deadly encounters, Gray concluded, produced "a quality of excitement scarcely experienced before or since."[4]

This sense of danger altered profoundly the priorities of soldiers' daily lives. They welcomed the change, for what was lost seemed to them commonplace and burdensome, and what was gained appeared extraordinary and liberating. Danger simplified living by rendering irrelevant numerous previous concerns. Institutionally, bureaucratic requirements diminished as one moved closer to battle. The enemy's presence on Guadalcanal, observed Marine captain Garrett Graham, had "cut all the red tape and blown away all the horesefeathers. . . ." Individually, those in and near combat relished the reduced compass of their lives, however fateful remained the considerations within. William Dreux, the American infantry officer who volunteered for OSS missions, described his work behind enemy lines in Brittany: "[One] of the qualities of that life was simplicity. All I wanted to know . . . was what lay around the next bend of the road, or whether that enemy machine gun in that clump of trees could cover the road to my left, or how soon it would be before I could stop and rest. Could I trust this Resistance leader? That barn we were hiding in, what was the best escape route if a German patrol came, and could we fight our way out? Most of the questions were like that, basic and uncomplicated. . . . The answers often were not easy, but you got them fast enough. You were not dealing with a lot of trivial matters, or if some of them were trivial they did not seem that way."[5]

A company officer with a Scottish battalion in North Africa found combat's strange simplicity at odds with the "complicated drama" he had expected. Only the war retained relevance. Food's sole purpose was to nourish soldiers. Daylight's *raison d'être* was that it permitted soldiers to see the enemy, darkness's that it concealed them from the enemy.[6]

And no one described better than Ernie Pyle the allure of plainness:

> The outstanding thing about life at the front was its magnificent simplicity. It was a life consisting only of the essentials—food, sleep, transportation, and what little warmth and safety a man could manage to wangle out of it by personal ingenuity. Ordinarily, . . . life . . . stripped to the bare necessities . . . is an

empty life and a boring one. But not at the front. Time for me had never passed so rapidly. I was never aware of the day of the week, and a whole month would be gone before I knew it.

At the front the usual responsibilities and obligations were gone. There were no appointments to keep, nobody cared how anybody looked, red tape was at a minimum. There were no desks, no designated hours, no washing of hands before eating, or afterward either.[7]

Soldiers also welcomed this simplification of life because it seemed to create a moral atmosphere superior to that of the rear echelon or the home front. Material values appeared to diminish in tandem with the worth of money. Garrett Graham discovered that "Money was of no possible value on Guadalcanal, except as poker chips and counters in a crap game. There was nothing whatever for which it could be spent. . . . There was no one to trade with, and nothing to buy." On a boat sailing to that island, correspondent Richard Tregaskis watched Marines take half-dollars from a large heap and skip them on the waves. Said one of the Leathernecks: "Oh, hell, money don't mean a thing out here anyhow. Even if you stay alive, you can't buy anythin'." In Europe, there was a similar, if less steep, depreciation. American combat surgeon Klaus Huebner reported that prior to D-Day, "I . . . play blackjack for twenty dollars a card with officers from Headquarters Company. I either go into this fight loaded or broke. What's the difference?" There thus disappeared, to Dreux's applause, the usual "need to consider a compromise between integrity and money. . . ."[8]

This sense of enhanced moral values nourished a widespread conviction that those at the front were better people than they had been before the war or than others were elsewhere. Pyle wrote to his editor that "the very simple, very uncomplicated" life of the battle zone was "devoid of all the jealousy and meanness that floats around a headquarters city." Cartoonist Bill Mauldin cited the "surprisingly little bickering and jealousy in combat outfits." Only at the front, averred Sevareid, was one able to find selflessness. GIs themselves sometimes developed exorbitant conceptions of combat-soldier virtue. After the war, Orval Faubus "longed for the manner in which the men of battle dealt with each other—in complete frankness and genuine honesty with all pretense and sham removed. . . . We yearned for the association with men of great differences, yet so devoid of prejudice and so imbued with loyalty that we could go out together to fight and die, for each other and for the common cause of freedom. We longed for the spirit of the men of combat—a spirit motivated by bravery, honor, compassion and sacrifice, with the absence of pettiness, envy, jealousy and falsehood. . . ."[9]

Their senses sharpened by danger, soldiers looked about them with new eyes. At people, for example. Soldier-writer Harry Brown explained that

> In peacetime you could go into a store and talk to a clerk, but by the time you had left the store you had completely forgotten the clerk's face. It was different in war. You might see a man's face in the flash of an exploding shell or in the cab of a truck or peering out of a slit trench, and though you had never seen the face before and never would see it again, you couldn't forget it. War left impressions of unbelievable sharpness. It was almost as though men, in losing identity, gained identity. Their faces and voices became intense. They clung to the mind.

And at terrain. As Margaret Bourke-White realized, "You become sensitized to topography. . . . [To] the individual the landscape takes on a personal intensity. . . . The landscape becomes as intimate as the features of someone you love." Combat soldiers would have shied from her last phrase, but they agreed that battle cast terrain in new perspective. Eric Sevareid brought to this experience an articulateness beyond that of most soldiers:

> There is an atmosphere at the front, a heightened feeling which can never be translated nor described. Until one becomes drugged with exhaustion, every scene is a vivid masterpiece of painting. The tree and the ditch ahead are all the trees and ditches of creation, informed with the distillation of sacred *tree*ness and *ditch*ness. Each common odor goes down to the final nerve endings; each turn of the road is stamped indelibly upon the brain; every unexplored house is bursting with portent; every casual word and gesture bears vibrant meaning; those who live are incredibly alive, and the others are stupefyingly dead. Obscure villages which were meaningless names on the map—Minturno, Castelforte, Santa Maria Infante—soon acquire the significance of one's native town, each street and each corner the custodian of intimate, imperishable acquaintance.[10]

A British officer, John Guest, agreed that combat, and notably its threat of imminent death, threw the milieu of the fighting soldier "into startling relief," and that "one snatched at it with a sense of urgency." Though it is difficult to find analogous civilian experiences, the situation may have been akin to that of the child recovering from a long illness abed who, on his first venture outdoors, feels as if he were seeing every object for the first time, with each one—leaf, stone, blade of grass—beautifully and keenly etched.[11]

If danger delighted because, inter alia, it liberated soldiers from many of civilian life's pedestrian pursuits, it also added piquancy to those that remained, and even to some that soldiers wished to reclaim, however briefly. Amid so much that was extraordinary, one soon again coveted touches of the ordinary. In one of Katsunori Tamai's autobiographical novels, a Japanese soldier fighting in China wrote to his brother of an episode in which he and his comrades made an outdoor bath of a great jar they had found:

> By the grace of good luck, I am still alive after a number of very bad days in the field. Death has been a constant companion. . . . Perhaps because of this, we are all very excited tonight about something that must seem to you to be very simple and childish. What is it? We are going to have a hot bath!
>
> The men are acting like kids. Well, to us, it is a thrill, a very great one. It shows you to what a minimum our pleasures have been reduced. . . . The joy of living, now, is contained merely in being alive. We find a keen, almost painful joy in the appreciation of things that formerly had little meaning, the animal pleasures of cooking and eating, bathing, washing our clothes, the feel of the sun, the sweet, fresh air. These are luxuries.

On another occasion his unit discovered an orange tree. "For a few moments, it caused complete confusion in our ranks, as the men broke out of line and began trying to bring down the fruit with bamboo poles. Then, Hayase . . . suddenly shinnied up the tree. . . . None of us got very many oranges, but even a few pieces seemed delicious. It seemed to me that I had never tasted anything quite so good. All our senses have been sharpened amazingly."[12]

An ensign in the Imperial Japanese Navy, eating candy between air assaults on the doomed battleship *Yamato,* found it "indescribably delicious." "A sense of delight bubbles secretly in my breast."[13]

Hence the elements constituting the delight in danger: "an inner excitement," in Ernie Pyle's words, "that built up into a buoyant tenseness seldom achieved in peacetime"; sharpened senses enhancing receptivity to people and surroundings; a narrowing focus sloughing off the routines and many of the commodities of workaday life; a heightened pleasure infusing those that remained; identification with a battle-zone atmosphere thought purged and morally superior. Many letters, journals, and newspaper dispatches reserved their most ethereal language for the exultation drawn from the soldier's success in remaining alive amid so much death. This was sometimes described as so profound an elevation of consciousness that the soldier could believe that he had, for some moments, transcended the limits of the self. Pyle caught superbly this quality of battlefield danger: "[War] is vastly exhilarating. . . . There is an intoxication about battle, and ordinary men can sometimes soar clear out of themselves on the wine of danger-emotion."[14]

"Delight in spectacle"

With combat serving initially to sharpen the senses, soldiers became especially receptive to the appeal that J. Glenn Gray termed the "delight in spectacle." Wartime travel brought them to sights new and strange and often compelling, so it was not surprising that soldiers responded in unaccustomed ways to scenes of natural beauty and to military tableaux, some of them common to the course of battle and others gathering impact from their rarity.

War's ambiance often worked to heighten emotional reaction to natural settings. John Guest, commanding a British antiaircraft unit, found the Italian countryside "piercingly beautiful." Guadalcanal, to Marine rifleman William Manchester, was "a spectacle of utter splendor." On a flight over the Atlas Mountains of western Algeria and Morocco, Ernie Pyle awoke from a nap and looked down just at sunset.

> The remnants of the sun streaked the cloud-banked horizon ahead, making it vividly red and savagely beautiful. . . . Below us were the green peaks . . . lovely in the softening shroud of dusk. Villages with red roofs nestled on the peak tops. . . .
>
> [It] seemed terribly dramatic that we should be there at all amid that darkening beauty so far away, so foreign, and so old.
>
> It was one of those moments impossible to transmit to another mind. A moment of overpowering beauty, of the surge of a marching world, of the relentlessness of our own fate. It made me want to cry.[15]

Phenomena of human design possessed an even greater power to move on-lookers.

Pyle described an evening in December 1940 when Luftwaffe bombers roared above the streets of London.

> [On] that night this old, old city was—even though I must bite my tongue in shame for saying it—the most beautiful sight I have ever seen.
>
> It was a night when London was ringed and stabbed with fire. . . .
>
> I gathered a couple of friends and went to a high, darkened balcony that gave us a view of a third of the entire circle of London. As we stepped out onto the balcony a vast inner excitement came over all of us—an excitement that had neither fear nor horror in it, because it was too full of awe.

You have all seen big fires, but I doubt if you have ever seen the whole horizon of a city lined with great fires—scores of them, perhaps hundreds.

There was something inspiring just in the awful savagery of it. . . . Immediately above the fires the sky was red and angry, and overhead, making a ceiling in the vast heavens, there was a cloud of smoke all in pink. Up in that pink shrouding there were tiny, brilliant specks of flashing light—antiaircraft shells bursting. . . .

[The] thing I shall always remember above all other things in my life is the monstrous loveliness of that one single view of London on a holiday night—London stabbed with great fires, shaken by explosions, its dark regions along the Thames sparkling with the pin points of white-hot bombs, all of it roofed over with a ceiling of pink that held bursting shells, balloons, flares and the grind of vicious engines. And in yourself the excitement and anticipation and wonder in your soul that this could be happening at all.

These things all went together to make the most hateful, most beautiful, single scene I have ever known.[16]

No less enchanted was Malcolm Muggeridge, who described the destruction of London landmarks:

Thenceforth, the Blitz was a nightly occurrence. I nearly always went out when it was on; often with Andreas [Mayor], occasionally with Graham Greene. This was not out of bravado, or a wish to be killed; just an instinctive movement towards where the noise was loudest, as people on a seaside beach gather where the throng is greatest. Also, there was something rather wonderful about London in the Blitz, with no street lights, no traffic and no pedestrians to speak of; just an empty, dark city, torn with great explosions, racked with ack-ack fire, lit with lurid flames, acrid smoke, its air full of the dust of fallen buildings. I remember particularly Regent's Park on a moonlit night, full of the fragrance of the rose gardens; the Nash Terraces, perfectly blacked-out, not a sign of a light anywhere, white stately shapes waiting to be toppled over—as they duly were, crumbling into rubble like melting snow. Andreas and I watched the great fires in the City and Fleet Street from St. James's Park. It was a great illumination, a mighty holocaust; the end of everything, surely. . . . I felt a terrible joy and exaltation at the sight and sound and taste and smell of all this destruction; at the lurid sky, the pall of smoke, the faces of bystanders wildly lit in the flames.[17]

The sense of spectacle could as easily take hold of those who bombed as of those being bombed. Anthony Cotterell, a ground signals officer in the British Army, flew with the RAF on a raid against Frankfurt.

We could see the clusters of searchlights, the flares, the fires and the flashes. . . . It was quite unlike what I expected. Everything was so neatly beautiful. . . .

We could see what looked like hundreds of thousands of electric light bulbs carpeting the ground. It took me some little time to realize that these were incendiaries. They looked so regular and artificial, so naively pretty, that one couldn't associate them with any work of destruction. . . . With the flares dropped by the pathfinders, the flares dropped by the enemy fighters, the waving searchlights, the bead-like pattern of incendiary fires on the ground, and the flashes of gunfire, there was a sense of supreme experience and excitement.[18]

Just as likely to evoke awe and aesthetic gratification were invasion fleets. Pyle wrote of those Allied vessels on their way to North African beaches: "Hour after hour I stood at the rail looking out over that armada of marching ships . . . and an almost choking sense of its beauty and power enveloped me." But it was Normandy that provided World War II's spectacle nonpareil. The scale was tremendous, and many stared at what they sensed was the greatest undertaking in the history of human beings. "No one, nowhere," said an American paratrooper in the 82d Airborne Division, "ever saw so damn many ships, barrage balloons, landing craft, tanks and soldiers"— 5,000 vessels ("like nothing ever seen before in the history of the world"); 200,000 men in the initial assault force; 2 million men landed over 109 days; 500,000 vehicles; 17 million ship tons of supplies. The most celebrated martial epics of Western culture arose from the water-borne expedition of the Greeks against Troy, but that was to Normandy as the fieldmouse to the elephant. Many gaped in wonder.[19]

Spectacle was not confined to grand, once-in-a-lifetime sights; it also appeared frequently in the course of battle. Firefights created extraordinary patterns of color and movement. A Marine general, Thomas Watson, described the "vivid pyrotechnics" on Saipan: "gun muzzles flashing yellow, tracers leaving red streaks, shells and grenades creating orange arcs with jagged edges." A correspondent for the *Chicago Daily Times* reported from the Pacific that phosphorus shells "burst in beautiful white puffs from which arch out myriad streamers of white, so that the explosion resembles a gigantic white chrysanthemum." Colonel Charles Codman of Patton's staff, suffering a bad head cold in Sicily, wrote home to his wife on the first day of August 1943: "And speaking of wonderful things, we had quite a show from the palace window last night. [The air raid] was very noisy but colorful in the extreme. The high-water mark—and perhaps the most beautiful as well as [most] satisfactory sight I have ever beheld—was a flaming enemy bomber spattering itself and its occupants against the side of a mountain. God, it was gorgeous—completely cured [my] sulfa hang-over."[20]

"Delight in destruction"

To civilians, the most surprising, puzzling, and ultimately incomprehensible of J. Glenn Gray's enduring appeals of battle was the delight in destruction. But, wrote Gray, "Anyone who has watched men on the battlefield . . . finds it hard to escape the conclusion that there is a delight in destruction. . . . Men who have lived in the zone of combat long enough to be veterans are sometimes possessed by a fury that makes them capable of anything. Blinded by the rage to destroy and supremely careless of consequences, they storm against the enemy. . . ."[21]

Some soldiers confined the impulse to the enemy's property. A Canadian recounted his actions in the German town of Udem:

> First I took a hammer and smashed over 100 plates, and the cups along with them. Then I took an axe to the china-cabinets and buffets. Next I smashed all the furniture and pulled the stuffing out of the big chairs. Then I took the hammer again and smashed all the elements on two electric stoves and broke the enamel off the stove fronts and sides. Then I put a grenade in the big piano, and after I poured a jar of molasses into it. I broke all the French doors and all the doors with mirrors in them and threw the lamps out into the street. I was so mad.[22]

Bert Damsky of the American 1st Infantry Division acknowledged "another instinct which we had—the desire to tear up and destroy. Whenever we saw something which was exceptionally nice, that we could not carry off ourselves and did not wish to leave for Jerry, we just smashed it with the butt of our rifles." In a German home, he and his friends did "one thing everyone has wanted to do": they ate from a table covered with a beautiful linen tablecloth, using fine china and crystal and silverware, and when they had finished, they wiped their mouths and hands on the tablecloth and ripped it to shreds, threw the china and crystal against the walls, and tossed the silverware out the windows. "It was really a great feeling!!!"[23]

The same emotional set, seizing soldiers in the course of battle, hurled them against the enemy. Lieutenant Paul Boesch, company commander in the 8th Infantry Division, remembered some of the fiercest fighting in the Western European theater: "It was a wild, terrible, awe-inspiring thing, this sweep through Huertgen." "Now the fight . . . was at its wildest. We dashed, struggled from one building to another shooting, bayoneting, clubbing.

Hand grenades roared, rifles cracked—buildings to the left and right burned with acrid smoke. Dust, smoke, and powder filled our lungs making us cough, spit. Automatic weapons chattered hoarsely while the heavier throats of mortars and artillery disgorged deafening explosions. The wounded and the dead—men in uniforms of both sides—lay in grotesque positions at every turn. From many the blood still flowed." "Never in my wildest imagination had I conceived that battle could be so incredibly impressive—awful, horrible, deadly, yet somehow thrilling, exhilarating."[24]

On Guadalcanal, Marine corporal Anthony Casamento, leader of a machine-gun section, lost to wounds or death all fourteen of his men. "Hell, I was mad then. . . . I lost my head, I guess; all my friends were shot and I was going to take revenge. The shells were booming and kerplunking all around, the shrapnel was whistling, the Japs were yelling, and it was a plain madhouse. Then I spotted them—two Jap machine guns. . . . They were the sons of bitches who got my men. So I got hold of my gun and fired at the first gun in front of me. I just let the whole belt go. God, it felt wonderful: just seeing the belt feed that way, knowing—well, I see the Japs suddenly pop up—I could see them hit—their stomachs sort of splitting open as though they were being cut in half, the blood spurting out, and then they'd tumble over on their faces, dead."[25]

The delight in destruction seemed especially sweet to those who felt it as a liberation from life's fetters. Against the backdrop of ebbing organizational power in combat, it could carry a culminating sense of release—from the military world's subjection to institutionalized discipline and even from the civilian world's subordination to law and responsibility for the welfare of others. James Jones portrayed the license a Pacific soldier felt as he took the life of a Japanese: "He had killed a human being, a man. He had done the most horrible thing a human being could do, worse than rape even. And nobody in the whole damned world . . . could do anything to him for it. He had gotten by with murder." Far from this extreme, and far more frequent, was the reaction of American military personnel in Cebu who worked to deny invading Japanese the use of various installations: a big Army warehouse: "We sprayed [gasoline] around . . . and ran along, touching matches here and there and feeling crazy"—and an office building: "We started piling up everything in the center of the floor . . . all the files . . . the chairs and tables and desks. . . . We tore down curtains and threw them in. . . . Then we set the place on fire and ran around throwing chairs through . . . the windows to make the draft better. It made us feel like kids letting loose."[26]

Soldiers in thrall to the delight in destruction elatedly cast off not only restraint but fear, notably the unrelenting apprehension that they would die in battle. While fighting for control of a Dutch dune, American paratroopers, tired, hungry, and suddenly infuriated at the enemy, sprang "beyond control": "in twos and threes they jumped on Germans in the foxholes, clubbing them, shooting them at point-blank range, diving for the next position." They were, as Laurence Critchell described them, "at that stage of blind anger where death was beside the point." An Army sergeant in the Pacific observed that during episodes of "wild exhilaration," soldiers regained the conviction that they were impervious "to missiles of a deadly nature." Corporal Casamento realized that in his utter absorption in machine-gunning Japanese soldiers, he had escaped his fear: "I didn't give a goddamn." His words anticipated what James Jones later described as one of the most powerful intoxicants of destruction, "The ultimate luxury of just *not giving a damn* anymore."[27]

Actually, the falling away of restraint and fear often went unnoticed, overborne by feelings of new power. Early in the war the Canadian Donald Pearce drew "quite a thrill out of seeing a city destroyed and left an ash-heap from end to end. It gave me a vicarious sense of power. I felt the romantic and histrionic emotion produced by seeing 'retribution' done; and an aesthetic emotion produced by beholding ruins . . ." Here was the counterpart, abstracted and rationalized, of those shouts that Casamento, with more than a dozen enemy bullets in him, hurled at the Japanese fifty yards away: "You come and get me, you little yellow bastards. You come and get me!"[28]

The words of a young American pilot in China laid bare the components of the delight in destruction: the sense of powerfulness, the loss of rationality, the childlike release, the fearlessness, the compulsion to wreck and ruin.

> I don't know just what it is, but when I get up there in that fighter and feel all that power responding to the touch of my hands, I almost go out of my mind. Sometimes I just yell out loud in the cockpit. I lose all fear, I feel I can do anything. I just want to speed, smash, fight. I guess I go mad for a while.[29]

J. Glenn Gray of course selected himself the terms by which he identified these reactions, and his choices—enduring appeals, delights, secret attractions—were forcefully positive. For him, the enduring appeals were the essence of the battle experience and represented gains rather than costs to the soldier. But seen from the perspective of the infantryman, they were far less central and far more injurious than Gray judged.

Their depiction drew on a literature of war here limited in several ways.

Much of the testimony limning the enduring appeals was that of correspondents or other non-combatant personnel whose views were not always those of fighting soldiers. True, at the outset, participants—correspondents, staff officers, support personnel, soldiers destined for combat—shared a single point of departure; but battle carried its acolytes where others could not follow, however much they wished to remain in step and thought that they had done so. What continued to separate newspeople from combat soldiers was the correspondents' shield, that vital space insulating them from the harsh week-after-week, month-after-month stringencies suffered by those on the line. Each correspondent came to combat when and at the distance he or she wished, and, more important, departed when he or she chose. Correspondents were, then, in important measure spectators, visitors who were not for any extended period utterly controlled by what went on around them. They were observers, occasionally and briefly touched directly by the fighting while ordinarily remaining at a safe remove. Given the nature of their access and of their craft, they found it difficult not to accentuate war's theatrical aspects. They seized on the dramatic and responded with awe ("This is wonderful!"), with a sense of privilege ("I'll never see anything like this again!"), and with gratitude ("I wouldn't have missed this for anything!").

To the problem of perspective must be added another, the absence from the literature of a corrective for a bias of social class. Combat soldiers did not often issue from those sectors of society given to the habit of recording experience. Even in an American army enlisting significant numbers of middle-class privates, those who bore the most extended combat did not often write, and those who wrote seldom sustained prolonged combat. The reactions of visitors rather than fighting men dominated the written record.

Soldiers being trained as infantrymen logically, if vaguely, anticipated that they would become participants in battle, but they at first thought of themselves as setting out "to see what it was like," that is, as observers. The British poet–tank commander Keith Douglas described his reaction to desert fighting prior to El Alamein: "I observed these battles partly as an exhibition—that is to say that I went through them a little like a visitor from the country going to a great show, or like a child in a factory—a child sees the brightness and efficiency of steel machines and endless belts slapping round and round, without caring or knowing what it is all there for. . . . [The] battlefield is the simple, central stage of the war: it is there that the interesting things happen." His was a common attitude marked for change, often during the first hours of battle, sometimes considerably later.[30]

Marine Robert Leckie remained an onlooker during the unopposed landing on Guadalcanal: "The boat struck the shore, lurched, came to a halt. Instantly I was up and over. The blue sky seemed to swing in a giant arc. I had a glimpse of palm fronds swaying gently above, the most delicate and exquisite sight I have ever seen." Later, as he approached a grassy knoll he feared might conceal enemy soldiers, he was ready to concede, lightly, that he had become a party to the events surrounding him. It was, he said, as if he and his comrades were playing games—Cowboys and Indians, Cops and Robbers, even Hide-and-Seek. At the conclusion of his first battle, however, as he watched flies swarming dead Japanese soldiers, he startled himself with the thought, "That could be me," and he was then only moments away from the point of no return: a settled conviction that he had become a target of death, a sense of self as likely or certain victim.[31]

In Sicily, it took American mortarman Hans Juergensen no more than seconds to move from delight in spectacle through empathy to preoccupation with his own jeopardy: "To our left we heard bombers and the rolling thumps of released bombs. Those weren't [our] B-17s, we realized. Oh, well. [Those German aircraft] are after ships[, not us]. Ack-ack and machine guns went into action, but not for long. A flame shot up out of the black, grew, and became a fan of orange, green, blue, and red. I couldn't help marveling at the beauty! At the same time I shuddered, thinking of how many lives were pulverized there. Immediately, another thought pushed through my consciousness. Good Lord, we must be perfect targets against that background!"[32]

Keith Douglas traced another abrupt transition. A German warplane, appearing in a clear North African sky, drew British antiaircraft fire. "The silver body . . . was surrounded by hundreds of little grey smudges, through which it sailed on serenely. From it there fell away, slowly and gracefully, an isolated shower of rain, a succession of glittering drops. I watched them descend a hundred feet before it occurred to me to consider their significance and forget their beauty. . . . 'Bombs!' I said into [my tank's] microphone."[33]

Ultimately, combat compelled soldiers to think of themselves—permanently, principally, and ofttimes exclusively—as targets. Robert Crisp described the moment of his realization: "One of those hurtling, innumerable bits of lead was going to hit me sooner or later. I couldn't be missed. So it was like this. Being shot at. Every half second within half a foot of death. Jeez, I was frightened." Even when caught earlier in the Blitz he had felt no such fear. "It couldn't only be because of all the whisky in London that night. This was more personal. . . . That must be it. These bullets were aimed at me.

They were meant to kill me personally. No careless indiscriminacy about them. Bombs in the night were quite different."[34]

Correspondents sympathized with the soldiers who repeatedly risked their lives and knew to heed their own safety in the war zone. A few contended frequently with their own deep fears of death's approach. For none was this as onerous as for Ernie Pyle, who drew nearer to battle and stayed longer than any other reporter. Of the Okinawa landings he wrote, "We were on the control boat about an hour. I felt miserable and an awful weight was on my heart. There's nothing whatever romantic in knowing that an hour from now you may be dead." But no correspondent—or headquarters officer or support solder—bore the veteran infantryman's relentless and unrelievable sense of self as target. Once acquired, it reshaped his reactions to the appeals of battle.[35]

"Movement into the spectacle"

The loss of observer detachment as distance between fighter and fighting diminished and as menace materialized reduced the combat soldier's responsiveness to the delight in spectacle. He did not become completely immune, but considerations of physical ease and, far more, safety dispelled aesthetic appreciation. From afar, Guadalcanal was William Manchester's "spectacle of utter splendor": "In the dazzling sunshine a breeze off the water stirred the distant fronds of coconut palms. The palm trees stood near the surf line in precise, orderly groves. . . . On the far horizon lay dun-colored foothills, dominated by hazy blue seven-thousand-foot mountains. Between the palms and the foothills lay the hogback ridges and the dense green mass of the Canal. Our eyes were riveted on it!" Movement *into* the spectacle, however, revealed that "except for occasional patches of shoulder-high kunai grass, the blades of which could lay a man's hand open as quickly as a scalpel," Guadalcanal was dense tropical forest: huge banyan, ipil, and eucalyptus trees, and between them "thick, steamy, matted, almost impenetrable screens of cassia, liana vines, and twisted creepers," infested by "plenty of real creatures"—serpents, crocodiles, centipedes, land crabs, scorpions, poisonous spiders, lizards, leeches, wasps, and "mosquitoes, mosquitoes, mosquitoes, all carriers of [a virulent] malaria."[36]

James Jones remembered "exactly the way [Guadalcanal] looked the day we came up on deck to go ashore": "God help me, it was beautiful. . . . the delicious sparkling tropic sea, the long beautiful beach, the minute palms of the copra plantation waving in the sea breeze, the dark green band of jungle

. . . the dun mass and power of the mountains rising behind it to rocky peaks. . . . From the mountain slopes in mid-afternoon with the sun at your back you could look back down to the beach and off across the straits to . . . one of the most beautiful views of tropic scenery on the planet." But Guadal-canal close at hand, Jones quickly realized, was "a pestilential hell hole." Yes, "a haunting beauty at a far remove," but not when one is caught in "the per-vasive mud . . . and jungle gloom," not when they are "all around you smoth-ering you. . . . When you are not straining and gasping to save your life, the act of [exerting to preserve yourself] can seem adventurous and exciting from a distance. The greater the distance, the greater the adventure." Prox-imity and danger transformed the soldier's perception of natural settings.[37]

In combat, smells further reduced susceptibility to spectacle. Aircraft mechanic James Johns reported that from his vessel moored off Guadalcanal, "You could smell the fragrance of the island with its flowers blooming bril-liantly in the tropical sunlight," but on the island, Manchester discovered its forest to be "a great toadlike beast . . . emitting faint whiffs of foul breath, a vile stench of rotting undergrowth and stink lilies." Beneath Guadalcanal's loveliness, Leckie uncovered "a mass of slops and stinks and pestilence." Combat odors aggravated revulsion. In the aftermath of their first battle, at Guadalcanal's Tenaru River, Leckie and his comrades were unable to sleep because of the stench of the dead. In Honolulu, writer-correspondent John Dos Passos met a sailor in whom smell had overridden sight: "Out there [in the Pacific war zone] it's all pretty scenery . . . too goddam pretty. I hate pretty scenery. I can't look at it without smellin' dead Japs."[38]

Battle brought the soldier new perceptions of the noises of combat. At a distance imposing though never musical, near at hand they were cacopho-nous and a terrifying harbinger of destruction. Richard Tobin recoiled from the nearby detonation of a German flying bomb: "With a noise that I hope I shall never hear again, and certainly I never imagined could come into the world . . . something straight ahead of me began to disintegrate into tiny par-ticles of noise. The explosion was a shaking and rushing of all the air in the world straight at me, and at no other human being."[39]

Even where there was little disparity between terrain viewed from far off and from close by, battle changed what the soldier saw before him. Beauty, whether the creation of natural or human forces, disappeared as soldiers quickly reduced landscapes to their combat components. Walter Bernstein contemplated an Italian vista: "It had been beautiful once, but now you could not look at it any more as a scene." Could those trees hide German 88s? Did that house harbor an enemy observation post? Was that valley a trap? "Normally," noted a medic, "we would gaze at these beautiful crags and peaks with the snow and mist on top with awe and appreciation of natural beauty, but it's not for us now. How are we going to take that hill? What perfect observation the Krauts must have of this whole valley from up there! Ping! Snipers up there. How will I get my casualties down these vertical cliffs? Somebody has to clean these hills out." It was as Erich Maria Remarque had said: for the fighting soldier, nature came to have "no significance in itself; it was simply good or bad in relation to the war. As protection or as danger."[40]

The dazzling lights of firefights continued to absorb the soldier—but in new ways. "The blackness of the rainfilled night was filled with arches of tracer bullets. [But] between each pair of tracers were four steel bullets that were unseen dealers of death." The correspondent who had discerned in those phosphorus-shell explosions "beautiful . . . puffs" creating "gigantic white chrysanthemum[s]" veered after a shell wounded him on Iwo Jima. "When one of those beautiful streamers strikes flesh it burns viciously, through clothing, skin, flesh, bone, and blood." "Men at war," he realized, "have little appreciation for the esthetic effects of white phosphorous."[41]

Even invasion spectacles suffered dramatic devaluation as the soldier's purview narrowed to combat. Were they not extraordinary sights? Yes, agreed Bill Mauldin: "Invasions are magnificent things to watch. . . ." But what of the soldier who was one of those thousands of fragments constituting the spectacle that so delighted distant observers? That more often invited feelings of impairment than of exaltation, of acute personal vulnerability rather than any reassuring sense of massive combined strength, as if such great numbers must inevitably diminish and ultimately overwhelm the individual. Magnificent to watch, but, Mauldin added, "awful things to be in."[42]

A few soldiers remained secure, confident that the invasion spectacle served them. The great concourse of vessels gathered in Ulithi Harbor for the invasion of Okinawa touched and heartened Marine Russell Davis:

There were transports, unending as common soldiers of the line. Patrol boats were like corporals; destroyers like sergeants; cruisers were lieutenants; carriers were colonels; and the battlewagons were generals. There was an army of ships arrayed in the anchorage at Ulithi. In such an army, the great Spanish Armada would have been run over and never sighted. There had never been as big a gathering before and there never has been anything as big since. Even the sickest and most bitter Marines came to the rail to look at the sea might of their country, and to feel, no matter how scared they were, some pride that the troops were the heart of the gathering. The great ships were there to serve and protect the troops.

But many came to feel differently, to believe themselves reduced almost to nothingness amid such numbers. Audie Murphy spoke acidly of the invasion of southern France: "Technically it was called a perfect landing. The vast operation designed to crack the enemy coastal defenses . . . had been calculated and prepared to the smallest detail; and it moved with the smooth precision of a machine. . . . But we do not know, we do not see the gigantic pattern of the offensive as we peer over the edge of the landing boats. . . . The battleships have given the beach a thorough pounding. . . . The rocket boat guns take over. . . . [The] men huddled in the boat . . . look as miserable as wet cats. . . . Suddenly I see the comedy of little men. . . ."[43]

After the war, James Jones worked as a screenwriter on Darryl F. Zanuck's epic Normandy invasion film, *The Longest Day.* "I had occasion to tramp all over the D-Day beaches . . . until I got to know them very well. . . . [At] Omaha I climbed up and sat a while on the edge of the bluff, and looked down into the cup-shaped area with the sea at its back." Jones knew combat—he had fought on Guadalcanal—and as he visualized D-Day, he pictured himself not as one of those in position to review the whole majestic fleet but as one of those waiting for the drop of the assault-craft ramp and the start of that desperate dash to the beach.

> It was easy to see what a murderous converging fire could be brought to bear on the beaches from the curving bluff. Especially to an old infantryman. And it was easy to half-close your eyes and imagine what it must have been like. The terror and total confusion, men screaming or sinking silently under the water, tanks sinking as their crews drowned inside, landing craft going up as a direct hit took them, or grating ashore to discharge their live cargo into the already scrambled mess, officers trying to get their men together, medics trying to find shelter for the wounded. . . . I sat there until my friends began to yell at me from down below, and I fervently thanked God or Whomever that I had not been there.

Omaha Beach had been "a bloodbath," and James Jones gave no thought to spectacle.[44]

Jones, in contemplation this time of the North African landings, saw such assemblages of power not with marvel but with despair; by marking the arrival of "massed, managerial, industrial-production technological warfare," they betokened the obsolescence of the individual. "A single infantryman in a war like that was about as noteworthy and important as a single mosquito in an airplane-launched DDT spray campaign: another fact the American soldier would take to sourly." Spectacle thus confirmed for Jones the soldier's loss of control, as his Sergeant Storm made clear in *The Thin Red Line:* "And the pageant, the spectacle, the challenge, the adventure of war they could wipe their ass on. It might be all right for field officers and up, who got to run it and decide what to do or not do. But everybody else was a tool—a tool with its serial number of manufacture stamped right on it. And Storm didn't like being no tool. Not, especially, when it could get you killed."[45]

Isolation and fear dominated the thoughts of invading soldiers. "You have a feeling you are making the invasion all by yourself." "God Almighty, the United States has picked me to crack [Germany's West Wall]. I was plenty scared. . . . In five minutes that ramp isn't going to be there and I am." "My heart stood still and my stomach turned over and over; I wanted to vomit everything I had eaten for the past few days. Oh, God, if I could only pray or something would happen to bring me out of this awful feeling. . . ."[46]

The rejection of spectacle in ground combat had its counterpart in the air war. Flak explosions at first fascinated B-17 pilot Joe Slavik. "They'd make colorful bursts of smoke all around you. Even the rockets [the Germans] fired at us were awesome. But you got over that fascination pretty quickly when you realized that they were trying to shoot you down, to kill you. Then you learned to be afraid of those bursts. They weren't pretty anymore." A B-24 pilot flying from an American airbase in Italy saw in the panorama on the ground none of the beauty that had moved Pyle on his flight over the Atlas Mountains; natural features were nothing more than guides to that day's target for his bombs. Airmen, Anthony Cotterell learned, came to know the great cities of Europe not by their buildings, boulevards, and monuments, "but simply by [the patterns of] their flak and searchlights barrages."[47]

The degradation of the delight in spectacle was not a neat, certain, clearly phased process. Some soldiers experienced in battle remained receptive. John George, who fought on Guadalcanal as an Army rifleman, reported that "Conversation centered mostly around . . . women, drinking, and city life. Only rarely was there any reference to the beautiful natural scenery surrounding us on all sides. . . . the unspeakably beautiful skies, the brilliantly blue ocean, and the complementing effects wrought both by blinding sunlight and gorgeously mellow moonlight. The whole little world we were living in was . . . no less than a fairy-land of natural beauty." But he knew that his friends did not share his view. "As one of the 'boys,' I was halfway afraid to call anyone's attention to [that beauty] . . . [and] its charm [was] regrettably lost to the greater portion of us." George, still susceptible to natural spectacle, was disappointed that those around him had become desensitized.[48]

Nonetheless, battle at first hedged soldiers' reactions to the beautiful and panoramic and ultimately suppressed them. Infantryman John Bassett soon reached the point at which he registered no emotional reaction to scenes that continued to draw delight from correspondents and visiting officers.

> The path turned upwards. Another 88 came in and hit well above us. The .50 caliber tracers from tanks were chattering over our heads in a continuous stream. They were covering the hills beyond us with protective overhead fire. The tracers were red. Someone lay dead by the side of the path. Who was it? A guy named Tex, they said. Then we stopped. I sat down on a bank and looked around me. The sound of the machine-gun fire beat on my head like hammers of the devil. A tank suddenly exploded below on the road: it was a mass of white flames. I could see the tracers plunking across the top of the bare hill ahead, plowing up the earth. We were getting up pretty high for overhead fire. We moved on and came to a vineyard. On a nearby hilltop a shell set off a German flare and rocket dump. Orange, red, green flares and brilliant parachute lights: the whole thing went up. And then we were climbing again—fast. I looked up and saw someone lying beside the path. "It's Jennings," someone said, "he's passed out." They were passing the word back for a medic to come forward. . . . Then we were in tall grass near the top. No one knew what to do. . . .[49]

Those soldiers conscious that their perceptions had changed struggled to find ways to express their new relationship to spectacle. A common solution was to incorporate in their language their discovery of spectacle's dual nature; highly moralistic terms would make clear that spectacle, whatever its gratifications, possessed the ability to harm them. A Marine general, a former enlisted man, described a night on Saipan: "American destroyers . . . sent up star shells that burst over the island and descended slowly . . . producing flickering shadows among the trees. . . ." Clashes with the Japanese created brilliant displays of yellows, reds, and oranges. For combatants, he concluded, "the setting was simply hellish"; for distant observers, "the combination of sound and color . . . had a kind of *wicked beauty.*" William Manchester's answer, though in more sophisticated form, was similar. In observing Guadalcanal from a distance, he "thought of Baudelaire['s poem]: *Fleurs du mal* [Flowers of Evil]. It was a vision of beauty, but of evil beauty." In earthier terms, one of Leon Uris's Marines, sailing from Guadalcanal and standing with his friends at the ship's rail for a last look, thought the island "calm and peaceful, like the day we first found her. Like an exotic Hollywood scene. But she had the body of a goddess and the soul of a witch." In this way soldiers signaled their conviction that in battle both natural and man-made spectacles ceased to bestow delight and became the source of such distress and danger that they deserved to be condemned as evil.[50]

Three other aspects of the combat experience—the burdens of inattentiveness, fatigue, and repetition—ensured that soldiers' reactions would be far different from those of visitors to the front. Soldiers fearing death felt it necessary to impose on themselves a constant caution that made the delight in spectacle first an unaffordable indulgence and then an outright menace.

Ernie Pyle learned that it was possible "to become so enthralled by some of the spectacles of war that a man is momentarily captivated away from his own danger." Indeed, no combat soldier suffered a more dramatic demonstration of that proposition than did Pyle himself. On July 25, 1944, he was one of a group assembled to watch at a distance of eight hundred yards the massive Allied carpet-bombing of Saint-Lô.

[The heavy bombers] came in flights of twelve, three flights to a group and in groups stretched out across the sky. . . . [They] came in a constant procession and I thought it would never end. . . .

But we were so fascinated by the spectacle overhead that it never occurred to us that we might need the foxholes. . . .

[For] an hour and a half that had in it the agonies of centuries, the bombs came down. . . .

As we watched, there crept into our consciousness a realization that the windrows of exploding bombs were easing back toward us, flight by flight, instead of gradually forward, as the plan called for. Then we were horrified by the suspicion that those machines, high in the sky and completely detached from us, were aiming their bombs at the smoke line on the ground—and a gentle breeze was drifting the smoke line back over us! An indescribable kind of panic came over us. We stood tensed in muscle and frozen in intellect, watching each flight approach and pass over, feeling trapped and completely helpless. And then all of an instant the universe became filled with a gigantic rattling as of huge ripe seeds in a mammoth dry gourd. . . . [I]nstinct told us what it was. It was bombs by the hundred, hurtling down through the air above us. . . .

[It] was chaos, and a waiting for darkness. . . . There was . . . dread in our hearts.[51]

The combat soldier needed only his daily round to warn him that any absorption in spectacle was a perilous relaxation of caution, a distraction from the danger that might confront his next step.

Fatigue also weakened spectacle's grip. Correspondent Robert Casey reported that there were times when "we were too numb mentally to appreciate the stirring and brilliant and sometimes ghastly panorama before us"; that did not mean, however, "that the pictures weren't there. They come back in retrospect more vivid and more startling than when tired eyes first looked upon them and seemingly failed to take them in." But bone-weary soldiers reached a point of emotionless stupor that correspondents seldom approached, and in any case combat allowed the soldier's thought few departures from the present to retrieve panoramic memories. James Jones wrote of the rifleman from whom "so much of so many different emotions had been drained . . . that his emotional reservoir was empty." Said a colonel of his soldiers fighting in France, "If a full moon shines on the glistening snow, most of the men are too cold and tired to see anything picturesque about it." During the battle for Okinawa, Manchester took refuge in a cave: "I was exhausted, and once inside my dry sanctuary I lay on my side . . . watching the kamikazes diving and exploding on our warships. It was one of the war's most extraordinary spectacles, but I was too weary to keep my eyes open." Ultimately, a state that Pyle called "cell-by-cell exhaustion" and Private Lester Atwell thought of as "feeling unreal with tiredness" confined soldiers to "the dullest, simplest observation[s]." Here the only spectacle possible was the mirage born of utter enervation.[52]

The final factor deadening receptivity to spectacle was repetition. "[All] things in war make a vivid impression on you because they are all new to you," recorded Bill Mauldin, ". . . But, as the months go on and you see more of war, the little things that are so vivid at first become routine." Soldiers who told one another, "We'll never see anything like this again," regularly did. Wrote medic Tsuchida from Austria during the spring of 1945, "Well[,] we still go on and on and being quite accustomed by now to . . . these far-off places of which I [previously] only read and saw pictures . . . we come [to] these historic and scenic spots very casually, our only thoughts being when the hell are we going to stop and sleep." Casey grew inured even to the invasion spectacle: "[We] had become so used to the pageant of ships that it no longer seemed worth a second glance."[53]

Thus did combat diminish and then dissolve the soldier's receptivity to the delight in spectacle. "Guadalcanal is an island of striking beauty," thought Marine captain Herbert Merillat, "—to anyone who does not remember the battles that have bloodied its soil or the men and ships that lie beneath the waters off its shores."[54]

"A sense of vulnerability"

Many of the forces that deflated spectacle also worked to lessen the delight in danger. At their center was again the combatant's acceptance of his vulnerability. "Risking all" was attractive only until the soldier realized that he was risking all all the time and would likely lose all. Repetitiveness fostered that sense of self as the target of death and quashed the titillation of danger as it did the pleasure of spectacle.

Mitsuru Yoshida, as an ensign in the Imperial Japanese Navy, became exhilarated during his "baptism of fire," an American air attack. He felt as if his chest were puffing up with pride. Then, sent to check the ship's radar compartment when it was struck by a bomb, he could not distinguish one corpse from another. Fellow officers and men were now all "hunks of flesh," and Yoshida immediately felt that he too was doomed, that he and those lumps were "one and the same, separated only by time." Danger was never again exciting.[55]

In July 1943, German pilot Johannes Steinhoff thought back on "the strange attraction" that had drawn him "almost compulsively" to aerial combat. It had endured "over the English Channel and then in Russia," but now, he realized, nothing was left of it. Air battle on the Eastern Front had been "little more than a harmless game," but in the West Luftwaffe pilots found themselves flying aircraft, state-of-the-art in 1939 but obsolete by 1943, against B-17s that Steinhoff believed came up to their *nom de guerre:* Flying Fortresses. The exciting air duel disappeared; three B-17s flying in formation were able to concentrate thirty machine guns on an attacking German aircraft. Allied technological advance had reduced German fliers' courage, discipline, and skill to irrelevancies, and had rendered the pilots "endangered human beings." "A sense of vulnerability" had entirely displaced the "strange attraction," and any mention of the delight in danger would have brought from the always polite Steinhoff a very sour smile.[56]

Correspondent Alan Moorehead described the episode that thenceforth made it impossible for him to feel excitement in danger. He was traveling with a British armored-car patrol in the North African desert when it was ambushed by Italians firing from a distance of only one hundred yards: "[T]racer bullets came down the road towards us in continuous streams of bright yellow light." Moorehead's driver fell "with a terrible wound in his arm." A shallow ditch provided only partial cover, and his other two comrades were soon hit. Crawling "inch by inch" away from burning vehicles, Moorehead thought, "this is too cruel, [the Italians] cannot realize what they are doing to us. If they were here with us they would see it and stop. No one . . . could inflict harm like this." Once darkness arrived, the four were able to struggle back to British lines, but Moorehead did not recover from the incident. Never again was combat attractive. Never again did he approach danger with elation or excitement or confidence or even simple dedication. Many soldiers, in reacting to such encounters with death, found that, in medic Tsuchida's words, the "appetite for excitement has been cured."[57]

For the ordinary ground soldier, the delight in danger was short-lived. Indeed, as suggested in the case of fatigue, the pressures of combat always pushed him to the opposite end of the emotional spectrum, away from sentience and toward insensitivity. For those compelled to remain within battle's orbit, the effects were sure to be dulling. Margaret Bourke-White noticed in American soldiers in Italy "the growing numbness that enveloped them like a shroud . . . their only defense against an anxiety that had become intolerable." Combat medic Keith Winston told those at home how foxhole soldiers went about their tasks "with a kind of deadened sense." "More and more, emotion seems to leave us," wrote Orval Faubus, "and we function more as machines." Concluding that feelings of excitement were baseless, bogus, or dangerous, fighting soldiers began to associate them with the disdained rear echelon. Neil McCallum recorded a day's activity during the Sicilian campaign: "Watched a battle to capture the town of Vizzini. The heat-hazed landscape of rugged hill and valley was smoke-covered and on fire. I was far enough away to feel the febrile excitement of staff-officers and other noncombatants."[58]

As for that "magnificent simplicity" to which danger and the exigencies of battle had stripped life at the front for Ernie Pyle, the soldier was able to hold in mind for only a short time the onerous aspects of his civilian existence from which war had liberated him. His prewar life, receding rapidly, became harder and harder to recall. Pyle himself, after two months with the forces campaigning in Tunisia, returned to Algiers and found "civilization" a "great thrill"—but only for a day. Thereafter his complaints returned and his dissatisfaction again became extreme; "all the confusion and regimentation of city life" made him wish for the front. It was a cycle of withdrawal and return, rejection and embrace, that Pyle would complete often during the war. But combat soldiers had few such opportunities to refresh earlier grievances with civilian living, and in any case, with the oppressive aspects of military life dominating their thought, they relished every prospect for a return to "civilization." Life on the line *was* simpler; it was also incomparably harsh. Even as he approached battle, BAR gunner Lester Atwell thought he saw clearly the nature of the soldier's existence at the front in France: "What a rotten life this was going to be! Always outdoors, always dirty, devitalized, tired from the broken sleep of guard duty."[59]

As for the superior moral atmosphere of the front, combat soldiers continued to extol the subordination of monetary values, the straightforward way comrade treated comrade, the contrast with rear-area deviousness, but no one was able to maintain for long that battle was making a better person of him. The crux of combat was the destruction of human beings, and as boys—at home, school, and church—American soldiers had been taught that killing another was wrong, a crime and a sin. Moreover, the coarsening compelled by combat subdued resistance to other practices that soldiers had believed sinful, unethical, unjust, or simply wrong. Many prayed that the war would cause no more than a temporary suspension of the moral precepts integral to their prewar lives, but few were confident that the problem would solve itself. Following a Pacific battle, Marine Eugene Sledge reckoned the moral costs in his own life and concluded that "something in me died at Peleliu"—his youthful propensity to believe "that man is basically good." William Manchester grieved that he and other Marines "came to hate the things we had to do, even when convinced that doing them was absolutely necessary; [we] had never understood the bestial, monstrous and vile means required to reach the objective"—that is, killing the enemy until Japan was compelled to surrender.[60]

As for those perceptions of terrain that danger electrified, exhaustion and a dire apprehension that overtook soldiers repeatedly committed to battle—that the the end of the war was continually receding—confined such gratifying reactions to correspondents and other visitors. It was not then, as Sevareid suggested, that "each turn of the road is stamped indelibly upon the brain," but that each turn became every other turn. Combat soldiers soon left behind the sphere of pleasurably heightened sensitivity; their problem became that of overcoming utter depletion in order to maintain a minimal sensitivity to the dangers of the terrain surrounding them.[61]

Frank Mathias "entered the Army as a sort of game tinged with the excitement of going out into the world." "I left with a thrill of adventure. . . ." During training, he continued to take pleasure in his "freedom from the earlier restrictions of civilian life. Few of us analyzed it, but we relished this temporary sense of well-earned irresponsibility as much as children delight in a circus or carnival midway." Assignment to the 37th Division band spared him much combat, but not all, and he came to feel "as if this war had lasted forever and would go on through eternity. It seemed to have swallowed my life, destroying things as they used to be before 1943. It was making me old before my time." Dread displaced excitement. The journey from draftee to combat veteran, begun in an emotional expansiveness, ended in emotional contraction.[62]

"You went too far!"

The delight in destruction seemed to promise that it would arrest the slide into emotional insensibility. The soldier who consigned himself to a storming violence cast off, at least temporarily, worry that he had lost all control and fear that he would die, two powerful inhibitions. Propelling himself forward furiously assured him that he was still alive, still sentient, still able to shed restraint and to act powerfully. Ironically, it was a reassertion of life directed at the destruction of other lives. Also ironically, in that rebellion against fright, emotionlessness, and regimentation lay a surrender of control over the self that, as he came to realize, placed his own life in greatest jeopardy.

What James Jones had called the delight in destruction's "ultimate luxury of just not giving a damn anymore" was far more dangerous than engrossment in spectacle. Manchester, during combat on Okinawa instructing six seventeen-year-old replacements direct from boot camp, recognized the problem. Feelings of elation, he told them, were "normal and OK as long as men didn't become suicidal; the moth-in-the-flame threat was always there." J. Glenn Gray, as a counterintelligence officer, did not see enough combat to grasp that the soldier, in feeling himself at the mercy of forces he was powerless to control and in acting to defy them, invited a further and fatal loss of control: that he could become as heedless of his own survival; that surrender to the delight in destruction often proffered as its ultimate step the destruction of self.[63]

This awareness came to Private John Bassett during combat in northern Italy:

> We were worried about the snipers to our rear [and] were really in a mess now. No one was moving forward anymore. . . .
>
> It was a little too open where I was, so I got up to run to a better place. I ran two steps and . . . C-r-rack!! The bullet hit the dirt beside my right foot and a small cloud of dust rose as it whined away into the woods. I turned sharply to my left and dove headlong into a clump of bushes. That was too close.
>
> "Hey Bassett? Don't let him get away with that!" Sabin yelled. . . .
>
> "Christ!" I yelled back. "Where is he?"

> Then I became enraged: there was no explaining it. I forgot fear temporarily. . . . I turned around and tried to locate that sniper. I stood up and ran along the densely wooded hill, disregarding all caution. As I dived towards another bush, several shots whistled over my head. I curled up in the bush and [then I] knew I'd made a mistake. My anger faded. Oh-oh boy, I thought, you went too far—you're alone out here—better get out of here and get back to the others—fast! I crawled out of the bush and crawled another ten yards and then got up and ran back.

He had, he knew, acted "foolishly . . . desperately."[64]

A Japanese American infantryman, caught up in the 442d Regimental Combat Team's determined effort to rescue a battalion of the 141st Infantry Regiment cut off in the Vosges Mountains, "let out a bloodcurdling cry that seemed to well up from the bottom of his lungs. . . ." Others yelled and moved to the attack. All around Sergeant Fujio Miyamoto "soldiers were stumbling and falling. His nerves and body were tattered. . . ." Each day he received a letter from his fiancée in Honolulu; he sent detailed replies. He was a gentle, soft-spoken person whose mother had wept when he volunteered. "But as he strode across the forest floor the glare in his eyes belonged to an entirely different person. Everything had vanished from his head—getting back alive, his fiancée, his father. . . . He didn't even think about his mother. . . . All he could think of was killing the enemy who had killed his buddies. Kill and kill again—that was the only thought running through his head."[65]

In the struggle for that Dutch dune, those American paratroopers of the 501st Regiment had fought so heedlessly that to them, as Critchell said, "death was beside the point." But for Americans, whose acute focus on personal survival was unequaled, death was *always* the point, and fighting men fortunate enough to survive onslaughts as reckless as those of the mountains and the dune realized—and realized quickly because "the intoxication of utter fearlessness . . . is something no one can sustain for long"—that they had to guard against exposing themselves again.[66]

Caution might not save the soldier's life, he knew, but it offered far better odds than yielding himself to emotion so powerful that it might even leave him with no consciousness of his wounds. "[Y]ou get so charged up," said Commando Kelly, "that often you don't notice [your injuries] until the tension eases off." To succumb to the destructive impulse, to abandon reason, was indeed to give over one's fate to what Creighton Abrams called "a crazy force."[67]

And as the costs of the delight in destruction were higher than Gray realized, so were the returns less gratifying than he had assumed.

When Audie Murphy's closest friend was shot down as he left cover to accept the surrender of those Germans who had shouted "*Kamerad!*," Murphy killed two nearby German soldiers with a grenade, picked up their machine gun, and started up the hill, firing on the position from which his comrade had been cut down. "I do not think of danger to myself. My whole being is concentrated on killing." He found those he was seeking. "As the lacerated bodies flop and squirm, I rake them again; and I do not stop firing while there is a quiver in them." But Audie Murphy, like other soldiers who have tried to describe themselves while in thrall to the delight in destruction, found in it no delight at all. "I remember the experience as I do a nightmare. A demon seems to have entered my body."[68]

The U.S. Army estimated that during battle in New Guinea, one man—David Rubitsky—killed five hundred Japanese soldiers. "So I would just shoot them and bayonet them, shoot them and bayonet them. I was completely an insane man. To think that a human being would do that [to] another human being, what I did."[69]

7 THE APPEALS OF BATTLE
Comradeship

Comradeship stood apart. Rather than addressing the relationship between the individual and the phenomena of battle, as did danger, destruction, and spectacle, comradeship spoke to the connection between the soldier and his fellows. Its impact extended beyond the visceral; its duration was far more extended, its effects far less transient. It penetrated almost every aspect of battlefield experience. Of all the delights, it seemed least subject to any impeachment; seldom did any who spoke of it evince any ambivalence as to its nature or influence.

No aspect of war has received more favorable consideration than comradeship. Observer-commentators reserved for it elevated, sometimes fulsome, descriptions. Correspondent Jack Belden spoke of "the community spirit of the battlefield" and the soldier's sense of belonging "to some great brotherhood motivated by . . . common purpose." Bill Mauldin claimed for fighting soldiers a "nobility and dignity" deriving from "the way they live unselfishly and risk their lives to help each other." A U.S. Army chaplain who followed the troops in Italy and France found in comradeship—"living and fighting and dying together"—"the true meaning of human fellowship." Ernie Pyle told his civilian readers about a "fraternalism in war" that those at home would find difficult to grasp. "Such companionship finally becomes a part of one's soul, and it cannot be obliterated." Lewis Mumford, living the war through the letters of his soldier son, concluded that those who fought "knew comradeship and experienced love, sometimes to a degree far beyond their civilian experience. . . . War, which plainly brutalized men, also raised some of them to a saintly level."[1]

The reactions of soldiers-commentators were no less ardent. Ben Tumey, as an artilleryman fighting in support of the 79th Division in Europe, believed that "'I am part of all that I have met' could apply to [all] the enlisted men of the battery. We are so awfully close together." Paratrooper Kurt Gabel was convinced that "the only permanency [lay in] the human relationships and bonds of friendship welding us together." At the end of the war in Europe, combat engineer Henry Giles contemplated the dissolution of his battalion, company, and platoon: "But what we had together was something awfully damned good, something I don't think we'll ever have again as long as we live. Nobody in his senses wants war, but maybe it takes war to make men feel as close to each other as we have felt. We'll never feel toward anyone else the way we have felt toward each other. . . . We are a little homesick for it already."[2]

American soldiers paid homage to comradeship by placing it within the framework that meant more to them than any other, that of family and home. Gabel realized that he and those around him had come to regard their unit "as our family, as our home." One's comrades, wrote home a Japanese American soldier, "became blood relations. . . ." In the Pacific, Eugene Sledge realized that "Company K . . . was home; it was 'my' company. I belonged in it and nowhere else." Indeed, its hold on some moved *beyond* the sway of the domestic. "There is a bond [in combat]," explained Newman Phillips, a Pacific replacement in the Army's 32d Division, "closer than family or friends [at home]." Harold Leinbaugh, too, found in the affinity between men in battle "a bonding beyond husband and wife." Loyalties, said Marine Russell Davis, "shrink down past country and family to one or two men. They become . . . more precious than father and mother, sister and brother, wife and girl."[3]

Comradeship was compelling as a rich, multifaceted phenomenon that served combat soldiers in varied ways. It met needs of practicality, of emotion, and—even amid combat—of idealism.

In very utilitarian ways, comradeship strengthened the individual for participation in battle. It provided a powerful motivation to fight, helped to overcome fear, enhanced safety, strengthened perseverance, protected against disintegration, and offered a basis for reconciliation with death.

What induced the American soldier to enter upon, and to persist in, World War II combat? No force urged him forward more powerfully than comradeship. William Manchester asserted comradeship's primacy in words that have attained an almost classic standing: "Men . . . do not fight for flag or country, for the Marine Corps or glory or any other abstraction. They fight for one another." The military adviser/historian S. L. A. Marshall agreed: "The only answer . . . supportable in all that I have seen of man on the battle-field is that he will be persuaded [to risk his life] by . . . friendship, loyalty to responsibility, and knowledge that he is a repository of the faith and confidence of others." Even the most vitriolic critic of the war, Paul Fussell, obliquely granted comradeship its place: Men, he said, "will attack only if young, athletic, credulous, and sustained by some equivalent of the buddy system." It remained for the French writer and pilot Antoine de Saint-Exupéry to place comradeship firmly at the center of war's experience: "The taste of bread shared among comrades made us accept the values of war."[4]

Comradeship heightened the soldier's determination to overcome his fear of battle. It could by itself make some feel more secure. Henry Giles, a victim of chronic ear infections, explained to a sympathetic doctor why he wished to return to his unit rather than be reclassified, temporarily at least, as a non-combat soldier. "I told [the doctor] I had been Weapon Sgt. with my outfit for two years—they were all my friends." "I said I thought I had a better chance of taking good care of myself with my own outfit than any other way. . . . They would do anything to help me. . . ." Returning from a dangerous patrol sent forward to draw enemy fire—it had; several replacements had been killed—Grady Arrington was warmed by the relief with which his comrade Jim Thaxton welcomed him back. "Having so dear a friend made me feel safer, more able to cope with anything the Germans might throw our way." The British writer Alexander Baron caught a litany that ran through the minds of many combat soldiers: "In battle other men were close to you; they admired you; they talked to you; they passed a mug of steaming tea to you; they crawled under a blanket with you. [You] marched with them; you felt safe and strong with them; you were one of them."[5]

To a soldier, it was incontestable that the presence of comrades improved the odds that he would survive the war. For the GI moving from battalion to "within range of bullets," advised Bill Mauldin, "the important thing from [the company] forward is to have a few acquaintances." George Thompson of an 84th Division rifle company was more direct: "We all were in it together. Each one's life depended on what the other one did. . . . [We] were trying to stick together for our own survival."[6]

They were right—and soldiers would, if pressed, cite instances of wounded friends. The high command worried that concern for comrades would divert energies from the assault to the fallen. Robert Houston and his fellow paratroopers of the 101st Airborne Division "had been taught to keep our minds on combat and let the medics take care of the casualties." It was a reasonable position. There were others, specially trained, to do the helping. It was a sound order. Other lives—and the success of the operation—were at stake. To do otherwise, one Marine agreed, would be "stupid": "If everybody stopped to pick up the pieces, the war would last forever." Still, affinity regularly subjugated both logic and discipline. Few soldiers could ignore the battlefield wail, "Oh my God, help me!" A Marine, one of Russell Davis's friends, proclaimed that "When a buddy of mine is hit, I'm going to bring him in, and they can jam this war for all I care." A member of Leinbaugh's company was so determined to secure aid for a wounded comrade that he threatened to shoot an aidman who was so petrified by heavy German fire that he had refused to crawl forward. "Stay where you are, soldier!" Arrington ordered a replacement soldier impatient to go to an injured friend, but Arrington immediately realized that had their situations been reversed, *he* would have gone to *his* friend. "No one could have kept me from going to his assistance. If ordered to stop, I would have disobeyed, even had I known I would be shot by the enemy, shot by my superior, or faced a court-martial." There was substance to the combat soldier's conviction that friends extended life.[7]

Soldiers who, for whatever reason, failed to draw strength from those around them might still be propelled forward by another aspect of comradeship, the threat of sanctions when its tenets were violated. The soldier drawn to respond to "Oh my God, help me!" was aware that failure to do so might subject him to terrible rebuke: "Where the fuck was you, Tom?" Comradeship's power pushed as well as pulled. With friends serving as the wellspring of strength, aid, and often survival, the fear of a rift with and ultimate banishment from fellowship was a potent one. Often when comradeship's positive components failed to impart the strength essential to overcome fear, its negative elements subordinated that fear, by replacing one set of dreaded consequences with another even more dreadful. Marine Eugene Sledge acknowledged the gravity of the situation: "What was worse than death was the indignation of your buddies. You couldn't let 'em down. It was stronger than flag and country." J. Glenn Gray focused on half of comradeship when he wrote that "the fighter is often sustained solely by the determination not to let down his comrades," and Newman Phillips on the other half when he declared that "I fought . . . because I did not want to appear as a coward to my buddies."[8]

An episode during preliminaries to the 1st Marine Division's amphibious assault on Peleliu offered a rare demonstration of rapid transition from support to pressure to compulsion. Assembled aboard ship for the landing, Marines noticed that one of their number, a runner unnamed in Russell Davis's account, was missing.

> I looked along the line and couldn't see him. Buck walked up ahead and couldn't find him. We went back under the LCI [Landing Craft, Infantry]— and he was sitting on his cot staring at his pack and rifle.
>
> "Get it on," Buck told him.
>
> "I don't know whether I can."
>
> "We'll help you," Buck said. He picked up the pack, spreading out the straps with his hands.
>
> "I mean I don't know whether I can go in."
>
> "You don't have any choice. There's no place in God's world for you to go but in." Buck began to stuff the runner's arms through the shoulder-straps.
>
> As soon as the man had his pack on he flopped back on the cot. He was crumpled and limp, with his arms splayed out.
>
> "Get up and get in line," Buck ordered him.
>
> "I want to pray." . . .
>
> Buck blew up again. I suppose he had been holding his own tension down all along and I hadn't noticed it. He screamed in the runner's face and shook his arms and tried to drag him off the cot. John came in under the LCI and crowded Buck gently aside. Together John and I got our arms under the runner's arms and walked him back to the rail.[9]

Seldom, however, was there anything approaching duress. Most, drawn by comradeship's powerful incentives, moved forward willingly, and if some were still reluctant to go along, there was a reinforcing impetus in that fear of shame. Just before the Okinawa invasion, Russell Davis became apprehensive.

> "We're going up," the rumors began. The whisper was everywhere.
>
> "Where to?" . . .
>
> "Wherever it is we're going, it will be rough. I mean *rough*. They're building scaling ladders, more coffins, more crosses."
>
> I began to sleep badly. Some nights I scarcely slept at all. I wasn't the only one. Late at night, when the tent flaps were turned up and I could look through into the other company areas, I saw a scattering of orange dots which marked men alone with their cigarettes and their thoughts and fears. They sat on the edges of their bunks and smoked through the night. . . . When someone stirred . . . someone else would wake and a conversation would begin, but it would be careful and guarded.

"That you, Jack?"

"It's me. Just having a smoke. Nothing wrong."

"What's the matter?"

"Nothing. I told you nothing is wrong. Not a thing."

[No] one would admit, aloud, that he was nervous in the night. Then he might become suspect by the others. . . . This was the time when a man needed all the friends he had. "[No] one wanted to be cut off from the rest." Ordinarily no other prod was required.[10]

As comradeship induced men to enter combat, so did it work to keep them there.

The most potent propaganda that the Germans directed at American combat soldiers aimed to isolate them. "Why are you fighting us?" it asked. "No one cares about you." James Fry, a regimental commander in the 88th Division on the Italian front, conceded the persuasiveness of the enemy's approach: "There can be no doubt but that some of it was effective. . . . [It] was responsible for some of the desertions that always occurred during combat." Fry knew that foxhole opinion resonated to the German theme because his thinking too clustered about "Who gives a damn what happens to me?" Most front-line soldiers came to accept as an article of faith the indifference of the high command and the home front. "Men who fight are damn fools" seemed the only conclusion when combat soldiers realized that they constituted only a fragment of the military's full complement of personnel, almost all of whom remained safe from harm. "The fellows in the rear and back home—they get the gravy." Fighting soldiers knew that those who remained at home were making record wages; they were convinced that rear-echelon supply units saved for themselves the best of the equipment and comfort items consigned to the front. "By this time tomorrow I may be dead somewhere among these damn rocks, with my face puffed up and ants running up my nose, just like that poor devil over along the trail that they haven't had a chance to pick up." Seventy percent of the war's military casualties were infantrymen. "God. Anything is better than this."[11]

To the Germans' assertion that "No one cares about you," then, only one rejoinder appeared possible: "My buddies do!" Comradeship stood between the infantryman and isolation. "There was," paratrooper Ross Carter believed, "no perceptible road to life visible [to] the front-line men in Italy in 1943 and 1944. To be wounded, killed or captured: these were the three roads to our destiny." "[The] pill of death . . . is bitter for youths in their teens and twenties, [but] they were prepared to swallow it, knowing that they had been set apart to die if need be." "Oldring, Hastings, Carlton, Olson and the Master would never march, camp, eat, drink, love or talk with us again [and they] wouldn't matter a damn to anybody except those of us left in the platoon. . . . But somehow I felt that comradeship with them and with jokers like Duquesne, Big Rodgers, Berkely, Finkelstein, Casey, and all the others had about it a value that in itself geared me to face whatever lay ahead as well if not better than my hatred for the enemy and his philosophy. . . . [Here was the] philosophy which carried me through the dark and bloody days that followed."[12]

Friends were indispensable to perseverance in combat; on that there was no disagreement. "I hold it to be one of the simplest truths of war," declared S. L. A. Marshall, "that the thing which enables an infantry soldier to keep going with his weapons is the near presence or the presumed presence of a comrade." Sledge said it, too—less pretentiously and less anemically: "The only thing that kept you going was your faith in your buddies."[13]

As the soldier's span in combat lengthened, comradeship also served to protect him against, or at least to retard, psychological disintegration. Paratrooper Laurence Critchell knew that it was friendship "that kept them sane." Comradeship, said an infantry scout wounded at Anzio, was "the main thing that keeps a guy from going haywire."[14]

Friends aided and accelerated that coarsening essential to the combat soldier. They put forward rationales for behavior unacceptable in civilian life; they assured him that in repressing sensitivity to the consequences of his conduct he did not place himself beyond humanness. Coarsening carried him far from his former self; comradeship promised that he had not gone too far. With an incisiveness rare so early in the war, British soldier John Guest grasped the connection: "I am undergoing a land-change into something coarse and strange. Every now and then the old self revives in a frenzied struggle with the new, and then I am in torment until [New] Self . . . has beaten [Old] Self . . . back and snapped the door on him. Were it not for [my] friends . . . I would find it insupportable."[15]

During an American counterattack launched in a desperate effort to reestablish the Pilar-Bagac defense line on Bataan, infantryman Sidney Stewart leaped into a crater to escape the blast of Japanese bombs—to discover that an enemy soldier had acted identically. Before the Japanese could raise his rifle, Stewart covered him with his .45, and the two were left "facing each other in a fantastic nightmare. . . . He didn't look as I had expected Nips to look, like the faces of the dead ones I had seen. His face was clean and clear-cut. Sort of simple, and his eyes were wide and brown and somehow honest.

Yet there was a hopeless look in them. . . . I knew I had to move on. I knew I couldn't take him prisoner. We didn't have time. We had to move up and there was no way to let him go. . . . He said something in Japanese. . . . I knew it was a surrender. . . . He didn't cringe or sneer, nor did he show any hatred. 'Why, I don't hate this guy. I can't hate him,' . . . [This] man was like a friend." But then from a distance other Americans urged Stewart to join them in moving forward. The Japanese, recognizing Stewart's hardening, sadly shook his head and took from his shirt pocket a small prayer board. Stewart killed him with a single shot.[16]

Though furious fighting filled the days that followed, Stewart's combativeness drained away. "I could not shake off the murderous feeling of having killed a helpless man." During a lull, his friends intervened. "Sid, you shouldn't let that thing worry you. You shouldn't think about it all the time. After all, boy, this is war, and that's just one of the things of war. . . . As long as men are men, and countries are made up of individuals, we'll have wars." There was laughter, and the conversation turned to other topics—medicines, food, reinforcements expected to arrive from the mainland—and then Japanese mortars resumed their fire. As in the aftermath of Paul Bäumer's shellhole encounter with the French soldier of World War I, a renowned, parallel episode in Remarque's *All Quiet on the Western Front,* Sidney Stewart did not think again of the enemy soldier whom he had killed.[17]

James Jones, too, explored comradeship as an instrument of exoneration. In *The Thin Red Line,* Bead, going off to relieve himself, looks up to discover an enemy soldier charging down on him. The American manages to tackle the Japanese, beat and bayonet him, and, when he still will not succumb, shoots and smashes at him with his rifle butt. Sobbing, wailing, and vomiting, Bead suffers an "oppressive guilt." "He could not escape a feeling that, especially now, after he'd both looked [at] and touched [the body], some agent of retribution would try to hold him responsible." He imagines their positions reversed and sees "himself spitted [by] that crude [Japanese bayonet] blade descending into the soft dark of his [own] chest cavity." Returning to the platoon, Bead shakes off questions and says only enough to send others in search of the body. When he confesses, "I feel guilty," his friends object. Think of yourself, they urge, not as the Japanese soldier being killed but as the Japanese soldier dominating *you,* killing *you.* "Guilty! What the hell for? It was him or you, wasn't it?" Hesitantly, Bead agrees to accept the dead soldier's wallet—and his rifle ("[You] won it. And won it the hard way"). Finally, a comrade confides that "I'll say one thing. When you set out to kill him, you really killed him." "You think so?" "[Yeah, and] I ain't the only one." Bead begins to grin.[18]

The captain, in remarks to Bead, places a social seal on the episode. "[We] really have no choice. We have to do as society demands. . . . That was what happened to you today. . . . Well, I just want you to know that you were morally justified in what you did. You had no choice, and you musn't worry or feel guilty about it. You did what any other good soldier would have done. . . ." It was one of those rare passages in which James Jones mislaid his touch for realism—enlisted men were not ordinarily concerned about society's demands or field captains interested in explaining them to enlisted men—but the words of Captain Stein and Bead's comrades did trace out the elements of the prevailing rationale. A great variety of situations created distress; the reassurances were few and fundamental—the absence of alternatives available to the individual soldier and thus the inevitability of the outcome; the irrelevancy of particular participants and thus the blamelessness of the soldier involved. Still beyond was the most telling assurance and final absolution: the pleading that those destroyed had either killed comrades or, if left alive, would have been sure to do so. Bead's friends had offered him this ultimate refuge of comradeship.[19]

Comradeship also served to divert the combat soldier from self-absorption, from obsession with his own cares and fears. The problem, a common one, was there in a letter that a British lieutenant, George Morrison of the Black Watch, wrote home from the North African desert in September 1942, a month before his death at El Alamein. "I find myself . . . worried about little things, like scratches that fester and tea being cold, and being occasionally constipated. But that is because all our interests revolve about ourselves, there being no outside interest or attraction whatever. . . . [We] are almost like the bed-ridden invalid whose one thought is himself." By contrast, Sidney Stewart found in comradeship the corrective for an acute self-centeredness riveted to his suffering. Made a prisoner of the Japanese after the fall of Bataan, often an experience no less severe than combat itself, he survived the Death March and lived to reach the stockade at Camp O'Donnell, Luzon. There, one day, Father Bill Cummings, a Manila priest who had chosen to accompany the troops to Bataan, spoke to a small group of prisoners, urging them to help one another. For himself, Father Cummings thought that, amid so many men suffering beyond his ability to offer relief, "if I can help a few, then maybe God will feel my life is justified." And then he added words that stirred Stewart deeply: "[And] when I worry about their suffering, I don't have time to think of myself." "Suddenly," Stewart recalled, "I felt my life depended on helping the others"—his comrades John, Hughes, Weldon, and Ross. Later in their imprisonment, they agreed that caring for a frail friend did "as much for [the stronger] as it has for [the weaker]."[20]

Comradeship was also valuable as a psychological sentinel. Fighting soldiers knew their friends well enough, and cared enough, to react to changes that they observed in those who remained oblivious to their own deterioration. This phenomenon interested two American psychiatrists visiting North Africa to investigate soldiers who had "cracked up." A nineteen-year-old corporal whom they interviewed did not deny that his comrades were susceptible to collapse.

> "Yeah, that's right. Some of them do [break down]. But you can see it comin' on, and sometimes the other guys can help out."
>
> "How do you mean, you can see it coming on?"
>
> "Why, first they get trigger happy. They go running all over the place lookin' for something to shoot at. Then, the next thing you know they got the battle jitters. They jump if you light a match and go diving for cover if someone bounces a tin hat off a rock. Any kind of a sudden noise and you can just about see them let out a mental scream to themselves. . . ."
>
> "How can the other fellows help out in a case like that?"
>
> The corporal looked down at his hands a little sheepishly.
>
> "Aw, you can kind of cover up for a guy like that before he's completely gone. He can be sent back to get ammo or something. You know and he knows he's gonna stay out of sight for a while, but you don't let on, see? Then he can pretend to himself he's got a reason for being back there and he still has his pride. Maybe he even gets his nerve back for the next time. . . ."[21]

Finally, comradeship was often able to provide the soldier a measure of reconciliation with death.

Infantrymen isolated from their fellows frequently found very painful thoughts of their deaths. Especially torturous was the realization that death struck individually, that it "takes a man by himself," in the historian Jonathan Marwil's phrase. Comrades, however, frequently disguised reality by visualizing death as a companionable experience. Paratrooper Ross Carter, for example, moved toward reassurance that he would not be alone in death by imagining that "if it were my destiny to die in battle," it would come "by T. L.'s side, surrounded by Berkely, the Arab, Duquesne, Casey, Gruening and the other stalwarts of the platoon." Indeed, even amid grief at the loss of a friend, that death might be made to appear a bridge between the current lives and prospective deaths of his comrades. When his best friend—first as college roommate and then as comrade-in-arms—was killed by a German sniper, Grady Arrington seemed almost to welcome the prospect of his own extinction. Was his dead friend not better off than he was? he wondered. Surely, he thought, he would not be compelled to endure life much beyond Thaxton's departure, a death, he said, that he had feared more than his own. Audie Murphy, too, found that the loss of friends diminished death's remote and hostile nature: "[A]t this moment the grave seems merely an open door that divides us from our comrades."[22]

The presence of comrades still alive, moreover, seemed to promise that those who did die would not simply disappear. A man's life might be, as Ross Carter believed, "a trifling thing, really important to almost no one but himself." But that "almost" loomed large; no one wished to be forgotten. The Army, thought Arrington, kept the dead soldier in mind "only long enough to bring in a replacement," but comrades "do not forget so quickly." Members of Franklyn Johnson's antitank company, like those in many units, adopted rites that enhanced remembrance. Comrades (with "wet eyes," wrote Johnson) sorted out the dead friend's possessions and then distributed among themselves and others in the outfit his toilet articles, his towels, even his underwear. Comradeship tried to pledge that one would go easier and would remain longer in the minds of the living.[23]

As comradeship met practical requirements in strengthening soldiers to take part in battle, so it fulfilled a number of their emotional needs.

Many soldiers, it was clear, took from the idea of "comrade" much of their sense of personal identity. Within the world of war, such alternative roles as "son"; "boyfriend," "sweetheart," or "lover"; "husband"; and "father" quickly became remote and at least temporarily irrelevant. Dominant American social values gave to "soldier" a set of meanings of little allure—and to "infantryman" even less. "Comrade," however, offered an immediate, material relationship in substitution for distant, weakening roles, and an intimacy promising to free the soldier from the isolating orbits both of self-absorption and of military depersonalization. Nothing supported the combat soldier's sense of himself as powerfully as the role of comrade.

Comradeship possessed as well a power to suppress alternative identities supportable in civilian society but dangerously divisive in combat. William Broyles, Jr., has described the ability of comradely affection to transcend "race and personality and education—all those things that would make a difference in peace." Several scenes in Leon Uris's World War II story *Battle Cry* suggest that ethnicity should also have found a place on Broyles's list. As Marines recuperated in New Zealand from combat on Guadalcanal, Danny Forrester became upset that in a minor argument Speedy's last words to Levin were "Don't go away mad, Jew boy." Speedy defended himself—"I don't like kikes. . . . We make it plenty damned rough for them in Texas"— but Seabags intervened on Forrester's side: "You don't like Levin because he's Jewish. You don't like Pedro because he's Mexican. You don't like New Zealanders because they talk funny. You don't like colored people—who *do* you like, Speedy?" "What the hell are you guys," Speedy shot back. "A bunch of Nigger lovers? [Levin] ain't nothing but a kike draftee. . . . They're all yellow. . . . He's yellow." But Mac, the squad leader, surprised Speedy and brought the argument to a close by telling him that Levin, "Golden Gloves welterweight champion of New York for two years," had turned down a spot on the Division boxing team because he wanted "to stick with the outfit . . . [and] to be a Marine like the rest of us."[24]

On a subsequent training march of great arduousness, Speedy, noticing Levin's bloody feet, expressed concern to Mac: "I don't want it out that I said this, but . . ." Later, just prior to the Marines' invasion of Tarawa, Speedy approached Levin.

> "Levin."
>
> "What do you want?"
>
> "I'd like to talk to you for a minute."
>
> "I ain't looking for no trouble."
>
> "Levin, since we're going into combat and . . . well, what the hell, let's shake hands and forget the crap."
>
> [Levin smiled] "Sure, Speedy, put her there."
>
> "Er, Levin, the guys was talking it over and . . . well . . . we all felt that . . . well here, Levin. [Speedy handed Levin a mock membership certificate.]
>
> "It's kind of a club we made up a long time ago. We sort of figure that you are a member now. All the guys signed it. You can sign my copy if you want to."
>
> "Jees, thanks, Speedy . . ."[25]

That the episode was as saccharine and glibly crafted as if designed for a Hollywood war film and that the denouement was bathetic—Levin was cut down by Japanese fire as he signaled naval craft for supplies critically needed; Speedy carried him to an aid station and nursed him as he died ("Hold my hand . . . will you, Speedy?")—need not obscure comradeship's ability to integrate soldiers of disparate backgrounds. Even from a training camp in California, draftee Eugene Gach was able to write, "Everyone is called the Dago, the Wop, the Greek, the Jew, the Heinie, the Polack, and there is no bitterness in any of it." And as comradeship leavened or inhibited intolerance, it also subjugated excessive tolerance. Many soldiers who, as a matter of conscience, had vowed never to fire their rifles at human enemies did so to save comrades whose lives were suddenly endangered. To those in the combat squad, non-violence could be just as dysfunctional as bigotry. Thus, as the comrade's role strengthened the soldier's sense of personal identity, comradeship worked simultaneously to diminish identities that divided.[26]

Nowhere was comradeship more important than in meeting the combat soldier's emotional need for intimacy—and even love.

Basic training's destruction of privacy and enforcement of physical intimacy often left sour tastes of deprivation and resentment. "We circled each other cautiously," reported Samuel Hynes of Navy ground school. "[We] shared nothing of the past, we shared everything in the present— . . . room, toilets, mess hall, classrooms, parade ground. And more than that we shared a hatred of the whole program, and a determination to survive it." But one of training's results—the shedding of soldiers' self-consciousness about their bodies—did much to advance comradeship. Most soldiers welcomed the escape from diffidence (perhaps more a middle-class than a working-class or upper-class phenomenon) and enjoyed the conversion of private embarrassment into group ritual.[27]

Gach spoke of "the silent and perfect communion of the four of us drinking a lot of beer at Bert's Place, and then going outside and standing shoulder-to-shoulder, pee-ing down the bluff." Many GIs remembered how, during truck-convoy rest stops, eyes had been riveted by the sight of a seemingly endless line of their fellows urinating in union over the edge of an embankment. Of richer significance was the desire of many to signal together their success in carrying the war to the enemy's homeland by standing with friends to moisten the first German soil or by lining bridges and peeing into the River Rhine. William Manchester did something in the Pacific that prior to the war he "wouldn't have dreamt of . . . carrying . . . out in full view of strangers." As a fallen tree brought his truck column to a short halt, he was "seized by a compelling need to empty my bowels." He bolted to the ground and squatted. When motors started up again, he shouted, "Wait for me!" completed his task, and sprinted for his vehicle, "pulling up my pants as all hands cheered."[28]

In relieving reserve, on a par with the lifting of bodily discomfiture was the almost universal use of language at odds with that of polite society.

"[M]uch of what we all said and sang," reported Hynes, "*was* obscene. Obscenity was a kind of intimacy, a shared language like the common toilet and the single room we slept in, a step past conventional reticences. . . . Our common vocabulary connected us with each other. . . ."[29]

Physical intimacy thus crossed what many had previously assumed were the fixed boundaries of selfhood, and with the pressures of training and approaching combat, prepared the way for emotional intimacy. Forced sharing of facilities fostered sharing of another quality. Wrote Army sergeant M. H. E. Marsden: "Companionship, robust and vital, real and alive. You just share your life with the men in the barracks. This has been going on for twelve weeks. Twelve weeks ago if someone had suggested that I even drink out of the same cup that someone else had taken a drink from I would most likely have retched, but that was twelve weeks ago. Now, five of us drink out of the same canteen. We share a bottle of Coke, taking turns guzzling, share a box of ice cream with the same spoon. We even wear each other's drawers and socks and shirts."[30]

Within war zones, reciprocity again intensified.

"Anybody got any ink? My pen's dry."

"Somebody loan me a pen?"

"I'm out of stamps. Anybody got any?"

"Who's got some writing paper?"

"Hell, I'm out of cigarettes. Who's got some?"

"Gimme a light, somebody. I've lost my goddamned lighter again."

"Hell, my last pair of socks are wet. Anybody got a dry pair?"

"I've got to wash my teeth or they're gonna fall out. Somebody gimme some toothpaste."

"We get to laughing sometimes," reported Sergeant Henry Giles, "about what one of us would do without all the others. Even in a family there are *some* things that are private, but in this platoon what one man owns, everybody owns. Well, nobody has asked to borrow [my] toothbrush yet, but I expect it any day."[31]

This communitarianism quickly expanded to requisition parcels sent to soldiers by their families. "We shared all packages immediately. . . ." "All food parcels are shared. We feast on innumerable delicacies. . . ." Next came a significant step up, to the contents of letters from home. "Mail call," Giles recorded in his diary. "Three letters from Janice. In one she said she was trying to learn to play Beethoven's 'Moonlight Sonata' really well. I read that part out loud. I often read parts of her letters aloud to the fellows, just as they read interesting things from their letters." The men's interest rapidly outran the casual as they invested themselves in their comrades' relationships with others. Another Giles entry read: "Mail call just now! And *ten,* count them, *ten* letters from Janice. . . . I feel just about 100% better. . . . I think I'm the happiest man in the outfit tonight. . . . [but] some of the boys are almost as glad for me. 'Giles heard from his girl!' 'She's all right!' [Giles's fiancée had undergone surgery on her hand.] What good joes they are. . . . Black Mac came in . . . with a big grin. 'Heard you got ten letters.' I fanned them out to show him. He said, 'I told you. Now, what the hell were you beating your brains out for?' So I told him . . . [that I'd feared] I'd never hear again[, that] maybe she had died. And it [had] just shriveled my soul. . . . He nodded and said he knew." A final entry revealed how dense the emotional mesh became. "For some reason I started making down my bed before writing my letter to Janice tonight. Everybody stopped and stared at me. Finally Pigg said, 'Aren't you going to write your letter tonight?' It really rocked me back on my heels. We know each other so well that to change the routine the least bit seems strange."[32]

In Italy, Audie Murphy's friend Brandon learned that his ten-year-old daughter wished to cut off her pigtails. Boys in school had been pulling her hair; it was difficult for her grandmother to braid; her girlfriends were getting permanents; etc. The squad gathered around Brandon as he read the letter aloud. "Granny won't let me unless you say ok so I hope you say ok." Debate ensued, with Horse-Face the most adamant: "Oh, no. Don't let her. Keep her a kid as long as you can." It was, said Audie Murphy, "a problem that concerns us deeply."[33]

A veteran of the New Georgia campaign whose name was Watson told Arthur Miller: "Sergeant Jones . . . got a . . . letter [and] came up . . . with this picture of his new baby that had just been born in the States. We passed this picture from one foxhole to another until it was rumpled. For about three days and three nights all we seemed to talk about was Jones's baby, as though it was ours. I mean it seemed like such a funny thing to be happening."[34]

Emotional communion engendered in turn a physical intimacy of still higher intensity. During engineers' training, a friend chaffed Marsden: "Cute fanny, kid." In retaliation, Marsden "gave him a good goose" and that set in train an extended physical byplay—"so we ended up laughing and he washed my back." And combat, when it came, countenanced further physicality, from simply sheltering against the elements to the sad but intimate care of wounded comrades to the exuberance of victory celebrations. GIs in Europe quickly shed self-consciousness about sharing blankets and body heat through winter nights. Wounded friends had to be helped to defecate; ailing friends suffering attacks of malaria had to be sponged. "In a tent, with a hundred and four [degree] fever and chills and pains ripping him up," wrote Leon Uris, "a man finds out what the word buddy means—to bathe a sick kid and feed and attend to him." And battlefield triumph had its own, very different intimacies. Recalled the New Georgia combat soldier Watson: "All the outfit were trying to be the first one onto a certain [Japanese] airfield. . . . [We] ran so fast we outdistanced the other outfits and almost got cut off [so] they pulled us back and we waited weeks for the jump off. Yeh, we really wanted that field. [Finally] we got our chance and stormed the field. . . . And, boy, you should have seen the crying. The guys kissed each other. I [even] kissed men I never saw before in my life."[35]

Richard Leacock, an Army private and combat cameraman, observed of young GIs with whom he stayed in Burma that "There's a strange closeness [among] the men. You've had no sleep for several days. There's pouring rain and constant [gun]fire. It's over and everybody just goes to sleep in big piles. It's a weird sight. Guys in each other's arms. You never see that except in the army."[36]

Such physicality posed questions about the relationship between combat, comradeship, and sexuality, an issue little discussed by the soldiers themselves and left without consensus. Judgments ranged across the spectrum—and remained tentative. James Jones was inclined to believe in the virtual hegemony of sexual feelings: "Could it be that *all* war was basically sexual? Not just in psych[ological] theory, but in fact, actually and emotionally? [Was war a] sort of sexual perversion? Or a complex of perversions?" If so, was there not "an almost sexual ecstasy" in comradeship? On the other extremity, Marine fighter pilot Samuel Hynes believed that combat anesthetized sexual longings. "We were young men at the peak of our sexual powers, but those powers slept." He speculated that male sexual activity and participation in war were both forms of aggression and that the latter drove out the former. "Were we living our sexual lives in the bombing and strafing?" Or were their sexual impulses being sublimated "in the comradeship of the all-male, committed life of the squadron?" He too was aware that he did not have answers. "I only know that for nearly a year we lived like monks—hard-drinking, obscene monks, but poor, obedient, and chaste." Neither comrades nor Okinawan women nor even American nurses, he claimed, often aroused explicit sexual reactions.[37]

Falling between these views were those of soldier Watson, who cast himself and most GIs with Hynes but allowed for significant exceptions.

About the women problem . . . we naturally can't do like the Japs. They have whores coming right into the foxholes with them. . . . What happened with us was this: The absence of women hits men in two ways. Some guys take on nasty habits. I've seen men do things I never believed anybody would do. And those men go from bad to worse and nothing can stop them. It's a terrible thing. But then there are men who it don't bother. Me, for instance. I just forgot about women. I think most of the men react this way. You just never think about it. You lose all your urge after a while. It's as though that part of your body went to sleep or died.[38]

Watson nowhere made explicit those "nasty habits" (masturbation? sexual encounters with island women? with comrades?) but one cannot ponder such relationships without considering the sexual mores that prevailed in the late 1930s and early 1940s. In a point of view held by many other American middle-class military personnel, William Manchester later found much contrast between wartime and postwar decades. Youth of the 1970s and 1980s, he argued, were in matters sexual far more worldly-wise than those of the war generation. "[In] our innocence we [soldiers] knew almost nothing about homosexuality. We had never heard of lesbians, and while we were aware that male homosexuals existed—they were regarded as degenerates and called 'sex perverts,' or simply 'perverts'—most of us had never, to our knowledge, encountered one. . . . There was [in our civilian lives] so much excitement (and apocrypha) about heterosexuality that we seldom gave its inversion a second thought."[39]

A reasonable estimate was that, as one component of the numbing process, sexual desire diminished as a function of time spent in combat, and that explicit sexual expression in comradeship was, in the 1940s, slight.

Nonetheless, frequent acknowledgments of feeling reflected the reactions of human beings who cared for one another and felt their friendship profoundly. His comrades, Manchester declared, "were closer to me than I can say, closer than any friends had been or ever would be." It should surprise no one then that, under the pressures of the battlefield, feelings of friendship intensified—and sometimes moved to love. True, that word was so powerfully and indissolubly bound to heterosexual relationships that its application to comrades was almost always hidden behind a curtain of reticence. When Arthur Miller described a soldier as "in love, in love with his comrades in arms," he prefaced his use of "love" with "For want of a better word. . . ." That one, he knew, had "certain sneering connotations"—a want of maleness and thus of toughness, a glint of abnormality. No, soldiers did not employ the word "love" in description of their feelings for one another in combat. Beyond battle, however, alcohol sometimes provided an acceptable excuse for some loosening of expression. Hynes recounted an aviators' party at which "affection flowed among young men [who] threw their arms around each other's shoulders and sang a roaring bawdy song. It isn't easy for young American males to express feelings for each other, but on those occasions, when we were together—all pilots, all drunk, shouting indecencies to music and laughing—it was all right. . . . It was possible, then, to feel comradeship, to be happy together without being emotional, or not visibly, and thus unmanly." Ordinarily, however, reserve remained firmly in place.[40]

When a platoon leader received "a bombshell"—news that his friend had been wounded ("Well, Paul, they got your buddy")—his thoughts traced all the concern of love: "Oh, dear God, please be with Jack. Don't let them kill him on the way back. Guide him to the aid station. Don't let him be hurt bad. Please, God! Please, God!" But the words that could be spoken when comrades were reunited, even with both wild with relief, were of another order. "Where in hell you been? Didn't you know the war is still going on? All the information I could get was that you had been promoted to the rear to march in a parade. . . . You dirty bastard!" "Hell, they can't kill you: you're too damn sorry!" Many settled for even less—with the usual disguise a flurry of epithets (e.g., "You kiss my old rusty dusty!"). When Audie Murphy hurried his release from hospital and rejoined his unit at Anzio, Snuffy and Kerrigan greeted him "with hearty curses, and I [returned] the compliment." All took care to speak of separations in ways sure to exclude emotion.

> "Say, have you been sucking around the old man again? I hear you got pushed up to staff?"
> "You heard right. I'm going to look for more respect from you characters."
> "Go to hell."

When comrades died, the injunction against emotion was often categorical.

> "You heard about Swope and Little Mike?"
> "Yeah. Anderson told me."
> "I always said that coffee would be the death of him."
> "How'd it happen?"
> "They went into a shack to heat up some java and got a direct hit from an 88. . . . [Swope] lost his right leg at the hip and part of a hand. [The] medic said he never made a sound and never had any expression at all on his face."
> "He had guts."

"Yeah. You can say that again. Mike was blown all to hell. Hardly enough of him left for identification. . . ."

"He was a good soldier."[41]

The medic who later told Audie Murphy that the wounded soldier Horse-Face had just died then asked,

"He was a pal?"

"We'd been together since North Africa."

"Jesus . . . that's too bad. I lost a buddy on Anzio. Was he married?"

"Yeah. He was married."

"Any kids?"

"No kids."

"Must've been a good joe."

"Yeah. He was all right."

"Well, that's war for you."

"Yeah."[42]

Comradely love, seldom spoken, did occasionally appear in letters sent to those at home themselves linked to soldier-writers by love. John Stradling, an infantry draftee later killed in the Italian campaign, wrote: "It takes the selfishness out of a fellow to be one of the boys, and to go through everything with every kind of person. You learn to love them all." (It was easier to own to deep feeling for a group of men than to admit love for one or two comrades.) Love appeared as well in plaintive "fictional" accounts by authors accustomed to recognizing and depicting emotion, sometimes with extraordinary claims for its properties. Leon Uris went far beyond a simple acknowledgment of comrades' love for one another. He described soldiers as "[loving] each other in a way that no woman could understand . . . and [giving] a tenderness to each other that even a woman couldn't duplicate." Correspondents, too, sometimes softened. "I had been accepted by these men," wrote Marine Corps combat correspondent Jim Lucas, "and learned to love them." Finally, love received some due, years later, in veterans' retrospective comprehension of their wartime experience. In the late 1970s, Manchester decided that his flight from the hospital back to his comrades had been "an act of love."[43]

During the war itself, candor was most likely to appear in frustrated soldiers' attempts to describe their feelings to those who had not experienced battle. It finally exploded from Watson as he tried to explain comradeship to Arthur Miller and gradually realized that any interpretation resting on friendship would be inadequate: "Friendship is the greatest thing out there. I mean real friendship, not because a guy can give you something you want. I tell you the truth: I would die for any one of thirty or forty men out there as easily as I'd flick out this match. I swear that's the truth. I don't expect you to understand it, but I swear it . . . I would die for them. I love them with everything in my heart."[44]

Thus, comradeship opened fighting soldiers to intimacy, physical and emotional, and it in turn led them to what J. Glenn Gray called "the higher reaches of the spirit"—the realization of their most idealistic impulses, to aid others unselfishly and ultimately to reach even beyond service to sacrifice.[45]

Henry Giles exulted in the selflessness of the members of his platoon.

> Not a one who wouldn't do anything in the world for you, and for each other. Give you anything they've got—from their last pair of dry socks to their last franc or Airmail stamp. Nobody finds a bottle and hides it—brings it straight to share. Nobody gets a package from home and hoards it. Usually the guy who gets the package has only one piece of candy, like everybody else, or one cookie or piece of cake. On cigarettes—as short as they are—nobody goes off and lights up by himself. He lights up, puffs it down a piece, then gives the butt to somebody. Goes short himself. It's a grand, grand outfit.

The combat soldier had no way to measure his contribution in advancing the war, but he could manifest and measure his usefulness to the small group around him. Innumerable requests for, and renderings of, aid were the threads with which trust, intimacy, and love were woven fast, and such service could reach beyond mutual aid to sacrifice.[46]

An American nurse on Bataan reported that the wounded frequently insisted, "Take my buddy, he's hurt worse than me." Infantryman Frank Mathias was witness on Luzon to battle action of the kind that to World War II Americans represented the acme of nobility: "PFC Anthony L. Krotiak and his squad were subjected to intense small-arms fire and grenades, driving them into an abandoned Jap trench. A grenade landed in their midst. Krotiak jammed it into the soft earth with his rifle butt, then fell over it, successfully shielding his men from the explosion. He died a few minutes later." Krotiak was awarded the Congressional Medal of Honor. On Iwo Jima, as two Marines—Sergeant Henry Hansen and PFC Donald Ruhl—ran to the top of a sand-covered pillbox and began to engage Japanese soldiers in nearby support trenches, "a demolitions charge came flying through the air and landed . . . in front of them. Shouting, 'Look out, Hank!,' Ruhl dived on the charge and absorbed its full blast. Hansen . . . was spotted with blood and bits of flesh. [He] reached up and grasped Ruhl by the foot [but Lieutenant] Wells, . . . crouching nearby, quickly ordered, 'Leave him alone. He's dead!'" Ruhl too received the Medal of Honor. That such episodes became the stock in trade of home-front propagandists and, depicted on the backs of bubble-gum cards, drew the excited admiration of small boys who knew nothing of war should not obscure reality: at the farthest reach of comradeship, they did occur.[47]

To the combat soldier, in the end, nothing held greater importance than comradeship. Indeed, as protracted campaigning darkened and dirtied everything else, it provoked an intensification of comradeship. "Friendship," said Eugene Sledge, "was the only comfort a man had." Comradeship—friends' love and loyalty and devotion to one another—seemed the only redeeming presence in war; it alone was able to sustain a world in which battle had reduced their consciousness to "us." As Kurt Gabel felt comradeship's force, "We would march in step for *us,* sing for *us,* excel for *us,* endure for *us,* and . . . suffer and die for *us.* For each other."[48]

Comradeship was less subject to impeachment than danger, spectacle, and destruction—unlike theirs, its nature was not misinterpreted by those who did not experience it from within battle—but it did possess shadowy and pernicious extensions that most veterans have forgotten today.

For most combat soldiers the crux of comradeship was not sacrifice but the survival of self. Wrote PFC Keith Winston in his war journal: "[T]here's a genuine bond—you might call it survival—that brings every type of man together." Comradeship did not require affinity; it opened to necessity. One could even argue, as did psychiatrist Rollo May, that with the unrelenting quest for survival at the core of comradeship, the soldier became a comrade in simply accepting a combat role. It followed then that when, for whatever reason, he failed to play his part, comradeship was subject to rapid disintegration. On a bombing mission against Nagoya, John Ciardi's B-29 suffered gun malfunctions; his investigation uncovered problems that "the most elementary inspection should have caught. . . . When I called [Tiger] on it he blew up in my face, and I blew back. He's a likable kid, but in no way Jap [fighter aircraft] will discount." Ciardi decided to make his own gun inspections. "Enemies have been made by less than that, but so have eleven dead men." With comradeship welded to survival, soldiers did not remain close to those who no longer helped them to go on living. Emotional affinity did not overcome neglect of function.[49]

Conversely, comradeship often banded soldiers of discordant temperaments who effectively performed mutually supportive jobs. As J. Glenn Gray knew, many wartime comrades would not have been friends before the war and would not remain friends afterwards. Indeed, some were not friends during the war. Said Bill Mauldin: "Some of the best Willie and Joe material I picked up was from listening to infantry partners who were personally incompatible or even hostile . . . but who worked as a team on patrols or when taking towns, and so clung together like sick kittens on a hot brick. To hell with personalities—they wanted to get home alive." And in recent years Mauldin has placed in this category Willie and Joe themselves: "The main thing about [them] was that . . . they were like two cops operating together as partners. . . . They don't particularly like each other. They aren't cut from the same cloth. They don't have the same friends. But they're damned good at what they do together, and each is the other guy's life-insurance policy. They're not devoted to each other, but they need each other."[50]

With survival establishing the hierarchy of soldiers' concerns, none of its rankings was more important than their heed to comrades before non-comrades. As coarsening advanced, combat soldiers progressively closed down consideration for non-comrades. Partiality is, to be sure, intrinsic to comradeship, but here the results were drastic.

The decline of interest in non-comrades began early. "A corpse . . . cries out for care," declared combat surgeon Brendan Phibbs. "[So we] always performed some small ritual . . ."—pulling a field jacket over torn viscera; turning the dead man on his stomach to cover his face; sticking a weapon in the ground and placing the casualty's helmet atop it. "[But we] learned to be selectively callous. . . . [Those] from our own battalions, our friends from our terribly close family of survivors, *their* deaths diminished us," but "German dead didn't count at all"—and "men from other units" didn't count as much. Concern diminished even within the platoon. When, during a nighttime lull in Pacific fighting, one Marine was shot and killed by another, very nervous and frightened Marine, Russell Davis noticed less distress around him because the dead man was without buddies. He was "a loner."[51]

And ordinarily, as comradeship strengthened within a group, it was not long before reaction to occurrences beyond the group slipped toward indifference. As a passenger in the RAF aircraft taking part in a night raid on Frankfurt, signalman Anthony Cotterell noticed that "the sense of interdependence between various members of the crew was complete. . . . Each one was conscious of his own important part in the crew." Once in the sky, there was almost palpable "a tremendous sense of comradeship with the other members of the crew. Your companionship with each other knows no inhibitions of temperament or prejudice. Friendship is perfect and complete." Over the target, however, amid enemy fighters and flak, Cotterell discovered the limits of that comradeship. He watched the bright shafts of German searchlights pinion another RAF bomber against the blackness. "The cruel thing is that one's only sensation is one of relief that the searchlights are temporarily diverted elsewhere. One feels no urge to go to the assistance of the unfortunate aircraft that is cornered. [O]bviously, it would be senseless to do so, but it seems extraordinary that one doesn't feel any urge to do so. I noticed the same indifference to the troubles of others when flying with the Americans. There is complete unity within the individual aircraft, but for some reason that is where it ends. Nor is it simply . . . my own . . . idiosyncrasy. It was obviously a general state of mind."[52]

Indifference often yielded to obliviousness. In training camp, U.S. Army private Wayne Weber anticipated feelings that came to most only with combat: "I had made a few friends in my company. These I stuck with; the rest, as far as I was concerned, didn't even exist." In the Pacific, Manchester made clear that he had no concern for anyone beyond his own circle. He was acidly critical of a replacement officer whom he could not dissuade from a frontal assault ("I'm going to lead these people over the top"). When the lieutenant barked out, "Men, I know you'd like to stay here. I would myself. But those yellow bastards down the beach are killing your buddies," he disastrously overestimated the compass of their comradeship. "He didn't even realize"—Manchester's words were contemptuous—"that a combat man's loyalty is confined to those around him, that as far as the Raggedy Ass Marines [Manchester's small group] were concerned the First Battalion might as well have belonged to a separate race." (The lieutenant rose from cover; pointed at the Japanese; shouted "Follow me!"; climbed the wall—and was immediately stitched up and down by bullets from a Nambu machine gun. No one else had moved.)[53]

With the disappearance of all sympathetic notice of others, comrades surprisingly renewed their attention to non-comrades—but not in the way the latter would have desired. It was as if thoughtful regard, in reaching the vanishing point, were then replaced by a new, negative interest that mounted steadily. Invidiousness began modestly. When, during the Battle of the Bulge, those in Leinbaugh's company gave thought to two of their battalion's other companies ordered to assault German positions through woods so dense that one could not see six feet forward, they "knew what [the attackers] were going up against but thought 'Better them than us.'" A rule among the men read, "Take anything you can from the army, but don't steal from other guys," but practice increasingly countenanced theft from other units—and targets not confined to the rear echelon. Grady Gallant's squad of Marines negotiated an agreement with one of their number, "a thug and a pickpocket." He was permitted to continue practicing his craft, but only beyond the squad. This willingness to exploit non-comrades led in turn to a far graver order of victimization. In combat, one turned first to survival.[54]

Bill Mauldin spoke more directly than most of comradeship's iron necessity. When he wrote that "A man was safer staying with his friends" and that "The infantryman can't live without friends," his eye was not entirely on enemy action. The outsider, the non-comrade American, was at risk from forces on his own side of the line.

> I tried to confine my visits to units where I knew people. One of the most fatuous and puzzling notions common among many inexperienced civilians and rear-echelon brass hats who actually get to the front is that the infantrymen up there are going to be solicitous about their visitors' welcome. If you are a stranger blundering your way toward a clump of enemies in a bush, the average dogface in his hole will assume that you know what you're doing, or that you are a souvenir hunter. Besides, it might be useful to him to see exactly where the fire is coming from when they shoot at you. If he knows you, on the other hand, he realizes you're an idiot and might holler a warning at you—unless it means exposing his own position. Before he'll do that you have to owe him a lot of money. Why should he feel otherwise about all this? His ass is on the line all the time, every day. You can leave anytime; he can't.

Beneath the bantering tone was deadly seriousness. Combat soldiers applied to strangers standards different from those that governed their reactions to friends. It was understandable that soldiers would not endanger their own lives in aid of a blundering idiot-visitor, but Mauldin pointed to another order of reality, that combat soldiers might benefit from the newcomer's jeopardy: "Besides, it might be useful to see exactly where the [enemy's] fire is coming from when they shoot at you."[55]

Here was an issue that fighting soldiers seldom talked or wrote about, and it was left to writers to fill out episodes that Mauldin only hinted at. In Irwin Shaw's *The Young Lions,* an experienced combat soldier urges an acquaintance to "Come along with me. You'll have a lot better chance of coming out of the war alive if you go into a company where you have friends," and Shaw then proceeds to illustrate the acuity of such advice:

> There were three soldiers, a Lieutenant and two Sergeants, from a Communications Zone Signal Corps message center, who had somehow arrived here [on the front lines] in a jeep on a tourist visit. . . .

The Lieutenant was wearing a beautiful officer's coat, brindle-colored and full. The last time he had been in New York, Michael had seen such a coat in the window of Abercrombie and Fitch. All three men were wearing parachute boots, although it was plain that they had never jumped from anything higher than a barstool. They were all large, tall men, clean shaven, well dressed, and fresh looking, and the bearded infantrymen with whom they were playing [a crap game] looked like neglected and rickety specimens of an inferior race. . . .

[Michael] guessed that you could only find people who laughed like that fifty miles back of the lines. . . .

"[We're] here on business, [said the Lieutenant]. We heard we could pick up some pretty good souvenirs in this neck of the woods. I get into Paris twice a month, and there's a good market for Lugers and cameras and binoculars, stuff like that. We're prepared to pay a fair price. How about it? You fellows got anything you want to sell?" . . .

[When no sellers came forward, the Lieutenant moved to his alternative plan] "OK, I'll look around for myself. I hear there was some action here last week, there should be plenty of stuff lying around. . . . Which way is the front?"

Later, platoon sergeant Houlihan becomes suspicious that between his position on a ridge and the river below the Germans have set an ambush. "There's a nest there, some place. They've got a machine gun set up there, and they're just . . . waiting for us." So when the company is ordered to advance, Houlihan protests—"They'll have five hundred yards of cleared land and the bridge to lay it on to us"—but the Captain will do no more than direct that a patrol be sent out, and Houlihan is left to organize the mission. "Keep going, in plain view, down to the river, if necessary, to draw fire. Then we can spot the place where the fire originates from, and [the Captain] will get the mortars working on it and wipe it out. . . . Any volunteers?" There are none. Then the Signal Corps lieutenant and his two sergeants arrive on the ridge.

"Sergeant, do you mind if we join you?"

"Sergeant [a member of the platoon interjects], the Lieutenant is here to hunt souvenirs to take back to Paris.

"By all means, Lieutenant. [W]e're honored to have you, we are indeed."

"I heard this was the Front. Is it?"

"In a manner of speaking, Sir."

"It's awfully quiet. I haven't heard a shot in two hours. Are you sure?"

"I'll tell you something, Sir. I do believe the Germans pulled out a week ago. . . ."

"Good. . . . I hear that a man could pick up some German souvenirs down there."

"Oh, yes, Sir, a man certainly could. That field is covered with helmets and Lugers and rare cameras."

"Louis, Steve, let's go down and take a look . . . Do you mind, Sergeant? . . ."

"Make yourself absolutely at home, Sir."

"You'll keep an eye on us, won't you, Sergeant?"

"I certainly will."

"Good. Come on, boys."

As the three begin sliding down the slope, one member of the platoon, a recent replacement, protests: "Houlihan, you can't do that! You can't let them go out there like that! . . . They'll be killed. . . . If you don't stop them, I'll put in a report, I swear to God I will. . . ."

> "Put in a report, eh? You want to go yourself, is that it? You want to get killed this afternoon yourself out there, you want Ackerman to get killed, Crane, Pfeiffer, you'd rather have your friends get it than three fat pigs from the Service of Supply. They're too good to be killed, is that it?"

German machine-gun fire suddenly breaks the conversation. The three men drop dead. Members of the platoon are able to locate the enemy's position. American mortars destroy it. The replacement submits no report.[56]

Rear-echelon personnel, headquarters staff, and correspondents are not the only ones whose lives are weighed differently.

> You go up as a replacement and your chances are awful. The men who are there are all friends, they feel responsible for each other, they'll do anything to save each other. That means every dirty, dangerous job they hand right over to the replacements. The Sergeants don't even bother to learn your name. They don't want to know anything about you. They just trade you in for their friends and wait for the next batch of replacements. You go into a new Company, all by yourself, and you'll be on every patrol, you'll be the point of every attack. If you ever get stuck out some place, and it's a question of saving you or saving one of the old boys, what do you think they'll do? . . . You've got to have friends. You can't let them send you any place where you don't have any friends to protect you. . . .

Here the words of an Irwin Shaw soldier described too harshly the situation confronting new arrivals—conscious, uniform intent of the sort depicted was a rarity—but comradely solidarity did exact a toll of others. After the war, James Jones met a Ranger staff sergeant who in the course of a drinking bout told him:

> One day at Anzio we got eight new replacements into my platoon. We were supposed to make a little feeling attack that same day. Well, by next day, all eight of them replacements were dead, buddy. But none of us old guys were. We weren't going to send our own guys out on point in a damnfool situation like that. . . . We were sewed up tight. And we'd been together through Africa, and Sicily, and Salerno. We sent the replacements out ahead. But how am I going to explain something like that to my wife? She'd think it was horrible. But it was right, man, right. How are we going to send our own guys out into that?

For every such episode driven by dark calculation there must have been many others propelled by subliminal but almost automatic partiality.[57]

Bill Mauldin saw in comradeship "the best life insurance," and GIs with extensive combat experience knew the rude reality beneath the cartoonist's words. Within the context of that actuality, those soldiers—wounded, injured, or ill, healed or unhealed—who broke out of hospitals, and others who escaped from replacement centers, to rejoin their units must be revisited.[58]

A few described their flight as a protest against boredom. A few cited shame. Wrote a wounded Third Army NCO whose attempt to return to his unit from a Paris hospital was on this occasion thwarted: "I was always feeling guilty of leading the 'Life of Riley' while my buddies were undoubtedly miserable." "[A] highly specific reaction to leaving one's immediate social group" was sociologist Samuel Stouffer's explanation for such guilt. Even Ernie Pyle, at home between the Sicily and mainland Italy campaigns, felt "like a deserter and a heel—not so much to the war effort, but to your friends who are still over there freezing and getting shot at." A few responded to impulses that others might characterize as noble. "Oh hell," Audie Murphy told a nurse; "As long as there's a man in the lines, maybe I feel that my place is up there beside him." Some found it intolerable that they were not present as battle decided the fates of friends. Henry Giles, vowing to go AWOL from a Liège replacement depot if his unit did not immediately send for him, complained, "Don't even know whether there *is* an outfit left and God knows . . . when I will know. Don't know which of my friends is living or dead or if all of them are gone. Like being in a fog."[59]

Some could not bear the thought that they had become part of that despised rear echelon, one of the malingering "Them." Many spoke as if impelled by a sense of responsibility born of the expectation of reciprocity. "They went back," wrote Mauldin, "because they knew their companies were very shorthanded, and they were sure that if somebody else in their own squad or section were in their own shoes . . . those friends would come back to make the load lighter on *them*." Whatever the propulsion, the decision to go AWOL was seldom easy. In typical fashion, Orval Faubus, while hospitalized, wished he were back in combat but realized simultaneously that once back in battle, "I'll find myself wishing to be [anywhere] away from the slaughter."[60]

Beneath such explanations often lay a more menacing consideration. In June 1945, William Manchester, suffering from "a superficial gunshot wound just above my right kneecap," was evacuated to a field hospital. There, though "warm, dry, and safe," when he "heard that my regiment was going to land behind enemy lines on Oroku Peninsula[,] I left my cot, jumped hospital, hitchhiked to the front, and made the landing on Monday." "Why," he asked, "had I returned to terror?" As we have seen, he decided in 1978 that his journey back to "almost certain death" had been "an act of love." But with Marines anticipating a savage and very costly invasion of the Japanese home islands, it may have been equally an act of fear, grounded in dismay that he might otherwise be reassigned to a unit in which he would be a stranger.[61]

Mauldin himself, wounded, hospitalized, and then transferred to a replacement depot, was told that his unit, only fifteen miles away, would send a truck for him; but he knew that others had been waiting three weeks, and that the longer he stayed the more likely it became that he would be declared a "casual" to be "snapped up eventually by some [unfamiliar] outfit. . . ." Over the wall he went. At the height of this war, to come among comrades as a stranger was to open oneself up to special risks of becoming a casualty.[62]

Combat engineer Giles had said of his friends that there was "Not a one who wouldn't do anything in the world for you, and for each other"—a claim requiring no corroboration in the minds of combat soldiers. In that willingness to do anything they thought indispensable to one another's survival lay the extraordinary power—and the foremost vulnerability—of comradeship. It created a powerful bond between soldiers, but only some soldiers, and as its protective focus narrowed and intensified, it courted an equally powerful corruption. Comradeship, said Ernie Pyle in some of the last words he wrote, "finally becomes a part of one's soul. . . ." But not always to the soul's elevation.[63]

Comradeship's costs were not confined to non-comrades. Coarsening not only closed out others but closed down the self, and this process, with prolonged combat, worked change in soldiers' views of old comrades, dead comrades, and prospective comrades.

Combat soldiers were surprised to discover the transiency of grief. Some were taken aback that, very early on, they felt so shallowly the deaths of soldiers who were acquaintances. On Guadalcanal, reported Marine Robert Leckie, it was "difficult to feel deep, wracking grief for the dead, and . . . hearing the lieutenant tolling off the names, I had to force my face into a mask of mourning, deliberately adorn my heart with black, as it were, for I was shocked to gaze inward and see no sorrow there. Rather than permit me to know myself a monster (as I seemed, then) I deliberately deluded myself by feigning bereavement. So did we all."[64]

Leckie was sure that his unresponsiveness would not extend to the loss of "one's close buddies," but many soldiers were startled as they registered their reactions to comrades' deaths. True, the initial pain was devastating—but often also surprisingly brief. Harold Leinbaugh offered almost a primer lesson in rapid recovery. When they learned that a friend had died just after reaching the aid station, squad members, gathered in a basement, "looked at one another with long faces." Then letters and parcels arrived. "In each of his two large Christmas packages Stewart found several little ones, each individually wrapped and tied."

> I opened them one at a time and passed them to Johnny, who then passed them to the others. Johnny and I were making cracks about so many little packages and outlandishly guessing what would be in the next one. The others mechanically passed them on, not cracking a smile. Finally Pop said something funny. The ice was broken, and in a few minutes everyone was normal again.[65]

Soldiers were learning what survival required and were developing within themselves that "core of hardness to anything that might happen." Marine corporal Curtis Allen Spach, in combat on Guadalcanal 110 days, wrote to his father: "My best buddie . . . was caught in the face by a full blast of machine gun fire and when the hole we were laying in became swamped by flies gathering about him and [he] being already dead, I had to roll him out of the small hole on top of the open ground and the dirty SOBs kept shooting him full of holes. Well anyway God spared my life and I am thankful for it."[66]

Introspective soldiers recognized not only what was happening to them but why. The problem, as Pyle grasped, was that if men "didn't toughen up inside they simply wouldn't be able to take it"; grieving conceded to death dominion over their destinies, a thought debilitating in battle. Observing the men in his company, British officer Peter Cochrane concluded that the rapid return to equanimity "was not stark insensitivity . . . but a realization that it would be impossible to go on if you thought too much about burying the friend with whom you'd shared a mess tin for months. It could lead to wondering who would bury you." The combat soldier, concluded Commando Kelly, "can't afford to let [death] work on his mind."[67]

Other battlefield imperatives colluded to propel soldiers quickly beyond the loss of friends. There was no time for the dead. Medic Keith Winston noticed that his thoughts no longer lingered over those who were gone. "For a time this worried me, thinking the Army was dehumanizing me, making me insensible to tragedy and sorrow." Then he realized that "there wasn't time to dwell on [them], with all the work and continual pressure of self-preservation—all of which was part of us 24 hours a day." And in battle, the needs of the moment were not long in reasserting themselves. "Some poor bastard stepped on a mine. . . . I hope we have time to get something to eat." On Christmas Day 1944, Lester Atwell reflected over a turkey dinner that the members of his unit "were safe momentarily, sheltered; we had warm food to eat; we were still alive. And how quickly those who had been killed were forgotten!"[68]

Another influence working to break off comradeship abruptly was the taint that some soldiers felt immediately in those, even comrades, who were wounded or killed. "Something strange seems to happen," James Jones reported, "when a man is hit. . . . [It] is as though he has passed through some veil . . . and has entered some realm where the others . . . cannot follow. The dead, of course, really *have* entered a different realm. . . . There is a sort of instinctive dislike of touching [the wounded and dead], as though what happened to them has contaminated them and might contaminate the toucher." The appearance of the bodies of the dead repulsed others. Corporal Ben Waldron learned that in war dying was "seldom done in [as] neat and tidy [a] manner as some funeral parlor might have it." On Corregidor, he saw bodies grotesquely contorted. "You could use your imagination forever, and never come up with all of the twisted and gross shapes of death on a battlefield." He had gone out in the wake of a Japanese shelling "and picked up Lieutenant Lacey in baskets, piece by piece." Deaths that left unrecognizable the lineaments of comrades in life often catapulted them from the consciousness of survivors.[69]

A perplexing mystery, moreover, hovered about every loss of a friend. Did it portend the soldier's own destruction because the friend's death was at bottom his own death drawing closer? The logic was blunt: his luck ran out;

we were together a long time; I did everything that he did; my luck must be running out; his fate places death's mark on me. Or was the friend's demise a propitiatory offering to war's appetite for deaths? Back at base camp after the invasion of Peleliu, a group of Marines felt the decline of "the precariousness, the suffering, the hardship, and the gore" that had absorbed them during the campaign. "Sorrow and bitterness from losses of friends, so strong at first, was tempered by a practical philosophy that was inescapably in our minds. 'Someone had to die. It was too bad that it was he.'" From the air war John Ciardi brought an even harsher perspective:

> You saw a plane break up. You saw it catch fire. . . . [The] truth . . . the dark truth [is that] you were secretly glad. It could have been you. It was a superstitious ritual we were playing. There were a certain number of blackballs to be passed out. Every time another plane went down, [one] was taken out of play. Somebody had to catch it, and somebody else caught it for you. It didn't make any sense, but that's the way we felt. That's a dirty, dark thing to say. . . .
>
> When the news came that so-and-so's crew . . . had gone down over Tokyo, you made sounds: Oh, my God. But somewhere, very deep down in your psyche is, It could have been me.[70]

Writers who, in the war's early years, described for the home front the nature of military life, and veterans who, years later, published their memoirs, often extolled comradeship in terms as expansive as those of draftee Gene Gach: "It's forming friendships that we know will last for the rest of our lives, friendships that make our previous civilian associations seem like mere politeness by comparison." Gach heedlessly assumed that his comrades would survive the war; and for almost all support personnel, for many artillery and armor combatants, even for a number of fortunate ground soldiers, events did not overthrow their identical supposition. Closer to the reality of the infantryman's wartime existence, however, with its collisions with loss and its far less effusive vision of comradeship, was this snippet of verse written by an American soldier who fought from Sicily to Anzio:

> I saw you die and cursed the fading night,
> Then raised my rifle to adjust the sight.[71]

Soldiers' reactions to separations from comrades for reasons other than death were equally revelatory. Experienced enlisted men grew to accept that wartime intimacy was a hothouse plant that blossomed—and withered—more rapidly than any peacetime variety. Sergeant Clarence Merson of a signal air-warning company described one quick flowering:

Sitting around a table in the smoke-filled P.X. at night, talking with fellows from Colorado, or Ohio, or perhaps Virginia, the momentary warmth of friendship flaming like a match—

Wheh y'all from? Allentown, Pa. You? Bristol, V'giny. Had a buddy went to Pennsylvania once. . . .

And so on into the night, these countless remembrances of things past. The whole intricate fabric of their lives is rewoven simply, sometimes naively and always without restraint. And for the moment these fellow soldiers sitting around the table smoking and drinking are the finest people you've ever known, and the bond of friendship is, perhaps, as complete and absolute as friendship can ever be.

However, in an hour, alone once more, walking under the stars, these very people become remote and their stories join the ten thousand others which clutter your brain.

Soldiers granted that, in the phrase of one Marine officer on Wake Island, "War makes friendships quickly, and breaks them as fast."[72]

The number of soldiers who parted with comrades from whom or about whom no word was ever received was extraordinary. Of the casualties in Leinbaugh's company, Doc Mellon said, "We never heard whether any of our wounded guys even made it to the field hospital." Charles Cawthon spoke of "the hundreds who shed blood in [the regiment's] ranks and then disappeared." Few returned—Leinbaugh estimated that only one in eight of the company's hospital evacuees returned before the war's end—and very few wrote. "It's funny," thought one of James Jones's soldiers, that so many had been hit and evacuated, and "We never really knew what happens to them." But then, when he was himself hospitalized, he felt no inclination to contact those back in the company. Others who were transferred out or even sent home on furlough often vanished without word. Comradeship having served survival in a time and a place, he—and many others—moved on.[73]

Some who departed relished their liberation from comradeship. Staff sergeant Miles Standish Babcock of the 37th Division in the Pacific thought of comradeship bitterly, as an instrument of the "mass personality" that the Army forced upon infantrymen. "Compelled by circumstances to accept [for months or years] the companionship of men with whom you have nothing in common . . . except [wartime conditions] . . . your personality and attitude [are] distorted to fit the eccentricities of the mob." More prevalent was simple relief—from an intimacy grown stale. Audie Murphy described a night scene during the Italian campaign: "The six occupants of the tent are all awake. Canteens clink, and flames spurt as cigarettes are lighted. I squint at the luminous dial of my watch. It is one o'clock in the morning. For a while we lie without speaking. We have been together so long and closely that there seems not a detail of one another's lives with which we are not familiar. Nothing remains to talk about." Lester Atwell spoke in like vein: "Sometimes I think we just get to know each other too well; there's never any relief."[74]

Many found in separations a welcome retrieval of privacy. To snatch any solitude in the war zone was virtually impossible and even to search for it, however forlornly, was often regarded as conduct "counter to [that] we-band-of-brothers camaraderie." When the withdrawal of a comrade required Atwell to pitch his own tent, he found himself smiling at the prospect of his first privacy in five months. "Once inside, there was no necessity to speak to anyone, see anyone, consider anyone, or compromise on space. That alone made for one of the happiest intervals in the Army." Thus, below comradeship's many gratifications were elements of strain sufficiently severe that many who left its orbit felt relief at the fracture of relationships that they had regarded as unnatural, or at least abnormal.[75]

V-E Day revealed how central survival was to comradeship; with the disappearance of necessity, bonds loosened rapidly. Lester Atwell returned to his combat medical unit in June 1945 following an assignment in personnel. One buddy, he discovered, had begun to act "so funny"—"he's not a bit friendly, the way he used to be." Another had gone off to live alone. Others had revealed unsuspected tempers. "Best friends had violent disagreements and sulked for days." Nicknames by which friends had long called one another suddenly became intolerable. One of two southern litter bearers, inseparable since their arrival, hailed his friend, in customary fashion, as "Turtle-eye." "Don't cohll me Tuttle-eye!" "But that's what I ohlways cohll you. . . ." "Well don't you say it again, goddamit!" The exchange climaxed in a chase and a flying ax that barely missed its target. The two, Atwell reported, never again spoke to one another. Others argued fiercely over minutiae.

> "That was a ninety-millimeter shell."
> "You're crazy, that's no ninety."
> "You're full of shit."
> "*You're* full of shit."[76]

Some, troubled by the flux of disintegrating relationships engulfing them, naively thought that they could restore comradeship to their lives simply by going elsewhere. A Kentucky soldier decided to switch back to his old outfit. "Got some good friends there, yes, sir! *Real* frien's. We get back to the States, Ah'm puttin' in for a transfer. Wouldn't want to go to the [Pacific] with these boys. Rather have frien's aroun' me there. Need 'em there." Atwell's caution—"[Y]ou'd probably be disappointed [there too]. . . . It'd be the same everywhere"—went unheeded. "It was something in the air. We knew each other too well and were tired of the companionships that had carried us over the months of combat. Friends fell out for no known reason, tried new friendships, clung fast to them for a few days, dropped them, and went off to look up their earliest acquaintances in the division." Much of that called comradeship had been shored up by the fear of dying in combat and thus disintegrated with the cessation of the shooting. "At every turn," Atwell concluded, "there was that sense of things that had sustained us, falling apart, ending."[77]

If some soldiers held comradeship so lightly that it became a restraint to be thrown off as rapidly as possible, others sought the same solitariness from an opposite set of mind. Their investment in comradeship had been so complete that, with the deaths of their friends, they had lost everything. Occasionally a soldier, prescient from the outset in judging the momentousness of the stakes, decided to withhold himself altogether. Leinbaugh told of a soldier who had chosen to remain a loner because "a guy could get hurt if he got too close to a buddy." Others were willing to commit to friendship—but reservedly. A German soldier on the Eastern Front felt both comradeship's appeal and its danger; he feared, with justification, that it would prove a way station on a journey from one loneliness to an even more desolate loneliness. "[In] the field a friend is a very special thing. At first you live in noisy solitude, in violent loneliness; then you find a friend [but] you know the whole time that he may be gone the next second, leaving you alone again in the din and solitude, with nothing."[78]

Those who risked most were soldiers so absorbed in wartime friendship that they cast over a single buddy the mantle of imperishability that they still thought theirs to share. A Japanese American trooper wrote home in shock at what often happened next: "You lose your buddies—fellows with whom you laughed, ate, slept, sweated. They grow to be more than mere buddies. [Then] they die before your eyes—not a pleasant, natural death, but an unimaginable kind of mutilation mixed with groans and prayers and ending with a gurgling last breath."[79]

No soldier's life embodied more poignantly than Audie Murphy's this evolution of comradeship. So fully did he believe that comradeship was war's sole redemptive element and thus that war's only positive function was as the vehicle of comradeship, that World War II became for him, in effect, a comrade. So, as he held in his arms the dead Brandon, he was disbelieving: "He is not dead. He can't be dead, because if he is dead, the war is all wrong; and Brandon has died in vain." Soon, following his private vengeance campaign and, finally, his admission that his friend was truly dead, he came to that state described by a member of his company: "You get so tired, you don't care. It doesn't matter [if the German tanks get you]. Nothing matters. You stand up and do the best you can, and then to hell with it." In a fierce fire-fight Audie Murphy sent his men to the rear, and then, in an attempt to hold back a German armor and infantry assault, called down American artillery fire atop himself. "Fifty over? That's your own position." "I don't give a damn. Fifty over." Somehow he survived the barrage and afterwards simply walked down the road: "If the Germans want to shoot me," he thought to himself, "let them. I am too weak from fear and exhaustion to care." With comradeship gone, all was gone.[80]

With comradeship bestowing benefits so numerous, its dissolution would of course exact costs. More significant was that many soldiers found those costs so high that they were led to renounce comradeship.

Rarely could soldiers regenerate this most intimate comradeship. Indeed, its rupture often plunged survivors into virtual isolation. The Japanese American soldier Rudy Tokiwa, bereft of friends made as long before as basic training, "swore to himself he would never again make a really close friend on the battlefield." When, in Italy, John Muirhead was transferred from a B-24 to a B-17 group in early 1944, he regretted that it was necessary to leave his crew. But "my disappointment was reconciled by a kind of relief. Anonymity had its advantages. Camaraderie among crews that had been together a long time made each member vulnerable and was a burden of love that couldn't flourish. It was better to be alone." Audie Murphy agreed: "Since Kerrigan [one of his last friends] got his, I have isolated myself as much as possible, desiring only to do my work and be left alone. I feel burnt out, emotionally and physically exhausted." Here Audie Murphy withdrew, in Roger Spiller's apt phrase, into "a fatalistic alienation from his fellow soldiers." He was essentially alone.[81]

The search for a feelingless solitude often brought first an apparent indifference to others and then a harshness constituting virtual disavowal of comradeship. Wrote Muirhead: "When we were back at our base, I didn't inquire about the plane that hadn't returned, except to verify that I didn't know the pilot or any of the crew. I sought to isolate myself from such things, which was a hopeless posture of evasion I persisted in trying to maintain. If I didn't know them, I would not grieve. If I didn't speak to them, I would not remember . . . whether they were fair or dark, or whether I liked them or disliked them." When another plane was lost, Muirhead asked an airman about the dead pilot. Told his name, Muirhead had a second question: "Was he new?" "No," replied the airman in surprise. "He was around for a while. . . . You don't seem to know anybody anymore." But that was as Muirhead wanted it. He knew nothing even of the crew with which he flew daily. "The men . . . with me had all done well, and it was to my satisfaction that I didn't have to know them."[82]

Even more disaffected than Muirhead, Audie Murphy evinced remorse that he had ever been or had a comrade. What comradeship had given him had proven, in the wake of Brandon's death, no compensation for what its destruction had taken from him, and he was left with a sundered spirit. His final words, in rejecting with harsh despair any possibility of new combat friendships, repudiated comradeship itself: "Let the hill be strewn with corpses so long as I do not have to turn over the bodies and find the . . . face of a friend."[83]

At its core, World War II comradeship was an agreement between soldiers that they would, in the service of self-preservation, help one another to survive battle. Seldom could its parties violate the terms of that basic compact and expect comradeship to survive. Some of its relationships, to be sure, transcended those conditions, inspiring conduct that Americans agreed entered the realm of the morally sublime. Love between men did sometimes move some to sacrifice their lives for others. Comradeship, however, also generated conduct that moved to the morally odious. If concern for, and even love of, a few fell within comradeship's boundaries, so did the withdrawal of all consideration for the many.

Some American soldiers reaped all the gratifications described in the first pages of this chapter. Comradeship served best a unit like that of Henry Giles, Company A of the 291st Engineer Combat Battalion. That unit saw extensive combat in the European theater from just after D-Day to V-E Day, and it distinguished itself. Its bridge was the first across the Rhine, at a cost of thirty-two grueling hours, thirty-one wounded, and one dead. But while proximity to battle created within its ranks a comradeship of high intensity, its fortunes were so generous that few of its members were called on to pay the costs of comradeship destroyed. Giles realized that because his company suffered fewer losses than infantry units, it was able to remain "together for so much longer . . . like a family." He and his friends committed much of themselves to comradeship—and, given a favorable fate, gained much. But in front-line rifle companies, whose personnel often turned over one or two or even three times during twelve to twenty-four months of combat—replacements replacing replacements—men wagered just as much, and lost far more, than Giles' engineers. To some, comradeship delivered its benefits and from them exacted few of its tolls. But it imposed on others—those in combat longest, those whose units suffered most severely—an intolerable strain: it permitted some of them to reach to a rarity in the male world, intimacy with other men—and then bullets and shells laid bare that theirs was the burden of a love that could not flourish.[84]

8 WAR FRONT AND HOME FRONT

Americans who contemplated World War II without experiencing battle thought of the conflict largely in terms of the nation's determination to deliver its power against distant enemies. The essential process required those at home to fabricate the profusion of armaments that their soldiers overseas would employ—with great effectiveness, no one doubted—against the Germans and the Japanese. In a popular image, endless, irresistible files of men and machines descended on Europe and Asia from great spans arching the oceans.

Clarity and logicality were the hallmarks of this pervasive design. Little in it was unfamiliar. To the minds of those in the United States, the war remained knowable.

In contrast, soldiers unprepared for what they met in battle quickly lost almost all sense of war's familiarity and solidity. They were unable to offer those at home a combatant's conception of the war. Changes bewildering and corroding denied them the substance necessary for an alternative vision; indeed, they felt themselves thrust into frightening voids. Distressed by the gulf opening between the war front and the home front, they failed first in attempts to make their experience of combat comprehensible and then in their plaintive, unconsidered pleas that those at home understand that experience. Finally, in confusion, frustration, and rising anger, they cast dark projections upon uncomprehending civilians.

Underpinning the departure of American soldiers for war was a profound attachment to home. They set out bearing an acute sense of sacrifice in leaving it, a resolve to destroy every threat to it, and an impatience to return to it.

Indeed, home—as family, locale, and nation—grew in their esteem with each mile from induction center to battlefield. Peering from the Pullman cars carrying them to the West Coast, Grady Gallant and his Marine friends felt borne in on them "the great wealth of our land and how precious it was to us." Artilleryman Ben Tumey reported that "Only after you are apart from your parents do you realize how splendid they are. How we love that place called home." Travel in war zones ordinarily enhanced the worthiness of home. "Yes, being over here has certainly taught us to appreciate America," an Army sergeant in Italy told Margaret Bourke-White. "It has really made us more patriotic. We've seen the poor Ayrabs, and we know how they live. We've seen the poor Eyetalians and they don't even have shower baths." Flying Tiger pilot Robert Scott described "the understanding that comes when you've seen the rest of the world, when you've glimpsed the filth and corruption of all the hell-holes that Americans are fighting in. . . . Then you know—for it's seared on your soul—that we have the best country in the Universe. . . ."[1]

Idealization prevailed. Bourke-White noticed that GIs near the Volturno "had had a lot of time to remember what their homeland was like, and the memory seemed to them beyond improvement." On this topic young soldiers indulged a sentimentality that they derided in others and would soon repudiate in themselves. Keith Winston wrote to his wife, "Now that the radio is working I get a wave of homesickness when I hear real American music. A complete hush falls over the group, 'eating' up every note. Darling, America is so wonderful. . . ." John Burns remembered how soldiers in Algiers "tended to gather round the waterfront, as though by going near water they were challenging the barrier that kept them from home." The United States became "the best country on this earth" or "the greatest country in the world" or "God's country," though sometimes locale took precedence over nation. "I have seen no metropolis that can match Seattle" . . . "Pickens, South Carolina is the best place in the whole wide world."[2]

A sociologist tracked such declarations to the "nostalgia effect," a "sentimental overvaluing of everything the serviceman . . . had left behind." But beneath the gush was a fundamental of soldier life: home lay at the center of the GI's conception of the war. Combat engineer Giles carried constantly a "picture of [all the] good things" he would do at home as soon as the war ended.

Prisoners of war often had nothing more: "I . . . built my dreams around the things that Jane and I were going to do when I returned home." When correspondents asked infantrymen why they were fighting, they often thought prosaic soldiers' most common response: "To get home." Ernie Pyle noticed a constancy in his conversations with those at the front. "Ten minutes hardly ever goes by without some nostalgic reference to home, how long you've been away, how long before you get back, what you'll do first when you hit the States, what your chances are for returning before the war is over."[3]

Home, medic Frank Irgang knew, permeated GI thought:

> A soldier's utmost desire is to go home. . . . He fights a war with this uppermost in his mind. Every day he is on the front is one more day nearer to the time he will be home. Every mile he walks is one more mile closer to home, though it be in the opposite direction. He thinks of this early and often; he believes it and lives it, even when the odds are a thousand to one against his living another minute.

In 1943 Orval Faubus tried to represent graphically for the readers of his hometown newspaper the sway of home. Soldiers bore to home, he wrote, a relationship like that of a wheel's spokes to its hub. They had left home, but their thoughts and memories "all run . . . back to the hub of our existence . . . the center and basis of all human life, the home."[4]

Soldiers setting out for war believed that their links with home would keep them securely connected. Sergeant Don Robinson, editor of the *45th Division News,* pictured clearly how this would be done:

> All my adult life, I've read about the disillusionment of war; of men who went to the front and never were the same spiritually again. This time, I think, it will be different.
>
> What makes the difference? Mail, for one thing. It keeps the boys in closer touch with the familiar. [Letters, V-mail, air mail—this] flood of information and endearment has kept the men feeling close to home, close to their civilian interests, close to their home towns. Then, there is radio. Not all the men can listen to it, but many do. These tell the others about what they hear. And when the outfits hit the rest areas, there are movies depicting scenes from civil life, keeping alive in their minds the way life is lived back home.
>
> And there are newspapers. . . .
>
> In Italy today, the *Stars and Stripes* rolls out the home news for the troops—not just the big news, but the little things that happen in Brooklyn, Atlanta, and Omaha. . . .
>
> And . . . the *45th Division News* . . . is like the home-town weekly in a terri-

tory served by a big daily. We treat the division like a community, even though it's a traveling community. . . .

We feel that we are part of the new conditions which are helping the boys to keep a wholesome outlook on things through this war.[5]

Mail from home gained an extraordinary prominence in the American military. "A soldier's life," Bill Mauldin knew, "revolves around his mail." The postmaster aboard a Navy vessel patrolling Alaskan waters weighed his shipmates' priorities: "The two most important necessities in a sailor's life are perhaps food and mail. I am not at all sure whether food should be given precedence, for many times I have seen chow neglected in favor of sweating out a mail line fifty men long." Airman John Muirhead, flying from a base in Italy, reported that "Letters from home, to me and to everyone else, were the most important event of any day. They were our communion with the past, our sacred past; they were our confirmation of life expressed in simple words of love." Each letter from home, observed infantryman Grady Arrington, was "looked upon with honest reverence."[6]

Annette Tapert's study of soldiers' mail concluded that letter-writing quickly became the soldier's main means "to stay in touch with his dreams and plans" at home. One Marine in the Pacific received thirty-five letters in a single delivery. "It made me feel wonderful to know everything was o.k. at home." Conversely, the absence of mail could seem calamitous. Staff officer Cornelius Whitney was in India three months without a letter, though he knew that his wife was writing each day. "We were green soldiers, uprooted suddenly from our homes. When we did not receive mail for long periods, our imaginations ran riot. We berated the whole war effort—if a detail like this was so badly handled back home, how could we win the war? Even worse, and of course quite unreasonably, we felt that our sweethearts and friends had deserted us." George Wilson, as an infantry replacement in France, told of a soldier who by the narrowest margin held back from shooting himself because he had not received letters; they arrived the next day.[7]

The war generated mountains of mail. In 1943, GIs received an average of fourteen pieces per week. On New Guinea, three-quarters of the soldiers wrote one or more letters each day. V-mail—a process that reduced 8½-by-11-inch letters to 16-mm film for transmission, then enlarged the transparencies for delivery as 4-by-6-inch letters—appeared during the summer of 1942; by September 1944, 789,539,390 V-mail letters had been sent from or received abroad. At war's end, the total probably exceeded 1 billion.[8]

What soldiers sought in letters from home was unmistakable. Morton Eustis wanted to know "what you did each day, and all the general gossip and chit chat." In soldiers' pleas for reports of "the little things," "the small things," "the ordinary everyday things," "the usual things," they solicited a ritual of reassurance that family and friends were doing what the soldier wished them to do, what he missed doing, what he would surely do again. "It is just the little things in life," as Seaman James Fahey told it, "that you look forward to when you go home. When you had them you thought nothing of them, you took them for granted. Now you look forward to meeting your family and friends, being able to go to the corner store and get the morning paper . . . or visit the drug-store for a big ice cream soda, looking at the buildings and going to Parish Church and the local theater." Ben Waldron cherished "a clean pair of socks or simply to sit in an easy chair or . . . to read a newspaper, or sit and munch on salted peanuts [or] to hold a Parker Pen . . . and write on a . . . paper that hadn't been used for something else [or] just to . . . ride two blocks in a taxi." On Bert Damsky's list was the same inner-spring mattress, in company with an icebox raid at midnight, a cold Coke, a cup of real coffee, and a weekend date "with dancing, dining, and a little loving."[9]

Once Pearl Harbor fixed in Americans' minds the necessity of fighting the war, the "little things" became soldiers' vehicle for discussing unembarrassedly with one another the grounds for their presence in combat; reclaiming as quickly as possible home life's favorite articles and activities was sufficient purpose for almost all soldiers and Marines. As long as they felt themselves at one with those at home, mail describing the commonplace continued to attest to both the worthiness and attainability of that goal.

Soldiers also asked the familiar, the roseate, and the immutable of the troupes and films sent out to entertain them. The social historian John Costello has called the movies that soldiers applauded "prepackaged sentimental bundles of home." A Marine private in the Pacific agreed: "I know what it is to be cut off from everything. . . . Those hours can stretch into centuries—and would, if it weren't for a movie now and then. Movies that stop us from thinking of ourselves and our surroundings. Movies that remind us that there are such things as pretty girls, gay music, and a civilization worth living for. . . ." Charles Cawthon's unit underwent eight days of refitting after combat in Normandy: "the motion pictures . . . ran all day in a blacked-out barn, the film spotty and jerky from constant use. These wartime films, like wartime writing, projected a streak of blatant unreality, but they were avidly attended, for this was the tenor of the times and we were all attuned to it."[10]

Secretary of War Henry Stimson declared American servicemen "the most homesick troops in the world."[11]

Early in combat, soldiers believed that their vision of home upheld them against insupportable stress. When letters reached Paul Boesch, "nothing could be too tough to take!" Others in crisis were sometimes able to find relief by summoning home's "small things." One airman struggling with anxiety on a bomb run over Europe distracted himself by imagining that in that moment Mom was making one of her wonderful apple pies, that Dad was at his workbench, that Tommie was out sliding in the snow. Just as Marine Wallace Reid refused an order to move forward on Guadalcanal, "pictures of the past" intervened. "There's Mom making coffee for Pop as he comes in from the rain" and "for a few seconds I'm happy." Whenever briefly relieved from combat, Reid and his friends retired to their "trysting place," a stretch of beach.

> It was here we came when soul and mind and body rebelled against this . . . wanton destruction of man by man. . . .
>
> On this beach the magic images of home dispelled momentarily the stench of death and the screams of our buddies. . . . Ski was playing his violin before a record audience, and Murphy was again shoveling the coal into the red hot belly of the Southern as she roared down the rails. . . . And Hammond was again wooing and winning the girls all over . . . Los Angeles. And I, I was again trudging through the woods with my dogs, hunting the wily partridge, rabbit or squirrel, or . . . sitting on the broad flat banks of the Okemulgee . . . with a fishing rod in my hand and all the world at my feet. . . .
>
> This was the one place in this whole island of destruction and catastrophe and chaos where we could summon up the memories of the things which we missed so much, the things we were fighting for, and dare not forget, lest we go mad.[12]

Some soldiers bargained with home as they did with God, pledging extended devotion and loyalty in exchange for immediate protection. Caught in a Huertgen Forest town under all-day German artillery bombardment, combat MP Michael McDonald pledged that "If I ever reach Philadelphia again, I'll never leave, so help me God. I won't even go down to Wildwood."[13]

Sustained by memories "beyond improvement," soldiers insisted that there be no change at home while they were away. Disgusted by what he saw as the filthiness and cruelty of North African Arabs and by the coarsening of friends around him, Johnny Stradling was adamant: "Mom, it's just *got to be* all right at home." While in battle on Okinawa, Marine Russell Davis heard the news of President Franklin Roosevelt's death, but "Nobody would be-lieve it. . . . Marines always found it difficult to believe that anyone was dying back home. . . ." The historian Allan Winkler has proposed that dur-ing World War II, Americans "wanted a better America within the frame-work of the past"; he might have made an exception for white combat soldiers, who wished exactly the America they had left as they tramped up the gangway.[14]

Forebodings of change, however, had come to some almost immediately. While still awaiting the call to the Navy's V-7 Officers Training Program—he would soon be summoned to Notre Dame—Douglas Leach confided to his diary that "one of my greatest fears in going away is that I shall return to find my world . . . greatly changed—friends gone away, married, no longer holding common interests, etc. I find it hard to face the fact that the Choir and [the Young People's Fellowship] will never be the same. . . ." Combat in-tensified such anxieties. Fighting in the New Hebrides, Army sergeant Arnold Gates wrote to his parents that "many of us fear that the way of things as we left them will be gone when we again set foot on American soil. We are concerned over the prospect of returning to find our folks, our sweet-hearts and our friends changed." Soldiers perceived that combat was chang-ing them. Holding all else steady was, they thought, their only chance of coping with the altered selves who might survive the war. Convinced that combat was increasing the distance between them and those at home, they insisted that society remain still, lest it extend the gap.[15]

Yet there was within this war another world that soldiers in combat could not long ignore. Home remained the lodestar, but its light began to fade and its image to dim, an evolution that could begin even before soldiers left the United States. While still at Camp Howze near Fort Worth, John Stradling complained that "You just darn near forget what home is like without getting a letter for a week or so." Overwhelmingly, however, it was battle that blurred the soldier's picture of home. As Orval Faubus moved forward in France, the sound of a German aircraft overhead called to his mind the buzzing of angry bees. "That reminds me . . . that I am pretty far removed from the vari-colored hollyhocks in which I used to trap bumblebees and which will soon be bloom-ing in the peaceful door yards around the farm houses of the Ozarks. Or per-haps they are blooming now. One forgets so much." Combat concussions shook remembrance. Irgang, the medic who professed that soldiers fight with the desire to go home uppermost in their minds, realized as he was evacuated with other wounded that in battle "the real picture of home fades and becomes distorted." Private John Sheehan wrote a poem reimagining his departure from home in the light of his battle experience.

> Along with the letter, keys and such, I'll leave
> My thoughts: civilian thoughts that cannot . . . breathe
> In gas masks. . . .
> Until the wars are won . . .
> I'll leave you here, my thoughts, where peace has stayed.[16]

Home's diminishing visibility in the mind's eye seemed to some soldiers to consign it to a dream state. Lieutenant Colonel Jacob Bealke of the 90th Infantry Division wrote to his wife in April 1944: "So many things have happened to me, I have come so far, travelled across an ocean, and been so busy in the past months that [the whole United States] now seems to be a highly desirable dream which is way out of reach." Spring stirred in Henry Giles thoughts of his home in Kentucky: "Dad is burning his tobacco bed about now and Mama is fussing about getting the garden plowed so she can plant potatoes and early peas. And the old short-core apple tree down by the barn is about to bloom. [But] sometimes I . . . wonder if I haven't just imagined the things I remember."[17]

No one caught better than Ernie Pyle the waning of home. As the North African campaign opened, he reported exuberantly that GIs always marched "with a feeling that at last we were beginning the final series of marches that would lead us home again—home, the one really profound goal that obsesses every one of the Americans marching on foreign shores." Five months later, however, with the surrender of Rommel's Afrika Korps, there had come a change.

> For a year, everywhere I went, soldiers inevitably asked me two questions: "When do you think we'll get to go home?" and "When will the war be over?" The home-going desire was once so dominant that I believe our soldiers over here would have voted . . . to go home immediately, even if it meant peace on terms of something less than unconditional surrender by the enemy.
>
> That isn't true now. Sure, they all still want to go home. So do I. But there is something deeper than that, which didn't exist six months ago. I can't quite put it into words. . . .
>
> Home gradually grows less vivid, the separation from it less agonizing. There finally comes a day . . . when a man is living almost wholly wherever he is. His life has caught up with his body, and his days become full war days, instead of American days simply transplanted to Africa.[18]

Here Pyle described the diminution of home as if it were part of a painless acclimatization, a healthy accommodation to "war days." Soldiers were
less sanguine. Many found the process wound round with trepidation, for
with home's withdrawal, only battle remained. Kurt Gabel and his fellow
paratroopers made their way through the Ardennes toward the Our River:

> Although Jake and I still carried on our verbal parody of suburbia, the exercise
> had become perfunctory. The old banter was gone. Even [film star] Gloria De
> Haven had lost her appeal, and Hollywood had faded into indistinct impres-
> sions of a long-ago experience. The bubbling letters from my mother still
> reached me, although in bunches and sporadically. So did letters from Ruth.
> But their power to reassure me that there were really people like that going to
> places like Mocambo or Trocadero [night clubs] or the Farmers Market and re-
> turning to pearl-gray luxury to sleep in warm bedrooms—that power had been
> dissipated. . . . The battalion moved out in single file. . . . Gloria De Haven was
> gone; Ruth was gone. There was no song and there were no images, just the tall
> machine gunner in front of me and snow in the five-yard space between us.[19]

For combatants, the experience of war proved no mere interval between
phases of their civilian lives. Within that gap were forces so powerful that
they imposed on soldiers a drastically altered existence. Within was a cosmos
of its own, the world within war.

It was an imagery that soldiers adopted easily as their consciousness of
home contracted. His own home at 108 Elm Street, said Jacob Bealke,
seemed "to belong to another world which I visited a long long time ago."
Soldiers had thought themselves inhabitants only of the world into which
they were born; there home presided. In the world of war, home was an increasingly awkward visitor—and not the only one threatened with expulsion. All except what was within the soldier's most immediate compass
retreated too. Grady Gallant, with the Marines on Guadalcanal, spoke of this
compression of the combatants' perspective: "We did not have the slightest
idea of what was going on in the world. We got no lectures on world developments or who we were fighting, or why—we all had sense enough to know
why we were fighting. We saw no magazines or newspapers. We received no
pinups, were not entertained by anyone but the Japanese—and they made it
interesting enough. There was a radio at headquarters, but we seldom got
any information concerning what had been received on it. . . . We lived in
holes . . . for four months and eight days."[20]

Gallant's words signaled no craving for more information; most soldiers
became utterly indifferent. While lying in his foxhole on a hill in the Huert-

gen, Paul Boesch mused "about how the war had suddenly diminished in size. Heretofore I had always tried to keep abreast of . . . broad strategy, to read about developments in all theaters. . . . But now . . . I didn't give a damn about these things. . . . I wanted to know [only] how our 3d Battalion was getting along, how many casualties Company F was taking from the shelling, what was being done to blast the stalemate . . . in our own particular, private little war."[21]

An exception reinforced the rule. As Marines at rest after the seizure of Peleliu played in the water, a "blond kid" shouted from shore, "Hey, fellers, we've taken Metz!" He stirred no interest. "Fellers, we've taken Metz. I just heard it over the radio." The swimmers paused to talk among themselves. "Where'n hell's Metz? Philippines?" "No, it's in Europe. France or Germany." "Sounds German to me." The blond persisted: "It's important, our taking Metz." "Sure, everything's important when you first get out here." "I've been out here fifteen months . . . ," the blond replied. "But even if I was here fifteen years I'd still want to know what's going on." "Well," came the dismissal of one of the swimmers, "I'll be back in the States soon and I'll write you." Laughing, they returned to their pursuit of an octopus.[22]

When, after five years and eight months, V-E Day brought to a close the war in Europe, Marine Eugene Sledge and those around him in the Pacific received the news with dense apathy. "Nazi Germany might as well have been on the moon."[23]

As their focus narrowed on combat, soldiers began to view differently even their most important links with home. Mail lost some of its prominence. Its demotion reflected in part the devaluation of all things associated with home. John Muirhead, who had earlier spoken of letters as "our communion with the . . . sacred past," reconsidered; viewed from his airbase at Foggia, Italy, "Even letters from home awakened nothing more than a vague recollection of the past, a past that was fading from me; it was as though they were speaking of someone else, and I had no right to read what they had written. . . ." In the Pacific, Sy Kahn noticed a change of feeling that infected both inbound and outbound letters. "As months became years, as our casualties increased and familiar faces disappeared, even the letters from family and friends became a chorus of diminished voices, speaking to us from another world." Laboring with shovel to reinforce a position on Cape Gloucester, his thoughts tried to leap the miles: "It's raining now, after a beautiful day, bordering on hot. The good weather reminds Kas and me of home. What a distant thought now. It gets more and more difficult to write home—especially to keep saying all is well."[24]

But it was not only the way home receded that altered attitudes; home voices were fainter, yet they also failed to speak the messages soldiers longed to hear. True, Americans were spared news of the order that desolated soldiers in other armies—the war-borne vicissitudes and deaths of family members. On the Volga, Russian lieutenant Hersch Gurewicz received an urgent summons: stepping on a mine, the nurse whom he loved had been reduced to a dying torso. Mail bearing news of friends and family killed in air raids upset everyone in Guy Sajer's Wehrmacht unit: "It seemed we were to be spared nothing." So it was for Tommies in the wake of the Blitz and for Japanese soldiers during the American bombing of home-island cities. Here some Americans came to realize their good fortune. Sergeant Don Robinson pondered the news of an Italian friend, that his mother was dead. "I found myself rejoicing that no one I knew was likely to be forced to walk three days to rejoin his family, only to find . . . that his mother had been killed by bombs. That is one thing that is appreciated by the American soldier in danger: he knows that his family is all right."[25]

Still, the exemption failed to allay the shock of other kinds of bad news: that daily life was not proceeding as soldiers had left it, that their closest relationships were not shielded against change. The most notorious missive was the "Dear John letter." In *Battle Cry,* Leon Uris caught its arrival among a group of Marines in the Pacific. Noticing that Ski was acting strangely, Mac confronted him, then wrestled from him a bottle of sleeping pills. "The little sonofabitch tried to kill himself." "Was it Susan?" "Did you get a letter?" Danny read it to the group: "She's going to have a baby, another guy's. They're going to be married. . . . [The] rest of it is just . . . apologies. . . ." Andy sounded the group's anger: "A Dear John letter. Them goddam women, them dirty no-good bitches." Frank Irgang's love did not even write. The medic was lying in the mud of a French field under German shellfire when he received a letter: stationed near Chicago, a soldier friend who was "having a gay time" wanted Irgang to know that "Morals [at home have] become very loose, especially among the young women." Even more casual and careless was the postscript: "Here is a newspaper clipping that may interest you"—the announcement that Mary ("my Mary") had married a farmer exempted from military service. Irgang roiled as he thought of her and "her exact words [at the railroad station], 'I'll wait right here for you until the day I die.'" Irgang "felt a fit of rage trying to seize me."[26]

Such reactions appeared more than histrionic to the Germans; they appreciated the devastating impact of Dear John letters on enemy morale and circulated among prisoners of war those they were able to intercept on their way to unfortunate addressees. An American Army psychiatrist recalled, "We had a saying that as many casualties were caused on Guadalcanal by the mail from home as [by] enemy bullets," and a British soldier explained why the connection was not a fanciful one: "These mail links with home were frightening . . . comforting but frightening. . . . The Infantryman had a tight grip on himself and had to think of only one thing—survival. The grip was tight, but delicately balanced, a man's sanity in its grasp. The slightest thing that disturbed that balance might be fatal." Thus, women who "in their 'Let's be sensible about this, dear . . .' vanity" wrote Dear John letters were "guilty of murder. These were our private letter-writing Fifth Column who knocked the guts out of the fighting men."[27]

In time, commonplace and even sympathetic letters could inflict pain. Leon Uris wrote of Marines who had just completed an island campaign: "The first mail call from the States, bringing in loads of back letters, was a Godsend but at the same time it only made the men realize how lost and alone they were, and how long the war was going to last. The GI Blues set in in a bad way. And there were the neatly wrapped . . . letters stamped [Killed in Action] to remind us that so many of our buddies were gone." Orval Faubus's young son dictated to his mother items to be incorporated in the family letter. "Tell him I saw *Snow White and the Seven Dwarfs*. . . ." "Tell him I've been outside playing with my tank." When it reached him, Faubus found the letter "infinitely touching. No more powerful or forceful reminder could be brought to me of the love and tenderness left behind. Such things one puts away in the back of the mind until something like [this letter] brings them again to the fore." But soldiers discovered that expressions of tender emotion, so avidly sought earlier, could cut even as they comforted. Faubus: "And then the fear, the longing and the sorrow wells up in the heart and is for a time overwhelming. . . . Sometimes in the hell of the conflict I think that one .50 caliber bullet would make [my little boy's] features unrecognizable; a mortar shell would blow him part; . . . cannon shells . . . would not leave even one tiny piece of him to be found." "I wonder why I had to love him so much."[28]

Once soldiers saw combat, their attitudes toward films also became less pristine and more problematic.

Young men had come to the military heavily influenced by movies they had seen as adolescents. "Once we polled a rifle company," remembered William Manchester, "asking each man why he had joined the Marines. A majority cited *To the Shores of Tripoli*, a marshmallow of a movie starring John Payne, Randolph Scott and Maureen O'Hara." Many recruits believed that they required no introduction to combat; they had seen at the Bijou what battle was like. Of this they were no less convinced than a British lieutenant scrambling to safety across an invasion beach: "[H]e felt free [Alexander Baron wrote], triumphant, detached somehow from all that was happening around him; as if he were seeing it on a cinema screen, as if all the noises were on a sound-track and there were no fleet bullets or whanging steel splinters to harm him. And everything—he puzzled about it—everything was so familiar. He had seen it all before, on newsreels, in war films, in the war books on which he had grown up. There was nothing new here, nothing to shock." Like him, American soldiers expected the close alignment of actuality and play-acting. "It was just like a movie" . . . "It was just like the playback of a movie scene" . . . "It was almost like the movies, watching the exciting action while sitting safely in the theater seats." Some green soldiers knew better and became cautious. PFC William Hogan returned by bus to his camp in the English countryside: "Outside, the hills and the land are black . . . but far down on the horizon sharp antiaircraft searchlights intertwine . . . making an eerie background, like something out of a spectacular motion picture. The important thing now is that it is *not* a motion picture anymore."29

Most, however, felt no qualm until gunfire rapidly persuaded them that they were not acquainted with battle, that they were not spectators, that they were not safe. Baron's lieutenant found "nothing new . . . nothing to shock" until a shell landing close by flung just next to him the limbless trunk of another soldier. Combat laid bare what Hollywood had prettified or passed over. "We have been seduced," wrote Anton Myrer, "by the ermine and the crimson sashes, the boots and mustachios and spurs aglitter on parqueted floors, by cuirasseurs sweeping down sunlit vales in plumed, cloak-waving charge towards sparkling little brass cannon where the old purple-and-gold standard flutters gaily. Errol Flynn, in brief: Errol Flynn. The dashing, resplendent hero we have been led to ape—the hero that never did exist. We have been bewitched, all of us, by the seductive abstractions that have nothing whatever to do with a man, a friend—even as you or I—holding up to you his shattered stump of a leg and sobbing piteously his anguish and bewilderment."30

Combatants quickly registered the unpretty facets of fighting that films never exposed. Where in invasion movies were those who lost their stomachs in rough waters or whose nervous bowels compelled them to stretch over the sides of landing craft? Keith Wheeler, evacuated to a hospital ship after a shrapnel wound on Iwo Jima, "wasn't doing any visiting . . . but what I could see from my own bed was enough to demonstrate that this was no movie version of tender white hands, peace, and beauty. The ship smelled of blood, vomit, corruption, and hot, feverish flesh. And the many voices of pain murmured always in the hot air." Many in the Pacific became convinced that Hollywood had counterfeited the whole theater. Those lush, moonlit tropic isles, so romantic on celluloid, had left them unprepared for the mud, mold, and disease, for Micronesian women who bore no resemblance to Dorothy Lamour ("[If] the girls at home are uneasy about competition from Micronesian belles—well, they should see one some time"). Marines, Grady Gallant angrily pointed out, rotted in that Technicolor "paradise" of Hollywood's South Pacific islands. Especially egregious, in the soldier view, were depictions of combat and of death in battle. So many war films featured pilots or Marines that the GI thought of himself as "the forgotten man," and when he did appear, none of those "Hollywood soldiers" looked anything like him.[31]

As for combat, the films frequently got it wrong—from the willingness to volunteer ("Somehow in the movies men always step forward briskly to ask for dangerous missions") to the prominence of the bayonet in battle to the way grenades were thrown to the distance between enemies ("usually just across a coconut log" in movies). More offensive was the crisp resolution of movie battles, an issue addressed by James Jones in his study of the survivor of a Japanese assault:

> If this were a movie . . . [the attack] would decide something. It would have a semblance of meaning and a semblance of . . . emotion. And immediately after, it would be over. The audience could go home and think about . . . the meaning and feel . . . the emotion. Even if the hero got killed, it would still make sense. Art . . . creative art . . . was shit.
>
> [Here in battle] the emotions were so many and so mixed up that they were indecipherable [and] could not be untangled. Nothing had been decided, nobody had learned anything. But most important . . . , nothing had ended.[32]

Most outrageous was the scene of death in battle wrapped around with the imagery of patriotism and traditional heroism. "Soldiers at the front," Ernie Pyle learned from GI audiences in Italy, "can't stomach flag-waving from back home." John Ciardi watched *A Guy Named Joe* on Saipan. "All about how to die in an airplane, but too noble. And there is no music up high. [The air war is] not pretty. I resent the Hollywood touch in it. The Jap our guns shot down a few days ago is the way it ends: a piece of jaw here, an arm there, and a dismembered torso smoking like a charred roast. There aren't enough speeches or parades or posters in the world to make it pretty."

A Coast Guardsman contrasted popular battle deaths with those he had watched aboard war vessels. At home, he knew, "death is dramatized constantly by the stage and screen. . . . The hero . . . wipes out an enemy garrison (usually single handed) and is mortally wounded, just as he completes the job. He is immediately surrounded by his comrades who frantically try to save his life. 'It's no use, fellows. . . . I'm done for.' He sinks into the arms of his best friend [and] takes a long time to depart. . . . Finally, when the audience is about to float away in their tears, our hero dies." But the narrator had seen his ship's signals officer struck by steel from an exploding bomb. "Every time he breathed, bubbles would pop out of the bloody hash that had been his face. His life flowed across the deck and trickled over the side. No last words. No cigarettes. No meretricious drama."[33]

Contrasts between what soldiers knew to be reality and what they saw on film infuriated them. Talking among themselves, they were blunt in their proposals for the war movie the homefolks should be watching. Offered Marine private Martin Culpepper on Iwo Jima, "Hell, every [fox] hole's got [Americans' feces] in it. . . . You know, they oughta make a movie showing war like it is. It would be sensational. People falling in crap, parts of people lying around, bodies flung apart, people getting shot while they was trying to take a crap." In earthiness, soldiers hoped they had found an antidote to the films' view of war, for they now thought Hollywood romanticism dangerous. Manchester came to despise war movies as part and parcel of "the scam that had lured so many of us to recruiting stations." From Germany, Lieutenant Karl Timmerman wrote timidly to his wife in Nebraska: "Maybe those who have never been in battle find [a] certain glory and glamour that doesn't exist. Perhaps they get it from the movies or the comic strips." Laurence Critchell was not at all tentative: war films "are a parcel of nonsense [and an] outstanding . . . contribution, at least in America, to the secret craving of each new generation to be a soldier." (Later, Vietnam recruits would trace their fascination with combat to the film *The Sands of Iwo Jima*.)[34]

Whatever the degree of their concern, soldiers possessed no confidence that they would be able to alter home-front depictions of the war. That left them with their outrage—and multiplied it. "All this play-acting is just so much rot, an insult to those who died in real battles." With filmmakers beyond reach, the soldier often directed his disdain and anger at those who merely continued to believe Hollywood's version, home-front movie audiences. People sitting in theaters at home, charged Martin Culpepper, "don't know [what war is really like] and they don't care." Manchester fumed at film suggestions that "combat would be a lark," that the soldier would return "spangled with decorations," that a nurse "like Maureen O'Hara would be waiting. . . . It was peacetime again when John Wayne appeared on the silver screen as Sergeant Stryker in *Sands of Iwo Jima,* but that film underscores the point: I went to see it with another ex-Marine, and we were asked to leave the theater because we couldn't stop laughing." James Jones described a soldier wounded in the Pacific who, on an outing from his American hospital, went to a war movie so "lousy" that he stalked out. "As he walked up the aisle he looked at the faces of the people bathed in the flickering light from the screen as they chewed handfuls of popcorn and watched the fighting with avid eyes, and for a brief insane moment wished he had two or three grenades with him, to toss in among them. And see how they liked it."[35]

The military's attempts to bring home-front support straight into war zones soon incited irritation rather than that sense of solidarity the organizers sought. Radio, film, and stage stars volunteering to entertain the troops suffered depreciation with all other links to home.

Combat infantry complained, with justification, that few troupes reached them. Asked his opinion of Special Services shows, a GI in the 88th Division responded that "None of this was available to front-line soldiers, not even in a rest area. It could be enjoyed only on a furlough to Rome." Faubus agreed: "Many of the stars made many appearances for the men of the armed forces, but the combat troops had few, if any, opportunities to see them." The Andrews Sisters sang all their songs at replacement centers, in extension of an official logic that aimed to entertain the largest numbers without placing the entertainers at risk—hence, shows for crowds, principally support soldiers, in the rear. Bing Crosby and Marlene Dietrich, Faubus reported, came as far forward as division headquarters; there it was in the interest both of stars and officer-hosts to exaggerate, to the dirt soldier's disgust, their proximity to battle. Bob Hope, Frances Langford, and Jerry Colona, reported an NCO in the Third Army, "even went to the front at times." Lily Pons delighted a chaplain's assistant by coming to sing "pretty near the front." She "seemed to have a real feeling for the boys. She has a way of looking at you that makes one feel like an absolute hero and you're confident that she would commit suicide if anything should happen to you."[36]

But the favorite, both in Europe and the Pacific, was the comedian Joe E. Brown. He traveled 200,000 miles to put on 742 shows. Performing at a service club hastily erected at a rest area in Italy, "He was very funny, just what the men liked—as much as they liked pretty girls." A Pacific veteran extolled his appearances there:

The guy who is going to heaven is Joe E. Brown. He put on shows right up at the front. Right the hell in the middle of the foxholes. Guys would see his show and walk miles through the jungle so they could see it again. They wanted to kiss him. He kept acting without a stop. I really thought they would have to carry him off that island on a stretcher. You ask any man off New Georgia and he'll tell you Joe E. Brown is the greatest guy who ever lived in this world.

Brown's determination to perform at the front, however, was exceptional—he was memorializing one of his sons, an aviator killed in a crash—and as much as soldiers enjoyed the comedy and music that did reach them, they agreed with Robert Welker, who, from his post in the rear, concluded that "a precious handsome head was seldom risked where the guns could be heard."[37]

More aggravating than the absence of entertainers were the miscalculated performances of Hollywood tough-guy celebrities. Bill Mauldin remembered a USO appearance by Humphrey Bogart, who "laid the biggest egg I'd ever seen. Bogart came out on the stage of the San Carlo Opera House [in Naples] and there was this . . . crowd of guys who'd come down off the mountain for four days' R-and-R. I think he was a little bit in the bag, and he got up on stage and said something dumb like, 'I'm going back to the States to put my mob back together. Any of you guys want to go with me?' He was greeted with stony silence. He went on with his tough-guy act and they gave him a nice hand, but they just didn't think he was very funny. Because not one of those guys had a prayer of going home." Later, when the cartoonist came to know the actor ("really a good guy"), Bogart said to him, "I'll never forget all those guys looking at me. I really put my foot in it."[38]

Another star, John Wayne, tried three times to enlist but, at age thirty-four, the father of three and restricted by an infirm shoulder, he suffered the "bitter disappointment" of rejection. He managed to enter war zones as a performer, but not always to his own or others' gratification. After William Manchester's evacuation from Okinawa, he watched a Wayne show with other wounded at a Naval hospital in Hawaii.

> [The] curtains parted and out stepped John Wayne, wearing a cowboy outfit—10-gallon hat, bandanna, checkered shirt, two pistols, chaps, boots, and spurs. He grinned his aw-shucks grin . . . and said, "Hi ya, guys!" He was greeted by a stony silence. Then somebody booed. Suddenly everyone was booing.
>
> This man was a symbol of the fake machismo we had come to hate, and we weren't going to listen to him. He tried and tried to make himself heard, but we drowned him out, and eventually he quit and left.
>
> . . . I had the enormous pleasure of seeing Wayne humiliated in person. . . .

Edwin Hoyt saw the point at issue: "there was nothing a [Bogart or Wayne] could suggest about toughness that matched the reality of combat."[39]

No one arrived overseas with less soldier goodwill than Frank Sinatra. Despised as a skinny 4-F who, inexplicably, had become the idol of soldiers' younger sisters (returning from combat to a hero's welcome, Commando Kelly cringed when high school girls prattled, "You're better than Frankie Sinatra!"), the singer nevertheless read accurately the experience of earlier troupes, and on his 1945 concert tour he was a target of derision only "until he melted the GIs' hostility with his talents as a balladeer." It was a reverie, not a war movie, that Sinatra offered his soldier audiences.[40]

Combat soldiers both praised and damned the work of another extension of home, the American Red Cross—and once again, their estimation declined as the war lengthened.

The organization's credits were impressive. Many POWs attributed to Red Cross food parcels distributed by the Germans (and far less frequently by the Japanese) the critical margin between maintenance and fatal malnutrition. Vital plasma transfusions were available to American wounded because of Red Cross blood drives. Keith Wheeler made his "first acquaintance" with Red Cross field representatives when he arrived at a Saipan hospital without toiletries. "The second day a couple of . . . workers . . . went through the ward asking what we needed. [Razor? Toothbrush? Slippers?] Some patients were startled when they learned it wasn't necessary to pay." Prior to his medical evacuation flight home, a Red Cross girl, "pretty and pleasant," "made hot chocolate, opened cans of fruit juice, ordered coffee, lighted cigarettes. It was a pleasure to have her around." In North Africa, Morton Eustis thought that in its officers' clubs and enlisted men's recreation centers the Red Cross was doing "a remarkable job." Johnny Stradling praised it for bringing to that theater "the one little spot of home . . . and the one touch of 'mother' you find when in trouble."[41]

Others, however, began to voice angry complaints. Often the Red Cross did charge soldiers for its services. Traveling in Normandy, Frank Irgang was outraged that he had to pay for Red Cross coffee and doughnuts: "What kind of a racket is this?" The organization was also vulnerable to the criticisms leveled at entertainment troupes, that its ministrations seldom reached the front and that its members cast their lot with officers rather than common soldiers. As one field director conceded, the Army's offer of simulated officer rank, with all of its privileges, often precluded any representation of enlisted men's views. "The [military] command didn't like a challenge to their control. You bunked with 'em, you ate with 'em, so this tension made the job difficult."[42]

Keith Winston's reactions moved in rough consonance with the evolution of combat soldiers' response to the work of the Red Cross. Shipping out, he was impressed: "A thing that touched me deeply was the warm way the Red Cross handled us as we were ready to march up that gangplank. What a wonderful feeling to know that somebody cared—even strangers—and [was] on hand to say goodbye. Besides the liberal refreshments, each of us was given a large pouch with a number of useful things in it." As his division fought through France, however, Winston's enthusiasm cooled. "At long last our [Battalion] was visited by the Red Cross. Two girls handed out doughnuts and coffee to the boys. It was wonderful to see American women and it made most of us homesick." But the Red Cross was not where it should have been nor even doing what it claimed to do. "Sure, they do a good job for the rear echelon. . . . But where it means the most . . . where [men are] in dismal discomfort and in a semi-state of shock, you just don't know the Red Cross exists." Combat soldiers needed writing paper, envelopes, reading materials, "But always some excuse." "[T]hey are not doing the job the folks back home think they're doing for the GI up front. I'm not saying they do nothing, but I do say that where it is needed most they're badly lacking."[43]

In the last days of the European War, Winston flung at his wife "something [that] annoyed me so much I can't help but get it off my chest." He had written to her of the deficiencies of the Red Cross; she had written to him of her five-dollar contribution to the Red Cross. That would be, he vowed, "the last money they ever receive from us. . . . "Consider yourself bawled out!" After V-E Day, he wrote of "a Red Cross Club [in Dijon] which serves coffee and cake all day long for a slight charge—and what is extremely distasteful is that they have a separate dining room for officers. Can you imagine American contributions going for anything so anti-democratic? I took pictures of it so I could prove it to skeptic Americans when I return home." The Red Cross was "a glamour outfit basking in the glory of 'overseas' and 'doing a fine job'"—while working only where it was safe.[44]

The deterioration of ties with home reflected the frustrations of a problem larger than the failure of films, entertainers, and Red Cross: how combat soldiers were to communicate to those at home an experience of war far from the one that soldiers had anticipated, and further still from the one that the homefolks believed was unfolding in Europe and the Pacific.

The soldiers' dilemma revealed itself in a series of groping propositions that traced no neat logic in either their content or their fit but did mirror the changing needs of men struggling to comprehend the relationships between themselves and battle and those at home.

"We do not want them to understand battle as we do."

Combat soldiers—and military authorities—agreed on the necessity to sanitize the home version of the battlefield experience. A British officer who described his letters to his wife as "remorselessly cheerful and very properly uninformative about our serious activities" might have been depicting as well millions of American soldiers' letters. Pretense was proper because candor would inflict suffering on families without bestowing on them any ability to relieve soldier suffering. "[My] own . . . letters [were] made up of lies," acknowledged Robert Welker. "I never let them know my feelings; I could see no profit in such forthrightness, either way. Cut away and immune from the sickness of military life, [the homefolks] could offer no remedy but their love, which I never doubted; yet meanwhile they would themselves suffer in sympathy, which I could not abide."[45]

Speak no ill of friendly dead was one of soldiers' first principles. They sought to persuade parents that combat had not coarsened their dead sons. "I never heard John swear an oath, smoke, or drink, and his thoughts were always clean, I'm sure." Here official sanction fitted with front-line inclination: commanding officers wrote only letters that upheld the character of the dead. "The 1st Sergeant spoke highly of him and said his job as scout was dangerous but that he performed his duties and missions in an exemplary manner. His duty came first and frequently at the risk of his own life he showed his loyalty to his Company and the desire to be a 'damn good soldier.'" A kindred enterprise in which men and high command colluded was the purging of personal effects. Garrett Graham described how Marines removed from the items to be sent home any "incriminating letters or matériel d'amour." Airmen were no less circumspect. "A man's personal effects had to be culled by his friends . . . things that would be painful for his family to see . . . pornographic books or pictures, indiscreet letters, things of that sort." Just a short step up was the falsification of death reports. A drunken GI, James Fry reported, attempted to rape a nine-year-old Italian girl and died on the tines of her father's pitchfork; those at home, the regimental doctor made certain, would grieve that the soldier lost his life defending his country. When a sniper brought down a man meandering about on a souvenir hunt and the major wrote up the death as "Not in the line of duty," medics carrying the body to the hospital changed the tag en route.[46]

Another routine misrepresentation was the insistence that soldiers succumbed to the clean death—fast and painless. "[He] was cut down by enemy gun fire. He was killed instantly" . . . "I feel sure that those who lost their lives didn't suffer, for which we thank . . . God above." None of the bodies of the dead, by report, suffered disfigurement; what James Jones called "the awful animal indecencies" were, by agreement, omitted. Nor did home versions allow for deaths either desolate or purposeless. "One man . . . had died while we were away [to obtain] litters. . . . What a horrible, lonely way to die—in a dirty, evil-smelling horse stable in a strange and far-away land. . . . I hoped that his . . . family might never know how the end had come, that they might always believe that death took him as he ran gallantly up the side of a hill in the sunlight, a picture-book hero." Each death glowed with significance, even if that required resort to ordinarily detested Hollywood heroism. Orval Faubus wrote to the widow of his friend Cull, killed in an assault against the Germans: "Do not forget that death must come to us all, and no finer, braver, or more glorious death could come to any one than that which came to him; fighting bravely for God and country in defense of freedom and the rights of humankind. He is already across the dark river . . . and has entered into the portals of that country which waits for the good and the brave."[47]

To be sure, soldiers were sharply aware that, beyond their own wishes, domestic pressures bent them toward affirmations of the clean death. Parents asked company commanders: How did he die? Was it quick? In early summer 1944, a Mrs. Castelli of the Bronx wrote to Douglas MacArthur: "Please General he was a good boy, wasn't he? Did he die a hard death General? Oh! Please won't you drop me a line and tell me if he suffered long or not." A new widow wrote Faubus's captain: "This may seem strange to you but it would be a relief to me to know where he was hit. If he thought he was going to be a cripple for life I know he didn't try to live.* You don't know how bad I wanted him to come back under any condition he could make it back to me. When a woman loves a man like I did him it's so hard to give him up. My heart has suffered a thousand deaths since I received that telegram." How else could an officer respond save to summon whatever sympathy lay within him? Commanders, moreover, were often compelled to conceal their igno-

---

*Almost always a misconception.

rance of the facts. From Dayton, Ohio, a mother described a vision of her son's death at Anzio. "The last time I dreamed of Bob was the night before we got the telegram. . . . I was over there with him . . . in a queer looking stone house. . . . Then a bomb burst just where he was. I saw him go up in pieces. . . ." She was anxious of course to know if her son had died in this way, but Captain Felix, "search his memory as he might . . . had absolutely no recollection of what happened to Sergeant Fremder." Reality was often as harsh as one English writer represented it: "A shell kills half a dozen men. In the soldier's world the men are forgotten. . . . But away in the other world half a dozen families, perhaps a hundred human beings, are rocked with grief." Rarely, then, would an officer hesitate to invent something that would meet a mother's expectations.[48]

Nurse Juanita Redmond, returning to the United States after her escape from Corregidor, suffered more sharply than field soldiers the anguish in this predicament. Everywhere in Washington—in hallways, on stairways—civilians asked about their soldiers. Sometimes she succeeded in sending them away "relieved of the worst of their anxiety. More often we could tell them nothing about their own boys. . . . And sometimes we could only say, 'He died like a good soldier.' . . . [It] was harder telling those mothers and wives and fathers about their boys, than anything on Bataan or Corregidor."[49]

Candor was either impossible or unthinkable—that was the point Audie Murphy demonstrated to himself by imagining a truthful report. When Mason was killed by a huge shell, Murphy hallucinated. "Briefly a picture trembles in my mind . . . a white-haired woman who stands before a cottage on a shady street in Savannah.

> "I am his mother. What were his last words?"
> "[He said,] 'Think I'll walk over there and twist his goddamned ears off.'"
> "Whose ears?"
> "Those of a German who [had been] trying to kill us."
> "My boy went to his God with a curse on his lips?"
> "His God will understand."

Murphy was, he feared, "going batty."[50]

In their own letters home, soldiers seldom sought to make clear the realities of their lives. A Marine officer whose job it was to censor his men's mail noted their first concern—"They didn't want anyone worrying about them"—so their letters were, like Grady Gallant's, "filled with sweet nothings." Soldiers sometimes contemplated some variation on the I-am-fine theme, but their attempts foundered. Deliberating on a Christmas letter for his family, Lester Atwell searched for words that "would not give rise to worry" but could be reread for comfort if he were killed. It was a prescription too complex; he was able to think of nothing "out of the ordinary."[51]

Another apprehension was that the homefolks would find wanting the soldier whose letters laid bare his emotional state. Those in the field had ceased early on to distinguish sharply the interplay of courage and cowardice, but traditional values persisted at home. Years after the war, a woman remembered her soldier boyfriend: "He was sent to Italy where the fighting was very intense for a long time, and he wrote to me whenever he could. Then, in one of those V-mail letters he told me he cried many nights during the heavy fighting. In my sheltered life with my stereotyped notions of what [constituted] a man . . . the thought of his crying turned my stomach. I was convinced I had loved a coward. I never wrote to him again." Sailor Robert Edson Lee often awoke in the morning "with the sudden realization that I was alone and in danger. None of this went into my letters home. I falsified those, lest someone discover me in my agony [and more, my] mortal terror." "No one," Paul Fussell knew, "wrote: 'Dear Mother, I am scared to death.'"[52]

A final, and less prevalent, anxiety lay in the belief, tantamount to a superstition, that to send letters less than cheerful invited the retaliation of the cosmos: Soldiers who wrote frankly would soon receive bad news from home.

Safer on all counts, the combat soldier concluded, to confine oneself to the casual and the cosmetic. Just prior to Christmas 1944, Ross Carter and his paratrooper friends learned that they were to be thrown into the Bulge to blunt the German offensive; all knew that the unit roster had already turned over twice, that their odds of survival were slim. "We all wrote short letters home telling everybody we were well and looking forward to a big Christmas. We wished the usual season's greetings and expressed the usual optimisms about the war's early end and anticipations of getting home maybe sooner than we expected." Marines bound for the invasion of Okinawa wrote "something like this": "Am at sea. . . . In case I am not able to write again for a while, don't worry. I'll be okay. Will write as soon as I can." The Please-don't-worry of soldier letters was the liturgical complement of the Please-be-careful of family letters. In any practical sense, they were idiot phrases. Were there any words that could persuade parents to feel less anxiety or soldiers to take greater care in combat? But such refrains were fundamental to a ritual exchange that no party could dare ignore.[53]

In concealing their fright and fury, soldiers chose to hide from home components basic to the infantryman's world. "It was amazing," thought

James Jones, "how little of [the soldier's] secret bitterness . . . he allowed to filter to the people at home. . . ."[54]

"We cannot explain battle in any way that will enable them to understand it."

In the immediate wake of the soldier's negative resolve—We do not want them to understand—came the suspicion that whatever his will, he lacked the capacity—And if we did want to explain, we couldn't.

At work here was the conviction that the battle experience was accessible only to those who passed through it. About this, soldiers were definite. Frank Irgang: "No one would ever know what it was like without the experience itself." Bill Mauldin: "[You] have to go through it to understand its horror. . . . You have to smell it and feel it all around you until you can't imagine what it used to be like when you walked on a sidewalk or tossed clubs up into the horse chestnut trees or fished for perch or when you did anything at all without a pack, a rifle, and a bunch of grenades." Orval Faubus pondered the value of photographs in depicting blasted villages: "but no one could ever fully grasp the horror and awfulness without actually being on the ground, not only to see, but to feel the presence . . . and to smell the sickening stench of the dead." "Only those who have lived in this world [of war] can ever know what it is like."[55]

Why must one undergo combat to comprehend it? Here soldiers were far less decisive. Because, some proposed, battle so outdistanced normalcy that it destroyed all usual standards of comparison. "[The] world of the infantryman," Pyle suggested, "is a world so far removed from anything normal that it can be no more than academic to the average person." Because, others believed, battle inflicted pain of a unique order, one that Richard Gabriel thought "far exceeds anything most civilians ever suffer or witness." (He allowed one exception: civilians incarcerated in mental hospitals.) Soldiers often held that their suffering surpassed any that others, or even soldiers' earlier selves, were able to imagine.[56]

The insistence on experience quickly acquired as its partner the assertion that the experience was not communicable by those who had borne it to those who had not. Mauldin: "But no matter how much we try we can never give the folks at home any idea of what war really is." Grady Arrington: "Any veteran trying to explain such scenes finds himself inadequate." Again, infantrymen found the cause of the problem elusive. When pressed, some cited once more the absence from homelife of equivalent experiences that would enable soldiers to illuminate battle for others. And at bottom all soldiers were at times less intent on communicating the fearfulness and horror than on repressing them. Writing out of utter demoralization, medic Tsuchida told his family from a French battlefield: "What a mess this whole business is. My mind is one confused conglomeration of incidents, the basic fears of night, and the waiting for daylight. The rest . . . I would just as soon forget because it is so rotten."[57]

No one struggled more earnestly than Ernie Pyle to portray the war realistically. The European theater's Supreme Commander, Dwight Eisenhower, wrote to applaud the correspondent's dedication to "going full out to tell the truth about the infantry combat soldier." That, indeed, was Pyle's goal. War front and home front, he sensed, were drawing apart, and if civilians could not be helped to comprehend combat, soldiers would be thrust into a desolate, inconsolable isolation. GIs understood what he was attempting. Sergeant Arnold Diamondstein wrote his mother of Pyle's landing in France during the first phase of the Normandy invasion: "He was . . . our spokesman. It was not that his column told us things we did not know or feel, but the fact that you folks at home could read it, and get to know and understand. . . ." Particularly hopeful were soldiers whose isolated eruptions of frankness had merely persuaded them of their own incapacity. Lieutenant Robert Lewin, wishing only to warn his parents that battle had altered him, wrote home from North Africa: "I have changed a little and am not as wild or careless as I used to be, and you will love me a lot better when I come back, but I mourn the fact that a lot of my pristine gayety and recklessness has forever vanished. [Here, perhaps fearful he had gone too far, he drew back.] Don't worry about me. I'm well, happy, and have many friends." Parents left to ponder a son no longer carefree but still happy could not have registered the message Lewin intended.[58]

Medic Tsuchida's excursion into candor brought from home not insight but rebuke. "My gosh but I didn't know I wrote Belle anything out of the ordinary. . . . I do remember when I wrote . . . it was right after I had pieced together a guy's leg. . . . [As] I began to cut his trousers and shoes away, the fleshy meat just plopped out. . . . I just picked up the meat with my fingers and wrapped it up with several compress bandages. . . . And then we had mail that night, which included [the] letter from Belle wondering 'how do you like places like Paris?' Well, I answered her letter but I wasn't feeling too happy that night." Tsuchida's letters to his brother reveal twisted intentions: I want to tell you but not our parents; I want to tell you, but you will not believe what I write; I do not want to tell you too much; I do not want to tell you, and I am glad you do not or cannot understand. His desires, like those of so many soldiers, flowed home in an impossible jumble, a failure of focus in sometimes (but only sometimes) wishing that those at home knew better what combat was like. Just a little, enough to enhance public sympathy and appreciation but still well short of the level of comprehension that would panic parents.[59]

No wonder most soldiers felt they must entrust the task to Ernie Pyle. As the correspondent joined an infantry company moving up to assault a German strongpoint in Cherbourg, a GI spoke to him "almost belligerently." "Why don't you tell the folks back home what this is like? . . . They don't know that for every hundred yards we advance somebody gets killed. Why don't you tell them how tough this life is?" Pyle, always patient with front-line infantrymen, swallowed any temptation to reply, "Why don't you, soldier?" and instead "told him that was what I tried to do all the time."[60]

And he did try—continuously, intently, aggressively. But he too failed, as he acknowledged in his reply to Eisenhower's letter: "I think we're both fighting a losing cause—for I've found that no matter how much we talk, or write, or show pictures, people who have not actually been in war are incapable of having any real conception of it. I don't really blame the people. . . . I think I have helped make America conscious of and sympathetic toward [the infantryman], but I haven't made them *feel* what he goes through. I believe it's impossible. But I'll keep on trying." Pyle persisted, but tenacity's reward was mounting frustration and impatience. In the column he was drafting when he died, he sent flying at "the people" words drawn from deep anger. Allying himself with veterans of combat, he spoke of those

> who have had burned into their brains forever the unnatural sight of cold dead men scattered over the hillsides and in the ditches. . . .
>
> Dead men by mass production. . . . Dead men in . . . monstrous infinity. . . .
>
> These are things that you at home need not even try to understand. To you . . . they are columns of figures, or he is a near one who went away and just didn't come back. You didn't see him lying so grotesque and pasty beside the gravel road in France.
>
> We saw him, saw him by the multiple thousands. That's the difference. . . .[61]

Ernie Pyle's columns were like soldiers' letters addressed to the nation rather than the family. They aimed to preserve that eve-of-departure unity embracing in shared understanding and warm-hearted emotion both servicemen and homefolks. Pyle's accomplishment was that, as soldier and civilian experience sundered, he was able to create a new footing for the emotional connection. His words cut far closer to the GI experience than did those of the military's publicity men. The empathy he engendered at home provided at least a basis for the combat soldier's eventual reconciliation with civilian society; in their unreality, the official refrains chanted throughout the war—How well the soldiers are being treated! How heroically they are conducting themselves!—did not.[62] True, the experience of combat had opened another gap in understanding rather than emotion that neither Pyle nor anyone else could bridge. But for GIs who knew themselves incapable of explaining war to those they loved, Pyle's achievement sufficed to secure what they thought they wanted. They would return to a society sympathetic but spared the fuller realism that would have inflicted the soldier's pain on those at home. Soldiers continued to revere Ernie Pyle.

"They cannot understand battle, nor do they wish to."

The conviction that only those who experienced combat could know what it was like, however powerful and widespread, did not prevent some soldiers from yielding to their need to instruct the homefolks in war's realities.

A source of urgency was GI apprehension that the big war of the headlines belittled the role of the foxhole soldier. A Japanese American soldier fighting on the Volturno prodded his family: "When you read that a town . . . or a certain hill was taken, remember that in the process of that accomplishment lives of fine fellows were lost, and also, that . . . for the participants, life was a horrifying massacre." But families seldom responded to or inquired further about such correctives. They thought themselves fully sympathetic to their soldiers and thus felt uncertain of their sons' purpose.[63]

More upsetting were encounters between homefolks and soldiers during medical treatment or rare furloughs. For the first time in his life, thought Paul Boesch during grim fighting in the Huertgen, he was "involved in something which I did not want to share with my wife, at least not until I could better measure my own reactions and find some way to transmit the strange feelings that were surging through me." Numbers of soldiers believed that their return home offered the way, that they would be able to do in person what had eluded them in letters. But the few opportunities to test results proved discouraging. Even face-to-face, soldiers immediately tripped on their inability to describe what they knew, and their frustration quickly turned into disgust, even for civilians striving to understand. A sympathetic "It must have been a horrible experience" seemed to convey little comprehension when an hour earlier the soldier had overheard that the wait in the meat-market line that morning had been "horrible." Few attempts were repeated.[64]

Arthur Miller described the return of a twenty-two-year-old Navy flier who, as he talked with his girlfriend, was "filled with a dull longing for something from her. . . . And he cannot find it. . . . One moment she is filled with pity for him, the next pride. He suffers for her and for his inability to know what it really is he wants her to feel. He recalls how easy it was to talk to the guys in the squadron, how simple to communicate without talking at all. She asks him how it was, and he says it was pretty bad in the beginning but it got all right later on, and suddenly he is very tired. . . . His going and his returning seemed to have left no deeper residue in her than a sadness at his going and a joy at his return. Is that all she was supposed to feel? Was she supposed to know what he had rescued for her out there in the world? Or had he rescued anything anywhere?" At home, shaving in "the old bathroom," he was struck by "the curious notion . . . that it will be good to get out of here again . . . to be going back." He talked with his mother. "God knows he doesn't want her calling him a hero. The heroes aren't coming home to mother any more." He was puzzled: "He wonders again what on earth he would have these people feel." And angry: "When are they going to start figuring out this war?" Between mouthfuls of food, he tried to answer his mother's questions. "'Well, in the beginning, it was pretty bad. But after a while . . . it was all right.' Oh hell [he thought to himself], let it go at that. It doesn't matter anyway."[65]

Soldiers who tried to explain war soon decided to discount all civilian expressions of interest in the nature of combat. Yes, the homefolks *asked* about it—often from the conviction that candor would rebuild intimacy between them and their soldier sons. Lewis Mumford "begged" his son Geddes "to put down his first experiences on paper, before they had lost their clarity . . . if only so that we could come closer to him, in our imaginations, from that time on." But soldiers decided that plain speaking seldom created closeness. Sometimes civilians missed entirely what GIs attempted to convey. Commando Kelly admired infantryman Pop Murray, who, though in his mid-thirties, a casualty at Salerno, and a victim of doddering knees entitling him to discharge, continued to soldier on. Brought home for a hero's tour, Kelly "told a few people about Joes like Pop Murray, but it didn't take long to discover the people I talked with didn't know much about what kind of people foot-soldiers are, and it griped me." Sometimes civilians took alarm that replies to their queries would intensify soldiers' trauma. People questioned Ed Stewart about his war, but as he began to describe it, they "interrupted and cut him off." (One can imagine them thinking, "Uh, oh, this gore can't be good for him!") "So the second time I was asked how it was, I cut myself off after a couple of words."[66]

Often stories so different from those expected sent civilians recoiling in nausea or disgust. American soldiers often attributed these various miscarriages to civilian skepticism or indifference rather than civilian considerateness or vulnerability. "It was clear," Stewart concluded, "that people didn't believe me, or even if they believed me they really were not interested in the raw experience. They wanted the embellishments, the glory, the success, the survival—but not the raw experience. People don't want that."[67]

The government was aware that popular perceptions of combat remained rooted in the heroic model. In order to harden civilian resolve and impel greater dedication to the war of production, it attempted gradually to introduce more realistic views. When, in July 1943, the Army released new training films emphasizing "the use of extreme toughness and cunning" to subdue the enemy, *Life* published stills demonstrating the use of thumbs to gouge German eyes and of rifle butts to break German jaws. A New Hampshire subscriber reacted with "shame and horror": ". . . these tactics are those we associate with the Japs—not American soldiers." A Texas reader objected that "To plan and practice maiming in such a cruel and heathenish manner is more the action of a Nazi barbarian than an American. I can't forgive *Life* for printing the devilish pictures." Early in 1943, Washington allowed newspapers and magazines to publish photographs of enemy dead—Japanese bodies, for example, awash in the New Guinea surf. To protest letters, an airman responded that if the objectors had only seen the American dead on New Guinea, "as we did . . . they'd realize dead Japs make good pictures. . . ." In late September 1943, the government, lifting its ban on pictures of American dead, released a photograph of three soldiers lapped by water at the Buna shoreline. No part of a face was visible; the bodies were intact, their positions restful rather than contorted; no crabs, ants, or maggots were within view. Death seemed gentle.[68]

Still, public opposition, though clearly diminishing, continued. A New Yorker wrote *Life* in "strong protest" that pictures of American corpses "make a mockery of sacrifice." Two months later, resistance re-ignited as photos of Marine dead at Tarawa dramatized, in a way many civilians found unbearable, the steep cost of that campaign: one thousand dead and two thousand wounded in just three days of fighting.[69]

Such eruptions puzzled and perturbed combat soldiers. The published photographs seemed to them antiseptic—"quite ordinary," Manchester called them. That they shocked a significant segment of the public once again widened the gap; those who protested them testified to their mulish denial of the line companies' daily realities. If we can endure the dying, soldiers angrily told one another, those at home should be able to tolerate pictures of our dead. The homefolks do not want to understand.[70]

"They ought to understand battle."

Despite evidence that soldiers wanted to tell no more than civilians wished to be told and that, even had there been strong urges on both sides, soldiers could have transmitted their perceptions of combat no more accurately than civilians would have received them, soldiers were unable to let the matter rest.

When Keith Winston's wife wrote to him of a quixotic proposal that soldiers' wives should visit them in Europe, his reaction reflected the soldier's initial protectiveness of those at home. "Over here we look upon that idea ... as a lot of baloney. Dear, we're on duty 24 hours a day, we travel regularly and we get no leaves. Nor do we desire to have our wives see the conditions under which we live—to say nothing of the danger they'd be in. Some guy must have been thinking of some General friend back in England when he suggested such a crazy idea." But the innocence of war that he here strove to maintain did in its larger forms increasingly agitate him. "People in our country don't begin to know the meaning of war—and don't care—until it hits them when one of their family is killed or wounded." "[They] just don't have the vaguest idea about war." "[I am] getting so sick of all this, especially after hearing that 86% of the U.S. people (who know nothing—zero—of the hell a soldier endures) want [to force] unconditional surrender [on] Japan. It's so easy to want all—when you give nothing."[71]

In Winston's agitation lay the soldier's fear that civilian incomprehension would permanently estrange him from those at home. That after all was the warning filtering back from the first returnees. "[O]ccasionally we received letters from old Company K buddies who had returned to the States," recalled Eugene Sledge. "Their early letters expressed relief over being back with family or with 'wine, women, and song.' But later the letters often became disturbingly bitter and filled with disillusionment. Some expressed a desire to return if they could get back into the old battalion. . . . [The] gist of their disillusionment was a feeling of alienation from everyone but their old comrades. . . ." Sledge worried that the soldiers' experience "seemed to set us apart forever from anyone who hadn't been in combat."[72]

So soldiers remained painfully suspended between their reluctance, their inability, and their necessity to explain battle. Orval Faubus re-visited the puzzle frequently, always in confusion. He desperately hoped that through the letters he sent to the home-town newspaper he would "make others see the horror and . . . cost of [the] war. . . ."—even as he denied his ability to do so. "[We] would like for others to understand us. . . . But I, for one, know that is impossible." The tension generated by such inconsistent impulses was endurable in the war's early stages. But as the fighting intensified, each letter, newspaper, and magazine from home seemed a reminder of civilian misinterpretation and too often a revelation of some new foolishness or stupidity deriving from it. Naïveté, at first worth a laugh, became offensive and then unbearable as a mirror of what civilians thought soldiers did.[73]

Just after an infantryman's death in combat, his comrades opened a corporate newsletter: there was his picture. "Private Michael Novak, 'Little Mike,' as he was familiarly known among his co-workers at Eureka, is now with the Seventh Army in Italy. That is bad news for the Germans. . . . We are expecting great things of him in the war. . . . Keep up the good work, Mike. We are proud of you." An Army nurse received a letter from home: "I hope you can send me some fine laces from one of those picturesque Italian towns." ("Lord, when we get to those towns there's nothing left of them.") Another nurse was similarly importuned: "Send me some souvenirs; I'll pay for them." ("The only souvenirs we can send are pieces of shrapnel.") In Germany, Private Lester Atwell pondered various queries from home. Had he stopped off at the Monopole-Metropole Hotel? Visited Cologne? Taken lunch on the Rhine? Tried a whole peach in champagne? The father of a Marine wrote to ask whether he should send on to Guadalcanal his son's full-dress blue uniform. During one of Ernie Pyle's visits home during the war, a man pressed him—"in complete good faith"—"Tell me now, just exactly what is it you don't like about war?"[74]

We don't want those at home to understand; we cannot enable them to understand; they cannot understand nor do they even wish to. And in the end, with logicality once more submissive, soldiers came to: But, damn it, they just *have* to understand! And when persuaded that they did not and would not, soldiers grew angry with them. James Jones often depicted this ire as almost explosive. His Sergeant Winch, returning from the Pacific aboard a hospital ship and impatient to be with a woman for the first time in a year, found in San Francisco a willing partner, but her conversation made clear that "She did not understand anything at all about any of [his war]. [Civilians] could not get it through their thick heads that all that out there has absolutely nothing to do with any of this back here. Suddenly he wanted to split her head open with the bottle. . . ."[75]

By the later stages of the war, infantrymen's anger had led to a lengthy indictment of the home front.

Soldiers blamed the home front's unrealistic view of war for America's failure to take seriously the enemies they were fighting. Today it startles us that Adolf Hitler, one of history's greatest destroyers, so often appeared on newspaper and magazine pages in dismissive comic caricature, a goose-stepping, self-important little man exposed by his sissy-boy mustache and haircut. In 1942, Spike Jones and his City Slickers recorded a novelty tune that quickly achieved national popularity:

> When der Führer says ve is der Master Race,
> We Heil [Bronx cheer], Heil [Bronx cheer], right in der Führer's face. . . .
> When Herr Goebbels says we own the world and space,
> We Heil . . .
> We Heil . . .
> Are we not der Supermen?
> Ya, we are der Supermen, super-dooper Supermen. . . .

Certain radio stations banned the song not because its flippancy demeaned the war effort but because of the impropriety of a sound like breaking wind in public. Japan's leaders and soldiers were similarly burlesqued. All this pained soldiers who had acquired good cause to view their adversaries grimly—and who had long forgotten their own lighthearted departure for war. (Troops shipping out as late as 1944 continued to strut their own shouts of "Banzai!" "Look out, Tojo," and "Heil, Hero.")[76]

Civilians seemed to view military life no more seriously than they did Japanese and Germans, and soldiers who themselves damned the service still found offensive those who so easily dismissed it. Early in the war a genre of "You're in the Army Now" literature and entertainment appeared that cast duty in the military somewhere between a novel outing and a minor chastisement for civilian truancies. Soldiers whose experience did not include combat duty but might have provided scripts for Sergeant Bilko's subsequent television escapades published a spate of books, variants on *My Military Misadventures* or *My War with the Army.* Irving Berlin's 1942 extravaganza, *This Is the Army,* sold out houses from Broadway to San Francisco with such songs as "The Army's Made a Man Out of Me" ("I used to sleep with Brother. But now I sleep alone. I used to be a tenor. But now I'm a baritone") and "This Is the Army, Mr. Jones" ("You've had your breakfast in bed before. But you won't have it there any more. . . . You had a house-maid to clean your floor. But she won't help you out any more"). Soldiers sleeping exposed to the weather in North Africa or on Guadalcanal while the show toured the

United States may not have been well enough acquainted with maid service to feel fully the burden of its loss.[77]

Soldiers' anger also converged, intermittently, on the treatment of prisoners of war held at home. A society failing to contemplate its enemies as dispensers of death confirmed, in soldiers' minds, its lack of *gravitas*. Wilma Parnell worked in the administration office of an Oklahoma POW camp.

> Our Saturday night dances always brought many of the townspeople of Tonkowa to the camp, and German prisoners routinely provided the intermission entertainment, singing *Lieder* and Christmas carols. When their concerts were over they would file into the bar, each to receive a single glass of beer before marching back to the compounds. They were always under guard and never spoke to us, but they seemed to love the break in their routine, and the townspeople thrilled to their music.

Reports of such entertainments, and of cake and ice cream socials, and of POW work protests and even stoppages reached soldiers in the field. POW treatment, insisted Bill Mauldin, should be "within the rules, but only within the rules." Russell Putman, returning from a graveside service, read a letter describing "a 'strike' of German prisoners . . . working in plants in the States. . . . It seems unbelievable. It makes me shudder to contemplate what will happen to an America that refuses to face the facts of life. . . . God help those who promote such insults to our dead as to fail even in the handling of prisoners sent back to our shores."[78]

Ingenuousness opened civilians to the attempts of military authorities to intensify production efforts by blazoning battle episodes opportune for moral exhortation. Front-line soldiers resented particularly those in which official publicists invoked the heroic model; as a GI complained, "All [the public] hear about is victories and a lot of glory stuff."[79]

One early incident that rankled was Wake Island's "Send us more Japs" message. Following the Marine repulse of the initial Japanese landing attempt, a distant headquarters inquired by radio, considerately but impractically, what the detachment most needed. The alleged reply, attributed to the Marine commander, Major James Devereux, was then trumpeted "as a snappy comeback . . . entirely worthy to take its place in history alongside 'We have not yet begun to fight!' . . . 'Don't give up the ship!' and other classic speeches of ringing virtue," though the phrase itself, in the most charitable interpretation, was a distortion of words used by Wake's radioman merely as requisite filler in his encoded message. Even during the war those who knew the reality protested. In a book published in 1943, the last man to leave the island prior to its capitulation described the Marines' reaction as "dour" and "singularly cold." Theirs was "a nasty and dangerous job," and "They would have asked for twenty or thirty battleships, a thousand pursuit planes, another thousand flying fortresses, and the rest of the . . . Marine Corps. . . . But Japs? No! If more Japs came they would handle them expertly, but they just couldn't see any sense in *asking* for them." After the war, liberated POW Devereux was far more brusque: "We heard ['Send us more Japs!'] from this fulsome [radio] commentator. . . . That was news to me. One of the Marines said, 'Anybody that wants it can sure have my share of the Japs we already got!' He spoke for every man on Wake. . . . We had all the Japs we could handle and a lot more, too. . . . I would not have been damn fool enough to send such an idiotic message."[80]

Four years later, Joe Rosenthal's fortuitous snap of a camera shutter, capturing forever an instant of remarkably poetic movement as six Marines raised a flag above Iwo Jima's Mount Suribachi, revealed the persistence of that divide. When President Roosevelt realized the photograph's dramatic power, he ordered that the flag-raisers be identified and returned home as heroes; the three still alive were soon on tour in support of a lagging war-bond drive. One of them, Ira Hayes, was in shock from the outset. His company had entered combat with a strength of 235; only 35 survived. As Hayes mourned the loss of three of his closest friends, officialdom's manufacture of heroism intensified his distress. Why had he been saved? Why should *he* be fêted and flattered? There had been nothing heroic or even exceptional about the flag-raising (except of course for that frozen flash of time).[81]

Others on the tour were also agitated, though more indignant than troubled. The Marine combat correspondent chosen to escort the flag-raisers fumed that the project was "a vaudeville act" designed to coax money for the war from "a bunch of fat cats . . . grown rich in the war. . . ." But Hayes, profoundly disturbed, began to drink, to muff his lines, and to miss engagements; pulled from a Chicago bar and summarily returned to the Pacific, he tried to explain to his family:

> I am back again . . . and I like it better this way. I have a reason. . . . There were a few guys who went all through the battle of Iwo with me. I've known them for a year, fought together and were scared most of the time together. And they were back here while I was in the States, just for raising a flag, and getting all the publicity and glory. That I could not see. . . . I know I am right. . . . Surprising how much a picture can do.

After the war, however, celebrity resumed its pursuit of Ira Hayes; he died of alcoholic misadventure in 1955.[82]

Soldiers directed a steadier anger at the war's inequality of sacrifice. They were required to relinquish much and, too often, all; those at home, they believed, gave up almost nothing. When the GI looked back, Mauldin reported, what he saw at home was selfishness. "All he knows is that he expected to make great sacrifices for little compensation, and he must make those sacrifices whether he likes it or not. Don't expect him to weigh [this] complicated problem before he gets sore. He knows he delivered and somebody else didn't." Observed surgeon Brendan Phibbs of the infantrymen around him, "They grasped slowly and in fragments what had been the truth of their lives all along: they were the ultimate sacrifice of the whole war. . . ."[83]

More serious than the disparity itself was society's failure, or refusal, to recognize it. Civilians seemed to miss vital distinctions between themselves and combat soldiers. As Eric Sevareid said, "The nation was encouraged to believe that it could produce its way to victory. . . ." In a war of production, producers were able to entertain thoughts that their contribution was almost commensurate with that of combatants. Civilians, moreover, often neglected to differentiate the roles of combat and support soldiers. The public, Marine sergeant Gilbert Bailey charged sardonically, "makes little . . . distinction between a man who faces death every day and another who is simply overseas. They all wear the same ribbons and tell the same stories."[84]

Without awareness of the distinct parts played by public, rear-echelon forces, and fighting men, civilians would never comprehend their own good fortune. A jungle rot case discharged early sent word back to his friends in the Pacific: "It's a small price the people back here pay for victory and they . . . will never understand how lucky they are." Worse, with no sense of how dramatically they were benefiting, civilians would not realize how little favored combat soldiers were. Phibbs was angry: Nobody "would know or care that they . . . had pulled the whole war machine forward." Clearly, many at home continued to measure their own situation with little regard for that of soldiers at the front.[85]

Almost all American families were better off because of the war effort. As early as 1940, seven million of the unemployed had found jobs—and soon another seven million who had not worked before. Between 1941 and 1945, wages rose 68 percent while the cost of living climbed only 23 percent. Americans' first reaction was to sigh in relief at their deliverance from the depression. A Kentucky woman remembered that

> The first work I had after the Depression was at a shell-loading plant in Viola. . . .
> We made the fabulous sum of thirty-two dollars a week. To us it was just an absolute miracle. Before that, we made nothing. . . . It didn't occur to us that we

were making these shells to kill people. It never entered my head. . . . We were just a bunch of hillbilly women laughin' and talkin'. It was like a social. Now we'd have money to buy shoes and a dress and pay rent and get some food on the table.[86]

Soon, however, the wartime level of economic activity became the basis of civilian expectations, and the new norm was already in place when government controls began to tighten. Heating oil and gasoline, meat, sugar, coffee, cooking oils, and fats were rationed; butter, bananas, and chocolate became scarce; race tracks were closed down and nightclubs subjected to curfews. Those who then surveyed their stations against returned prosperity began to feel deprivation—and to include in their letters overseas expressions of their dissatisfaction. Many no doubt wrote in well-meant efforts to suggest to their soldiers that they too were sacrificing, but front-line reaction was scathing. Marines in the Pacific who learned that Mrs. Roosevelt had resolved not to serve butter at the White House thought it "Too God-damned bad!" In Europe, Lester Atwell mocked civilian sacrifice: "I had no idea of the privations at home! The things one went through at the butcher shops!" Audie Murphy met a friend returning to the front following treatment for trench foot.

> While waiting at the aid station, I read some old Chicago papers.
> What's new? . . .
> The cigarette shortage continues; and people are demanding an explanation for the scarcity of tobacco.
> My piles bleed for them.
> The public is warned that meat rationing will be more severe in coming months.
> Meat?
> Yeah. The kind that doesn't come in cans. Remember?
> Lord, yes. Steak.
> Night clubs may be forced to close at midnight to conserve fuel and the energies of factory workers who like to guzzle too late.
> I can't stand it. . . .[87]

There emerged among soldiers a new civilian composite—lazy, easily diverted by the prospect of partying, uncaring, corruptible—and news from home became a major source of grievance. Most alarming were domestic developments soldiers judged directly antagonistic to their survival, notably production failures that created deficiencies in materiel.

When gunner Odell Dobson's B-24 was shot down over Europe, his legs were mangled as he parachuted from the plane. On the ground, in piercing pain, he rummaged in his kit. The morphine phial was there—but it was empty! Furious, he cast about for the culprit. A fraudulent contractor, a negligent inspector, a lazy woman worker?[88]

As Ernie Pyle visited an artillery battery, one of its gun crews discovered that it was about to use a charge with the required quantity of powder promised on the outside of the bag but only half of that quantity actually in it. "If we'd shot that little one the shell would have landed on the battery just ahead." The artillerymen too speculated on culpability. "Some defense worker who had to work on Sunday made that one. He was too tired to fill it up, the poor fellow" . . . "Guess somebody had worked eight hours already . . . and made twenty or thirty dollars for it and had to work overtime at time-and-a-half and was just worn out" . . . "Or somebody who had to drive all of three or four miles after work to a cocktail bar and he was in too big a hurry to finish this one. It sure is tough on the poor defense workers."[89]

On Guadalcanal, James Jones recounted, a grenade exploded a half-second after leaving the hand of an American lieutenant who, if he was lucky, may have lost only fingers. "Some lady defense-plant worker in sexy bluejeans had been talking to her neighbor on the assembly-line," Jones imagined, "about her new dress or new lover and mismeasured her fuse-cutting."[90]

Infantrymen about to assault a German position near Herrlisheim discovered that their artillery support had shells sufficient for only two minutes of covering fire. "All them goddamn factories, Pittsburgh, Detroit" . . . "Nobody shooting at them; they got enough to eat, they got good places to sleep. You'd think they could make enough ammunition."[91]

Civilian assembly-line mistakes were reprehensible, but the intentional withholding of production was unpardonable. No subject agitated soldiers as did civilian strikes. "There was one thing concerning home life that soldiers were absolutely rabid on," wrote Ernie Pyle from North Africa, ". . . strikes. Just mention a strike at home to either a soldier or officer, living on monotonous rations in the mud under frequent bombing, and you had a raving maniac on your hands." Coast artilleryman Win Stracke remembered in the same theater "heated discussions when John L. Lewis pulled out the miners. Oh, the terrible bitterness. 'Those sons-o-bitchin' miners are makin' a hundred and fifty or two hundred bucks a week and we're bustin' our asses for a hundred dollars a month. They oughta string 'em up.'" "I have only one regret," a Marine on Tarawa told a correspondent, "that John L. Lewis is not beside me." "He wouldn't be alive," interjected another Marine, "if he was beside me. I don't mean the Japs would kill him. I would." At a supply depot on Eniwetok, a logistics officer entreated John Dos Passos: "What I want you to explain to me is why we tolerate these strikes back home. My men get all hot and bothered so that they can't do their work; whenever they get a home town paper or a letter in the mail they just about blow their top."[92]

Worse, labor problems pursued soldiers even into the war zones. "And then we get these merchant marine boys[, crewmen who] can't do this and can't do that because the union won't let them. Looks like the only thing the union would let them do is to sit on their ass and get paid. There have been cases where Marines have been taken out of action when there weren't enough able-bodied men left to defend the perimeter because our gallant merchant seamen refused to unload the ships. . . . Christ!" Robert Sherrod found that soldier attitudes toward labor were "savage"; he pictured "some ten million angry men." Strikes seemed the cruelest consequence of the homefolks' fundamental misconception of the war: "Surely, no sane man would dream of striking against his own soldiers if he understood what war was like."[93]

Business did not escape criticism—not entirely. There was disgust with corporations whose newspaper and magazine advertisements puffed products they claimed were winning the war, but such boasting was an affront to the soldier's amour propre, not a threat to his survival. The black market did involve businessmen—small-scale rather than large, local storeowners rather than chains, independent butchers rather than major packers—but seldom did evasions of price control and rationing, or even cases of profiteering and corruption, reach (in recognizable form) all the way to the front. Corporations drew some irritation from soldiers but little of the ire directed at unions.[94]

Soldiers did not exempt businessmen, or any other civilian, from their most comprehensive indictment, that materialism had overwhelmed American society. As money became less useful to the soldiers, they easily concluded that it had become far too vital to those at home. In mid-1942, Technical Sergeant Lee Merson wrote to his father: "What is going on there? . . . [My] July 13 issue of *Time* [with its news of a failed scrap rubber drive, low war-bond sales, and worker demands] makes me sick and bitter. . . . While all over the world men are being shot to pieces, other men . . . are quibbling about dollars. . . . [Everyone] is out to get whatever he can from this unprecedented opportunity. . . . [Complacent] people are playing with human lives!" For many servicemen, money-grubbing became a dominant image of home. As Samuel Hynes and other Marine pilots partied in an officers club on Saipan, his friend Joe sang a "Casey Jones" whose lyrics he altered to lament a plane crash rather than a train wreck. The search for the pilot, he recounted, uncovered only spots, "hundreds and hundreds of spots"; all then joined in a chorus anticipating the government's payment of insurance benefits to the dead man's survivors:

> Ten thousand dollars going home to the folks.
> Ten thousand dollars going home to the folks.
> Oh won't they be delighted!
> Won't they be excited!
> Think of all the things that they can buy![95]

At bottom, such sentiments signaled the distress of soldiers attempting to accommodate two social environments, both vital to them (one enduringly; one only transiently, they hoped). They tried—and failed, their efforts broken by the dissonance between battle and economic boom. To GIs, it was, in James Jones's phrase, "a new world that seemed to have gone crazy with both destruction and a lavish prosperity."[96]

One of the few letters less welcome than those describing the deprivations thought to be suffered at home was that from the acquaintance who bragged that he knew everyone and, wartime regulations not withstanding, could get everything. The soldier's fear that American society had become replete with "operators," many little older than he, aggravated an earlier grievance against all of his male peers who had remained civilians. PFC Thomas Raulston, a paratrooper wounded in Normandy, wrote to his parents from a hospital bed in England: "How the guys at home can lift their heads is beyond me." "When I think of some of those 4-F, draft-dodging bastards I know back home," Kerrigan railed at Audie Murphy, "I want to spit nails." In that category of civilians that he labeled the "most despised," Paul Fussell placed "the 4-F or physically unfit and thus defective, the more despicable the more invisible the defect, like a heart murmur, punctured ear-drum or flat feet." Maladies; disqualifying conditions? What GI had not collected both in the course of campaigning?[97]

Fighting men leaped easily from any contemplation of contemporaries who remained where soldiers wished to be, doing what soldiers wished to do, to the conviction they were deficient morally and socially. In August 1944, Henry Giles met with fellow soldiers, "Sammie and other fellows from near home," to exchange news of Kentucky. "By the time we got it all put together we had a pretty good picture of what it's like back there. One thing is sure. All the fellows our age have gone to war." But seven months later, alarmed when he read in *Stars and Stripes* that units in Europe would be transferred rapidly and directly to fight the Japanese in the Pacific, Giles trembled with anger. Why pick on us? he argued, when there were at home "4-Fs by the millions."

The more fragile became the soldier's sense of his own survival, the more intolerable grew the thought of contemporaries safe at home.[98]

Lee Merson concluded that querulous letter to his father, "[My] mind becomes corroded with what I read [of the home front]. What a ludicrous and tragic situation that soldiers must beg, actually beg, for arms to defend people who, by their very actions, don't seem to give a damn. Yes, Dad, tell them that my mind is sick and bitter." It was true, indeed tragic, that civilians lacked all but a semblance of the soldiers' view of war, but the sweep and severity of Merson's censure, so common among infantrymen in the last phases of the war, lacked any reasonable foundation. With soldiers and civilians dominated by dramatically different perspectives, the soldiers' view of home was as unfair as civilians' view of the war front was uncomprehending.[99]

Contrary to front-line conviction, most civilians were aware that soldiers sacrificed as they did not. Studying the polls, Allan Winkler reported that "By the middle of the conflict, nearly seven of ten people in the United States said they had not had to make any 'real sacrifices' as a result of the war." Most worked hard in behalf of the war effort. Michigan's Willow Run B-24 bomber plant operated the clock around; ten-hour workdays, six-day workweeks were common. Design engineer George Sunal considered work there "strictly business. There were no coffee breaks and music wasn't allowed. . . . You felt you were a part of each plane we made. You were at the plant so much you practically lived there." Stephen Ailes, who worked for the Office of Price Administration, the federal agency administering the rationing system, reported, "You just routinely worked till midnight; you worked Saturdays. You always had in mind the fact that all these guys were in foxholes someplace or sitting out on some cold deck somewhere. All of us had relatives and pals doing that." Merson's cry that those at home were "people who . . . don't seem to give a damn" drew on soldier anger, not social reality.[100]

The effort at home, beyond setting in motion the economic recovery that quickly roared into prosperity, bolstered citizens' attitudes toward the nation. A California shipyard worker rose from third-class machinist to progressman and, with pay and overtime, found himself with "more money than I had ever heard of." "[The] war did great things for me"—and for his estimate of the United States. "During the Depression, I was really feeling bad about this country," but the mammoth, cooperative exertion of the mobilization for war had led him to "really love [it] again. It made you think you were living in a great country. It made you proud to be an American." When in the early war years radio brought "The Star-Spangled Banner" into living rooms, families commonly rose to their feet. A sense of shared purpose fostered an excitement that seemed almost palpable. A teacher turned war factory worker explained: "In knowing that I am REALLY doing something to help us beat the Axis, there is a certain calm, yet thrilling feeling of satisfaction which can be compared with no compensation from any other type of work." The nation was not as united a people as the government professed or as white Americans assumed, but the perception of a singular enterprise requiring and meriting the efforts of all—"You just felt that the stranger sitting next to you, in a restaurant or someplace, felt the same way you did"— was more comprehensive and compelling than at any other time in this century.[101]

Nothing served to connect people more rapidly or cohesively than direct participation in war production; but beyond that work lay a realm of almost equivalent psychological import, quasi-military mobilization. Adults flocked to local defense groups to train as block wardens, blackout checkers, aircraft spotters, first-aid medics, auxiliary police, and the collection drive volunteers who solicited their neighbors' kitchen fats, old newspapers, tin cans, scrap metal, and rubber. Many of those who remained beyond such organizations still engendered a spirit of participation by conserving scarce materials, by growing vegetables in backyard "victory gardens," by buying war stamps and war bonds.[102]

And many of these activities made room for children. A twelve-year-old Wichita girl purchased a war stamp each time she was able to accumulate twenty-five cents in coins; saved the family's newspapers, metal, rubber; rode her bicycle sparingly (to save tire wear); and, with other Girl Scouts, ran errands and baby-sat for war-worker families. Boys too participated—and moved on to make common cause with combat soldiers via Saturday-afternoon war movies, late weekday afternoon radio serials, *True* and *Action* comic books. Informal neighborhood enlistments introduced them to vacant-lot foxholes, tree-hut observation posts, pipe and broomstick rifles; to firepumps, hoses, helmets, and gas masks temporarily appropriated from their warden fathers; to war games waged against the gang down the block.[103]

Anne Bosanko Green, a WAC during the war, remembered "the slight tingle of danger and the unknown [that] gave the kind of excitement that leads today's adventurers to polar expeditions and space exploration. We were all adventurers in those days." A jot of jeopardy; a cause incontrovertible yet sufficiently urgent to prod the linking of effort; engrossing activities appearing to advance the cause (and thus justifying any economic dividends that might accrue)—civilians believed that *they were* fighting the war. That many soldiers were persuaded they were not would have astonished them.[104]

Americans who returned from overseas during the war rediscovered, in accord with individual perspective, one of two very different Americas. Photographer-writer Carl Mydans, released from a relatively mild internment in a Japanese camp for civilians; correspondent Robert Sherrod, with the battle for Tarawa still vivid in his mind; Army nurse Theresa Archard, evacuated in exhaustion after ministering to the wounded of North African and Sicilian campaigns—all three came home in December 1943 or January 1944.

The nation he had not seen in three years deeply impressed Mydans: "The national adjustment had been completed and the . . . entire war effort was, in an American way, moving along a kind of never-ending conveyor belt. And coming out of another world, we found the United States awesome, dramatically resolved, powerful beyond belief: a homeland inspired"—and, he added, suffering a sense of guilt that others were being shot at and bombed. Sherrod, in contrast, weighed home scenes against the Marine casualties he had witnessed and found "a nation wallowing in unprecedented prosperity"; everywhere people indulged strikes while themselves "lobbying for special privilege." Home-front Americans "were not prepared psychologically to accept the cruel facts of war." Nurse Archard's view was like Sherrod's: "[S]o many people insensitive to the reality of a world at war and its tragedies beyond number, concerned only with the way it might be inconveniencing them . . . [complaining] because of a shortage of luxuries. . . . Many Americans . . . were doing their part. . . . But there were all too many who were not worthy to be called Americans—people who were making more money [and] hoping to continue to do so at the expense of the lives, the misery, and the sacrifices of others." The contrast between battlefront and home front was too stark to be borne; the shock that jolted Archard, Sherrod, and early returning combat soldiers colored darkly their reactions to the homeland.[105]

Yes, civilians complained; but set against the extent to which a people not directly threatened by war accepted wartime controls, resistance and evasion remained of minor consequence. The extensive exposure of non-cooperation won approval as a means of bringing down shame and punishment on the violators of wartime norms. Soldiers, however, read those stories as indicators of common conduct. Coming upon a newspaper account of a young woman convicted of disorderly conduct and fined ten dollars for "meeting and entertaining" a prisoner of war working in her cannery, GIs were likely to pass over her chastisement and subsequent isolation, and to find in her story a confirmation of their worst fears of change at home: American women were sleeping with German soldiers. *Conquer the Clock*, a

film in RKO's *This Is America* series, told a cautionary tale of a female defense worker who left the assembly line long enough to sneak a cigarette in
the restroom; cartridges that passed without primers while she was away
caused a weapon to misfire and a soldier to die. Such narratives were exhorta-
tions to raise production standards, not acknowledgments that carelessness
was the standard.[106]

Soldiers could not see behind accounts of strikes and black marketeering
the coalescence of attitudes almost as disapproving, if not as heartfelt, as their
own. Historian Geoffrey Perrett found at home "a widespread demand that
labor, especially in defense plants, be denied the right to strike." Economist
John Kenneth Galbraith concluded that "There was a black market, but it was
small. There were troublesome moments in the case of meat, but there was a
great deal of obloquy attached to illegal behavior." Passengers on a Kentucky
bus who overheard a woman say that she hoped the war would not end until
she completed payments on her refrigerator did nothing to restrain the old man
who shouted "How dare you!" and hit her over the head with his umbrella. The
home front wielded its own Don't-they-know-there's-a-war-on complaints almost as disdainfully as soldiers mobilized them against the home front.[107]

A few soldiers, to be sure, evinced insight into difficult aspects of home
life that most of their comrades seldom considered. Infantrymen loathed the
waiting—between training and first combat, prior to landings and ground
assaults, and so on—but rarely did they give thought to the onerousness of
waiting at home. An exception was John Dye, who while still in pilot training began "to realize how much tougher it is for the ones we . . . leave behind. Those of us who . . . 'do the job' are really so very much more fortunate
than are those who fight our single battle for us . . . a hundred times more
fiercely in the imagination of a quiet night. For they must 'sweat out' every
moment of every long day while we must only brace our minds and bodies
for the rough going periodically. . . ." Dye held in his mind the family of a
friend killed in the explosion of his plane: its members must be begging "for
an answer where no answer is. . . . For [the dead pilot] it was a problem for
ten seconds—and then he had his answer. . . . But who can tell how long his
mother will have to wait for her answer?" War correspondent Richard Tobin,
thinking of his wife as he left for the war zone in April 1944, suddenly understood that "It is far easier for a man to face danger or pain himself than
for someone who loves him but cannot be there, cannot feel and share the
actual pain," but would fear it nonetheless and would imagine it repeatedly
until the arrival of the government's telegram or the return of the soldier.[108]

On rare occasions GIs did debate the issue. When Grady Arrington received a letter from a woman whose feelings for him were cooling and read there her complaints about shortages at home, he exploded.

> Isn't it just too God-damn bad that those poor civilians can't live exactly as they did before the war! Man, they've really got it rough—sugar and coffee rationed; maybe can't have but three or four cups a day now! Hell, they can't find a big juicy T-bone in every restaurant . . . can't get rubber tires for pleasure [riding] . . . have to walk once in a while. Walk! Walk! Get that, Thaxton, *walk!*

"I don't know, buddy"—Thaxton gentled his irate friend—"their part in this war is not too damn easy. Sometimes it is harder on our parents . . . who pray and wait, not knowing whether we're dead or alive. Death doesn't come so cheaply to them as it does to us; we see it every day." But Thaxton's case was grounded in speculation about the reactions of distant others; it could not carry the force of those battlefield realities responsible for the infantryman's immediate distress. The sarcasm of "Man, they've really got it rough" prevailed.[109]

Toward the end of the war, soldier feelings about the home front, intensified by the infantry's sense of separation from other arms and the rear echelon, often incorporated visions of conspiracy and betrayal edging on paranoia. Soldiers envisaging themselves as targets had long before conceded that they might at any time become victims of the enemy; now they also felt assailable by all who were more distant from battle than the regimental command post.

John George set out the reasoning of GIs around him on Guadalcanal.

> A Doughboy's weapon is broken or worn out—so . . . Ordnance is no good; he is short of food—so the [Quartermaster] is a bunch of fat-butted, useless deadheads; his head is tight and buzzing with fever, so the Medical Corps—other than his own Infantry medics—is an aggregation of military drones. The soldier sees himself the victim of a huge conspiracy, with the enemy, the elements, and even his own countrymen allied against him. If he lives through his ordeal of combat without becoming a confirmed cynic, he is lucky.[110]

Combat surgeon Phibbs later testified to that hostility soldiers' imaginations stretched from just behind the line to their doorsteps at home and should have extended, he thought, from their wartime present to their peacetime futures.

> . . . the world behind them drank the liquor they had liberated and slept in the beds they had fought for and made fortunes selling them stuff to fight with and screwed their girlfriends and stole their jobs.

[And] all their sacrifice was going to mean exactly nothing when they went home. . . . They were going to be poor while others would have grown rich. Fat, safe generals from plush-lined headquarters would make speeches at banquets and hand each other medals and call each other heroes, and at American Legion halls the parasites from the quartermaster battalions would wave flags and scream about patriotism. . . .[111]

From his own suspicion that many countrymen were desecrating the infantry's sacrifice Klaus Huebner drew images even more malignant: "My mother speaks of threatened unemployment in the U.S.A. since war contracts are rumored to be on the decline. It sounds as though some folks at home are enjoying this endless killing and are afraid that it may come to a sudden end and some may lose their well-paying jobs."[112]

Such was the explosive expansion of anxiety about the battlefield enemy to encompass all who would not grasp war as a process of killing and above all of dying. Here soldiers became so angry that they wished first to summon civilians to share their suffering and then to send home samples of war's destructiveness. "News from home is good," Sy Kahn recorded in his diary. "Dick and Ginger write that the war is still far away from them. [In these damnable bombings] it's not far away from me. . . . I got a little angry last night, pacing up and down the tent, after reading in some letters about dances, gay weekends, college. If only they could experience one raid, even one alert, sitting next to [my] foxhole, half asleep in the dark, nerves raw to every sound." Marine Eugene Sledge "heard more than one buddy express the opinion, as we sat in the mud, that civilians would 'understand' if the Japanese or the Germans bombed an American city." Tom Harmon, All-American football player become P-38 pilot in China, included in a number of his wartime speeches at home and in his 1944 autobiography the view that "perhaps it was too bad that the United States had never been bombed because Americans didn't seem to appreciate the horrors of war and the sacrifices it imposed. . . ."[113]

At bottom, such imprecations signaled more pain than malice. Many of the particulars of the infantry's indictment of the home front possessed some substance; others were baseless or, more often, exaggerated. But in accounting for the combat soldier's breach with home, the materiality of the charges was far less crucial than the persistence of the two ineradicable facts to which he owed his separation from all except the comrades around him: Others did not understand the experience through which he was passing, and, most commanding, while they were elsewhere, he was there, in battle.

CONCLUSION
The World Within War

Soldiers more and more aware of their separation from earlier sources of support in and beyond the war zone contended at the same time with battle's capacity to deepen their isolation by drawing them deep within its own sphere. At risk were relationships that soldiers had assumed so fundamental to their existence as to be immutable.

Combat altered the fighting man's sense of time, first by erasing the accustomed markers of its passage. Lost were those familiar points of the day that had signaled regular changes of activity. On Guadalcanal, Grady Gallant sensed, battle created "a new order of living"; it "wipes out the meal hours" and "removes bedtime." Mornings and afternoons so coalesced that it meant nothing "whether it is 8 a.m., or 11 a.m., or 3 p.m." Even days and nights merged when fighting, and its fears persisted around the clock. Brooding over 144 unbroken hours under fire, Geddes Mumford realized that his "conception of time in terms of days and nights was completely gone. I can remember experiences but not with relativity to days. . . ." Gallant too: "Now the day is really twenty-four hours long with no discernible division between it and the day before, or the day following."[1]

As awareness of daily cycles waned, so did any sensitivity to the day's position in such larger indices as days of the week or dates of the month. When his thoughts singled out a day in November 1944, Henry Giles was surprised. "Saturday. It was always the day back in the states when we all got passes, went into town and painted it red. Just another day, now. Have to look at the calendar to know what day of the week or month it is. You couldn't tell by anything that happens." All consciousness of day and date slipped away from

Frank Irgang: "[I]t did not matter." Days special at home lost themselves in the anonymity of days at the front. "Pinkie just stuck his head in and said the mail wouldn't be up tonight . . . ," Giles recorded in his journal. "He drew his head back, then stuck it back in. 'Did you know today is Easter?' I said I didn't. He said, 'It is.' And that was that. Just another day to us."[2]

Time, playing other tricks on men under fire, alternately compressed and extended its movement. When rare excitation dominated the soldier's emotions, time sped. "I do not know how long I lay watching all this," reported Ralph Ingersoll of an early North African battle, "or when the intense excitement of the scene began to wear off. . . . [T]here seemed [to be] no time." Only when a leg messaged that it had cramped did he realize that time had passed. When fright filled the soldier, time slowed almost intolerably. As his aircraft approached the target on Maloelap, navigator Bernard McKenna nervously consulted his watch five times—"and each time it said ten minutes to one." During the enemy's conquest of Corregidor, Ben Waldron "shot two or three Japs with my .45. . . . I was out of breath and scared to die. It seemed as if I had been fighting for hours when actually the skirmish only lasted a few minutes. Everything seemed to move in slow motion. You could shoot a man and watch all his reflex actions before he fell to the ground."[3]

The bunching and stretching of minutes was, however, particular to intense combat and thus of limited duration. More momentous was the soldier's enduring sense that time had flattened out and would extend itself infinitely in replication of the present instant. The moment came to dominate the consciousness of combat veterans, a development requiring no effort on their part. Ernest Hemingway's advice that soldiers focus themselves to live "completely in the very second of the present minute" was gratuitous; combat pressed them to it. An assault on Saint-Lô exhausted PFC Frank Globuschutz. "I didn't know if I could go on much longer. This seemed like the end of everything. . . . There was no memory of any time before being here, under fire. [Combat] was all there was." Paratrooper Critchell and his friends "had become veteran troops. . . . We had no memories and no future; we lived . . . completely in the present." Battle obliterated the past. A serious but survivable wound, capture, or the end of the war might restore a future; but fighters believing death far more certain did not resist combat's compelling immediacy, even when what remained of time, the moment multiplied perpetually, became an unbearable vision. "Now time becomes a dreary succession of light and darkness," Audie Murphy cried out; ". . . the endless cycle of hours ticks its way into eternity."[4]

This conviction that combat had reduced soldiers' lives to an infinite extension of what Gallant called "the living instant" became partner to another, that the war itself would be without end. As the moment overwhelmed time, subjugating past and future; as combat came to control the moment, even when soldiers were temporarily freed of fighting; as each clash succeeded the last in sheer iteration of tactics and techniques, battle became limitless. The termination of an attack brought the survivors nothing beyond the shallowest relief, as James Jones knew. "Even if they had captured this whole ridge, nothing would have ended. Because tomorrow, or the day after, or the day after that, they would be called upon to do the same thing again—maybe under even worse circumstances. The concept was so overpowering, so numbing that it shook [the soldier]. Island after island, hill after hill, beachhead after beachhead. It staggered him." And its end (presuming there was one) would be so remote as to have "no connection with any individual engaged now. *Some* men would survive, but no *one* individual man [fighting today] *could* survive." Wrote Harry Brown,

> In the last war, they sent a guy to France. That was all there was to it. . . . Then he went home. . . . Real simple. . . . But what do they do this time? . . . They send you to Tunisia, and then they send you to Sicily, and they send you to Italy. God knows where they'll send you after that. Maybe we'll be in France next year. . . . Then we work our way east. Yugoslavia. Greece. Turkey. No, not Turkey. All I know is, in 1958, we're going to fight the Battle of Tibet.

"I sit down beside Kerrigan," Audie Murphy remembered. "My eyeballs burn; my bones ache; and my muscles twitch from exhaustion. Oh, to sleep and never awaken. The war is without beginning, without end. It goes on forever."[5]

Absorption in the moment set off other shifts in basic behavior premised on the relevance of a past and the assurance of a future. Soldiers' intellectual interests and even cognitive concentration eroded. The minority to whom books had been sustaining soon found the contents trivial and extraneous to their war lives: "Whatever I read, even about the war, seems to vanish into [an] abyss." Many combat soldiers became anxious that they had ceased to learn anything new and were losing all acuity of thought. Marine David Brown blamed the Pacific environment: "The sun and the sand, the sea and the unvaried scenery seem to leave the mind to rot and stagnate like a sultry swamp." But John Dye found the problem no less distressing in Foggia, Italy, even as he hoped that its effects would disappear if the war were ever to end. "It is almost as if the mental processes had closed up shop and [were] merely riding out a kind of storm."[6]

Simultaneous with the shriveling of mental activity, but more pronounced, was the smothering of affect. Drastically diminished feeling attended the men's debilitation ("We were all too exhausted to react, and almost nothing stirred our emotions"); their coarsening ("we learned to live . . . as simple as animals without hope for ourselves or pity for one another"); and their resignation in the face of forces more powerful than they ("But now I was just a paratrooper captain . . . reduced to insignificance by all [those] big, lumbering Sherman tanks"). "The war," Lester Atwell noticed, "seemed to affect many of our men that way. Nothing went deeply; no impression remained. Just get the main facts as quickly as possible, then the hell, forget it, move on to something else." Amid intense fighting, the captain's return to the company relieved Audie Murphy of command and suddenly opened to him a liaison assignment removed from combat. Here, amazingly, was "the gift of life," he knew; but no "inward emotion" rose to meet his release from imminent death. "I am so much a part of the war now that it does not matter."[7]

As combat merged past and future with the present, so did it dissolve distinctions between other fundamental concepts that soldiers had thought autonomous.

Whatever verdict headquarters officers and correspondents attached to a particular clash—that is, to a small segment snatched from the soldier's seemingly indivisible band of battle—for him continuous warmaking melded victory and defeat. Winning and losing bled into one another. Early in the war, soldiers had ceased to interest themselves in the outcome of battles on other fronts, a situation on which Bill Mauldin turned his customary candor: "If nothing is happening to [the GI in his foxhole] and he is able to relax that day, then it is a good war, no matter what is going on elsewhere." And soon soldiers lost much of the differentiation between winning and losing even within their own sphere. Ernie Pyle watched a column of infantrymen plod up a path through North African hills. "In their eyes . . . was no hatred, no excitement, no despair, no tonic of their victory—there was just the simple expression of being there as if they had been there doing that forever, and nothing else."[8]

Those at home would have been shocked to learn that within their soldiers' altered framework, even life and death became fuzzy and equivocal. To men who each day regarded their existence as less anchored in the realm of the living, life and death yielded their polarity and moved toward fusion. Battle took from Marine captain Cord Meyer, Jr., almost all the friends who had passed through Brigade School with him; on Guam, a Japanese grenade took three of his teeth, an eye, and nearly his life. He was, he began to feel, "a little out of place among the living." On Okinawa, the dead summoned Elvis Lane. "Corpses litter the gray, muddy landscape. There [is] an occasional head. . . . Some of the corpses seem to be grinning. . . . I am afraid that if I stare, one [of them] might ask: 'Don't you belong with us?' And another . . . : 'The war isn't over! You'll soon be joining us!'" For the twenty-six who remained alive after the 296 infantrymen of Company B, 115th Regiment, 29th Division, had twice futilely attacked Normandy's Sainte-Marguerite, death had relinquished its alien quality; it beckoned, in a fashion not unfriendly, as their only reprieve from battle. "They figured that they were committed to die, that there would be no rest until they did."9

When he wrote to his sister from the Pacific, David Brown first erased most of the line separating life and death, and then he too drew death as scarcely less appealing than life. "[All] of us feel the reality of death in a new way, as if *we ourselves* had already gone over *there.* . . ." With so many of his comrades dead, only half of him remained alive; the other half had

> gone into that land of shadow—which is also destined to be ours. . . . [It] would be just as cheerful for us over there as here, with so many friends gone over. It seems quite *natural:* except that we shrink from whatever pain there is, and don't want to leave undone whatever we might accomplish in a normally long life. . . . [But when] we see how quickly good men fall, it is plain . . . to see all that's left [for us]. That *this* life is the shadow, not the other.10

As the soldier became more persuaded that he was moving toward his end, the less compelling became the forces of life ordinarily sustaining stout resistance to death.

The loss of mental focus on all save the rudiments of survival; the petrifaction of emotional reaction to events in and beyond battle; the reiteration of the combat moment into an apparently endless war whose sole movement was the approach of one's death, now resisted less by the will than by habit and reflex—here was the play of forces that immured combat veterans within the world of war.

Young American men had entered the war effortlessly accepting that home, the world they were leaving, was the only world, and that their military service would function solely as an intermission in their stateside lives. They knew they would find in war no extension of home life, but they expected to remain firmly attached to home throughout an experience they undertook as intriguing and important. Collisions with military discipline and with conditions in other nations at war shook them, but dissonance at first only lent poignancy to the everyday life left behind. Home shone brighter than ever. Once contending with combat, however, soldiers realized that they would be unable to confine war within their accustomed orders of experience. Violence, fear, hardship, and hurt quickly vaulted them beyond the mere contemplation of differences between war and home to an awareness of stark separation from home. "The thousands of miles," fretted David Brown on New Britain, "seem like thousands of years, as if everything were happening on a different planet." Soon war created an alternative world—"It seems," said John Toole, "like war has become a way of life"—and compelled soldiers to concede that it was encasing them. Orval Faubus surely puzzled those at home when he told them, "The war is our world and our life"—and then alarmed them: ". . . and the other one we know fades away."[11]

So imperious were front-line demands that they threatened to obliterate that other, very recent existence. Said Watson of the fighting on New Georgia: "I got so, after being in the line for almost two months, that I forgot I had ever lived any place else." "Does that other world exist?" wondered one of John Burns's soldiers. "I can't remember the time when I was a part of it." Marines on Guadalcanal, Jim Lucas reported, became convinced that "There had never been any life but this one. The rest was a mirage." Here soldiers arrived at a juncture signaling change profound and irrevocable. James Johns watched the evacuation of casualties from Guadalcanal. "They were dirty, sick, ragged; their eyes looked as if they had been to hell and back. I remember wondering how they could ever be the same again. . . . Many of them never were. I don't suppose any of us ever were." Combat soldiers began to think of themselves as perpetually set apart.[12]

Like the prisoner without possibility of parole gradually accustoming himself to his cell, the soldier gauged that any chance of survival lay in totally inuring himself to the world within war. Thoughts of that other, fading world would only resuscitate hope of returning to it; hope would revive the fear that it could not possibly happen and the aching futility of wishing that it could. Here was the way to demoralization. Better not to think of those one had loved at home. "I'm sure it is best," Faubus knew, "that we do not remember too much. Perhaps it is nature's way of protecting us from a memory that would be too painful because of its remoteness and inaccessibility. As for me, I have put my pictures and mementos away and may . . . not look at them again until this business is well over with."[13]

Another thrust toward divorce from home emerged from the soldier's consciousness of the moral disparity between his actions in the two worlds. "We fought," infantryman Leon Standifer was sure, ". . . because we believed that we would be able to serve honorably. I am afraid we all found that that is impossible." A despondent Grady Arrington realized that in one day of battle he had trespassed, lied, cheated, stolen, and killed. Would the soldier be forgiven, he pondered, when such acts were forced upon him? With questions so agonizing and answers so elusive, fighting men saw in retreat from the civilian world an escape from its moral accountability. "I was an altogether different person in combat than I was before or after," declared Jim Sterner, "just like a different human being." "Drinking and sex and war, they all go together. Doesn't matter if you should or shouldn't, you do," Henry Giles discovered. "[But it's] got nothing to do with the kind of guy you were back home or want to be when you go back." By disconnecting memberships, Grady Arrington for one found the footing to insist that "Only those men who have faced a similar circumstance are capable of judging the rightness of our actions."[14]

Soldiers strove not only to contain such depleting emotion as prolonged fear and anxiety but, as Faubus proposed, to put down sympathetic emotion that, surprisingly, left them equally vulnerable to prostration. Their efforts to confine thought to the basics of battle, sustenance, and survival again constricted the already tight compass of their war lives. In the last of Guadalcanal's battles, Gallant reported, he and his fellow Marines were "in a state of extreme fatigue, malnutrition, and disgust. We had lost our emotions for happiness and enthusiasm. . . . [Our] thoughts turned around a very narrow field, the center of which was food. . . . There was nothing to distract us from the business at hand." Pondering his "Stone Age Life" at the front, William Manchester observed that "Our vision of the war was largely tunnel vision. To each of us the most important place in the world was his foxhole." To Commando Kelly, the combat mind was "single-tracked," turning itself only to such problems as "finding another weapon as fast as I used [this] one up so I could keep on blazing away."[15]

In shrinking thought, soldiers hoped to attain the centerpoint of the world within war, one of a perfect, steady, impenetrable stolidity, a point beyond hope. Marines, wrote James Lucas, "left girl friends and wives back home, and their big desire was to get home to them. But none of them dared dream that that could ever happen." As Watson landed on New Georgia, he "felt something I never felt before. . . . I walked up the beach and I saw the jungle and I knew . . . I was going to the place where I would die." Convinced that "every friend I ever had in the world" was either dead or still fighting near him and that "everything I know about" was on that island, he felt himself utterly absorbed by the world within war.[16]

But soldiers who not long before had been required to repel from their war lives the people and experiences most important to them seldom achieved the impervious stoicism they sought. They contrived varying periods of impassivity, only to find them broken by the intrusion of thoughts or feelings that flayed their senses. Letters from home could pierce their reserve, but so could commonplace experience—the glance, for example, of a soldier almost inured to GI existence at an object not General Issue. Wounded by German fire, Ed Stewart received skilled care at the hands of medics in a schoolhouse-hospital, but then, "They made a deadly mistake. They put white sheets on [the beds]. You looked at those . . . sheets. . . . [Their] white innocence . . . was more than you could bear."[17]

Slight ameliorations might touch off dear, dangerous memories. Faubus considered himself "reconciled to [combat] conditions and danger"—until he received his first clean clothes in three weeks. "If you happen to get a touch of the comforts of peace and civilization it brings back a longing for them that hurts and hurts." Wisps of music could be just as damaging. From a building in a French town, John Toole looked out at a tank in the roadway. "Its radio is playing popular American tunes. The music makes me aware that there is indeed another world devoid of death and suffering. I go into a slump of inexpressible sadness." On Saipan, John Ciardi watched the film *Rhapsody in Blue*. "It was a strong thing to hear Gershwin again. It's too terrific. It fascinated me and suddenly it scared me. . . . I listened to the Rhapsody in Blue and thought I didn't want to die. . . ."[18]

During the fighting's final stages, soldiers bore a crushing sense of the costs that the war had thrust upon them—and of the absence of any reparative return. Far more troubling than deteriorating mental function and cramping emotion was their recognition that they could no longer *act* at accustomed levels of individual effectiveness. In the heedless confidence that they brought to military service, they had been sure they would remain at or near the center of events in which they participated. Military authoritarianism soon stripped some of that faith but still left them unprepared for combat, or for a loss of efficacy so complete that they often felt helpless. Consider the ordinary pattern of movement at the front—troops told little, rousted with only minutes' notice, ordered to march or mount trucks, deposited at destinations unknown to them, sent just as peremptorily into battle or into reserve. Conscious of themselves as captives of repetitive, mechanical movement, contending with unrelenting fear, infantrymen too long in combat came to feel numb, spent, and enfeebled. John Bassett caught in his journal a brief span indistinguishable from the whole of the Italian campaign: "I pushed up tight against the bank. It's no good to keep going, it's all fucked up, it's crazy, but what the hell can I do? Just move along when they tell me to. The line moved again and I with it. . . . It didn't matter where we were going either. I was just going somewhere with my squad. . . . Here and there a man would never rise again to move in the line. So it was; while most of us went forward, there were some who stayed behind."[19]

But no matter how determinedly infantrymen tried to harden themselves against combat's shocks by yielding themselves to its current, no matter how separated they felt from the support of other arms, military authority, and the home front, seldom did they achieve any sense of reconciliation with their existence in war. They could not always fend off thoughts that carried them homeward. That they renounced their chances of survival—repeatedly—signaled that they had not dispelled hope of survival. But, had they been successful in sealing themselves within combat, they still would have found there nothing of sufficient worth to justify their presence. Of war, as experience and institution, they became unrelievedly critical; they described it as senseless, wasteful, and futile. Particularly poignant as Allied victory approached was their verdict that there would be no human winners. Watching German POWs, Audie Murphy realized that he shared with them "the knowledge that we carry in our hearts that nobody ultimately wins. . . . Force used tyrannically is our common enemy. Why align ourselves with it in whatever shape or fashion?" William Manchester envisioned Japanese and American participants "united by death, the one great victor in modern war." "The cost in grief and devastation," concluded George Wilson, ". . . is so immensely expensive that no one really wins."[20]

Combat soldiers thus found themselves in painful suspension between the worlds of war and home. Only a dire fatalism offered any alleviation. "Everybody died. What difference did it make? We were trifles in time, a flicker of an eyelash in a million light-years. Death came, sooner or later, and there was no perceptible difference between the two." Perhaps the furies of war would pass by one so little resistant that he would admit both his insignificance as an individual soldier and the impossibility of his survival.[21]

The isolation of the combat soldier manifested itself in a loneliness he seldom discussed. Such feelings were at odds with the masculine ethic. To write of them risked exposing a weakness that those at home might find disappointing or even disgusting. To speak of one's loneliness, even within close relationships surmounting manliness, would rebuke those whose companionship had proved wanting. "We avoided the topic," said Fred Olson of Leinbaugh's company, "as if it didn't exist." Orval Faubus did acknowledge meditating on the subject as he stared at a night sky above Fresnes, France, in November 1944: "the loneliness and longing, which at times wells from our hearts" would, he thought, fill all the space within his gaze and then that ". . . well out beyond the silent stars." After the war, George Gieszl was able to call up his sense of isolation, vivid even amid comrades. "The terrible thing . . . is the utter, complete aloneness. There isn't anything else—just you. Someone can be just two feet from you, but there's nothing there. It's like you're shot into space and there you are [with] that utter aloneness. . . . It's against nature to be in a place like that." Soldiers in battle were uninterested in all but the proximate sources of their loneliness. Whether it inhered in their culture, arising from Americans' "extreme emphasis on individual responsibility," as Rollo May submitted, or whether it proceeded from such military policies as that which brought so many men to battle singly, they left unexamined. Bereft of any broad emotional support that might have checked some of combat's denaturant effects, they simply hurt. Worse, loneliness increased their vulnerability to battlefield disintegration.[22]

In an Army that held its divisions at the front rather than withdrawing them periodically for rest, refitting, and replenishment, soldiers came to feel that they were kept fighting all the time. In 1945, front-line units who were asked in a War Department poll what they would most like changed in the Army responded decisively: "relief from the hard grind of combat." They wanted Washington either to begin the regular rotation of units or to set a limit on the soldier's time in battle. Without hope that either would become policy, however, soldiers grew to accept that continuing in combat made breakdown unavoidable. They were alert to antecedent conditions, beginning with the exhaustion that so often gripped them. Though they acknowledged the medical corps' efforts to treat severe cases, often effectively, with bed and barbiturates, they knew that their problem extended far beyond exhaustion, and they resented the insistence of many commanders that the stress of battle could cause physical but not psychological damage. General Patton, ordinarily solicitous of soldiers felled by combat exhaustion, disdained cases of "so-called" battle fatigue. "A large proportion of men allegedly suffering from [it]," he maintained, "are really using an easy way out." Quick to find cowardice in others, he was certain that "Any man who says he has battle fatigue is avoiding danger." Thinking to enlist soldiers in preventing its spread, he urged them, to no avail, to "make fun" of those who thought themselves afflicted. The commanding officer of the 29th Division,

Major General Norman Cota, pounced on psychiatrists who referred to battle fatigue as a disease. "[N]othing's wrong with most of [those soldiers] that a few hours' rest won't cure."[23]

In the Pacific, too, ranking officers repudiated any psychological component. While in a Guadalcanal field hospital recovering from shrapnel wounds, "Chesty" Puller met an enlisted patient who babbled, whimpered, and trembled. Suspecting artifice, the colonel said to the private, "There's no such thing as shell shock or battle fatigue. All in the mind. Until I got in this war, I never saw a bit of it. We fought all up and down Haiti and Nicaragua without it. You'll be okay." The patient, however, failed to rally, and when Puller found him crying over a photograph of his girlfriend, he was so exasperated that he turned to threats: the Marine Corps would put up pictures of its shirkers in post offices at home; the private's girl would learn of his collapse; she would never look at him again. Dismayed, the young Marine rifleman returned to combat. A hospital doctor congratulated Puller. The ward corpsman tried to put him on report for brutalizing a patient.[24]

To the men on the line, neuropsychiatric collapse was no phantom. They took issue both with those commanders who denied its reality and with those psychiatrists who, while granting its existence, attributed it to the "accumulation of experience" beginning at birth and thus held that soldiers who faltered in battle were those who had entered the service already impaired. Combat soldiers thought otherwise; they had watched the collapse of men they knew to be weak and strong, deceitful and straightforward, doubting and devout. They at first associated psychological damage with weapons injuries, notably blows to the brain, but soon decided that long exposure to deprivation, danger, and the deaths of friends was ample cause. They found no way to determine why some broke down and others went on, why some recovered and others stayed disordered; but with time in combat every man, they became convinced, would arrive at his breaking point.[25]

Soldiers developed their own symptomatology of nervous collapse—at the onset, inattention; then behavior more and more robotic; then the vacant look. The latter, variously called the Thousand- or Two-Thousand-Yard Stare, the Bulkhead Stare, or the Gooney Bird Stare, seemed to mirror, as Pyle proposed, "the accumulated blur, and the hurting vagueness of being too long in the lines." Without medical intervention, such signs presaged crackups of striking variety: spastic tremors; the inane repetition of words or phrases; amnesia; infantile regression; paroxysms of crying, laughing, shrieking; and so on.[26]

In Bioncourt, Faubus met a friend whom he recognized was hovering close to collapse. "He has faded away until he is almost a shadow. His clothes hang loosely. . . . His face is seamed . . . with the many tragedies he has witnessed. His voice is somewhat broken and it is easy to tell, when you hear him speak and look into his eyes, that he is near the breaking point." In Normandy, Glover Johns gaped at a soldier lying on a litter, his eyes closed, his face "twisting horribly," his body jerking, his legs slamming into the air. On Guadalcanal, Marine PFC John Conroy lived "the life of a savage," with "little food or hope—fighting and dying each day—four hours sleep out of seventy-two. . . ." So many of his platoon mates had been killed that he could not sleep ". . . without seeing them die all over again." He suffered a breakdown—and later wrote his parents from a hospital bed: "You keep asking me so I'll tell you. I have been shell-shocked and bomb-shocked. My memory is very dim regarding my civilian days. [The doctors] feel that [another] sudden shock in action now would affect my sanity." In the same campaign, one of Lieutenant Paul Moore's Marines "flipped and went into total hysterics, screaming and yelling in the middle of the night"; then a weapons sergeant cracked, positioned himself tightly against a tree, and threatened to grenade anyone who approached. "This kind of thing," Moore allowed, "happened all the time."[27]

High-command opinion, accepted by many rear-echelon personnel, some psychiatrists, and even some medical investigators, held that the average GI could withstand between 200 and 240 days in combat. Infantrymen countered that experience on the line relegated such claims to grotesque exaggeration. In the Pacific, Sledge estimated, the Stare appeared on fighters' faces after fifteen days. Leinbaugh reckoned that the soldiers around him in the European theater were able to endure seventeen to twenty-one days without breaking. Two psychologists, following the advance beyond Normandy to determine the pattern of deterioration, found that "after the 30th day in combat, the soldier's effectiveness began to decline precipitously, and by the 45th day . . . soldiers . . . were close to a vegetative state." The British ordinarily withdrew their units after twelve days of fighting; many American formations in Europe remained without real respite for sixty days. (Faubus counted his unit's days out of the line during a 184-day period, July 1944–January 1945: fifteen.) The average Marine rifleman serving from Pearl Harbor to the Japanese surrender passed 120 days in combat. The results, however indecipherable in precise magnitudes of collapse, were stark in their aggregate. On Okinawa, American losses totaled 7,613 killed and missing, 31,807 wounded—and 26,211 psychiatric casualties. In European campaigning during 1944, 26 percent of American soldiers suffered nervous breaks. Neuropsychiatric cases accounted for the same proportion of all World War II medical evacuations, one in four.[28]

Trained as a rifleman in the spring of 1944, Aleck Hovsepian soon persuaded his battalion commander to allow him to transfer to G-2 work gathering combat intelligence. After six months on or near the front lines in France, he received his second wound. It alarmed him more than the first because he recognized that the damage was only partially physical. "I'm not badly injured . . . ," he wrote in one of many letters of uncommon candor addressed to his father. "But I guess I'm hurt, Pop. Hurt inside—in my brain. Now, don't get panicky and imagine your son is ready for the booby-hatch. I'm not. I'm just scared. I'm not a coward, Pop. I guess I've proved that . . . but I'm scared of memories. You see, as soon as I'm left with them at night, the little bastards begin to crawl in my brain. . . . [T]hings in life happen and are gone, but [war] memories live and crawl. . . . And there's no way to shake them off."

His memory-bastards were numerous—glimpsing a German corpse whose rigid arms seemed to be "reaching up to God"; leaping upon an enemy whom he was sure was feigning death, only to discover that the man had died twelve hours earlier; coming upon the body of a high-school friend, captured and then bayoneted; standing helplessly as a French friend flashed back to her incarceration in a concentration camp and, mistaking him for a Nazi, slashed first at his breast and then at her own. The worst came while crossing a river just inside Germany. Given sole custody of twenty-five German prisoners to be escorted back within American lines, Hovsepian ordered them to row across the fog-bound water. Then in mid-passage, at a word from their officer, they ceased to pull on their oars and the boat drifted toward a German position. Hovsepian commanded them to resume; they sat still. Riffling thoughts wildly, he could think of only one thing to do: "I was getting pretty scared, so I just shot the first man and pushed him overboard with my foot." Though he waited after each execution, he killed six in five minutes before the Germans sprang to comply. "When the last of them was ashore, the gun fell out of my hand and I went to pieces."

During hospitalization, Hovsepian spoke with a sympathetic psychiatrist who helped arrange a transfer to the Army post office in Paris. There, photographing and developing V-mail, he soon felt rested—but not recovered. "I've got a lot of things to live down in my soul, a lot of memories to get rid of." He had "gone through a living hell," had "seen men torn to pieces" and had "killed a lot of men . . . four of them with my own bare hands." (Two years and one day earlier he had written from training camp, "I pity the guy who gets into a fight with me. I can kill any man with my bare hands in 10 seconds flat. . . .") Finally, with orders in hand, he prepared to return to Los Angeles. "Today I'm on top of the world. I am going home. I am twice as big as I was, and have glamor and medals all over me. After the hell I've gone through I am a nice guy, I hope, and I know I am a man. But deep inside my soul, I'm scared." Reunited with his family on January 7, 1946, he began his struggle to overcome what is today readily recognizable as post-traumatic stress disorder: a sense of morbid futility, sleeping disorders and nightmares, nervousness and withdrawal, restlessness and hair-trigger anger. He was, he thought, "one of those men who look OK outside, but are empty and aching inside, a sort of walking ghost full of memories that shouldn't have happened to them."

In late November 1945, just four months after his twenty-first birthday, Aleck Hovsepian had told his parents in a letter from Brussels that combat had aged him ten years. His mother, reading only the scrubbed accounts that he addressed to her, judged him twenty years older.[29]

In the wake of World War II, Americans continued to ground their corporate judgments of the combat experience in their wartime views of how the war was waged. Common-wisdom estimates shut out much of the grimness of duty overseas, but returning soldiers, whether front-line or rear-echelon, seldom moved to challenge them.

Civilians accounted support troops as men who had "fought for their country," and welcomed them home with a heartiness undiminished by the absence of combat records. Such returnees knew that, whatever the deprivations they had borne, the war had dealt more harshly with others; to be acclaimed heroes with standing to share equally in all the benefits of the GI Bill gladdened them. They possessed neither grounds nor need to contest the public's view of the war.

Reacting viscerally to some of their first postwar experiences, returned combat soldiers often felt impelled to rattle the home folks to the realities of battle. In theaters showing war films they erupted in raucous laughter or in insults shouted at the screen; seeing rare snatches of realism, they longed somehow to insist that the audience pay heed to what they had endured. But such impulses flared briefly. However it might continue to grate that while the combat veteran alone might know the nature of his experience, "everyone else wants to tell him," returnees became aware that formidable obstacles blocked any revision of the public's picture. They had already tripped on the snags of trying to tell others what battle was "really" like. They knew too that any stories of theirs would be far less welcome than the more palatable tales of the 90 percent. And soon after the war they sensed the movement of public interest away from the ground combat their compatriots were confident they understood to aspects of the war unique, portentous, and perplexing—the atomic bomb and the Holocaust.[30]

In any case, all inclination to dispute public perceptions quickly yielded to the necessity to close the divide that combat soldiers felt between them and home. They had already moved through amazement—the war would never end, but it had; front-line soldiers could not live, but many had—to at least partial relief. Once able to accept their survival, they determined to put the war behind them as rapidly and thoroughly as possible. They meant to forget their war memories, not revivify them in public debate; to reintegrate themselves, not foster a wider separation. They too basked in the public's gratitude, but they sensed an undercurrent of worry that those longest in combat might have become "killers" or "freaks." In truth, that issue provoked greater anxiety in soldiers than in civilians. "We had dogs trained to kill," recounted ex-Ranger Robert Shore. "When the war was over, we untrained them; we made them mild again. But not so with men. The Army didn't believe in unlearning us." Returning combat soldiers were thus intent on demonstrating that they were normal human beings completely dedicated, as indeed they were, to the pursuit of the "good life"—a decent job, marriage, and a family. Any exasperation with the public's incomprehension of what lay behind them, any reiteration of "They'll never understand," would be reserved for other ex-soldiers.[31]

The chief recourse of World War II veterans striving to heal themselves was repression. They were already familiar with its consolations; the attempt to exclude painful thoughts had begun with first combat. "[The] strong and constant urge in all of us," observed Army sergeant Arnold Gates in the Pacific, "is ever toward the day when we can forget the mud and filth and the smell of bloated death. The natural tendency with all men is to forget the unpleasant quickly and almost thoroughly." It had seemed to work for Marine George Hunt, who just six weeks after vicious island fighting reported that "time had swallowed up Peleliu. [It] appeared inconceivable that we had ever been there at all." Repression, moreover, was the medical establishment's principal prescription for recovery. Many received the advice that a Navy doctor gave Marine Robert Charles: "Time will help. In fact, it is the only medicine. Try to put the war behind you. . . . Don't look back. Don't talk about it. Try not to even think about it. There are nicer things to think about." Often, in fact, such formulas simply bolstered the men's own intentions. Hovsepian attempted to stifle all those memories that continued to crawl. John Emerick, too, "just tried to forget. That is what you try to do." And civilians oblivious of all that veterans were attempting to expel commended their reticence as a modesty especially becoming in those acclaimed as heroes.[32]

On one level—the restoration of soldiers' sense of their ability to act effectively—home visions of the war advanced recovery dramatically. Civilians offered men striving to throw off feelings of purposelessness, powerlessness, and emptiness repeated affirmations of their accomplishment in war. To soldiers' families, the conflict had been one of utmost moral clarity; victory had turned on the almost perfect congruence of American power and American morality. They thus cast their soldiers' achievement within such terms as "right" and "wrong," "justice" and "injustice," "courage" and "cowardice." There were, to be sure, limits to combat veterans' willingness to return to moralization. Significant numbers were angry that mainstream veterans' organizations gave themselves over to a boisterous, flag-wrapped patriotism, a development that brought renewed, though quiet, denunciations of "quartermaster parasites" turned legionnaires. But in the end the civilian insistence on the worthiness of the Cause, victory over tyranny, did much to dispel veterans' fears of inefficacy.[33]

Similarly, civilian assumptions that combat was a positive experience soon gave a new cast to the soldier's survival. What had appeared on May 8 or August 15, 1945, against a backdrop of powerlessness, utterly amazing seemed at home to assume significant individual accomplishment. "You're a survivor," the doctor told Robert Charles. "You've proved that." He contributed to his own survival, surely, and might have ensured it by acting as he had, by invoking in combat crises his own personal qualities. Soon, in reply to the question, "What did you do in the war?" the combat veteran's first answer, the minimal, "I survived," yielded to larger and more constructive characterizations. Pondering his postwar years, William Dreux observed that "Some of the things I saw [in the war] have acquired a richer meaning which I then saw dimly, if at all." Ex-paratrooper Clay Christiansen did retain a memory of his fear prior to the drop on Normandy—"I was very scared"—but retrospect rapidly shrank both the fright and "the deep sense of loneliness" that had assailed him on June 6, 1944: "I didn't fully realize then that I was playing an important role in the greatest and most powerful military invasion in the history of the world."[34]

Civilians' idealization of comradeship, in part a nostalgia for the sense of common purpose lost at home with the war's end, worked to relieve soldiers' memories of isolation. It was understandable that over time veterans would dwell on sacrifice for others rather than on the sacrifice of others; would summon the affinities that had joined soldiers rather than deeds that, in the drive for self-preservation, had divided them; and would recall the excitements of a high-stakes wartime existence rather than the relentless fear of their own deaths. It was understandable that veterans would ignore comradeship's inability to regenerate itself and its disintegration when, at war's end, survival was suddenly no longer at stake. It was understandable that decades later veterans would brush over the many postwar years they had remained without ties to wartime buddies, would abruptly reinfuse with feeling relationships with men who could be remembered as paying undivided attention to one another without the competing claims of careers, wives, and children, and would declare them the closest friendships of their lives. Nowhere did comradeship flourish as it did in veterans' memories.[35]

The decisive step away from the combat soldier's wartime conclusions came with his emergent conviction that the war had made its participants better persons. Their experience, veterans began to profess, had left them more mature, more manly, more proficient, more knowledgeable of people and the world. Many, grateful for advantageous turns in their lives soon after the war, recast their service as one that had opened to them educations and jobs at previously inaccessible levels. They more readily attributed career achievement to the war's returns than to the strengths developed in recovering from it. Almost entirely eclipsed was a fact that had appeared so unmistakable in 1944–45: that in World War II battle was a disintegrative experience.[36]

A number of veterans, it is true, continued to wrestle with private traumas seemingly beyond the reach of public reassurance—friends' deaths so bitter that they could not be redeemed; opportunities to help fellow soldiers or hapless civilians unheeded at the time and still haunting; killings that remained difficult to justify. For them, some relief arrived much later with the outspokenness of the veterans of the war in Vietnam, whose struggles with post-traumatic stress disorder seem to have licensed older veterans to own to their identical symptoms. Recently published memoirs of World War II combat soldiers, especially those who were also POWs, have acknowledged, and thus perhaps begun to exorcise, an anguish unrecognized by the public for half a century. Sy Kahn was one of those soldiers who, as he met his welcoming family at Pennsylvania Station in November 1945, expected his feelings of "strangeness and alienation" to pass; they never did. "I was changed by the war, haunted in dreams and memory, rendered restless and sometimes alienated, sometimes more at home abroad than in the United States, sometimes a stranger everywhere, and in mysterious ways beyond my knowing, perhaps a casualty." Clearly, however, most veterans were far more successful at that which they called "becoming themselves again." For each one of the

Sy Kahns unable to forget enough there were many Ray Whitings. "You know, there were plenty of bad times in that war," said the ex–combat engineer who had cleared mines from Omaha Beach. "But it's odd. Now . . . all these years later, you remember the good times, the funny things that happened. . . . Thank God, it's the laughs you remember." The veteran's vision of combat was not that of the combat soldier.[37]

Few veterans recognized the extent of change within themselves or the sweep of the process among their fellows, and fewer still grasped its social consequence. In the last stages of the war, soldiers vowed, in what became almost a rite of foxhole existence, that their sons would be spared the experience of combat. Ernie Pyle looked for but failed to find foolery in the words of a GI proposing extreme measures: "As soon as I get home I'm going to put ten-pound weights in [my son's] hands and make him jump off the garage roof, to break down his arches. I'm going to feed him a little ground glass to give him a bad stomach, and I'm going to make him read by candlelight all the time to ruin his eyes. When I get through with him he'll be double-4 double-F." In the postwar period, soldiers' sons were fortunate to escape such inflictions; less so to be denied their fathers' plain speaking.[38]

Veterans could neither reopen themselves to the sources of their pain nor cause distress to those they loved. Some said nothing; some summoned pleasantries; all skirted the terrors of battle. Thirty-five years after combat duty in Europe, Jack Short recounted: "I never discuss what I did in the service with my children. I told them some of the funnier stories. They do not know all the things that happened during the World War. I prefer that they don't." "My husband had been in the South Pacific," reported a California nurse, Betty Hutchinson. "You could never get the father of my four children to talk about the war. It was like we put blinders on the past. . . . That's the way we lived in suburbia, raising our children, not telling them about war. I don't think it was just [us]. It was everybody. You wouldn't fill your children full of these horror stories, would you?" Into this vacuum moved home-front images of warfare still expansive, dramatic, valorous. The cost of healing was that the next generation would acquire an expurgated version of combat, 1941–45.[39]

With lonely prescience, James Jones understood as early as 1962 how far psychic revision would carry veterans from the war of 1944–45. One among a group of comrades, he proposed, would write a book capturing their experience as they had registered it during the fighting—"but none of them would believe [the book], because none of them would remember it that way."[40]

NOTES

1. Battle: Expectation, Encounter, Reaction

1. Sabatelli: Horan and Frank, 136; seaman on light cruiser: Fahey, 15; Eustis, 171; *road back to America:* Babcock, 59.
2. Horan and Frank, 137; Pyle, *Brave Men,* 27.
3. Eustis, 200.
4. Graham, 66.
5. James Johns, 19; Mumford, 319.
6. Eustis, 99; Marine private: Horan and Frank, 197; James Jones, *WWII,* 34–36.
7. Hoyt, 193; Eustis, 121, 131, 148, 150, 154, 227.
8. Babcock, 79; Tregaskis, 3–4.
9. Eustis, 182, 183, 214.
10. Gabriel, 82; Wolfe, 143; Keith Wheeler, 125; Hilsman, 62.
11. Gallant, *On Valor's Side,* 227; Sledge, 20.
12. Dreux, 90; Owens, 63.
13. O'Sheel, 83; Boesch, 184.
14. Eustis, 121; *combat as a test:* William Hochman in Fuller, 164, 167–168; *strengthening the strong:* Marshall, 184; Leinbaugh, 2; Randall, 30.
15. Gabriel, 82; Mumford, 306–307, 319–320; *soldiers were rarely hit:* Eustis, 95.
16. Arthur Miller, *Situation Normal,* 116; Ciardi, 27.
17. Uris, 399; Bayler, 226; *I just want to kill:* Tregaskis, 29; *to kill his Jap:* Tregaskis, 143, emphasis added.
18. Arthur Miller, *Situation Normal,* 1, 69–70.
19. Gallant, 95.
20. Tregaskis, 15; Horan and Frank, 136.
21. Ingersoll, 173.
22. Robert Scott, 131–132.
23. Russell Davis, 1.
24. Gallant, *On Valor's Side,* 207; Owens, 62–63.
25. Fry, 35, 287.
26. Arrington, 156.

27. Robert Houston: Critchell, 42; *cannot realize:* Moorehead, *A Late Education,* 128.
28. Gallant, *On Valor's Side,* 227.
29. Hoyt, 112.
30. *Some envisioned:* Sledge, 130; *Some considered:* Waldron, 49; *Some granted:* Hynes, 75.
31. Russell Davis, 50, 69; Wingfield, 177–178.
32. Frank Mercurio: Wolfe, 185; *with satisfaction:* Kelly, 36; *with indifference:* Eustis, 154; Moore: Mason, 130–131.
33. Hoyt, 119.
34. Mowat, 199.
35. Pyle, *Brave Men,* 247; Janice Giles, 39; Keith Wheeler, 26; Lamb, 40.
36. Shirer, 514; Critchell, 90; Pereira, 9; Sabatelli: Horan and Frank, 141; Boesch, 15; James Jones, *Whistle,* 73, 75.
37. Hynes, 75.
38. Sledge, 75; Atwell, 50; Bernstein, 149.
39. Sledge, 75; Atwell, 50; Bernstein, 149.
40. *Often GIs caught:* Fry, 55; Mumford, 325; Sledge, 77; Pyle: Nichols, 130.
41. Cochrane, 34–35; Graham, 141.
42. Bourke-White, 62.
43. Currey, 88; Critchell, 72.
44. *Preconceptions of combat:* Keller 6; George Wilson, 112.
45. Dreux, 232; Critchell, 72; *As the war moved forward:* Irgang, 177; Faubus, 453; George Wilson, 112; *One can only try:* Breuer, *Storming Hitler's Rhine,* 52.
46. George Wilson, 111–112.
47. Mowat, 144; Atwell, 33.
48. Crisp, *Brazen Chariots,* 39.
49. Eustis, 136, 142, 143, 159, 200, 229.
50. Eustis, 231, 233–234.
51. Mumford, 318; Hunt, 21; George, 80.
52. Irgang, 29.
53. Atwell, 22; Sevareid, 388; Kennett, 134.
54. Pearce, 150; Murphy, 4; Ingersoll, 148, 150.
55. Leinbaugh, 53, 248.
56. Tregaskis, 137; Sledge, 143.
57. Gabel, 173; George Wilson, 114, 116.
58. Toole, xvii.
59. McHugh, 5–6.
60. Thompson, 35–36.
61. Wolfe, 185.
62. Weigley, *Eisenhower's Lieutenants,* 12; McHugh, 34–35; Theodore Wilson, 72; Janice Giles, 318.
63. Phibbs, 78–79.
64. Irgang, 196–197; Janice Giles, 318.
65. Cawthon, 86; Fry, 2, 43; Hunt, 111.
66. Arrington, 50; Leinbaugh, 76; Fahey, 81; *Are we going to look like that?* Piercy, 214.
67. Arrington, 73–74.
68. Stiles, 66.
69. Tobin, 139; Randall, 45.
70. Hoyt, 283–285.
71. Eustis, 95; Myrer, *The Big War,* 190.
72. Marshall, 131, 132, 136, 137.

73. *Convinced that death:* Lavender, 10; Eustis, 153.
74. Johnson, 66; Randall, 25–26; Harry Brown, 44; Atwell, 65; James Jones, *Whistle,* 7.
75. Eustis, 142, 223; Huebner, 117; James Jones, *Whistle,* 7.
76. *But when Horse-Face:* Murphy, 158; Sledge, 303; Crisp, *Brazen Chariots,* 195–196.
77. Lindsay, 114–115, 216, 248; *Each escape from death:* McCallum, 69.
78. Irgang, 31; Bassett, 52; McHugh, 5.
79. Whitaker, 210; Breuer, *Death of a Nazi Army,* 81; Russell Davis, 210.
80. Mauldin, *Bill Mauldin's Army,* 158; Whitaker, 214; Lavender, 66.
81. Lavender, 62; Tsuchida, 49.
82. *Often they expressed:* Johnson, 51.
83. *When each morning in Belgium:* Wingfield, 79.
84. Weigley, "The American Military" ("TAM"), 41–42; Irgang, 95.
85. George, ix; Winston, 253; Manchester, *Goodbye, Darkness,* 103.
86. Mathias, 118–119; Currey, 199.
87. Boesch, 54–55, 62; Faubus, 570.
88. Faubus, 357; George, ix; Nichols, 201; Pyle, *Brave Men,* 178.
89. O'Sheel, 205; Nichols, 201; Whiting, 159.
90. George Wilson, 58; Faubus, 212; Mauldin, *Bill Mauldin's Army,* 289, 299; Murphy, 194–195.
91. *Recognition, too, came:* Stouffer, vol. II, 347.
92. Cooke, 60; Tapert, *Lines of Battle,* 113; Perrett, *A Country Made by War,* 404.
93. Fry, 241.
94. Stiles, 131, 134; Martin, 206; Ciardi, 35.
95. Stiles, 131; Ardery, 202; Werrell, 705; Doolittle, 43; Muirhead, 3; Cubbins, 17.
96. Vietor, 130; Irving, 123; Sherry, 204–205; Theodore Wilson, 325.
97. Cubbins, 16; Ardery, 143, 155; Muirhead, 3, 4, 9.
98. Irgang, 174; Nichols, 76–77, 205; Pyle, *Brave Men,* 157.
99. Tapert, *Lines of Battle,* 111–113; Irving, 122–123; Cotterell, 112.
100. Tapert, *Lines of Battle,* 111, 113; Pyle, *Last Chapter,* 32–33.
101. Tapert, *Lines of Battle,* 111–112; Muirhead, 134–135.
102. Perrett, *A Country Made by War,* 406; Stiles, 167–168.
103. Ciardi, 90–91, 101–102.
104. Janice Giles, 103; Boesch, 55–56.
105. Fry, 240.
106. Bourke-White, 87.
107. Weigley, "TAM," 37–38; Stouffer, II, 88; Marshall, 16.
108. Crisp, *Brazen Chariots,* 113–114; Van Creveld, 89.
109. Tapert, *Lines of Battle,* 80; Stouffer, vol. II, 88; Irgang, 174; Faubus, 157.
110. Boesch, 216–217.

2. *Battle: Coping with Combat*
1. Janice Giles, 3–4; Lee, 30, 37.
2. Ardery, 225.
3. Lee, 162; Rock, 19; Uris, 377; Boesch, 143.
4. Tapert, *Lines of Battle,* 215–216.
5. Martin, 371; Rock, 19; Stradling, 162.
6. Marsden, 193; Saint-Exupéry, 134.
7. O'Sheel, 104; Faubus, 109, 136.
8. Muirhead, 149.
9. Howard and Whitley, v–vi.

10. Hill, Veterans Survey Project; Neimeyer, Veterans Survey Project; Perkins, 566.
11. Leinbaugh, 80; Russell Davis, 16; Moorehead, *Eclipse,* 101.
12. Hogan, 64; Russell Davis, 12; Joly, 98; Boesch, 21, 27.
13. Huebner, 110–111; Phibbs, 110.
14. Huebner, 111–112 (emphasis added).
15. Boesch, 231–232.
16. Leinbaugh, conversation with author, February 21, 1989.
17. Boesch, 158.
18. Wolfe, 167; Gallant, *On Valor's Side,* 335; Weston, Veterans Survey Project.
19. *Metaphorical imaginations:* Gallant, *On Valor's Side,* 335; sound of shells: Carter, 56; Myrer, 252; Wingfield, 27.
20. Hersey, *Into the Valley,* 79, 84–85; Hoyt, 122; Cochrane, 22.
21. Dreux, 254; Hoyt, 453; Henniker, 212; Pearce, 62–63; Butterfield, 83.
22. Irgang, 202; Breuer, *Death of a Nazy Army,* 224.
23. Irgang, 199–201; Randall, 61.
24. Irgang, 202.
25. Huebner, 110; Hoyt, 363.
26. Gabel, 231; Janice Giles, 33; *Similarly, battle endorsed:* Toole, 41.
27. Hoyt, 241; Cawthon, 121.
28. *Did the soldier know:* Irgang, 177; *That on patrol:* Randall, 20; *That the original bazooka:* Slingduff, Veterans Survey Project; *That the red circle* [and next three questions]: Martin, 129; *That in welcoming:* Boroughs, 201–202.
29. Belden, 294; Wolfe, 167; James Jones, *WWII,* 113, 116.
30. Wolfe, 132; Gallant, *On Valor's Side,* 250–251.
31. Remarque, *All Quiet on the Western Front, (All Quiet),* 270.
32. Muirhead, 153; Richard Wheeler, 124.
33. Faubus, 156; Mauldin, *Bill Mauldin's Army,* 163.
34. Belden, 294; Hunt, 99–100; Muirhead, 153.
35. Gallant, *On Valor's Side,* 335–336; Leinbaugh, conversation with author, February 21, 1989.
36. Hunt, 99; George Wilson, 46.
37. Hoyt, 107–108; Hunt, 11.
38. Lee Miller, 411.
39. Hunt, 11–12; Horan and Frank, 15.
40. Stouffer, vol. II, 174; Kennett, 138; *I just asked:* Stouffer, vol. II, 186; Arrington, 107.
41. Hunt, 127–128; Eustis, 203, 228.
42. Glasser, 151; Stouffer, vol. II, 186–187.
43. Muirhead, 122–123.
44. Boyington, 235, 239.
45. Keith Wheeler, 17.
46. Muirhead, 123; Breuer, *Storming Hitler's Rhine,* 108; Devereux, 125–127.
47. Pyle, *Last Chapter,* 44; Lay, 24; Renfro, 62; Keith Wheeler, 17; Russell Davis, 11.
48. Leinbaugh, 171; James Jones, *The Thin Red Line,* 148–149.
49. Hunt, 113, 128.
50. Leinbaugh, 119.
51. Devereux, 137–138; Leinbaugh, 128.
52. Muirhead, 122–125.
53. Muirhead, 125.
54. Lifton, 31–34; Bourke-White, 163.
55. Steinbeck, 199–201; Waldron, 95.
56. Ciardi, 82; Carter, 214–215.

57. Duus, 213; James Jones, *The Thin Red Line,* 388; Lea, 12.

58. Redmond, 166; Sajer, 254.

59. Whitaker, 89; James Jones, *WWII,* 196; Murphy, 248.

60. Myrer, 313; Hunt, 74.

61. Janice Giles, 238; Murphy, 106–107.

62. Leinbaugh, 54.

63. Bassett, 43.

64. Harry Brown, 148.

65. George Wilson, 18–22.

66. Gallant, *On Valor's Side,* 159; Burns, 87; George Wilson, 98; Muirhead, 99.

67. Mathias, 185; Fahey, 190–191; Huebner, 188.

68. Pyle, *Here is Your War,* 298–299.

69. Sledge, 66–67.

70. Babcock, 87.

71. James Johns, 16.

72. Pereira, 120; Sajer, 188; Kelly, 126.

73. Sledge, 254–255; Fry, 190; Mason, 137.

74. Bassett, 40–41.

75. Murphy, 187–188.

76. Plievier, *Stalingrad,* 13; Gabel, 201.

77. James Jones, *The Thin Red Line,* 452, 468, 481, 495.

78. Murphy, 53; Hunt, 119.

79. Waldron, 95; Gray, 102; Hunt, 119.

80. Russell Davis, 110.

81. Wolfe, 173.

82. Owens, 52–53.

83. Bond, 106.

84. Sevareid, 419–420.

85. James Jones, *Whistle,* 111.

86. *"If the bullet's":* Duus, 109, Arrington, 211; *Chance also informed:* Boesch, 169, Damsky, Veterans Survey Project; *Minor variants appeared:* Leckie, *Helmet For My Pillow (Helmet),* 104, Owens, 62–63; Atwell, 132.

87. Bassett, 20; Dreux, 44; Eustis, 142; Ingersoll, 123, 137.

88. Randall, 26–28; Bassett, 20.

89. Wolfe, 126–127; Damsky, VSP.

90. Belden, 294, 296, 298; Boesch, 169.

91. Leckie, *Helmet,* 283.

92. Pearce, 150.

93. Ciardi, xi, xix.

94. Lea, 24; James Jones, *WWII,* 54.

95. Sledge, 130; Duus, 109; James Jones, *WWII,* 122, 196.

96. Sledge, 130.

97. *"Just do":* Shaw, 545; *They learned:* Tsuchida, 52; *Field officers worked:* Huebner, 85.

3. Fighting the Germans: The War of Rules

1. *It was true that:* Emmrich, 33, Henniker, 49, Stahlberg, 143; *and that numerous:* Neumann, 89; *German SS:* Sydnor, 314; *Luftwaffe aircraft:* Henniker, 20; *German bomber assaults:* A. J. P. Taylor, 78.

2. Joly, 329; Pyle, *Here is Your War,* 265; Von Luck, 123, 273.

3. Moorehead, *A Late Education,* 120, 142–143; Duus, 184.

4. Moorehead, *A Late Education,* 59, 60; McCallum, 42; Crawford, 84–86.
5. Samwell, 34–35, 45.
6. Samwell, 23–24; Von Luck, 99–100; Joly, 149.
7. Crawford, 37; Von Luck, 100, 105, 110, 123.
8. Douglas, 69–72.
9. Samwell, 15, 136, 137.
10. *Sniping was a:* Nichols, 293, Kennett, 160, Moorehead, *Eclipse,* 133.
11. Galloway, 92.
12. Moorehead, *A Late Education,* 61; *Numerous British soldiers:* Samwell, 135; McCallum, 153; Moorehead, ibid., 62, 120–121, 137.
13. Samwell, 136; Dreux, 35; Henniker, 113; Irving, frontispiece, 373; Zeno, 197.
14. Tapert, *Lines of Battles,* 79.
15. Galloway, 54; Wingfield, 94, 95; McKee, 52.
16. *To many Germans:* Montyn, 47, 58, Sajer, 245; Windsor, 34.
17. Von Luck, 78.
18. Dalderup, 126; Archard, 96; Carter, 52.
19. Douglas, 72; *So American Soldiers:* Vietor, 31–33, A. J. P. Taylor, 226; *And again, one whose background:* Abzug, 33; Tapert, *Lines of Battle,* 77, 79.
20. *The Goums:* Hoyt, 188, Huebner, 81, Martin, 143, Roche, Veterans Survey Projects; McCallum, 123; Von Luck, 86.
21. McKee, 57; Samwell, 32, 135, 138.
22. Pyle, *Here is Your War,* 265; Martin, 60; Stahlberg, 143; Joly, 187, 292.
23. McKee, 57; Wingfield, 97; Von Luck, 102.
24. Bartov, 80, 83; Sydnor, 153.
25. Neumann, 107; Conot, 219; Stahlberg, 160.
26. Whiting, 173–174.
27. Pruller, 108; Sauer, 5; *True to Type,* 20, 22; *The welcome accorded:* Skrjabina, 6, Pabel, 63.
28. Sajer, 118, 186; Emmrich, 36, 78, 111, 112; Conot, 222; Bartov, 153.
29. Neumann, 137, 163.
30. *True to Type,* 22, 23, 45, 51; Polyakov, 13, 27; Neumann, 163.
31. Neumann, 209; Theodore Wilson, 136.
32. Samwell, 136; Moorehead, *Eclipse,* 71; Bernstein, 83; Cochrane, 109.
33. Leinbaugh, 134; Kennett, 155.
34. Currey, 95.
35. Leinbaugh, 225–226.
36. Cawthon, 126; Henniker, 258; Whitaker, 239; Breuer, *Death of a Nazi Amy,* 270; Zeno, 260.
37. Currey, 181.
38. Lavender, 74.
39. Currey, 151.
40. Glover Johns, 93–94.
41. Currey, 240–243.
42. Phibbs, 137–138.
43. Currey, 151; Irgang, 37.
44. Critchell, 197; Bassett, 10.
45. Randall, 94; Irgang, 53; Arrington, 224.
46. Irgang, 53; Leinbaugh, 92, 222; Randall, 93–94.
47. Tapert, *Lines of Battle,* 227; Boroughs, 88–89.
48. Putman, 240–241; Boesch, 80.
49. Hoyt, 500; Gabel, 175–176; Shomon, 41.

50. Irgang, 119–120; MacDonald, 207–209.
51. Fry, 337–338.
52. Keller, 127; Dreux, 196.
53. Hoyt, 409, 583; Irgang, 212; Toole, 138–139.
54. Boesch, 89–90; Critchell, 151; Fry, 308, 342–343.
55. Lavender, 68.
56. McWane, 63–64.
57. Irgang, 235; Faubus, 433.
58. Irgang, 234–235.
59. Terkel, 5, 259, 380.
60. Tobin, 133–134; *And when in one sector:* Currey, 88; Irving, 352; McHugh, 23–24; *Notwithstanding the Americans:* Breuer, *Storming Hitler's Rhine,* 84, Whitaker, 260.
61. Whitaker, 54; Irgang, 177; Shomon, 37.
62. Tobin, 137–138.
63. Tobin, 138; Whitaker, 206; Bourke-White, 28.
64. Shomon, 37; Irgang, 178; Hoyt, 465.
65. Whitaker, 70, 180; Breuer, *Death of a Nazi Army,* 121; Zeno, 264–265.
66. Boesch, 53; Critchell, 172; Huie, 139–140; Glover Johns, 138.
67. Lay, 124; Noonan, Veterans Survey Project; Huebner, 79; Carter, 240.
68. Nichols, 293; Whiting, 66.
69. Atwell, 298; Irving, 96; Whiting, 66.
70. Carter, 234; Atwell, 298–299.
71. . . . *and later at Bayeux: Time* Magazine, May 28, 1984, 29.
72. *Time,* May 28, 1984, 32; Terkel, 5, 259, 382.
73. Raff, 204.
74. Carter, 28; Irgang, 26; Burgett, 115–116.
75. Burgett, 111–112.
76. Terkel, 382.
77. Perkins, 565.
78. Sevareid, 388.
79. Sevareid, 389–391.
80. Atwell, 154.
81. Mydans, 172.
82. Breuer, *Storming Hitler's Rhine,* 280.
83. Faubus, 211.
84. Arrington, 87; Bernstein, 90, 98–99.
85. Feinberg, Veterans Survey Project.
86. Murphy, 176–177; Leinbaugh, 148; Randall, 104–105.
87. Arrington, 165–166, 227.
88. Houston, 61; Duus, 214.
89. Atwell, 380–382.
90. Bassett, 11.
91. Leinbaugh, 253.
92. Leinbaugh, 163.
93. Leinbaugh, 204–205.
94. Atwell, 392–393.
95. Atwell, 375–376.
96. Toole, 82; Irgang, 138.
97. Irving, 368; Abzug, 30; Ambrose, 63, 65; Slaughter, Veterans Survey Project.
98. Ambrose, 83; Critchell, 65.

99. Atwell, 428–429, 493–496.
100. Irving, 96–97.
101. Lavender, 43–44; Carter, 132, 134; Critchell, 68.
102. Atwell, 79; Currey, 138–139, 151, 243.
103. Huebner, 88; Archard, 99.
104. Breuer, *Death of a Nazi Army*, 103; Winston, 87.
105. Breuer, ibid., 103.
106. Winston, 210; Boesch, 9.
107. Huebner, 134; Burgett, 178.
108. Irgang, 86–87; Currey, 151.
109. Winston, 89; Breuer, *Death of a Nazi Army*, 103; Irgang, 11, 55, 71, 138.
110. Whitaker, 70.
111. Irgang, 76–77.
112. Kertzer, 71–72.
113. Currey, 151; Irving, 11.
114. Lay, 124; Boesch, 54; Janice Giles, 185, 199–200.
115. Breuer, *Death of a Nazi Army*, 268 (emphasis added); Wingfield, 31; Irgang, 86 (emphasis added); Carter, 44.
116. Moorehead, *Eclipse*, xii.
117. Hoyt, 521–524.
118. Hoyt, xiv, 525; Leinbaugh, 134 (emphasis added); Janice Giles, 179.
119. Lavender, 22; Pergrin, 193–194; Whiting, 192; Hoyt, 525.
120. Murphy, 39; *In a Normandy assault:* Burgett, 164–165; Arrington, 165.
121. Burgett, 130–131.
122. Arrington, 79, 191.
123. Pergrin, 194; Leinbaugh, 154.
124. Gabel, 177–180.
125. Murphy, 100.
126. Walzer, 23.

4. Fighting the Japanese: War Unrestrained

For a sharply contrastive interpretation of the dynamic between American and Japanese soldiers in the Pacific, see John Dower's book, *War Without Mercy.*
1. Falk, 241; Cassell, 569, 576.
2. Scidmore, 53, 87, 155, 289; Harries and Harries, 96.
3. Harries and Harries, 338; Kennedy, 214; *Life,* August 21, 1939, 28.
4. Falk, 241; Russell, 54, 235; Knox, 154; Congdon, 79–80; Fujita, 85.
5. Falk, 55, 191; Swinson, 73; Hieb, 93, 98, 119.
6. Mason, 203; Lawrence Taylor, 39, 52.
7. Lawton, 8; Falk, 78.
8. *Life,* August 21, 1939, 28.
9. Thompson, 149; Coleman, 64; Martin, 21; Grashio, 19; Hieb, 123.
10. Arthur, 132; Holland Smith, 193; *Even ordinary ailments:* Fitzpatrick, 82, 145; Stanley Smith, 25, 65.
11. Mathias, 180.
12. Donald Giles, 51; Whitman, 221; Coleman, 56.
13. Hough, 82; Becker and Thobaben, 171.
14. Kenneth Davis, 155; Manchester, *Goodbye, Darkness,* 183; Sledge, 37, 60–61; Horan and Frank, 150; Lucas, 102. See also Burke Davis, 129.
15. Okumiya, 327–328; Onoda, 37.

16. O'Sheel, 236; Reynolds, 57.
17. Schratz, 105; Fahey, 75; Hashimoto, 80–81; Sakai, 176–177.
18. Whitman, 269, 287–288, 291–292; Wainwright, 57; Young, 133, 146.
19. *Life,* May 11, 1942, 106; Young, 114; Whitman, 260; O'Sheel, 227–228.
20. Grashio, 18; Young, 74–75, 174; Hough, 84; Dyess, 41; Harries and Harries, 481.
21. Fahey, 46.
22. Tenney, 66–67.
23. Burke Davis, 147; Cook, 360, 365.
24. Cook, 475. See also *Life,* May 11, 1942, 106.
25. O'Sheel, 227; Lucas, 102; Wainwright, 77, 297.
26. Thompson, 155.
27. Young, 242–246, 272; Redmond, 21, 94–97, 99, 106, 109, 110, 117–118.
28. Bayler, 55–56.
29. Stewart, 66; Mellnik, 81, 104.
30. Ashton, x–xi; Grashio, 18; Tenney, 43.
31. Hieb, 155–156, 317; Falk, 204; *Life,* September 7, 1942, 23; Paull, 156, 164, 270; Toland, *The Rising Sun,* 439; *Although Washington withheld:* Becker and Thobaben, 119, Cawthon, 17.
32. Hough, 49; Richard Wheeler, 55; Frank, 129–130.
33. Vandegrift, 142.
34. Gallant, *On Valor's Side,* 292, 294–295, 297.
35. Clint O'Connor, 1–1; Mathias, 89; *Life,* February 21, 1944, 36; Richard Wheeler, 392. See also Routledge, 70.
36. *Life,* September 27, 1943, 37; *Life,* December 27, 1943, 51. See also National Research Council, 123.
37. Hough, 82; Camp, 230, 235.
38. Gallant, *On Valor's Side,* 342.
39. Kahn, 86–87.
40. Kenneth Davis, 154; Vandegrift, 142.
41. Tenney, 51–52; Donald Giles, 88.
42. Dyess, 25, 80; Charles, 37; Knox, 115.
43. Cook, 169; Hough, 363; *Life,* October 19, 1942, 20; Morale Services Division, July 1944, 8–9.
44. Horan and Frank, 11; Owens, 68.
45. Fahey, 149; Russell Davis, 83, 184–185; Scott, 191.
46. O'Sheel, 220, 222–223; Nichols, 373.
47. Camp, 200–201; Frank, 152.
48. Hough, 52–55, 81; George, 113.
49. Hough, 81, 245–246; Hemingway, 69; Twining, 195.
50. Dyess, 43; *Life,* February 21, 1944, 34; Congdon, 467–468.
51. Nichols, 373–374.
52. Myrer, 309; Morris, 303.
53. Bird, 3–5; Horan and Frank, 145, 150; Camp, 230.
54. *Life,* December 27, 1943, 51; Steenstra, Veterans Survey Project.
55. Gallant, *On Valor's Side,* 288; Holland Smith, 9; *Life,* November 9, 1942, 36; Hersey, *Into the Valley,* 82.
56. *Life,* December 27, 1943, 51; Fahey, 48.
57. Bird, 20; Cary, 116.
58. *Life,* August 16, 1943, 97; Babcock, 26; Arthur, 226; Uris, 272; Pyle, *Last Chapter,* 23; Bayler, 92; Dyess, 42; Horan and Frank, 24; Angel, Veterans Survey Project; *Life,* January 24, 1944, 30.
59. Butterfield, 66; Nichols, 374; Terkel, 27.

60. Robert Scott, 191; Hersey, *Into the Valley,* 82; *Life,* September 14, 1942, 2.
61. James Jones, *The Thin Red Line,* 52.
62. Moorehead, *A Late Education,* 61–62; James Jones, *The Thin Red Line,* 60; *Life,* December 27, 1943, 75; Hersey, *Into the Valley,* 49.
63. Kenneth Davis, 308.
64. Hersey, *Into the Valley,* 49, 56; Kenneth Davis, 308; Leckie, *Delivered from Evil,* 408; Babcock, 27.
65. Kenneth Davis, 308; *Life,* May 11, 1942, 98; June 26, 1944, 55, February 21, 1944, 34.
66. Valentine, 26; *Life,* February 22, 1943, 24; Congdon, 400; Hemingway, 28, 71.
67. *"Were like phantoms"*: Valentine, 26; *"This enemy was"*: *Life,* February 22, 1943, 24; Nichols, 374.
68. Young, 130; James Johns, 26.
69. Sherrod, 46; Horan and Frank, 150; Hunt, 13.
70. *Life,* August 16, 1943, 93; Emmerson, 155; *Life,* August 13, 1945, 34.
71. Twining, 86.
72. Gallant, *On Valor's Side,* 207.
73. Twining, 143; Gallant, ibid., 207–208.
74. *Life,* November 1, 1943, 52–57, February 21, 1944, 11, October 4, 1943, 57; Standifer, 19.
75. Cook, 147–149, 158–167.
76. Cary, 202, 207, 209, 216.
77. Swinson, 170–171.
78. Holland Smith, 200, 211; Richard Wheeler, 280; Leckie, *Delivered from Evil,* 712; Toland, *The Rising Sun,* 721.
79. Lawrence Taylor, 124–126.
80. Conot, 416; Cook, 357.
81. Cary, 173.
82. *Life,* January 24, 1944, 30; Calvert, 69–70.
83. Kahn, 58.
84. *"Possum Patrols"*: Congdon, 492, 526, Dyess, 41–42, and McCormick, 140; Harrington, 337; Routledge, 214.
85. Kahn, 58; Cary, 37.
86. Terkel, 61–62; Harrington, 216; Kahn, 152; Arthur Miller, *Situation Normal,* 148.
87. McCormick, 82–85.
88. Sledge, 122.
89. Sledge, 122; Cary, 37; Terkel, 62; Harrington, 193.
90. McCormick, 240; Richard Wheeler, 38, 231.
91. Harrington, 193, 288–289; Cary, 37–38.
92. Kahn, 68–69, 82; Cary, 173.
93. Standifer, 19; *Life,* May 22, 1944, 34, June 12, 1944, 6.
94. *Life,* May 22, 1944, 34, February 1, 1943, 21, February 22, 1943, 8, March 15, 1943, 4; *high-command directives:* Fussell, 117; *Censors continued:* Harrington, 193.
95. Harrington, 265.
96. Sledge, 155–156.
97. Terkel, 62–63.
98. Terkel, 62, 64.
99. Clint O'Connor, 4–1.

5. Discipline: Not the American Way

1. Stouffer, vol. I, 410, and II, 97; Serumgard, 120.
2. Stouffer, vol. I, 411; Orlin manuscript, chapter 4, 2; Buchwald, 135–136.

3. Keith Winston, 66; Old Sarge, 125.
4. Chapman, 29; Neimeyer, Veterans Survey Project.
5. Chapman, 31; Neimeyer, ibid., Babcock, 52.
6. Becker and Thobaben, 11.
7. Ibid., 133.
8. Keith Winston, 101; Leach, 39; Welker, 129.
9. Tobin, 12.
10. Myrer, 192; Fussell, 103; Babcock, 98, 100; Lee, 73.
11. Lee, 84; McWane, 93; Mathias, 67; Sledge, 319; Mauldin, *Bill Muldin's Army,* 280.
12. Boroughs, 250.
13. Tsuchida, 5.
14. Leckie, *Helmet,* 276; Babcock, 67, 82.
15. Boroughs, 222; Arrington, 31.
16. Walker, 132, 134; Cawthon, 22; Weber, 39; Tumey, 56–57.
17. Gallant, *On Valor's Side,* 308; Boroughs, 139; Mauldin, *Bill Mauldin's Army,* 297.
18. Tapert, *Lines of Battle,* xix; Kennett, 118; Critchell, 107; Graham, 75; Boesch, 68; Hynes, 213, 214.
19. Kennett, 118.
20. Hynes, 213; Leinbaugh, 11–12; Pergrin, 11.
21. Janice Giles, 107.
22. Myrer, 84–85, 228; Kahn, 31; Atwell, 256.
23. Leckie, *Helmet,* 118–119; Keith Winston, 26.
24. Tumey, 21.
25. Weber, 47; Mathias, 214; Atwell, 308; George Baker, "Funny Story."
26. Ehrgott, Veterans' Survey Project.
27. Mauldin, *Up Front,* 184; Noonan, Veterans Survey Project.
28. Leckie, *Helmet,* 139.
29. Mauldin, *Bill Mauldin's Army,* 300.
30. Wolfe, 257–258.
31. Atwell, 376–377; Burns, 122; Keith Winston, 51, 299; George Baker, "Inspection."
32. *Time,* September 1, 1975, 59.
33. Shaw, 468; James Jones, *The Thin Red Line,* 475–476.
34. Gustafson, 12; Leckie, *Helmet,* 244; Ehrgott, Veterans Survey Project.
35. Leckie, *Helmet,* 119; Culwell, 7.
36. Wolfe, xxiii.
37. Weber, 112; Keith Winston, 110; Tumey, 22.
38. Bassett, 16.
39. Robinson, 54; Boesch, 129; MacDonald, 75; Janice Giles, 79.
40. Arrington, 31; Breger, *GI Joe,* Foreword; Lamb, 41.
41. Welker, 267–268; Owens, 212, Faubus, 66.
42. Stein and Brown, "This Is a Furlough"; Gach, 152; James Jones, *From Here to Eternity,* 434–435; Breger, *GI Joe,* "Making Money."
43. McCormick, 181.
44. McCormick, 181–182.
45. Stouffer, vol. II, 119; Ingersoll, 76; Sledge, 319.
46. Arthur Miller, *Situation Normal,* 146; Russell Davis, 108; Gabel, 249; Ehrgott, Veterans Survey Project.
47. Ehrgott, Veterans Survey Project; Leinbaugh, 239–240; Burgett, 169–170.
48. Critchell, 104.
49. Toole, 22, 29, 31–33, 38–39.

50. Glover Johns, 95; MacDonald, 71.
51. Burgett, 155–157.
52. Welker, 103; Bassett, 62; Russell Davis, 222–223.
53. Keith Winston, 51; Ciardi, 46; Fahey, 70.
54. Gustafson, 21, 26; Tumey, 22–23; Kelly, 147.
55. Mauldin, *Bill Mauldin's Army,* 306, 309.
56. Phibbs, 125.
57. Arrington, 187–189; Arthur Miller, *Situation Normal,* 146.
58. Sledge, 319; Morale Services Division, August 1944, 2; Tumey, 21–22; Glover Johns, 75.
59. Standifer, 98; Stannard, 238; Ambrose, 35, 45.
60. Butterfield, 18; Ambrose, 45.
61. Hoyt, 257–258.
62. Boroughs, 250.
63. Gabel, 204–205.
64. Terkel, 67; Valentine, 23–24.
65. Valentine, 7–8.
66. Walzer, 30.
67. Leinbaugh, 179; George Wilson, 141; Currey, 39.
68. Duus, 121; Toole, 81; Boesch, 220.
69. Boesch, 220; Duus, 167, 197.
70. Gabel, 7, 220.
71. Lavender, 63.
72. Russell Davis, 186–188.
73. George Wilson, 114–117.
74. Roche, Veterans Survey Project; Ambrose, 241; Spiller, "Reverberations," 10.
75. Toole, 43; Roche, ibid.; Leckie, *Helmet,* 265; Fussell, 80–81.
76. Martin, 171–172.
77. Hastings, 251–252. See also Leckie, *Delivered from Evil,* 737.
78. Sevareid, 40; "*Winston Churchill:* Peter M. Dawkins in *Infantry,* September–October 1965, 2.
79. Manchester, *Goodbye, Darkness,* 277–278; Tapert, *Lines of Battle,* 109; *Those thus convinced:* Cawthon, 141; Perrett, *A Country Made by War,* 411; *and from the Bulge:* Pergrin, 98–99, 103–104; Moorehead, *Eclipse,* 224.
80. Bird, 27; Waldron, 103.
81. Kerr, 184. See also Jackson Scott, 170–171.
82. Charles, 44; Knox, 351, 385–386.
83. Knox, 163–164, 202, 225, 253, 448.
84. Knox, 296.
85. Coleman, 94; Berry, 139–140.
86. Stewart, 159, 161–163.
87. Bird, 6; Knox, 341–342.
88. Charles, 50; Fujita, 116.
89. Fujita, 116–117.
90. Fujita, 116; Knox, 403, 405; Congdon, 97.
91. Knox, 403.
92. Knox, 225, 394–395, 407–408, 421.
93. Russell, 122, 124, 132–134; Knox, 338.
94. Knox, 406.
95. Gallant, *On Valor's Side,* 82–84.

96. Ibid., 61, 96, 104–105.
97. Ibid., 20; Noonan, Veterans Survey Project.
98. Tregaskis, 83, 89; Richard Wheeler, 152, 430–431; Burke Davis, 169.
99. Graham, 79, 124; Gallant, *On Valor's Side,* 139; Burke Davis, 110–111, 113; O'Sheel, 165.
100. Cochrane, 173.
101. Graham, 29, 31, 37–38, 41–42, 44–46.
102. David Brown, 79.
103. Gallant, *On Valor's Side,* 214–217.
104. Blankfort, 8, 12, 21.
105. *Life,* September 20, 1943, 58; Graham, 126.
106. Blankfort, 20, 300.
107. Blankfort, 28, 31–32, 305–306, 310, 313, 315–316; Lucas, 100; Uris, 384.
108. Blankfort, 21; Lucas, 105.
109. Blankfort, 354.
110. Shomon, 135.
111. Leinbaugh, 277, 283.
112. Toole, 149–150.
113. Faubus, 654–656; Shomon, 134; Toole, 149; Kertzer, 111.
114. Owens, 229; O'Sheel, 219.
115. Faubus, 660; Lee, 163–164, 171–172; Welker, 342, 354.
116. Steinhoff, 193.

6. *The Appeals of Battle: Spectacle, Danger, Destruction*
1. Gray, x, 28–29, 51.
2. James Jones, *The Thin Red Line,* 200; Lee, 153; Cawthon, 67; Sevareid, 501.
3. Bielenberg, 176; Hanley, 74.
4. Cawthon, 67; James Jones, *The Thin Red Line,* 200; Belden, 254; Gray, 14.
5. Graham, 137; Dreux, 314–315.
6. McCallum, 54.
7. Pyle, *Here is Your War,* 212–213.
8. Graham, 123; Tregaskis, 25; Huebner, 61; Dreux, 314.
9. Miller, 240; Mauldin, *Up Front,* 61; Faubus, 703–704.
10. Harry Brown, 116; Bourke-White, 147–148; Sevareid, 388.
11. Guest, 83.
12. Tamai, *Wheat and Soldiers,* 105–107.
13. Yoshida, 95.
14. Pyle, *Here is Your War,* 214, 303–304.
15. Guest, 207; Manchester, *Goodbye, Darkness,* 159; Pyle, *Brave Men,* 295.
16. Pyle, *Ernie Pyle in England,* 31–33.
17. Muggeridge, 103–104.
18. Cotterell, 182–183.
19. Pyle, *Here is Your War,* 14; Boroughs, 82; Casey, 95; Whiting, 19.
20. Richard Wheeler, 253; Keith Wheeler, 159; Codman, 110.
21. Gray, 51.
22. Pearce, 147.
23. Damsky, Veterans Survey Project.
24. Boesch, 226–227.
25. Horan and Frank, 16.
26. James Jones, *The Thin Red Line,* 198; Wolfert, 20–21.
27. Critchell, 157–158; Babcock, 37; Horan and Frank, 16; James Jones, *WWII,* 38.

28. Pearce, 151; Horan and Frank, 18.
29. Sevareid, 335.
30. Douglas, 15.
31. Leckie, *Helmet,* 61, 63, 88.
32. Juergensen, 24.
33. Douglas, 27–28.
34. Crisp, *The Gods Were Neutral,* 12.
35. Pyle, *Last Chapter,* 99.
36. Manchester, *Goodbye, Darkness,* 159–160; Richard Wheeler, 36.
37. James Jones, *WWII,* 48.
38. James Johns, 21; Manchester *Goodbye, Darkness,* 160; Leckie, *Delivered from Evil,* 413, and *Helmet,* 88; Dos Passos, 7.
39. Tobin, 93.
40. Bernstein, 126; Tsuchida, 124; Remarque, *A Time to Love and a Time to Die,* 55.
41. Irgang, 70; Keith Wheeler, 159.
42. Mauldin, *Up Front,* 196.
43. Russell Davis, 174–175; Murphy, 169–170.
44. James Jones, *WWII,* 162–163, 165.
45. James Jones, ibid., 62, and *The Thin Red Line,* 356.
46. Slingduff, Veterans Survey Project; Wolfe, 121.
47. Treml, "Combat Pilot," A1; Cubbins, 85; Cotterell, 184.
48. George, 59–60.
49. Bassett, 65–66.
50. Richard Wheeler, 253; Manchester, *Goodbye, Darkness,* 160; Uris, 286.
51. Pyle, *Brave Men,* 434–438.
52. Casey, 122; James Jones, *The Thin Red Line,* 266; Tapert, *Lines of Battle,* 229; Manchester, *Goodbye, Darkness,* 366; Pyle, *Brave Men,* 451; Atwell, 65; Carter, 86.
53. Mauldin, *Up Front,* 40–41; Tsuchida, 123; Casey, 122.
54. O'Sheel, 278.
55. Yoshida, 64, 70–71.
56. Steinhoff, 38, 82, 119, 124, 145–146, 252, 256.
57. Moorehead, *A Late Education,* 126–129; Tsuchida, 31.
58. Bourke-White, 63; Winston, 178; Faubus, 216; McCallum, 153.
59. Pyle, *Here is Your War,* 193, 212; Atwell, 29.
60. Sledge, 160; Manchester, "The Bloodiest Battle of All," 42.
61. Sevareid, 388.
62. Mathias, vii, ix, 18, 175, 184.
63. James Jones, *WWII,* 38; Manchester, *Goodbye, Darkness,* 367.
64. Bassett, 11–12.
65. Duus, 205.
66. Critchell, 157–158.
67. Kelly, 71; Phibbs, 76.
68. Murphy, 176–177.
69. Schmidt, B9.

7. The Appeals of Battle: Comradeship

1. Belden, 26; Mauldin, *Up Front,* 14–15; Kertzer, 10; Pyle, *Last Chapter,* 45; Nichols, 419; Mumford, 289.
2. Tumey, 39; Gabel, 134; Janice Giles, 377.

3. Gabel, 134; Duus, 100; Sledge, 101; Phillips, Veterans Survey Project; Leinbaugh, conversation with author, February 21, 1989; Russell Davis, 12.

4. Manchester, *Goodbye, Darkness,* 391; Marshall, 160–161; Fussell, 4; Saint-Exupéry, 7.

5. Janice Giles, 232; Arrington, 168; Baron, 157.

6. Mauldin, *The Brass Ring,* 169; Leinbaugh, 193.

7. Houston, 35; Russell Davis, 78; Leinbaugh, 167; Arrington, 168, 176.

8. Phibbs, 148; Sledge, 60; Gray, 40; Phillips, Veterans Survey Project.

9. Russell Davis, 8–9.

10. Ibid., 162–163.

11. Fry, 178.

12. Carter, 139–140.

13. Marshall, 42; Sledge, 60.

14. Critchell, 290–291; Newman, Veterans Survey Project.

15. Guest, 5.

16. Stewart, 51–53.

17. Stewart, 54–56; Remarque, 218–231.

18. James Jones, *The Thin Red Line,* 164–166, 168–169, 173–174.

19. Ibid., 174–175.

20. Tapert, *Despatches from the Heart,* 74; Stewart, 36, 87, 187.

21. Cooke, 150.

22. Marwil, conversation with author, May 30, 1997; Carter, 207; Arrington, 220, 222–223; Murphy, 158.

23. Carter, 138; Arrington, 47; Johnson, 107.

24. Broyles, 59; Uris, 333–334.

25. Uris, 366, 391–392.

26. Ibid., 451–452; Gach, 61.

27. Hynes, 31.

28. Gach, 276; Manchester, *Goodbye, Darkness,* 352–353.

29. Hynes, 44.

30. Marsden, 68.

31. Janice Giles, 302–303.

32. Welch, Veterans Survey Project; Huebner, 160; Janice Giles, 88, 277, 349.

33. Murphy, 147.

34. Arthur Miller, *Situation Normal,* 145.

35. Marsden, 91, 93; Uris, 316; Arthur Miller, *Situation Normal,* 148.

36. Terkel, 378.

37. James Jones, *The Thin Red Line,* 277, 309; Hynes, 247.

38. Arthur Miller, *Situation Normal,* 147.

39. Manchester, *Goodbye, Darkness,* 100.

40. Ibid., 391; Arthur Miller, *Situation Normal,* 155; Hynes, 129–130.

41. Boesch, 228–229; Arrington, 142, 153; Murphy, 94.

42. Murphy, 156–157.

43. Stradling, 98; Uris, 316; Lucas, 104; Manchester, *Goodbye, Darkness,* 391.

44. Arthur Miller, *Situation Normal,* 145.

45. Gray, 50.

46. Janice Giles, 130–131.

47. Redmond, 22; Mathias, 174; Richard Wheeler, 373.

48. Sledge, 223; Gabel, 72.

49. Winston, 29; Ciardi, 66.

50. Gray, 89–90; Mauldin, *The Brass Ring*, 232; Lamb, 40.
51. Phibbs, 8; Russell Davis, 88.
52. Cotterell, 176–177, 182–183.
53. Weber, 22–23; Manchester, *Goodbye, Darkness*, 234–237.
54. Leinbaugh, 150, 152; Welker, 134; Gallant, *On Valor's Side*, 143–144.
55. Mauldin, *The Brass Ring*, 170.
56. Shaw, 623, 646, 649, 651, 653–657.
57. Shaw, 624; James Jones, *WWII*, 255.
58. Mauldin, *The Brass Ring*, 232.
59. McHugh, 32; Stouffer, vol. II, 137; Murphy, 139; Janice Giles, 149.
60. Mauldin, *Up Front*, 60; Faubus, 564.
61. Manchester, *Goodbye, Darkness*, 11–12; 391.
62. Mauldin, *Up Front*, 125–127, and *The Brass Ring*, 172–173.
63. Janice Giles, 130; Nichols, 419.
64. Leckie, *Helmet*, 86.
65. Ibid., 86; Leinbaugh, 127–128.
66. Tapert, *Lines of Battle*, 73.
67. Pyle, *Here is Your War*, 135; Cochrane, 139; Kelly, 150.
68. Winston, 257; Bernstein, 119; Atwell, 91.
69. James Jones, *WWII*, 86; Waldron, 74, 93.
70. Hunt, 145–146; Terkel, 202.
71. Gach, 276–277; Juergensen, 35.
72. Tapert, *Lines of Battle*, 6–7; Bayler, 195.
73. Leinbaugh, 30, 208; Cawthon, 127; James Jones, *Whistle*, 42.
74. Babcock, 59; Murphy, 62; Atwell, 471.
75. Muirhead, 39; Atwell, 458.
76. Atwell, 458–459.
77. Atwell, 459, 470–471.
78. Leinbaugh, 85–86; Hassel, 110.
79. Duus, 100.
80. Murphy, 177, 232, 242–243.
81. Duus, 178; Muirhead, 5–6; Murphy, 208; Spiller, "Hero Against Fire," 15.
82. Muirhead, 174, 177.
83. Murphy, 208.
84. Janice Giles, 292, 321.

8. War Front and Home Front

1. Gallant, *On Valor's Side*, 163; Tumey, 35; Bourke-White, 73; Robert Scott, 190.
2. Bourke-White, 73; Winston, 68, 161–162; Burns, 153; Fahey, 206; Connelly, 42; Boroughs, 13.
3. Kennett, 74; Janice Giles, 247; Waldron, 164; Bourke-White, 73; Nichols, 181.
4. Irgang, 110; Faubus, 85.
5. Robinson, 155–156, 158.
6. Mauldin, *Up Front*, 24; Wolfe, 64–65; Muirhead, 36; Arrington, 210.
7. Tapert, *Lines of Battle*, xviii; Horan and Frank, 143; Whitney, 39; George Wilson, 11.
8. Kennett, 73; Bowker, 35; *On New Guinea:* Morale Services Division, December 1943, 15; Tapert, *Lines of Battle*, xviii–xix.
9. Eustis, 67; Tapert, *Lines of Battle*, 147; Fahey, 182; Waldron, 208; Damsky, Veterans Survey Project.
10. Costello, 144; Cawthon, 107–108, 144.

11. Laffin, *Americans in Battle,* 134.
12. Boesch, 47; Wolfe, 75–76, 78, 111.
13. Currey, 140.
14. Stradling, 217; Russell Davis, 192–193; Winkler, 2.
15. Leach, 10; Tapert, *Lines of Battle,* 186.
16. Stradling, 147; Faubus, 181; Irgang, 110; Tapert, *Lines of Battle,* 2.
17. Tapert, *Lines of Battle,* 147; Janice Giles, 312.
18. Pyle, *Here is Your War,* 15, 297–298.
19. Gabel, 210.
20. Tapert, *Lines of Battle,* 147; Gallant, *On Valor's Side,* 351.
21. Boesch, 25.
22. O'Sheel, 323–324.
23. Sledge, 228.
24. Muirhead, 166–167; Kahn, xxi, 76.
25. Craig, 143; Sajer, 318; Robinson, 142.
26. Uris, 154–156; Irgang, 96–97.
27. Kennett, 73; Wingfield, 174.
28. Uris, 459; Faubus, 322–323.
29. Manchester, "The Bloodiest Battle of All," 81; Baron, 139; Fahey, 167; O'Sheel, 129; Boroughs, 115; *PFC William Hogan:* Martin, 27.
30. Baron, 139; Myrer, 352.
31. Keith Wheeler, 72; O'Sheel, 345; Gallant, *On Valor's Side,* 212; *So many war films:* Kelly, 152.
32. Boesch, 114; James Jones, *Whistle,* 204, and *The Thin Red Line,* 229–230.
33. Pyle, *Brave Men,* 172; Ciardi, 44; Wolfe, 186–187.
34. Martin, 325; Manchester, "The Bloodiest Battle of All," 81; Breuer, *Storming Hitler's Rhine,* 124; Critchell, 21.
35. Wolfe, 186; Martin, 325; Manchester, "The Bloodiest Battle of All," 81, 84; James Jones, *Whistle,* 204–205.
36. Roche, Veterans Survey Project; Faubus, 575; Terkel, 296; McHugh, 34; Connelly, 81–82.
37. Joe E. Brown, 258, 271–272, 274, 285; Hoyt, 272; Arthur Miller, *Situation Normal,* 147; Welker, 273.
38. Lamb, 40.
39. Zolotow, 169; Manchester, "The Bloodiest Battle of All," 84; Hoyt, 272.
40. Kelly, 175; Costello, 130.
41. Vietor, 119; Keith Wheeler, 82, 91; Eustis, 97; Stradling, 224.
42. Irgang, 124; Terkel, 561–562.
43. Winston, 98, 164–165.
44. Winston, 200, 271–272.
45. Cochrane, xi; Welker, 166–167.
46. Stradling, 280; Mumford, 339; Graham, 115; Muirhead, 66; Fry, 122; Boroughs, 200.
47. Mumford, 339; Stradling, 278; James Jones, *WWII,* 16; Boesch, 14; Faubus, 267.
48. Litoff and Smith, 231; Faubus, 309; Hoyt, 282; Baron, 198.
49. Redmond, 164–166.
50. Murphy, 102.
51. Graham, 76; Gallant, *On Valor's Side,* 220; Atwell, 77.
52. Costello, 198; Lee, 90; Fussell, 145.
53. Carter, 280; Richard Wheeler, 341; Dreux, 72.
54. James Jones, *WWII,* 76.
55. Irgang, 96; Mauldin, *Up Front,* 30; Faubus, 185, 361.

56. Miller, 400; Gabriel, 88.
57. Mauldin, *Up Front,* 129–130; Arrington, 69; Tsuchida, 15.
58. Lee Miller, 329, 399; Tapert, *Lines of Battle,* 40.
59. Tsuchida, 40–41.
60. Pyle, *Brave Men,* 399–400.
61. Miller, 400; Nichols, 419.
62. Laffin, *Americans in Battle,* 145; Sherrod, 114–115.
63. Duus, 100.
64. Boesch, 21.
65. Arthur Miller, *Situation Normal,* 175, 177–179.
66. Mumford, 304; Kelly, 148–149.
67. Leinbaugh, 294.
68. *Life,* February 1, 1943, 27; February 15, 1943, 8; February 22, 1943, 27; March 15, 1943, 2; July 26, 1943, 47; August 16, 1943, 6; September 20, 1943, 35.
69. *Life,* October 11, 1943, 4, 6; December 13, 1943, 27.
70. Manchester, *Goodbye, Darkness,* 242; Richard Wheeler, 209.
71. Winston, 119, 176, 178, 259.
72. Sledge, 272–273.
73. Faubus, 361.
74. Murphy, 130; Bourke-White, 131; Atwell, 361–362; Leckie, *Helmet,* 135; Nichols, 363.
75. James Jones, *Whistle,* 78.
76. Mirtle, 46–52; Coughlin, 127.
77. Bergreen, 402, 415, 559; Freeland, 210, 214.
78. Parnell, 86–87; Mauldin, *Up Front,* 53–54; Putman, 185–186.
79. Pyle, *Brave Men,* 399.
80. Bayler, 101–103; Devereux, 114–115.
81. Hemingway, 112–113, 125.
82. Ibid., 130–132, 134–135, 158; Toland, *The Rising Sun,* 658.
83. Mauldin, *Up Front,* 128; Phibbs, 16.
84. Sevareid, 215; O'Sheel, 183.
85. Tumey, 44–45; Phibbs, 16.
86. Millett and Maslowski, 408–409; Terkel, 108.
87. Green, 69; Catton, 292; *Marines in the Pacific:* Graham, 120; Atwell, 362; Murphy, 136–137.
88. Lewis, 29, 33, 38.
89. Nichols, 180.
90. James Jones, *The Thin Red Line,* 471–472.
91. Phibbs, 158.
92. Pyle, *Here is Your War,* 96; Terkel, 160; Sherrod, 114; Dos Passos, 44.
93. Dos Passos, 44; Sherrod, 114–115.
94. Goodman, 49; Terkel, 316.
95. Tapert, *Lines of Battle,* 25–26; Hynes, 195.
96. James Jones, *WWII,* 82.
97. Tapert, *Lines of Battle,* 156; Murphy, 94–95; Fussell, 116.
98. Janice Giles, 68, 270–271.
99. Tapert, *Lines of Battle,* 26.
100. Winkler, 47; Kane, 3; Lance Morrow's review of Roy Hoopes, *Americans Remember the Home Front, Time,* August 1, 1977; Tapert, *Lines of Battle,* 26.
101. David Kennedy's review of film *The Home Front,* AHA Perspectives, Fall 1986; Terkel, 120; *American History Illustrated,* July 1979, 12, 14.

102. Winkler, 30–32.
103. Litoff and Smith, 265–266; Coughlin, 69.
104. Green, 307; Polenberg, 132.
105. Mydans, 122; Sherrod, 151; Archard, 181–182.
106. Irgang, 97; Lingeman, 190.
107. Perrett, *Days of Sadness, Years of Triumph,* 73; Terkel, 112, 323.
108. Dye, 156–157; Tobin, 7.
109. Arrington, 198, 210–211.
110. George, x–xi.
111. Phibbs, 16.
112. Huebner, 59.
113. Kahn, 78; Sledge, 273; *Michigan Today,* October 1986.

Conclusion: The World Within War
  1. Gallant, *On Valor's Side,* 249–250; Mumford, 325.
  2. Janice Giles, 129, 324; Irgang, 75–76.
  3. Ingersoll, 154; Howard and Whitley, 174; Waldron, 80.
  4. Belden, 16; Hoyt, 436; Critchell, 305–306; Murphy, 109.
  5. Gallant, *On Valor's Side,* 251; James Jones, *The Thin Red Line,* 230; Harry Brown, 27–28; Murphy, 46.
  6. David Brown, 56, 78–79; Dye, 201.
  7. Sajer, 254; Muirhead, 3; Dreux, 208; Atwell, 147–148; Murphy, 263–264.
  8. Mauldin, *Up Front,* 19; Pyle, *Here is Your War,* 247–248.
  9. O'Sheel, 164; Richard Wheeler, 434; Hoyt, 421.
 10. David Brown, 83.
 11. David Brown, 56; Toole, 165; Faubus, 181–182.
 12. Arthur Miller, *Situation Normal,* 145; Burns, 337; Lucas, 104; James Johns, 21.
 13. Faubus, 181–182.
 14. Standifer, 248–249; Arrington, 102, 166; Leinbaugh, 294; Janice Giles, 72–73.
 15. Gallant, *On Valor's Side,* 350–351; Manchester, *Goodbye, Darkness,* 262; Kelly, 89.
 16. Lucas, 104; Arthur Miller, *Situation Normal,* 142.
 17. Leinbaugh, 207.
 18. Faubus, 189; Toole, 51; Ciardi, 83.
 19. Bassett, 7.
 20. Winston, 271; Sledge, 323; Terkel, 387; Murphy, 269; George Wilson, 267.
 21. Muirhead, 146.
 22. Leinbaugh, 303–304; Faubus, 412; May, 168.
 23. Morale Services Division, September 1945, 12; *Though they acknowledged:* Archard, 107–108, and Cooke, 137; Laffin, *Americans in Battle,* 160; Huie, 159.
 24. Burke Davis, 169–170, 182.
 25. *"accumulation of experience":* Cooke, 138 and Keith Wheeler, 142; *Combat soldiers:* Arrington, 229, Spiller, "The Thousand Yard Stare," 10, and Bowker, 82; *They found no way:* Bond, 130–131, and Belden, 25.
 26. *Soldiers developed:* James Jones, *WWII,* 113, 116, Lea, 34, Sledge, 128, and Gallant, *On Valor's Side,* 349; Pyle, *Brave Men,* 451; Keith Wheeler, 141.
 27. Faubus, 356; Glover Johns, 51; Tapert, *Lines of Battle,* 49; Mason, 132–133.
 28. *High-command opinion:* Spiller, "The Thousand Yard Stare," 14–15, and Whiting, 69; Sledge, 128, 321; Leinbaugh, conversation with author, February 21, 1989; Faubus, 500; Schratz, ix; Van Creveld, 95; Hastings, 246; Ingraham and Manning, 3.
 29. Hovsepian, 12, 165, 167–168, 171–173, 181, 183–184, 186, 191, 196, 199, 200.

30. Roche, Veterans Survey Project; O'Sheel, 349.
31. Coble, Veterans Survey Project; Wolfe, xxii; Burke Davis, 234.
32. Tapert, *Lines of Battle,* 186 (see also Mauldin, *Up Front,* 9–10, and Knox, 468); Hunt, 146; Charles, 178; Bird, 8.
33. Phibbs, 16; Lamb, 44.
34. Charles, 178; Dreux, xiii; Boroughs, 254.
35. *It was understandable that decades later:* Boroughs, 3–4, Orlin, Introduction, and Standifer, 241.
36. *Their experience:* Leinbaugh, 289, and Wolfe, 236.
37. Kahn, xxv, 329; Treml, "Mine Patrol," A3.
38. Nichols, 194–195.
39. Terkel, 133, 145–146.
40. James Jones, *The Thin Red Line,* 495.

REFERENCES AND
BIBLIOGRAPHY

Abzug, Robert H. *Inside the Vicious Heart: Americans and the Liberation of Nazi Concentration Camps*. New York and Oxford: Oxford University Press, 1985.

Aikawa, Takaaki. *Unwilling Patriot*. Tokyo: The Jordan Press, 1960.

Ambrose, Stephen E. *Band of Brothers: E Company, 506th Regiment, 101st Airborne from Normandy to Hitler's Eagle's Nest*. New York: Simon & Schuster, 1992.

Archard, Theresa. *G.I. Nightingale*. New York: W. W. Norton, 1945.

Ardery, Philip. *Bomber Pilot*. Lexington: The University Press of Kentucky, 1978.

Arrington, Grady P. *Infantryman at the Front*. New York: Vantage Press, 1959.

Arthur, Anthony. *Deliverance at Los Baños*. New York: St. Martin's Press, 1985.

Ashton, Paul. *Bataan Diary*. Santa Barbara: Ashton Publications, 1984.

Atwell, Lester. *Private*. New York: Simon & Schuster, 1958.

Babcock, Myles Standish. *A Guy Who Knows*. St. Paul: Ramaley Printing, 1946.

Baker, George. *The Sad Sack*. New York: Simon & Schuster, 1944.

Baker, Russell. *Growing Up*. New York: Congdon & Weed, 1982.

Baron, Alexander. *From the City, From the Plough*. New York: Ives Washburn, 1949.

Bartov, Omer. *The Eastern Front, 1941–45: German Troops and the Barbarisation of Warfare*. London: Macmillan, 1985.

Bassett, John T. *War Journal of an Innocent Soldier*. Hamden, CT: Shoe String Press, 1989.

Bayler, Walter. *Last Man Off Wake Island*. Indianapolis and New York: The Bobbs-Merrill Company, 1943.

Becker, Carl M., and Thobaben, Robert G. *Common Warfare: Parallel Memoirs by Two World War II GIs in the Pacific*. Jefferson, NC: McFarland, 1992.

Belden, Jack. *Still Time to Die*. New York and London: Harper & Brothers, 1943.

Benedict, Ruth. *The Chrysanthemum and the Sword*. Boston: Houghton Mifflin, 1946.

Bergreen, Laurence. *As Thousands Cheer: The Life of Irving Berlin*. New York: Viking, 1990.

Bernstein, Walter. *Keep Your Head Down*. New York: Viking Press, 1945.

Berry, William A. *Prisoner of the Rising Sun*. Norman: University of Oklahoma Press, 1993.

Bielenberg, Christabel. *The Past Is Myself*. London: Chatto and Windus, 1968.

Bilyeu, Dick. *Lost in Action.* Jefferson, NC, and London: McFarland, 1991.

Bird, Tom. *American POWs of World War II.* Westport, CT: Praeger Publishers, 1992.

Blankfort, Michael. *The Big Yankee: The Life of Carlson of the Raiders.* Boston: Little, Brown, 1947.

Blum, John Morton. *V Was for Victory.* New York and London: Harcourt Brace Jovanovich, 1976.

Boesch, Paul. *Road to Huertgen, Forest in Hell.* Houston: Gulf Publishing Company, 1962.

Bond, Harold L. *Return to Cassino.* Garden City, NY: Doubleday, 1964.

Boroughs, Ralph Zeigler ("Zig"). *A Private's View of World War II.* Greenwood, SC: Clew Books, 1987.

Boulle, Pierre. *The Bridge Over the River Kwai.* New York: Vanguard Press, 1954.

Bourke-White, Margaret. *Purple Heart Valley.* New York: Simon & Schuster, 1944.

Bowker, Benjamin C. *Out of Uniform.* New York: W. W. Norton. 1946.

Boyington, Gregory ("Pappy"). *Baa Baa Black Sheep.* New York: G. P. Putnam's Sons, 1958.

Brain, Philip S., Jr. *Soldier of Bataan.* Minneapolis: Rotary Club of Minneapolis, 1990.

Braly, William C. *The Hard Way Home.* Washington, DC: Infantry Journal Press, 1947.

Breger, Dave. *GI Joe.* Garden City, NY: Blue Ribbon Books, 1945.

——————. *Private Breger.* New York: Rand McNally and Company, 1942.

Breuer, William B. *Death of a Nazi Army.* New York: Stein and Day, 1985.

——————. *Storming Hitler's Rhine.* New York: St. Martin's Press, 1985.

Brown, David Tucker, Jr. *Marine from Virginia.* Chapel Hill: University of North Carolina Press, 1947.

Brown, Harry. *A Walk in the Sun.* New York: Alfred A. Knopf, 1944.

Brown, Joe E. *Laughter is a Wonderful Thing.* New York: A. S. Barnes and Company, 1956.

Broyles, William, Jr. "Why Men Love War." *Esquire* (November 1984), 55–65.

Buchwald, Art. *Leaving Home.* New York: G. P. Putnam's Sons, 1993.

Burgett, Donald R. *Currahee!* Boston: Houghton Mifflin Company, 1967.

Burns, John Horne. *The Gallery.* New York and London: Harper & Brothers, 1947.

Butterfield, Roger. *Al Schmid, Marine.* New York: W. W. Norton, 1944.

Calvert, James F. *Silent Running.* New York: John Wiley & Sons, 1995.

Camp, William. *Retreat, Hell!* New York and London: D. Appleton-Century Company, 1943.

Carter, Ross S. *Those Devils in Baggy Pants.* New York: Appleton-Century-Crofts, 1951.

Cary, Otis. *War-Wasted Asia: Letters, 1945–46.* Tokyo and New York: Kodansha International, 1975.

Casey, Robert J. *This Is Where I Came In.* New York and Indianapolis: The Bobbs-Merrill Company, 1945.

Cassell's History of the Russo-Japanese War. 5 vols. London and Paris: Cassell and Company, 1905.

Catton, Bruce. *The War Lords of Washington.* New York: Harcourt Brace, 1948.

Cawthon, Charles R. *Other Clay.* Niwot, CO: The University Press of Colorado, 1990.

Chapman, Robert B. *Tell It to the Chaplain.* New York: Exposition Press, 1952.

Charles, H. Robert. *Last Man Out.* Austin, TX: Eakin Press, 1988.

Ciardi, John. *Saipan.* Fayetteville and London: The University of Arkansas Press, 1988.

Cochrane, Peter. *Charlie Company.* London: Chatto and Windus, 1977.

Codman, Charles R. *Drive.* Boston and Toronto: Little, Brown, 1957.

Coleman, John S., Jr. *Bataan and Beyond.* College Station and London: Texas A & M University Press, 1978.

Congdon, Don. *Combat WWII: Pacific Theater of Operations.* New York: Arbor House, 1958.

Connelly, Kenneth A., Jr. *Chaplain's Assistant.* Seattle: Craftsman Press, 1945.

Conot, Robert. *Justice at Nuremberg.* New York: Harper & Row, 1983.

Cook, Haruko Taya, and Cook, Theodore F. *Japan at War.* New York: The New Press, 1992.

Cooke, Elliot D. *All But Thee and Me: Psychiatry at the Foxhole Level.* Washington, DC: Infantry Press Journal, 1946.

Costello, John. *Virtue under Fire.* Boston and Toronto: Little, Brown, 1985.

Cotterell, Anthony. *An Apple for the Sergeant.* London: Hutchinson and Company, n.d.

Coughlin, Gene. *Assistant Hero.* New York: Thomas Y. Crowell Company, 1944.

Craig, William. *Enemy at the Gates: The Battle for Stalingrad.* New York: Reader's Digest Press and E. P. Dutton, 1973.

Crawford, Robert John. *I Was an Eighth Army Soldier.* London: Victor Gollancz Limited, 1944.

Crisp, Robert. *Brazen Chariots.* New York: W. W. Norton, 1959.

——————. *The Gods Were Neutral.* New York: W. W. Norton, 1960.

Critchell, Laurence. *Four Stars of Hell.* New York: The Declan X. McMullen Company, 1947.

Cubbins, William R. *The War of the Cotton-Tails.* Chapel Hill, NC: Algonquin Books, 1989.

Culwell, Ben. *Adrenalin Hour: The South Pacific, World War II.* Houston: Menil Collection, 1987.

Currey, Cecil B. *Follow Me and Die.* New York: Stein and Day, Publishers, 1984.

Dalderup, Leo. *The Other Side.* London: Hodder and Stoughton, 1954.

Davis, Burke. *Marine! The Life of Lieutenant General Lewis B. (Chesty) Puller.* Boston and Toronto: Little, Brown, 1962.

Davis, Kenneth S. *Experience of War.* Garden City, NY: Doubleday, 1965.

Davis, Russell. *Marine at War.* New York: Scholastic Book Services, 1970.

Devereux, James P. S. *The Story of Wake Island.* Philadelphia and New York: J. B. Lippincott Company, 1947.

Domantay, Pat. *My Terrible Days and Survival in World War II.* New York: Vantage Press, 1972.

Doolittle, James. "Impact: Daylight Precision Bombing." *American History Illustrated* 10 (February 1980): 8–12, 41–47.

Dos Passos, John. *Tour of Duty.* Boston: Houghton Mifflin Company, 1946.

Douglas, Keith. *Alamein to Zem Zem.* London: PL Editions Poetry, 1946.

Doward, Jan. *Battleground.* Nashville: Southern Publishing Association, 1954.

Dower, John W. *War Without Mercy.* New York: Pantheon Books, 1986.

Drea, Edward J. "In the Army Barracks of Imperial Japan," *Armed Forces and Society* 3 (Spring 1989), 329–348.

Dreux, William B. *No Bridges Blown.* Notre Dame and London: University of Notre Dame Press, 1971.

Duus, Masayo Umezawa. *Unlikely Liberators: The Men of the 100th and 442nd.* Honolulu: University of Hawaii Press, 1987.

Dye, John Thomas III. *Golden Leaves.* Los Angeles: The Ward Ritchie Press, 1962.

Dyess, William E. *The Dyess Story.* New York: G. P. Putnam's Sons, 1944.

Emmerson, John K. *The Japanese Thread.* New York: Holt, Rinehart and Winston, 1978.

Emmrich, Kurt. *The Invisible Flag.* New York: The John Day Company, 1956.

Eustis, Edith Morton. *War Letters of Morton Eustis to his Mother.* New York: The Spiral Press, 1945.

Fahey, James J. *Pacific War Diary, 1942–1945.* Boston: Houghton Mifflin, 1963.

Falk, Stanley L. *Bataan: The March of Death.* New York: W. W. Norton, 1962.

Faubus, Orval Eugene. *In This Faraway Land.* Conway, AR: River Road Press, 1971.

Firbank, Thomas. *I Bought a Star.* London: George G. Harrup and Company, 1951.

FitzPatrick, Bernard T. *The Hike into the Sun.* Jefferson, NC, and London: McFarland, 1993.

Frank, Richard B. *Guadalcanal.* New York: Random House, 1990.

Freedland, Michael. *Irving Berlin.* New York: Stein and Day, 1974.

Fry, James C. *Combat Soldier.* Washington, DC: The National Press, 1968.

Fuchs, Karl. *Sieg Heil! War Letters of Tank Gunner Karl Fuchs, 1937–1941.* Hamden, CT: Archon Books, 1987.

Fujita, Frank. *Foo: A Japanese-American Prisoner of the Rising Sun.* Denton, TX: University of North Texas Press, 1993.

Fuller, Timothy. *Something of Great Constancy, Essays in Honor of the Memory of J. Glenn Gray, 1913–1977.* Colorado Springs: Colorado College, 1979.

Fussell, Paul. *Wartime.* New York: Oxford University Press, 1989.

Gabel, Kurt. *The Making of a Paratrooper.* Lawrence: University Press of Kansas, 1990.

Gabriel, Richard A. *No More Heroes: Madness and Psychiatry in War.* New York: Hill & Wang, 1987.

Gach, Gene. *In the Army Now.* New York: Dodd, Mead and Company, 1942.

Gallant, T. Grady. *The Friendly Dead.* Garden City, NY: Doubleday, 1964.

————. *On Valor's Side.* Garden City, NY: Doubleday, 1963.

Galloway, Strome. *With the Irish Against Rommel.* Langley, British Columbia: Battleline Books, 1984.

Garrett, George. *James Jones.* San Diego: Harcourt Brace Jovanovich, 1984.

George, John B. *Shots Fired in Anger.* Plantersville, SC: Small Arms Technical Publishing Company, 1947.

Giles, Donald T. *Captive of the Rising Sun.* Annapolis: Naval Institute Press, 1994.

Giles, Janice Holt. *The GI Journal of Sergeant Giles.* Boston: Houghton Mifflin, and Cambridge: The Riverside Press, 1965.

Glasser, Arthur F. *And Some Believed: A Chaplain's Experiences with the Marines in the South Pacific.* Chicago: Moody Press, 1946.

Goodman, Jack. *While You Were Gone: A Report on Wartime Life in the United States.* New York: Simon & Schuster, 1946.

Graham, Garrett. *Banzai Noel!* New York: The Vanguard Press, 1944.

Grashio, Samuel C. *Return to Freedom.* Tulsa: MCN Press, 1982.

Gray, Jesse Glenn. *The Warriors: Reflections on Men in Battle.* New York: Harper & Row, 1959.

Green, Anne Bosanko. *One Woman's War.* St. Paul: Minnesota Historical Society Press, 1989.

Green, Vincent. *Extreme Justice.* New York: Pocket Books, 1995.

Guest, John. *Broken Images: A Journal.* London: Longmans, Green, 1949.

Gunther, John. *Inside Asia.* New York and London: Harper & Brothers, 1939.

Gustafson, Walter. *My Time in the Army.* Chicago: Adams Press, 1968.

Habe, Hans. *A Thousand Shall Fall.* New York: Harcourt, Brace & Company, 1941.

Hanley, Lynne. *Writing War.* Amherst: The Unversity of Massachusetts Press, 1991.

Harmon, Tom. *Pilots Also Pray.* New York: Thomas Y. Crowell, 1944.

Harries, Meirion, and Harries, Susie. *Soldiers of the Sun: The Rise and Fall of the Imperial Japanese Army.* New York: Random House, 1991.

Harrington, Joseph D. *Yankee Samurai.* Detroit: Pettigrew Enterprises, 1979.

Harrison, Kenneth. *The Brave Japanese.* London: Angus and Robertson, and Adelaide: Rigby Limited, 1967.

Hashimoto, Mochitsura. *Sunk: The Story of the Japanese Submarine Fleet, 1941–1945.* New York: Henry Holt, 1954.

Hassel, Sven. *The Legion of the Damned.* New York: Farrar, Straus & Cudahy, 1957.

Havens, Thomas R. H. *Valley of Darkness: The Japanese People and World War Two.* Lanham, MD: University Press of America, 1986.

Hayashi, Saburo, *Kōgun: The Japanese Army in the Pacific War.* Quantico, VA: The Marine Corps Association, 1959.

Hayes, Thomas. *Bilibid Diary.* Hamden, CT: Archon Books, 1987.

Heinrich, Willi. *The Cross of Iron.* New York and Indianapolis: The Bobbs-Merrill Company, 1956.

Hemingway, Albert. *Ira Hayes: Pima Marine.* Lanham, MD: University Press of America, 1988.

Henniker, Mark. *An Image of War.* London: Leo Cooper, 1987.

Hersey, John. *Into the Valley.* New York, Alfred A. Knopf, 1943.

——————. *Men on Bataan.* New York: Alfred A. Knopf, 1942.

Hess, Gary R. *The United States at War, 1941–1945.* Arlington Heights, Ill.: Harlan Davidson, 1986.

Hieb, Harley F. *Heart of Iron.* Lodi, CA: Pacifica Publishing, 1987.

Hilsman, Roger. *American Guerrilla: My War Behind Japanese Lines.* Washington, DC: Brassey's (US), 1990.

Hogan, John J. *I Am Not Alone.* Washington, DC: Mackinac Press, 1947.

Holmes, Richard. *Acts of War: The Behavior of Men in Battle.* New York: The Free Press, 1985.

Horan, James D., and Frank, Gerold. *Out in the Boondocks: Marines in Action in the Pacific.* New York: G. P. Putnam's Sons, 1943.

Hough, Frank O. *The Island War.* Philadelphia and New York: J.B. Lippincott, 1947.

Houston, Robert J. *D-Day to Bastogne.* Smithtown, NY: Exposition Press, 1980.

Hovsepian, Aramais. *Your Son and Mine.* New York: Duell, Sloan and Pearce, 1950.

Howard, Clive, and Whitley, Joe. *One Damned Island After Another.* Chapel Hill: The University of North Carolina Press, 1946.

Hoyt, Edwin P. *The GI's War.* New York: McGraw-Hill, 1988.

Huebner, Klaus H. *Long Walk Through War.* College Station: Texas A & M University Press, 1987.

Huie, William B. *The Execution of Private Slovik.* New York: Duell, Sloan and Pearce, and Boston: Little, Brown, 1954.

Hunt, George P. *Coral Comes High.* New York and London: Harper & Brothers, 1946.

Hynes, Samuel. *Flights of Passage.* New York: Frederic C. Beil, and Annapolis: Naval Institute Press, 1988.

Ind, Allison. *Bataan: The Judgment Seat.* New York: Macmillan, 1944.

Ingersoll, Ralph. *The Battle Is the Pay-Off.* New York: Harcourt, Brace and Company, 1943.

Ingraham, Larry, and Manning, Frederick. "Cohesion." *Military Review* 6 (June 1981), 2–12.

Irgang, Frank J. *Etched In Purple.* Caldwell, ID: The Caxton Printers, 1949.

Irving, David. *The War Between the Generals.* London: Allen Lane, 1981.

Johns, Glover S., Jr. *The Clay Pigeons of St. Lo.* Harrisburg: The Military Service Publishing Company, 1958.

Johns, James M., and Compton, Bill. *Guadalcanal Twice-Told.* New York: Vantage Press, 1978.

Johnson, Franklyn A. *One More Hill.* New York: Funk & Wagnalls, 1949.

Joly, Cyril. *Take These Men.* London: Constable, 1955.

Jones, Don. *Oba, The Last Samurai.* Novato, Calif.: Presidio Press, 1986.

Jones, James. *From Here to Eternity.* New York: Charles Scribner's Sons, 1951.

——————. *The Pistol.* New York: Charles Scribner's Sons, 1958.

——————. *The Thin Red Line.* New York: Charles Scribner's Sons, 1962.

——————. *Whistle.* New York: Delacorte Press, 1978.

——————. *WWII.* New York: Grosset and Dunlap, 1975.

Juergensen, Hans. *Beachheads and Mountains: Campaigning from Sicily to Anzio.* Tampa: American Studies Press, 1984.

Kahn, E. J., Jr. *GI Jungle.* New York: Simon & Schuster, 1943.

Kahn, Sy M. *Between Tedium and Terror.* Urbana and Chicago: University of Illinois Press, 1993.

Kane, Jim, "V-E Day: A Special Memory," Ann Arbor *News,* May 7, 1979.

Kato, Masuo. *The Lost War.* New York: Alfred A. Knopf, 1946.

Keller, Julius. *From Riva Ridge to Riva.* New York: Vantage Press, 1974.

Kellett, Anthony. *Combat Motivation: The Behavior of Soldiers in Battle.* Boston: Kluwer-Nijhoff Publishing, 1982.

Kelley, Kitty. *His Way: The Unauthorized Biography of Frank Sinatra.* Toronto: Bantam Books, 1986.

Kelly, Charles E. (Commando). *One Man's War.* New York: Alfred A. Knopf, 1944.

Kennedy, Malcolm D. *The Military Side of Japanese Life.* Westport, CT: Greenwood Press, 1973 (1924).

Kennett, Lee. *GI: The American Soldier in WWII.* New York: Charles Scribner's Sons, 1987.

Kerr, E. Bartlett. *Surrender and Survival: The Experience of American POWs in the Pacific, 1941–1945.* New York: William Morrow, 1985.

Kersh, Gerald. *They Die with Their Boots Clean.* London: Readers Union Limited and William Heinemann Limited, 1942.

Kertzer, Morris N. *With an H on My Dog Tag.* New York: Behrman House, 1947.

Kirst, Hans Hellmut. *Forward, Gunner Asch!* Boston and Toronto: Little, Brown, 1956.

Knappe, Siegfried. *Soldat: Reflections of a German Soldier, 1936–1949.* New York: Orion Books, 1992.

Knightley, Phillip. *The First Casualty.* New York: Harcourt Brace Jovanovich, 1975.

Knox, Donald. *Death March: The Survivors of Bataan.* New York: Harcourt Brace Jovanovich, 1981.

Kodama, Yoshio. *Sugamo Diary.* Tokyo: Radiopress, 1960.

Laffin, John. *Americans in Battle.* New York: Crown Publishers, 1973.

——————. *Jackboot: The Story of the German Soldier.* London: Cassell, 1965.

Lamb, David. "Bill, Willie and Joe." *Military History Quarterly* 4 (Summer 1989), 36–45.

Lartéguy, Jean. *The Sun Goes Down: Last Letters from Japanese Suicide-Pilots and Soldiers.* London: The New English Library, 1975 (1956).

Lavender, Don. "Nudge Blue: A Chronicle of World War II Experience." Typescript prepared in 1964; copy on file at Military History Institute, Carlisle, Pa.

Lawton, Manny. *Some Survived.* Chapel Hill: Algonquin Books, 1984.

Lay, Beirne, Jr. *I've Had It: The Survival of a Bomb Group Commander.* New York and London: Harper & Brothers, 1945.

Lea, Tom. *Peleliu Landing.* El Paso: Carl Hertzog, 1945.

Leach, Douglas E. *Now Hear This.* Kent, Ohio, and London: The Kent State University Press, 1987.

Leckie, Robert. *Delivered from Evil: The Saga of World War II.* New York: Harper & Row, 1987.

——————. *Helmet for My Pillow.* New York: Random House, 1957.

Lee, Robert E. *To the War.* New York: Alfred A. Knopf, 1968.

Leinbaugh, Harold P., and Campbell, John D. *The Men of Company K.* New York: Bantam, 1987.

Levering, Robert W. *Horror Trek.* New York: Carlton Press, 1979 (1948).

Lewis, Bruce. *Four Men Went to War.* New York: St. Martin's Press, 1987.

Life Goes to War: A Picture History of World War II. New York: Simon & Schuster, 1977.

Life's Picture History of World War II. New York: Time Inc., 1950.

Lifton, Robert Jay. *Death in Life.* New York: Random House, 1967.

Lindsay, Martin. *So Few Got Through.* London: Collins, 1946.

Lingeman, Richard R. *Don't You Know There's a War On? The American Home Front, 1941–1945.* New York: G. P. Putnam's Sons, 1970.

Litoff, Judy Barrett and Smith, David. *Since You Went Away: World War II Letters from American Women on the Home Front*. New York: Oxford University Press, 1991.

Lucas, Jim. *Combat Correspondent*. New York: Reynal and Hitchcock, 1944.

MacDonald, Charles B. *Company Commander*. Washington DC: Infantry Journal Press, 1947.

Mallonée, Richard C. *The Naked Flagpole: Battle for Bataan*. San Rafael, CA: Presidio Press, 1980.

Manchester, William. *Goodbye, Darkness: A Memoir of the Pacific War*. Boston: Little, Brown, 1979.

—————. "The Bloodiest Battle of All," *New York Times Magazine*, June 14, 1987.

Marsden, M. H. E. *Khaki Is More Than A Color*. Garden City, NY: Doubleday, Doran, 1943.

Marshall, Samuel L. A. *Men Against Fire*. New York: William Morrow, 1947.

Martin, Ralph G. *The GI War, 1941–1945*. Boston and Toronto: Little, Brown, 1967.

Marwil, Jonathan. *Frederic Manning: An Unfinished Life*. Durham: Duke University Press, 1988.

Masashi, Ito. *The Emperor's Last Soldiers*. New York: Coward-McCann, 1967.

Mason, John T., Jr. *The Pacific War Remembered*. Annapolis: Naval Institute Press, 1986.

Masters, John. *The Road Past Mandalay*. New York: Harper & Brothers, 1961.

Mathias, Frank F. *GI Jive: An Army Bandsman in World War II*. Lexington: The University Press of Kentucky, 1982.

Mauldin, Bill. *Up Front*. Cleveland and New York: World Publishing Company, 1945.

—————. *Bill Mauldin's Army*. New York: William Sloane Associates, 1944.

—————. *The Brass Ring*. New York: W. W. Norton, 1952.

May, Rollo. *Power and Innocence*. New York: W. W. Norton, 1972.

McCallum, Neil. *Journey With a Pistol: A Diary of War*. London: Victor Gollancz, 1959.

McCormick, John. *The Right Kind of War*. Annapolis: Naval Institute Press, 1992.

McHugh, Vernon D. *From Hell to Heaven: Memoirs from Patton's Third Army*. Ardmore, PA: Dorrance, 1980.

McKee, Alexander. "The Defeat and Death of General Rommel." *New York Times Magazine*, October 22, 1967.

McWane, Fred W. *Memoirs*. Lynchburg, VA: published by author, 1951.

Mellnik, Stephen M. *Philippine War Diary, 1939–1945*. New York: Van Nostrand Reinhold, 1981 (1969).

Military Intelligence Service. *Soldier's Guide to the Japanese Army*. Washington, DC: The War Department, 1944.

Miller, Arthur. *Situation Normal*. New York: Reynal and Hitchcock, 1944.

—————. *Timebends: A Life*. New York: Grove Press, 1987.

Miller, Lee G. *The Story of Ernie Pyle*. New York: Viking Press, 1950.

Millett, Allan R., and Maslowski, Peter. *For the Common Defense*. New York: The Free Press, and London: Collier Macmillan, 1984.

Millot, Bernard. *Divine Thunder: The Life and Death of the Kamikazes*. New York: McCall Publishing, 1971.

Mirtle, Jack. *Thank You Music Lovers: A Biography of Spike Jones and his City Slickers*. Westport, CT: Greenwood, 1986.

Montyn, Jan. *A Lamb to Slaughter*. London: Souvenir Press, 1982.

Moorehead, Alan. *Eclipse*. New York and Evanston: Harper & Row, 1968 (1945).

—————. *A Late Education*. London: Hamish Hamilton, 1970.

Morale Services Division, Army Services Forces. *What the Soldier Thinks: A Monthly Digest of War Department Studies on the Attitudes of American Troops*. Washington, December 1943–September 1945.

Moriya, Tadashi. *No Requiem.* Tokyo: Hokuseido Press, 1968.

Morris, Ivan. *The Nobility of Failure.* New York: Holt, Rinehart and Winston, 1975.

Mowat, Farley. *And No Birds Sang.* Toronto: McClelland and Stewart, 1979.

Muggeridge, Malcolm. *Chronicles of Wasted Time.* Vol. 2: The Infernal Grove. London: Collins, 1973.

Muirhead, John. *Those Who Fall.* New York: Random House, 1986.

Mumford, Lewis. *Green Memories: The Story of Geddes Mumford.* New York: Harcourt, Brace, 1947.

Murphy, Audie. *To Hell and Back.* New York: Henry Holt, 1949.

Mydans, Carl. *More Than Meets the Eye.* New York: Harper & Brothers, 1959.

Myrer, Anton. *The Big War.* New York: Appleton-Century-Crofts, 1957.

——. *Once An Eagle.* New York: Holt, Rinehart and Winston, 1968.

Nagatsuka, Ryuji. *I Was a Kamikaze.* London: Abelard-Schuman, 1973.

Naito, Hatsuho. *Thunder Gods: The Kamikaze Pilots Tell Their Story.* Tokyo and New York: Kodansha International, 1982.

National Research Council. *Psychology for the Fighting Man.* Washington, DC: The Infantry Journal, 1943.

Neumann, Peter. *Other Men's Graves.* London: Weidenfeld and Nicolson, 1958.

Nichols, David. *Ernie's War: The Best of Ernie Pyle's World War II Dispatches.* New York: Random House, 1986.

O'Connor, Clint. "Fighting Snipers, Bugs and Jungle Rot in Burma." Cleveland *Plain Dealer.* March 27, 1994.

O'Connor, Richard. *Jack London.* London: Victor Gollancz, 1965.

Ogawa, Tetsuro. *Terraced Hell.* Rutland, Vermont, and Tokyo: Charles E. Tuttle Company, 1972.

Okumiya, Masatake, and Horikoshi, Jiro. *Zero!* New York: E. P. Dutton, 1956.

Onoda, Hiroo. *No Surrender: My Thirty-Year War.* Tokyo: Kodansha International, 1974.

Orlin, Louis L. "Just Over the Next Hill: A Memoir of Two Years in the Army During World War II." Unpublished manuscript written 1992–93.

O'Sheel, Patrick, and Cook, Gene. *Semper Fidelis: The U.S. Marines in the Pacific, 1942–1945.* New York: William Sloane Associates, 1947.

Ott, Wolfgang. *Sharks and Little Fish.* New York: Pantheon Books, 1957.

Owens, William A. *Eye-Deep in Hell: A Memoir of the Liberation of the Philippines, 1944–1945.* Dallas: Southern Methodist University Press, 1989.

Pabel, Reinhold. *Enemies Are Human.* Philadelphia: John C. Winston, 1955.

Padover, Saul K. *Experiment in Germany: The Story of an American Intelligence Officer.* New York: Duell, Sloan and Pearce, 1946.

Parnell, Wilma. *The Killing of Corporal Kunze.* Secaucus, NJ: Lyle Stuart, 1981.

Paull, Raymond. *Retreat from Kokoda.* Melbourne: William H. Heinemann, 1958.

Pearce, Donald. *Journal of a War.* Toronto: Macmillan of Canada, 1965.

Pereira, Jocelyn. *A Distant Drum.* Aldershot (U.K.): Gale and Polden, 1948.

Pergrin, David E. *First Across the Rhine.* New York, Atheneum, 1989.

Perkins, Bradford. "Impressions of Wartime," *Journal of American History* 2 (September 1990), 563–568.

Perrett, Geoffrey. *Days of Sadness, Years of Triumph.* New York: Coward, McCann and Geoghegan, 1973.

——. *A Country Made by War.* New York: Random House, 1989.

Petak, Joseph A. *Never Plan Tomorrow.* Fullerton, CA: Aquataur, 1991.

Petillo, Carol M. *The Ordeal of Elizabeth Vaughan.* Athens: The University of Georgia Press, 1985.

Phibbs, Brendan. *The Other Side of Time: A Combat Surgeon in World War II.* Boston and Toronto: Little, Brown, 1987.

Piercy, Marge. *Gone to Soldiers.* New York: Ballantine Books, 1988.

Plievier, Theodor. *Moscow.* New York: Doubleday and Company, 1954.

————. *Stalingrad.* New York: Appleton-Century-Crofts, 1948.

Polenberg, Richard. *War and Society: The United States, 1941–1945.* Philadelphia: J. B. Lippincott, 1972.

Polyakov, A. *With a Soviet Unit through the Nazi Lines.* London: Hutchinson and Company, 1942.

Prange, Gordon W. *God's Samurai.* Washington, DC: Brassey's (US), 1990.

Pruller, Wilhelm. *Diary of a German Soldier.* New York: Coward-McCann, 1963.

Putman, Russell L. *Sincerely, Put: Letters to his Friends. . . .* Privately printed, 1945.

Pyle, Ernie. *Ernie Pyle in England.* New York: Robert M. McBride, 1941.

————. *Here Is Your War.* New York: Lancer Books, 1943.

————. *Brave Men.* New York: Henry Holt and Company, 1944.

————. *Last Chapter.* New York: Henry Holt and Company, 1946.

Raff, Edson D. *We Jumped to Fight.* New York: Eagle Books, 1944.

Randall, Howard M. *Dirt and Doughfeet: Combat Experiences of a Rifle-Platoon Leader.* New York: Exposition Press, 1955.

Rawlings, Leo. *And the Dawn Camp Up Like Thunder.* London: Rawlings, Chapman Publications, 1972.

Redmond, Juanita. *I Served on Bataan.* Philadelphia and New York: J. B. Lippincott, 1943.

Reischauer, Edwin O. *The Japanese.* Cambridge and London: Belknap Press of Harvard University Press, 1977.

Remarque, Erich M. *All Quiet on the Western Front.* Boston: Little, Brown, 1929.

————. *A Time to Love and a Time to Die.* New York: Harcourt, Brace & World, 1954.

Renfro, Robert. "Three American Novelists at War." Ph.D. dissertation, University of Texas, 1984.

Reynolds, Bob. *Of Rice and Men.* Philadelphia: Dorrance, 1947.

Robinson, Don. *News of the 45th.* Norman: University of Oklahoma Press, 1944.

Rock, Norman. "General James Doolittle: 'Just Taking Care of America,'" *Friendly Exchange* (May 1987): 19–20.

Roeder, George H., Jr. *The Censored War.* New Haven and London: Yale University Press, 1993.

Routledge, Joseph E. *Eighty Days on Okinawa.* Bellflower, CA: Shade Tree Books, 1993.

Russell, Lord, of Liverpool. *The Knights of Bushido.* New York: E. P. Dutton, 1958.

Saint-Exupéry, Antoine de. *Wartime Writings, 1939–1944.* San Diego: Harcourt Brace Jovanovich, 1986 (1982).

St. John, Joseph F. *Leyte Calling.* New York: Vanguard Press, 1945.

Sajer, Guy. *The Forgotten Soldier.* New York: Harper & Row, 1971.

Sakai, Saburo. *Samurai!* New York: E. P. Dutton, 1957.

Sakamaki, Kazuo. *I Attacked Pearl Harbor.* New York: Association Press, 1949.

Samwell, H. P. *An Infantry Officer with the Eighth Army.* Edinburgh and London: William Blackwood and Sons, 1945.

Sauer, Wolfgang. "A Nation Paralyzed." *University Publishing* (Spring 1979): 5.

Scidmore, Eliza R. *As The Hague Ordains: Journal of a Russian Prisoner's Wife in Japan.* New York: Henry Holt and Company, 1907.

Schmidt, William E. "Jewish Vet May Finally Get Medal." Ann Arbor *News,* November 5, 1989.

Schratz, Paul R. *Submarine Commander.* Lexington: The University Press of Kentucky, 1988.

Scott, Robert L., Jr. *God Is My Co-Pilot.* New York: Ballantine Books, 1956 (1943).

Scott, R. Jackson. *90 Days of Rice*. Pioneer, CA: California Traveler, 1975.

Serumgard, Arthur K. *Old Sarge: How to Get Along in the Army*. New York and London: D. Appleton-Century Company, 1942.

Sevareid, Eric. *Not So Wild a Dream*. New York: Atheneum, 1976 (1946).

Shaw, Irwin. *The Young Lions*. New York: Random House, 1948.

Sherrod, Robert. *Tarawa: The Story of a Battle*. New York: Duell, Sloan and Pearce, 1944.

Sherry, Michael S. *The Rise of American Air Power*. New Haven and London: Yale University Press, 1987.

Shirer, William L. *20th Century Journey*. Vol. 2: *The Nightmare Years*. Boston and Toronto: Little, Brown, 1984.

Shomon, Joseph J. *Crosses in the Wind*. New York: Stratford House, 1947.

Skrjabina, Elena. *After Leningrad*. Carbondale and Edwardsville: Southern Illinois University Press, 1978.

Sledge, Eugene B. *With the Old Breed at Peleliu and Okinawa*. New York: Bantam, 1983.

Smith, Holland M. *Coral and Brass*. New York: Charles Scribner's Sons, 1949.

Smith, Stanley W. *Prisoner of the Emperor*. Niwot: The University Press of Colorado, 1991.

Spector, Ronald. *Eagle Against the Sun: The American War with Japan*. New York: The Free Press, 1985.

Spiller, Roger J. "The Thousand Yard Stare: Psychodynamics of Combat in World War II."

——————. "Repression of War Experience."

——————. "Hero Against Fire: Audie Murphy and his War."

——————. "'Reverberations'—An Interview with Paul Fussell."

Stahlberg, Alexander. *Bounden Duty*. London: Brassey's (UK), 1990.

Standifer, Leon C. *Not In Vain: A Rifleman Remembers World War II*. Baton Rouge and London: Louisiana State University Press, 1992.

Stannard, Richard M. *Infantry: An Oral History of a World War II American Infantry Battalion*. New York: Twayne Publishers, 1993.

Stein, Ralph, and Brown, Harry. *It's a Cinch, Private Finch!* New York and London: McGraw-Hill, 1943.

Steinbeck, John. *Once There Was a War*. New York: Viking Press, 1958.

Steinhoff, Johannes. *Messerschmitts Over Sicily*. Baltimore: The Nautical and Aviation Publishing Company of America, 1987.

Steinhoff, Johannes, Pechel, Peter, and Showalter, Dennis. *Voices from the Third Reich: An Oral History*. Washington, DC: Regnery Gateway, 1989.

Stewart, Sidney. *Give Us This Day*. New York: W. W. Norton, 1956.

Stiles, Bert. *Serenade to the Big Bird*. New York: W. W. Norton, 1952.

Stouffer, Samuel A., et al. *The American Soldier*. 4 vols. Princeton: Princeton University Press, 1949.

Stradling, Harriet, J. *Johnny*. Salt Lake City: Bookcraft, 1946.

Sulzberger, C. L. *World War II*. New York: American Heritage, 1966.

Swinson, Arthur. *Four Samurai*. London: Hutchinson, 1968.

Sydnor, Charles W. *Soldiers of Destruction: The SS Death's Head Division, 1933–1945*. Princeton: Princeton University Press, 1977.

Tamai, Katsunori. *Wheat and Soldiers*. New York and Toronto: Farrar and Rinehart, 1939.

——————. *Mud and Soldiers*. Tokyo: Kenkyusha, 1939.

Tapert, Annette. *Despatches from the Heart*. London: Hamish Hamilton, 1984.

——————. *Lines of Battle: Letters from American Servicemen, 1941–1945*. New York: Times Books, 1987.

Taylor, A. J. P. *The Second World War*. New York: Paragon Books, 1979.

Taylor, Lawrence. *A Trial of Generals*. South Bend: Icarus Press, 1981.

Tenney, Lester I. *My Hitch in Hell: The Bataan Death March.* Washington and London: Brassey's, 1995.

Terasaki, Gwen. *Bridge to the Sun.* Chapel Hill: University of North Carolina Press, 1957.

Terkel, Studs. *"The Good War": An Oral History of World War Two.* New York: Pantheon Books, 1984.

Thompson, Paul W., et al. *How the Jap Army Fights.* Washington, DC: Infantry Journal and New York: Penguin Books, 1942.

Tobin, Richard L. *Invasion Journal.* New York: E. P. Dutton, 1944.

Toland, John. *The Rising Sun.* New York: Random House, 1970.

—————. *But Not In Shame.* New York: Ballantine, 1974 (1961).

Toole, John H. *Battle Diary.* Missoula, MT: Vigilante Press, 1978.

Tregaskis, Richard. *Guadalcanal Diary.* New York: Random House, 1943.

Treml, William. "Mine Patrol." Ann Arbor *News,* June 3, 1984.

—————. "Combat Pilot Donates $50,000 to Preserve Historic B-17 Plane." Ann Arbor *News,* August 5, 1986.

(No author) *True to Type: A Selection from Letters and Diaries of German Soldiers and Civilians Collected on the Soviet-German Front.* London and New York: Hutchinson, 1945.

Tsuchida, William S. *Wear It Proudly.* Berkeley and Los Angeles: University of California Press, 1947.

Tumey, Ben. *GI's View of World War II: The Diary of a Combat Private.* New York: Exposition Press, 1959.

Twining, Merrill B. *No Bended Knee: The Battle for Guadalcanal.* Novato, CA: Presidio Press, 1996.

Uno, Kazumaro. *Corregidor: Isle of Delusion.* Shanghai: Mercury Press, 1942.

Uris, Leon M. *Battle Cry.* New York: G. P. Putnam's Sons, 1953.

Valentine, Douglas. *The Hotel Tacloban.* Westport, CT: Lawrence Hill and Company, 1984.

van Creveld, Martin. *Fighting Power: German and U.S. Army Performance, 1939–1945.* Westport, CT: Greenwood Press, 1982.

Vandegrift, Archer A. *Once a Marine: The Memoirs of General A. A. Vandegrift.* New York: W. W. Norton and Company, 1964.

Veterans Survey Project. U.S. Army Military History Institute, Carlisle Barracks, Pennsylvania.

Vietor, John A. *Time Out: American Airmen at Stalag Luft I.* New York: Richard R. Smith Publisher, 1951.

von Luck, Hans. *Panzer Commander.* New York: Praeger Publishers, 1989.

von Kardorff, Ursula. *Diary of a Nightmare: Berlin, 1942–1945.* London: Rupert Hart-Davis, 1965.

von Staden, Wendelgard. *Darkness Over the Valley.* New York: Ticknor and Fields, 1981.

Wainwright, Jonathan M. *General Wainwright's Story.* Garden City, NY: Doubleday, 1946.

Waldron, Ben D. *Corregidor: From Paradise to Hell.* Freeman, SD: Pine Hill Press, 1988.

Walzer, Michael. *Just and Unjust Wars.* New York: Basic Books, 1977.

Weber, Wayne M. *My War with the U.S. Army.* New York: Pageant Press, 1957.

Weigley, Russell. *Eisenhower's Lieutenants.* Bloomington: Indiana University Press, 1981.

—————. "The American Military and the Principle of Civilian Control from McClellan to Powell." Paper read at Institute for Advanced Study, Princeton, March 12, 1993.

Welker, Robert H. *A Different Drummer.* Boston: Beacon Press, 1958.

Werrell, Kenneth. "The Strategic Bombing of Germany in World War II: Costs and Accomplishments." *Journal of American History* 73 (December 1986): 702–713.

Wheeler, Keith. *We Are the Wounded.* New York: E. P. Dutton and Company, 1945.

Wheeler, Richard. *A Special Valor: The U.S. Marines and the Pacific War.* New York: Harper & Row, 1983.

Whitaker, W. Denis and Shelagh. *Rhineland: The Battle to End the War.* New York: St. Martin's Press, 1989.

Whiting, Charles. *'44: In Combat from Normandy to the Ardennes.* New York: Stein and Day Publishers, 1984.

Whitman, John W. *Bataan: Our Last Ditch.* New York: Hippocrene Books, 1990.

Whitney, Cornelius V. *Lone and Level Sands.* New York: Farrar, Straus & Young, 1951.

Wilson, George. *If You Survive.* New York: Ivy Books, 1987.

Wilson, Theodore A. *WW2.* New York: Charles Scribner's Sons, 1972.

Windsor, John. *The Mouth of the Wolf.* London: Hodder and Stoughton, 1967.

Wingfield, R. M. *The Only Way Out.* London: Hutchinson, 1955.

Winkler, Allan M. *Home Front U.S.A.: America During World War II.* Arlington Heights, IL: Harlan Davidson, 1986.

Winston, Keith. *V . . . -Mail: Letters of a World War II Combat Medic.* Chapel Hill: Algonquin Books, 1985.

Wolfe, Don M. *The Purple Testament.* Garden City, NY: Doubleday, 1947.

Wolfert, Ira. *American Guerrilla in the Philippines.* New York: Simon & Schuster, 1945.

Woltersdorf, Hans W. *Gods of War: A Memoir of a German Soldier.* Novato, CA: Presidio Press, 1990.

Wouk, Herman. *The Winds of War.* Boston: Little, Brown, 1971.

————————. *War and Remembrance.* Boston: Little, Brown, 1978.

Wright, John M., Jr. *Captured on Corregidor.* Jefferson, NC, and London: McFarland, 1988.

Yoshida, Mitsuru. *Requiem for Battleship Yamato.* Seattle: University of Washington Press, 1985.

Young, Donald J. *The Battle of Bataan.* Jefferson, NC, and London: McFarland, 1992.

Zeno. *The Cauldron.* London: Macmillan, 1966.

Ziemer, Gregor. *Education for Death.* London: Oxford University Press, 1941.

Zolotow, Maurice. *Shooting Star: A Biography of John Wayne.* New York: Simon & Schuster, 1974.

Zorns, Bruce C. *I Walk Through the Valley: A World War II Infantryman's Memoir of War, Imprisonment and Love.* Jefferson, NC, and London: McFarland, 1991.

INDEX